Excavations at Mount Sandel 1973–77

COUNTY LONDONDERRY

Frontispiece   Air view of Mesolithic site (lower left), Mountsandel Fort and River Bann from north (October 1973)

DEPARTMENT OF THE ENVIRONMENT FOR
NORTHERN IRELAND

Excavations at Mount Sandel 1973–77

COUNTY LONDONDERRY

P C WOODMAN

Professor of Archaeology
University College, Cork

NORTHERN IRELAND
ARCHAEOLOGICAL MONOGRAPHS: No 2

General Editor
ANN HAMLIN

BELFAST: HER MAJESTY'S STATIONERY OFFICE

© *Crown copyright* 1985
First published 1985

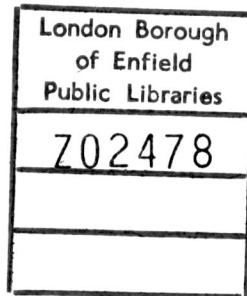

Printed for Her Majesty's Stationery Office by The Universities Press (Belfast) Ltd.

Dd. 738938 C7 6/85

ISBN 0 337 08194 8

Contents

Preface

An excavation of this type is a co-operative venture which over a period of eight years has involved many institutions and individuals. I would like to thank the Historic Monuments and Buildings Branch of the Department of the Environment (NI), formerly Finance, which initially undertook the financing of the excavation. I am particularly grateful to the late Dudley Waterman without whose support the excavation would not have been possible, and to Pat Collins who had directed previous excavations in the Mount Sandel area. The Director, Trustees and Keeper of Antiquities of the Ulster Museum must be thanked for allowing me to undertake the excavation and (with Historic Monuments and Buildings Branch) for providing financial support for post-excavation work on the preparation of the excavation report. This has been supplemented by a generous grant from the British Academy which helped defray the cost of preparing the illustrations.

In spite of the complications arising from the temporary abandonment of the building project and the subsequent change of ownership, both owners, George Wimpey and Sons and Coleraine Developments, gave us their full co-operation. The excavation eventually took us onto land owned by the Forest Service of the Department of Agriculture which was not only generous in allowing us to excavate but, in particular through the good offices of Mr Hutchinson (Head Forester, Somerset Forest), was an invaluable source of support and even, during one season, of labour. The Divisional Planning Office of the Department of the Environment at Coleraine County Hall helped with detailed maps of the area and provided temporary bench marks along the River Bann. The New University of Ulster also provided equipment and was a constant source of advice and help.

Other help and advice was given by Dr Macallister and Dr McConaghey of the Department of Agriculture, New Forge, Belfast, while Dr Kennedy of the Fisheries Research Laboratory provided information on fish movements in the Bann valley.

Any excavator relies extensively on his supervisors and planners so I would like to thank Mike Baillie, Vic Buckley, Sarah Costley, Liz Francis, Paul Gosling, Laurence May and Tom McErlean. Off-site assistance was given by David Cartmill, Dee Dixon, Don Emerson and Fiona McGregor who coped with the tedious task of sieving, sorting and counting the material from Mount Sandel.

Drawings were provided by Deirdre Crone, Rae Gillespie, Libby Lawson, Terence Reeves-Smyth and Jackie Stewart. Miss P Auterson typed the various versions of this report. Dr J Mallory and Laurence Flanagan provided many helpful criticisms of the original draft while my wife Toni helped patiently with the corrections and proof reading. I am grateful to Ann Hamlin and Emer O'Boyle for their editorial work, but any remaining imperfections are my own. The excavation archive will be deposited with the finds in the Ulster Museum.

Editorial Note

The text was finished in 1981, but the long editorial task was completed only in 1984, resulting in a delay of almost three years in the appearance of the book. I am very grateful to Emer O'Boyle for much editorial help and to Marion McLornan for drawing Fig 97.

Ann Hamlin *General Editor of Monograph Series*

List of Illustrations

FIGURES

I–II are at the end of the report

I   Site plan showing all features (main features numbered and lines of sections shown)

II East–west sections

TABLES

PLATES

Contributors

Peter Woodman, project director and main author, was at the time of the excavation Assistant Keeper in prehistoric archaeology at the Ulster Museum, Belfast. In 1982 he was appointed to the chair of archaeology at University College, Cork. The institutions of the other contributors are listed below.

D Bannon: School of Biological and Environmental Sciences, New University of Ulster, Coleraine

R W Battarbee: Department of Geography, University College, London

N F Brannon: Historic Monuments and Buildings Branch, Department of the Environment for Northern Ireland

J Cruickshank: Department of Geography, Queen's University, Belfast

L R Dalzell: School of Biological and Environmental Sciences, New University of Ulster, Coleraine

R Doggart: Department of Archaeology, Queen's University, Belfast

J V Dumont: Donald Baden-Powell Quaternary Research Centre, University of Oxford

P Francis: c/o Palaeoecology Centre, Queen's University, Belfast

A Hamilton: School of Biological and Environmental Sciences, New University of Ulster, Coleraine

F W Hamond: 75 Locksley Park, Belfast 10

R Heslip: Department of Local History, Ulster Museum, Belfast

I Johnston: Department of Geology, Queen's University, Belfast

B P Lenehan: School of Biological and Environmental Sciences, New University of Ulster, Coleraine

B J McDonagh: School of Biological and Environmental Sciences, New University of Ulster, Coleraine

M A Monk: Department of Archaeology, University College, Cork

J P Pals: Albert Egges van Giffen Institute for Pre- and Protohistory, University of Amsterdam

S J Phethean: Palaeoecology Laboratory, Department of Geography, University College, London

R Scaife: University of London Institute of Archaeology

M L Simpson: Carrickfergus Excavations Publication Project, c/o Ulster Museum, Belfast

Louise H van Wijngaarden-Bakker: Albert Egges van Giffen Institute for Pre- and Protohistory, University of Amsterdam

R Warner: Department of Antiquities, Ulster Museum, Belfast

CHAPTER I

Introduction to the excavations at Mount Sandel

The Site

The excavations on which this report is based took place in the townland of Mount Sandel which lies south of Coleraine and on the east side of the River Bann. This area is dominated by a ridge of fluvio-glacial gravels which run parallel to the River Bann. The ridge usually lies just below 100 ft OD and to its east is a lower area of clays which are close to 50 ft OD. The ridge is relatively flat with occasional knolls of slightly higher ground and at least one major depression—the Mount Sandel kettle-hole (Appendix 3).

The ridge drops to the River Bann as a steep escarpment which is today covered with a mixed conifer and deciduous forest. The river at this point is estuarine with the limit of the Bann estuary at the Cutts, about 1 km south of Mount Sandel. This limit of tidal rise, rather than salt water, is formed by a ridge of rock. The river does not differ significantly in character immediately above or below the Cutts as it runs through a relatively narrow, steep-sided valley which broadens in places. The narrows are a product of the glacial geomorphology and underlying bedrock rather than the nature of the river regime at any point. Thus the valley does not have a broad estuarine flood plain until it reaches the Bann mouth itself (Fig 1). Essentially the river can be described as a narrow channel cutting through a relatively flat landscape which lies below 200 ft and is a product of either the North Antrim Ice Sheet or outwash deposits associated with it (Creighton 1974).

The site is located in fields north-east of Mountsandel Fort (Fig 97).* Thus it is placed on one of the higher parts of the Mount Sandel ridge and is on the edge of the escarpment as it survives today, at a point where the river temporarily widens out (Pl 1). The excavation site not only straddled two fields but continued into the forest. The demesne bank which marked the boundary of the forest cut across the site and overlay part of it.

---

*Although the townland appears on Ordnance Survey maps as Mount Sandel, the fort appears as Mountsandel Fort, and this usage is followed in this report.

The Excavations

The original reason for excavation was the scheduling of an area of fields adjacent to Mountsandel Fort for development as a housing estate. In 1972 these fields were ploughed and as those closest to the fort produced a substantial quantity of flint artefacts a small rescue excavation was undertaken in 1973. It was assumed that as this area had been under cultivation very little of archaeological significance would have survived *in situ*. Although, as will be shown in Chapter 2, extensive areas had been eroded, considerably more than was expected had survived intact. The main emphasis was on the excavation of an extensive Mesolithic settlement which required four seasons of excavation, in 1973, 1974, 1976 and 1977. In total approximately 700 square metres were explored. The main purpose was the examination of a sufficiently large area to see whether different types of activities, as well as dwelling units, could be identified. This eventually led to the excavation of parts of the site which lay beyond the threatened area, but investigation of them was considered essential to reveal the total area of settlement.

The most striking evidence of Mesolithic occupation was the dwelling hollow found in the central portion of the eastern half of the site. Here arcs of post-holes were found round what appeared to be hearths. To the east and north of this area there appeared to be other hearths and arcs of post-holes which may have represented the partly eroded remnants of other huts. Miscellaneous pits were scattered to the north of this hollow as were traces of a smaller structure delimited by a series of narrow gullies. To the west lay an area where pits, hearths and other features were relatively scarce, though large quantities of industrial waste were uncovered. Few traces of Mesolithic activity were found south of the dwelling hollow.

Considering the strategic location of the site it is hardly surprising that there were traces of other periods of occupation. On the southern extremities of the site, and in the north-western parts, were scatters of Neolithic pottery, while two features produced ^{14}C dates which could indicate Late Bronze Age or Early

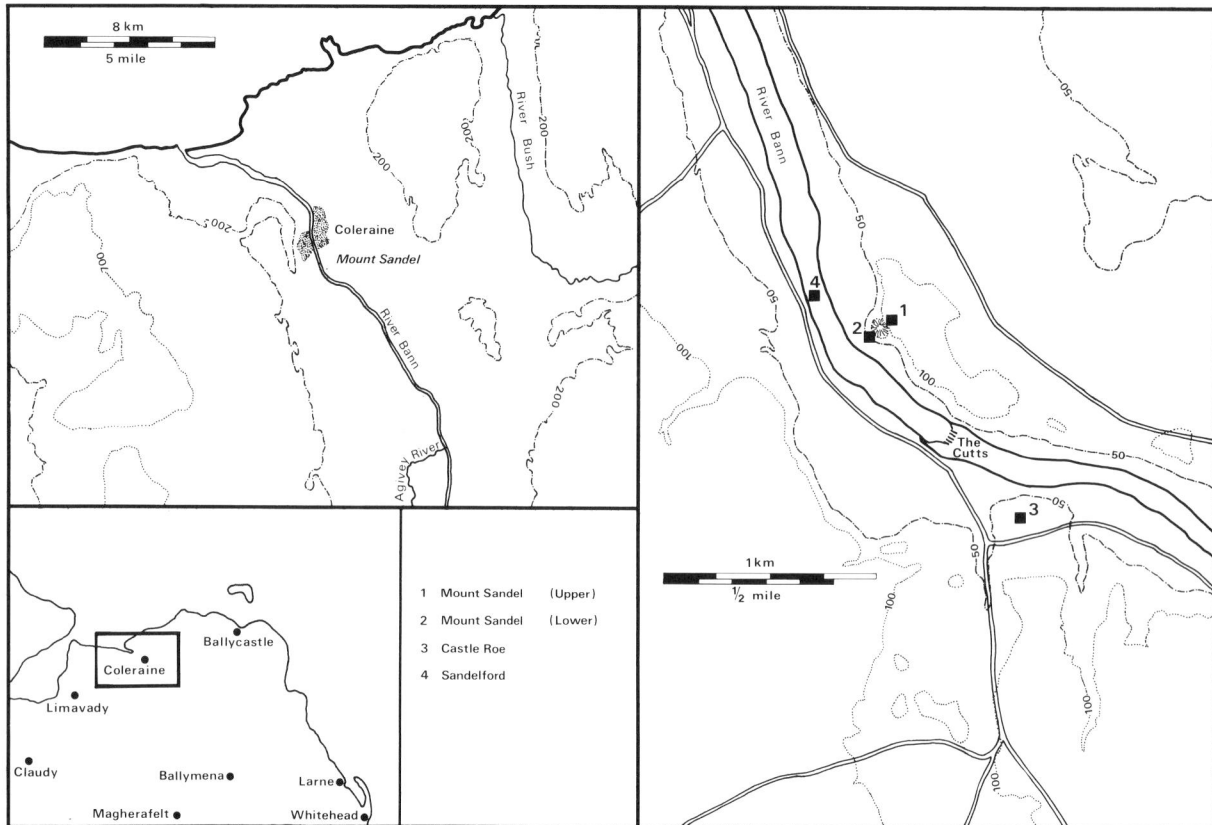

Fig 1   Mount Sandel and surrounding area

Iron Age occupation. Slight traces of occupation, perhaps associated with the nearby fort, were found in the form of souterrain ware. The final phases of occupation were associated with a post-medieval refortification of the fort which included the construction of a bank and ditch, which were to become the basis for the demesne bank. The most enigmatic structures were a pair of long gullies running along the south-eastern edge of the site. There is no clear evidence for their date.

History of Investigations

The Mount Sandel area has been associated with the study of the Irish Mesolithic for nearly one hundred years, in fact since before it was realized that there was such a period as the Mesolithic. The earliest reference to Mount Sandel is in Gray's 1888 paper on flint axes from Co Antrim, in which he noted that axes of the so-called Koekjenmidden type (flake axes) were found not only at Portrush but 'in the field behind Mount Sandel Fort'. Seaton F Milligan had already donated to the National Museum of Ireland some axes 'dug from a hole in a field at Mount Sandel'.

By the 1920s Knowles and Gray had amassed large quantities of material from surface collections so that eventually there were nearly one hundred flint axes from this area in museum collections. To these could be added the occasional so-called 'pigmy flint' and core. Although the location was never very specific, occasional items of the same type were found in the 'River Bann at Coleraine'. The tradition of collecting in this area was continued by the May family and J Batty, who added to the number of known axes and microliths from Mount Sandel (eg Batty 1938), while D MacLaughlin recovered a similar type of industry from the ford across the Bann at Mount Sandel.

Ironically at this point in the 1930s interest in Mount Sandel waned. Evidence from the Bann valley and typological comparisons with groups of material found in Europe (Whelan 1938) appeared to suggest that industries in which the flake axe played a significant role could be placed at the end of the Mesolithic, and so the 'Irish Campignian' was created. Emphasis in research was directed more towards the beach sites where material could be found in a stratified and datable context—thus the creation by Movius of the Larnian (1942). The myth of the lateness of the flake axe continued into the 1970s until ^{14}C dating evidence, combined with better dated typological comparisons in Britain, forced the author to revise the dating of this type of industry (Woodman 1974a, postscript, where a dramatic shift of opinion takes place).

Although the emphasis in Mesolithic studies had changed, work in the Mount Sandel area was never totally abandoned. In the mid 1950s A McL May noted a landslip below Mountsandel Fort, examination of which produced a selection of very fresh Mesolithic material. This encouraged A E P Collins of the Archaeological Survey to carry out a series of excavations through the deposits lying on a ledge between Mountsandel Fort and the River Bann. This site is usually referred to as Mount Sandel (Lower) (Collins 1983).

Methods

The location of the area of excavation was chosen on the basis of observations of charcoal spreads and flint density after the field had been ploughed in 1972. The area was divided up using a one metre grid system (Fig 2: letters, omitting I and O, east/west,

numbers north/south). Two one metre wide trenches were excavated through the very thin topsoil in the corner of the main field. One ran from 31 to 50 along line K and the other from C to T along line 40. For the remainder of 1973 the excavation concentrated on excavating the main hut hollow as well as attempting to define the maximum extent of a palisade gully. In 1974 further excavation round the hut hollow was carried out and by the end of this season a trial trench through the demesne bank had revealed further traces of Mesolithic occupation below the bank. The last two seasons were devoted to finding the maximum extent of the visible traces of Mesolithic occupation.

While all *in situ* traces of Mesolithic or later prehistoric occupation were excavated, using a one metre grid system, the large quantities of lithic material found in the overburden clearly did not warrant the same attention. While the plough zones of the original exploratory trenches were very carefully removed, the rest obviously could not be excavated with the same care. Besides the abundance

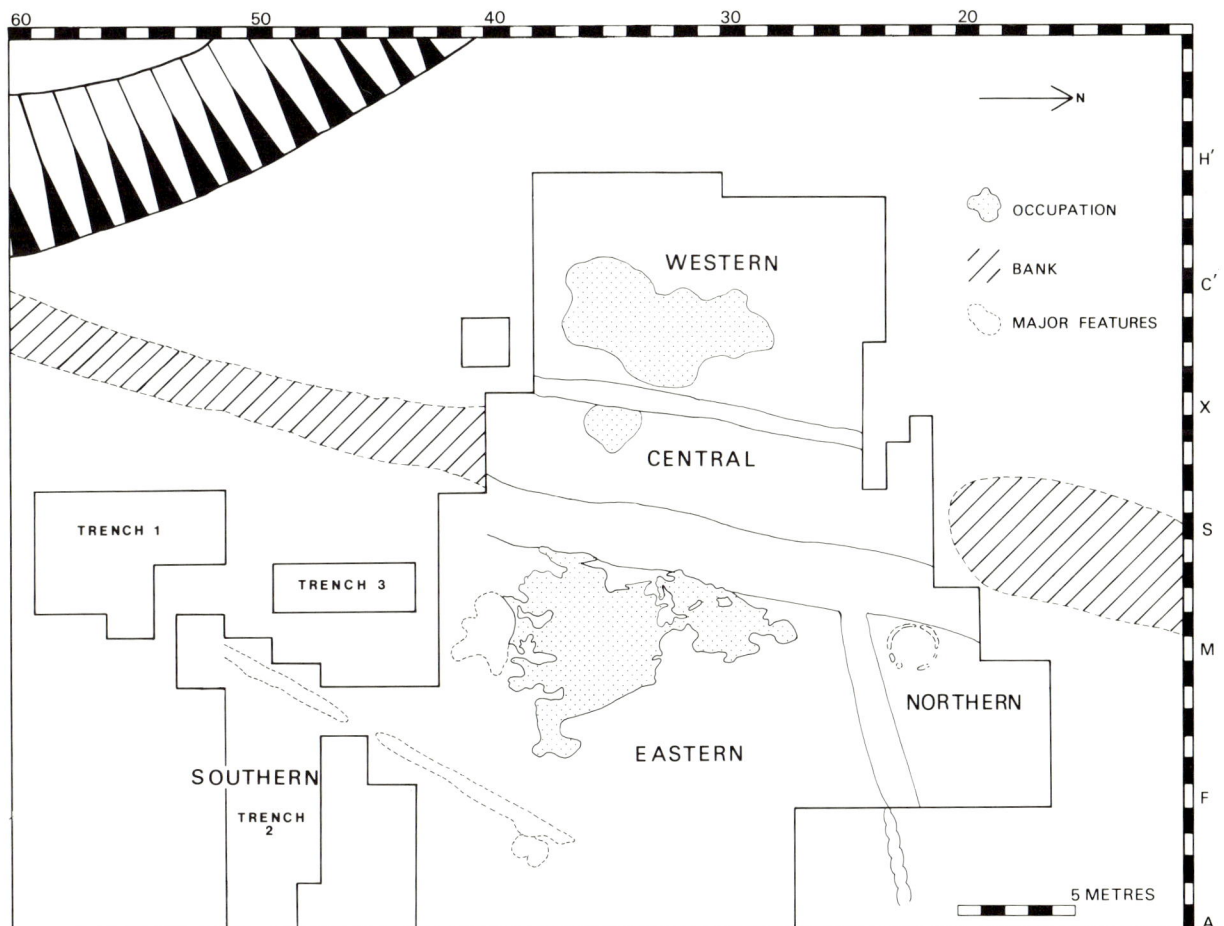

Fig 2 Area of excavation and internal divisions

of material it soon became clear that the area had been drastically affected by numerous reoccupations, and the contextless Mesolithic material had been subjected to significant disturbance. To these problems of preservation can be added the fact that without rigorous control, such as sieving, artefact recovery is subject to variation caused by the vagaries of soil conditions and human vision. Therefore the policy adopted was to strip the site to the Mesolithic or other undisturbed levels, ignoring most of the disturbed material. As will be seen below, some use has been made of the disturbed material, but perhaps if a sampling strategy had been adopted considerably more information could have been recovered.

The *in situ* deposits were excavated within a recovery grid of one metre squares, thus all material can be located within a metre square, while certain forms are recorded to the nearest centimetre. These include any retouched tools, cores and flakes where more than 50% of the surface is covered with cortex. Owing to a lack of experience on the part of many of those taking part in the excavation, other forms such as micro-burins and axe-sharpening flakes could not be guaranteed to be consistently recognized on site and were therefore only recorded by square metre.

During the first season blades (defined as parallel-sided flakes with length more than twice breadth) were also recorded to the nearest centimetre, but later this slightly subjective division was abandoned and each flake was recorded by a dot, but was not kept separately with its own three dimensional record of location. These flakes and blades were always kept by their metre grid square. The original keeping and noting of the location of blades was combined with a record of their orientation and declination. It was assumed that these long objects would be more susceptible to the recording of post-depositional disturbance, such as pits and hearths being cut through a pre-existing layer. As the features were all filled with black soil the usual colour changes could often not be used to detect the sequence of features on site. While this recording technique proved to be exceptionally useful (Chapter 11) it was eventually realized that the same result could be achieved by noting those blades which were lying at more than 45° from the horizontal. Unfortunately as field conditions were never again suitable, that is offering a combination of occupation soil and a group of features, the revised method was never tested.

During the excavation a 3 mm mesh sieve was used for all Mesolithic deposits. In the first season a dry-sieving technique was used, but in the following years a large water tank was used for on-site wet-sieving. Shortly after the start of excavations it became clear that some layers in certain features contained too much material, mostly burnt bone and hazel nut shells, for the rather rough and ready

on-site sieves. Therefore if a layer was thought to be organically rich the whole layer was removed to the Ulster Museum. Here H_2O_2 and NH_3OH were added to break down the clay element, a standard macrobotanical technique. The soil was then wet-sieved through a 1.5 mm and 850 micron mesh, dried and hand-sorted. In certain instances, when it was thought that a layer had not been contaminated by modern roots, the residue was placed in water and some charcoal and seeds were collected through flotation. As these techniques were, however, rather robust and could destroy seeds Mr M Monk of University College, Cork, undertook the more careful examination of a small residue of samples (Chapter 6).

Retrospect

It must be admitted that the excavation at Mount Sandel was notably lacking in two respects. First there was no conscious policy of using pedological information. Much of the pedological information was therefore derived from post-excavation studies of the bulk samples removed from the site for other purposes. Fortunately the work of Dr Hamond under the guidance of Mr Cruickshank of the Geography Department, Queen's University, Belfast, has partly retrieved the situation (Chapter 7 and Appendix 2a). Secondly, in the euphoria of discovering layers of soil containing bone fragments, there was no policy of setting up controls to allow estimation of the densities of bones, hazel nuts and similar material. Layers which were rich were removed *in toto*, while poorer layers were only sampled in an *ad hoc* fashion.

It must also be admitted that this excavation should not be taken as a model for problem-orientated excavations. It was not approached with any awareness of the need to create a methodological framework to examine the problems of Mesolithic settlement; it was assumed that the site would be mostly destroyed and that only a minimum would be preserved. The initial aim of the excavation, therefore, was to recover sufficient *in situ* archaeological material to enable this distinctive type of industry to be placed in a chronological context. The excavation's failure to make use of certain aids stems from this low expectation of recovery rather than from the circumstances of it being a rescue excavation. Similarly, while the nature of the site might never have been determined through preliminary sampling, the nature of the excavation was a product of the level at which Irish Mesolithic studies stood in 1973.

The Form of the Report

The site report has been divided into a descriptive section and a discussion followed by a series of appendices. In view of the rather complex nature of the site, arising from the numerous reoccupations of this area, it was decided to separate the descriptive and interpretative aspects of the report—particularly because of the unique nature of some of the evidence from the Mesolithic phases of occupation. However, as much of the material came from a series of pits, much of the repetitive detail has been relegated to Appendix 1a. The main body of the text, therefore, provides a general descriptive narrative of the degree of preservation of various parts of the site, as well as the context and inter-relationships of various pits, post-holes and other features. Similarly general descriptions of the archaeological material have been given in Chapter 3, while detailed accounts of where the material was found are reserved for Appendix 1b.

The function of the second section of the report (Chapters 11–13) is to provide an interpretation of the various facets of the evidence: the size and numbers of huts found on the site, the nature of the various pits as well as the nature and seasonality of the occupation. Chapter 14 offers a short summary of the evidence, the conclusions, and some outstanding problems.

CHAPTER 2

Description of the excavations

Introduction

A relatively large area was excavated, and the degree of preservation of evidence, ranging from Mesolithic to post-medieval, varied greatly across the site. It has therefore proved convenient to divide the description into areas where the degree of preservation was similar. These areas are (Fig 2) *Southern*—the area adjacent to the fort; *Eastern*—the area adjacent to the dwelling hollow; *Northern*—the northern periphery of the site divided off by an east-west boundary; *Central*—the area covered by the post-medieval bank; and *Western*—the area between the post-medieval bank and the escarpment. A detailed plan showing the location of all the features and one figure of sections have been provided in a pocket at the back of the report. These are distinguished by Roman numerals (Figs I–II). In them a single line denotes post-holes or other features cut into pre-existing ones. They also provide the main key to the numbering of features. The reader is also referred to Appendix 1a and Fig 92 (both in microfiche) for further details and profiles of excavated features.

Southern Area

This area can be best described as peripheral to the main excavations (Fig 3). The original exploratory trench, which was one metre wide and ran along line K from 30 to 50, revealed Features 6, 7 and 10. Trenches were then opened in various directions to ascertain if the two gullies 6 and 7 continued. However, the lack of archaeological dating evidence other than the overlap of 6, 7 and 10 suggested that there would be little purpose in opening large areas to expose and excavate what might remain a group of structures of unknown date. It was presumed, until a ^{14}C date of 435 ± 70 bc was obtained for Feature 10, that these features related to the post-medieval phase of Mount Sandel. The ^{14}C date provides one indication that part, at least, of this complex could be significantly earlier.

The excavation began on the assumption that there was virtually nothing preserved *in situ* above the subsoil, yet an intermittent, reddish-brown old soil

level was found. Part of the reason for the existence of this soil may be the change from a sandy gravel to a clayey loam. The only significant extent of the soil was in Trench 2 where it was up to 50 mm thick. In comparison with the main area of occupation this soil contained relatively little of archaeological significance. It was flecked with charcoal and produced two sherds of Neolithic pottery and a scatter of flint debitage.

Obviously the dominant features in this area were 6 and 7 (Fig 4). These conveniently overlapped in the area of a hearth and the sequence was gully (Feature 6), hearth (Feature 10) and finally gully (Feature 7).[*] The later gully also appeared to cut into the palaeosol referred to above. This gully was traced for over 13 m and contained only a small quantity of the ubiquitous Mesolithic flintwork. It was at its deepest and broadest at the eastern end of Trench 2, where it was over 250 mm deep and nearly 300 mm across. To the west it gradually became shallower until in Trench 3 it had become a rather narrow, elusive feature. Where F7 had cut F6 and the hearth (F10) its fill contained stones derived from F6 and quantities of charcoal derived from the hearth. The hearth was preserved as a small spread of charcoal at the base of the plough zone. It rested in a very shallow depression and overlay the fill of F6: the intervening soil layer has been burnt (Fig 4B).

F6 has to be considered with F11. These formed an intermittent gully which was 16 m in length, with a gap of about 1 m between the two sections. In the centre was a pair of very slight post-holes: one was only 40 mm deep. They were significantly slighter than any others in the immediate vicinity. Trench 1 was opened to ascertain whether this gully extended as far as Mountsandel Fort, as the southern end of F6 had been terminated by a lazy bed[†] in Trench 2. It did not reappear in Trench 1, where only a

---

[*] Subsequently F will indicate a Feature.

[†] Lazy bed is a term used in Ireland for a cultivation trench, especially associated with potato growing and particularly common in the period before the famine of the 1840s.

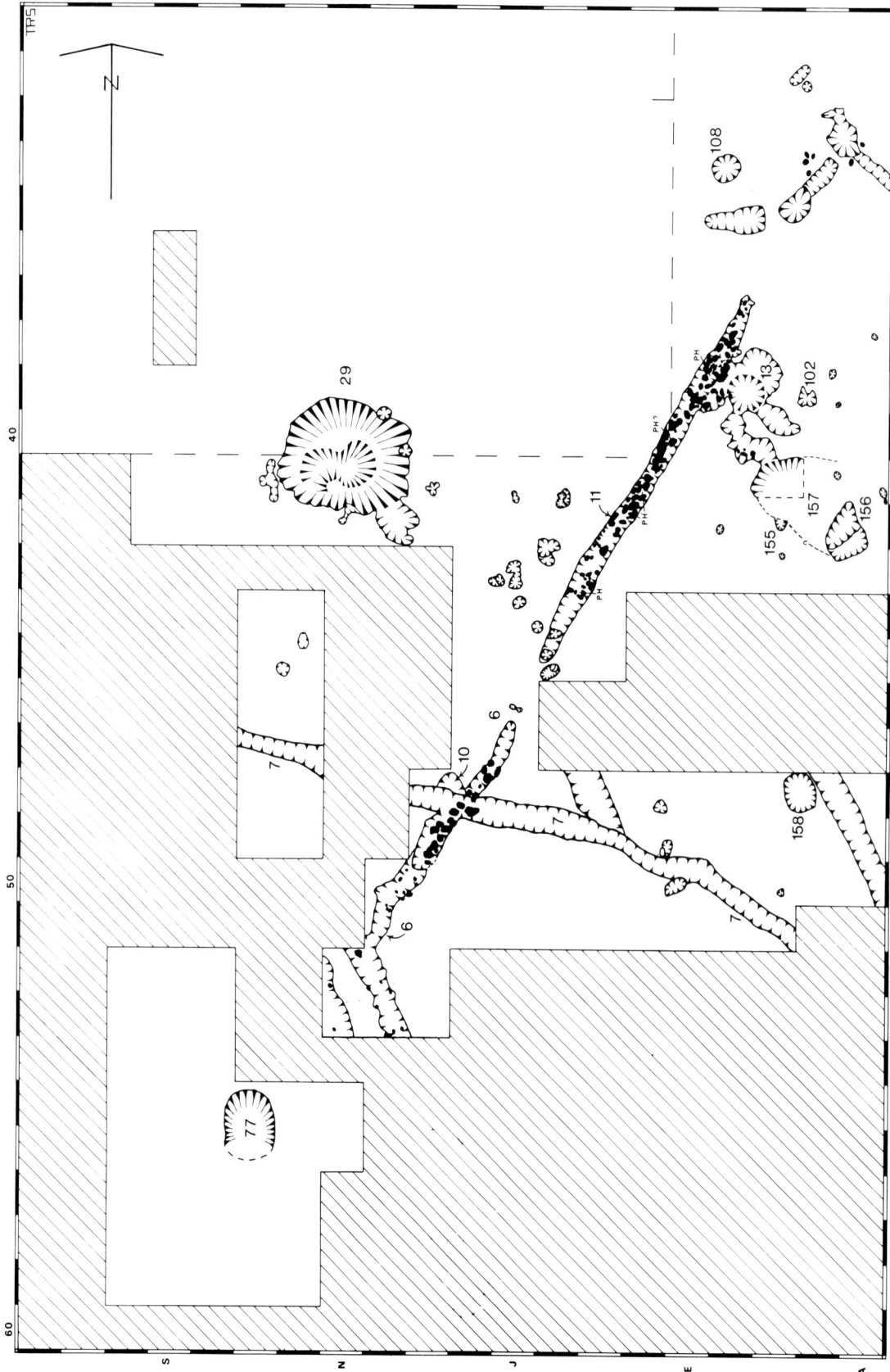

Fig 3   Southern area: plan

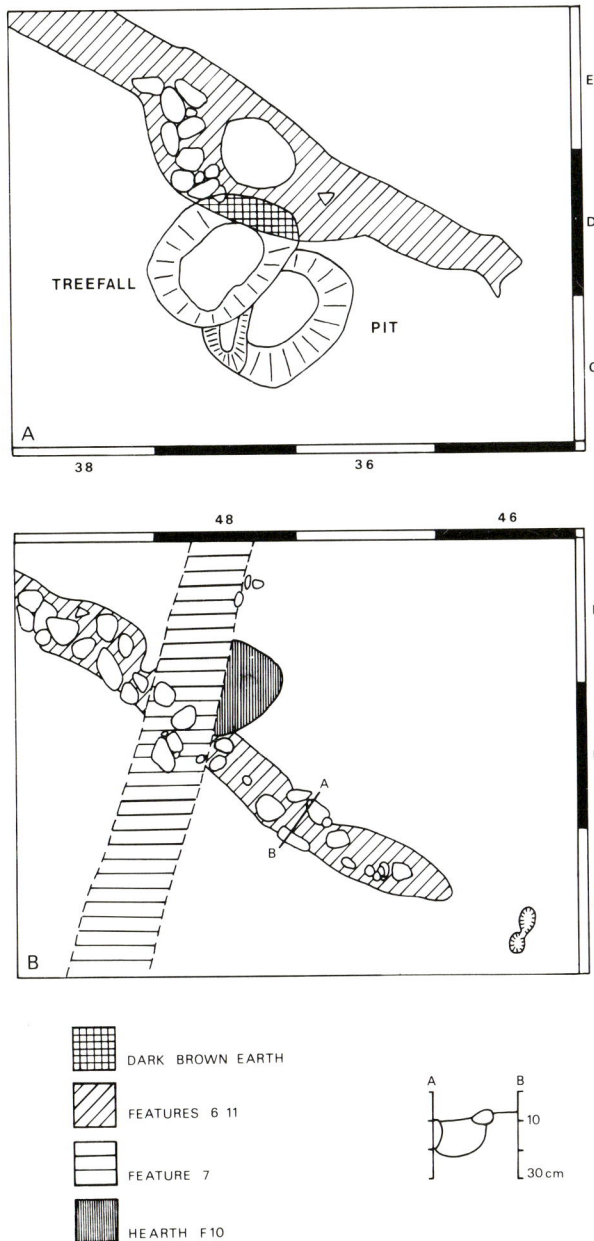

Fig 4   Plans of (A) FS11 and 13 and (B) FS6, 7 and 10, with section of F6

and were lying either at the bottom of the gully or in the brown soil, but occasionally stones were still *in situ* at the edge of the gully. At these points there appeared to have been voids for posts. It is possible that a continuous series of posts had been placed side by side in this trench and that the intermittent voids were a product of a later disturbance, probably ploughing. The presence of two slight post-holes cut into the base of the southern end of F11, and the large number of stones at certain points along the trench, suggest that large posts had been placed at intervals along these gullies. Presumably a lighter superstructure was then added. The squared shape of several of the voids did suggest that rectangular timbers might have been placed in them (Fig 4B, A–B). Certainly the relative narrowness of the slot indicates that the timbers could not have been very broad. As found the slot was up to 250 mm deep and 300 mm across, though presumably it was cut from an old ground surface that has since been eroded, and it could originally have been slightly deeper.

A complication arose at the northern end of F11 where the gully broadened, leaving an island of gravel in the centre of the trench (Fig 4A). F13 created an additional problem in this area. This can now be recognized as both a pit and a later tree-fall, but as it was the first and ironically the most complex tree-fall to be investigated, it was not fully understood during excavation. The sequence of F13 and F11 appeared to be as follows: first there was a pit, F13, up to 350 mm deep and nearly 1 m across, filled with the dark charcoal-stained soil found in the area of Mesolithic occupation; next F11 was dug, at one point cutting F13; subsequently the whole area was disturbed by the tree-fall. One result of the fall was that a V-shaped gully was gouged out at the junction of the original pit and the tree-fall. This was about 150 mm deeper than the pit and obliterated part of it, leaving a vertical junction between the redeposited gravel of the tree-fall and the slumped black soil of the pit. Gravel, presumably from the time of the tree-fall, partly covered F11. Another result of the tree-fall was to truncate the edge of the foundation slot. The only archaeological finds associated with this feature-complex were a sherd of Neolithic pottery in the tree-fall, fragments of brick in a lens of gravel overlying F11 adjacent to F13, and a scatter of Mesolithic material including a significant concentration in the original black layer of F13.

The other extensive evidence of human activity at the southern edge of the site was the line of post-holes which ran from north-west to south-east across it. Diagnostic archaeological material was unfortunately lacking in these post-holes and, beyond the fact that the extension to this line cut through the Mesolithic deposits, there was no stratigraphic dating evidence. One identifiable line of post-holes, just under 1 m

depression created by a large tree-fall was found (F77), containing a scatter of flint debitage and two sherds of Neolithic pottery. Similarly there was only one very slight possible extension to F11 at its northern end, though this was by no means certain, as it was separated by a 2 m gap and was relatively short. These gullies, F6 and F11, were filled with brown soil and contained in both their northern and southern lengths a number of rounded field stones (Fig 4). Many of these had been knocked out of place

apart, had a light brown fill, 10 YR 3/2,* and were often over 200 mm in diameter. They tended to vary in depth, at least in part because of erosion of the old ground surface from which they were cut. They were in the region of 130–180 mm deep and had straight sides and broad flat bottoms. This line ran across the southern end of F11 at a very acute angle. This might imply that these two linear complexes were not contemporary, though it was noticeable that the post-holes at the shallow southern end of F11 were of approximately the same size and depth as those in the row of post-holes.

Other traces of human activity in this area included a second tree-fall, first noted as a semicircle of black soil cut into the subsoil (F157). This example was about 2 m across but contained soil in only about half of its hollow. The rest of the hollow was filled with a disturbed sandy gravel (pecked outline in Fig 3). The result of the creation of this hollow was the partial destruction of a small pit, F155. In this area another sherd of Neolithic pottery was found. F156 appeared to overlie and cut the eastern edge of the tree-fall, F157. Other slight traces of gullies—usually filled with plough soil—were assumed to be a product of modern agricultural activities.

Evidence of Mesolithic occupation on this south-eastern edge of the site was thus relatively scarce. Small pits were found in Trenches 2 and 3, as well as two pits with a greasy black soil which were near F13 (F102 in C/39 and F108 in D–E/34).

Eastern Area

This area, shown in Figs 9 and 15, was delimited to the east by the edge of the excavation and to the west by a pair of ditches running approximately north–south. The northern boundary was provided by an east–west field boundary while the southern edge overlapped slightly with the area considered in the previous section.

The ditch systems were obviously later than the other features and will be considered first. The earlier ditch was F4, V-shaped and running north–south on the western edge of the area. For most of its length it was separated from F5, a shallow flat-bottomed ditch, by a narrow ridge but to the north they converged and F5 cut across it. Neither ditch was deep, F4 being at its maximum only 800 mm deep, and both were filled with a homogeneous brown soil. A mortar slick occurred in the base of F4. The east–west ditch (F82), which delimits the northern boundary of this area, was again relatively sterile, but as it cut through the mortar slick and its bottom was flat, it was probably contemporary with the other flat-bottomed ditches

(see also page 24, below). A few stones were found at its most westerly end. The plan of F82 suggested two phases (Fig 15), but disturbance by a hedge made it impossible to confirm this.

The charcoal-rich soil, shown cross-hatched in Fig 5, dominated the eastern area, which had in part survived the serious erosion which, elsewhere, had even cut into the subsoil. This erosion was at its most extensive on the eastern edge of the eastern area where the gravel ridge had taken the brunt of the ploughing. The result was that this edge contained relatively fewer features than elsewhere and it was uncertain how much of the B horizon had been removed. It has been noted already (p 7) that much of the site lay on a compact sandy soil. The B horizion along the extreme eastern edge was found to consist of a hard, very compact gravel, and it may be that in this area extensive ploughing had removed the upper, more sandy component, perhaps reducing the B horizon by 100 to 150 mm.

Along the northerly edge of the area there was a greater depth of soil and erosion had not been quite so extensive. In fact the recent accumulation of soil had become so thick that very little Mesolithic material was found here during surface collection. The reason for the increased depth appears to have been soil drift from slightly higher ground to the north and west. Unfortunately this happened at too late a date to prevent erosion: the palaeosol had already been removed from on top of the B horizon. The thicker soil layer did, however, provide protection from extensive damage during the more recent agricultural activity.

Although the occupation soil and the hollow in which much of it lay were without doubt the most significant part of the whole site, the area involved was relatively small. The total extent of the occupation soil was only 37 m². It had only survived because of the existence of a slight hollow and, on its northern edge, increased depth of soil. The expanse of occupation soil was roughly triangular, with the apex to the north. Its maximum length (north–south) was 10 m and its width 7 m. The only substantial volume of soil was that found in the main dwelling hollow. The northern area, though a welcome addition, was rather small and thin except in the area adjacent to the section (Fig 11).

The dwelling hollow was a slight depression cut into the sands and gravels (Fig 6; Pl 2). It was in reality an arc of slightly under 180 degrees which faced south-west. This was probably a natural fold in the sands which had been modified by man and required only the removal of sands and gravels in a chord of about 4 m across. The ridge had been cut to a maximum depth of 150 mm exposing the under-lying gravels. The rest of the hollow had a relatively flat sandy floor. In two places, M–N/39 and

---

* This and subsequent references are to the *Munsell Soil Color Charts* notations.

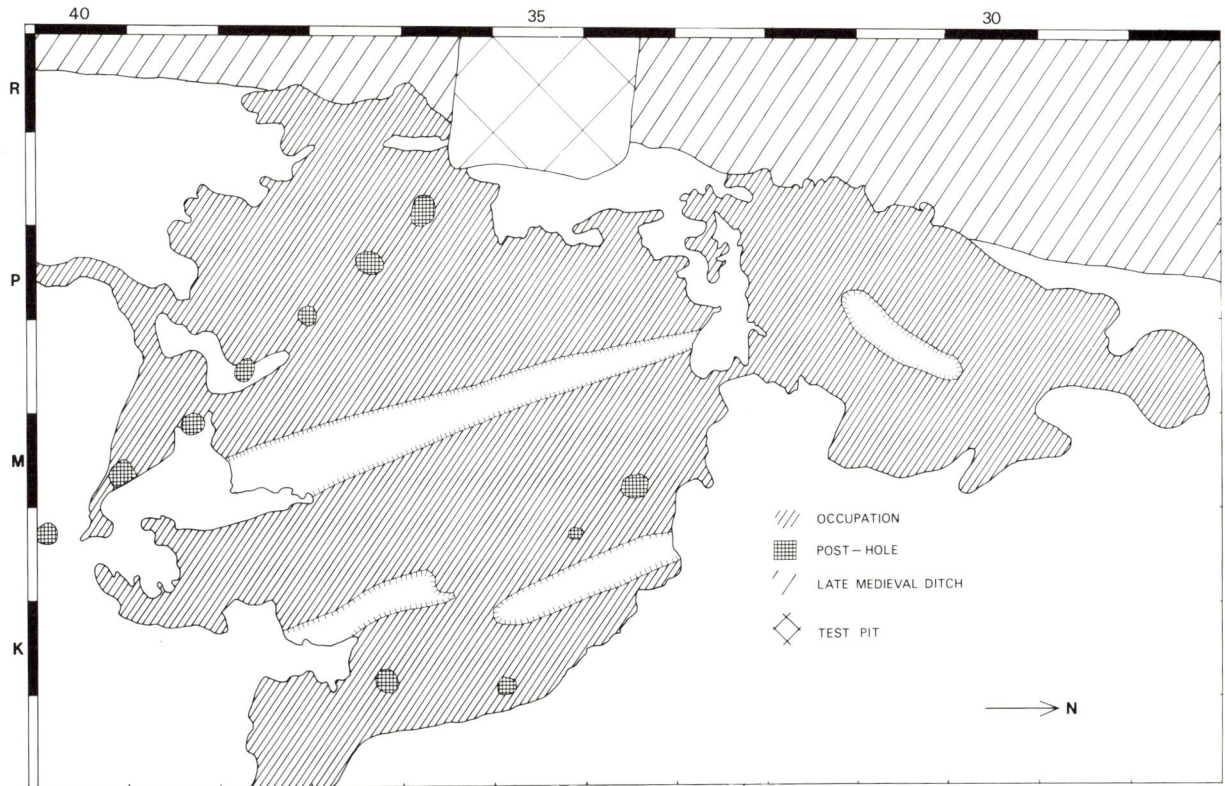

Fig 5 Plan showing extent of occupation soil and later disturbance in eastern area

P–Q/36–37, the remnants of what appeared to be elongated shallow depressions were found (shown in Fig 9). These were less than 50 mm deep and flat-bottomed, but unfortunately they were badly cut up by other, later features.

The occupation soil was of very uneven thickness (Fig 6), with a maximum depth of 100 mm in the deepest part of the hollow. However, this was only a tiny remnant of the original extent of the charcoal-stained soil, as it had accumulated in many of the features in eroded areas and could of course be found in the western part of the site.

The major sources of disturbance in this area (Fig 5) were the lazy beds which cut across it on the north-west to south-east axis and the post-holes which were noticeably larger than those to the south, probably because there had been less plough damage. As well as the one definite line of post-holes, several other scattered examples of varying size were cut into the occupation soil. These post-holes ranged from massive examples such as ph 1 (L/31, Fig 15) to a group of rather small post-holes which were found in the F31 area (Fig 9). As in the southern area these post-holes tended to be relatively straight-sided and flat-bottomed and were usually filled with a light brown soil, 5 YR 3/4.

Obviously there is a problem in estimating the proportion of occupation soil which has been removed from this part of the site. Not only did it originally extend over a much greater area, but it can be assumed that it had been much thicker and that a post-Mesolithic old ground surface had been totally removed along with most of the Mesolithic occupation soil. The presence of a Neolithic potsherd in the fill of a tree-fall (F29, L–N/40–42) was an indication of Neolithic occupation on a higher, now destroyed, old ground surface. Although no other item of post-Mesolithic date was found mixed with the occupation soil, the presence of this potsherd washed into the hollow at a date prior to the extensive post-medieval agricultural activities suggested that even in areas where the occupation soil was relatively thick, several tens of millimetres of occupation soil and a later level of occupation had been obliterated.

The Mesolithic occupation soil could not be described as homogeneous as certain areas were darker than others. This was due in part to the amount of root penetration, mostly by the tiny rootlets from the cereal crops growing in the field, though hedge roots did penetrate along the western edge of the hollow. One noticeable feature of this soil was the relative scarcity of stones and stone-holes which occurred quite frequently in the western area. There was also no evidence for any palaeosol

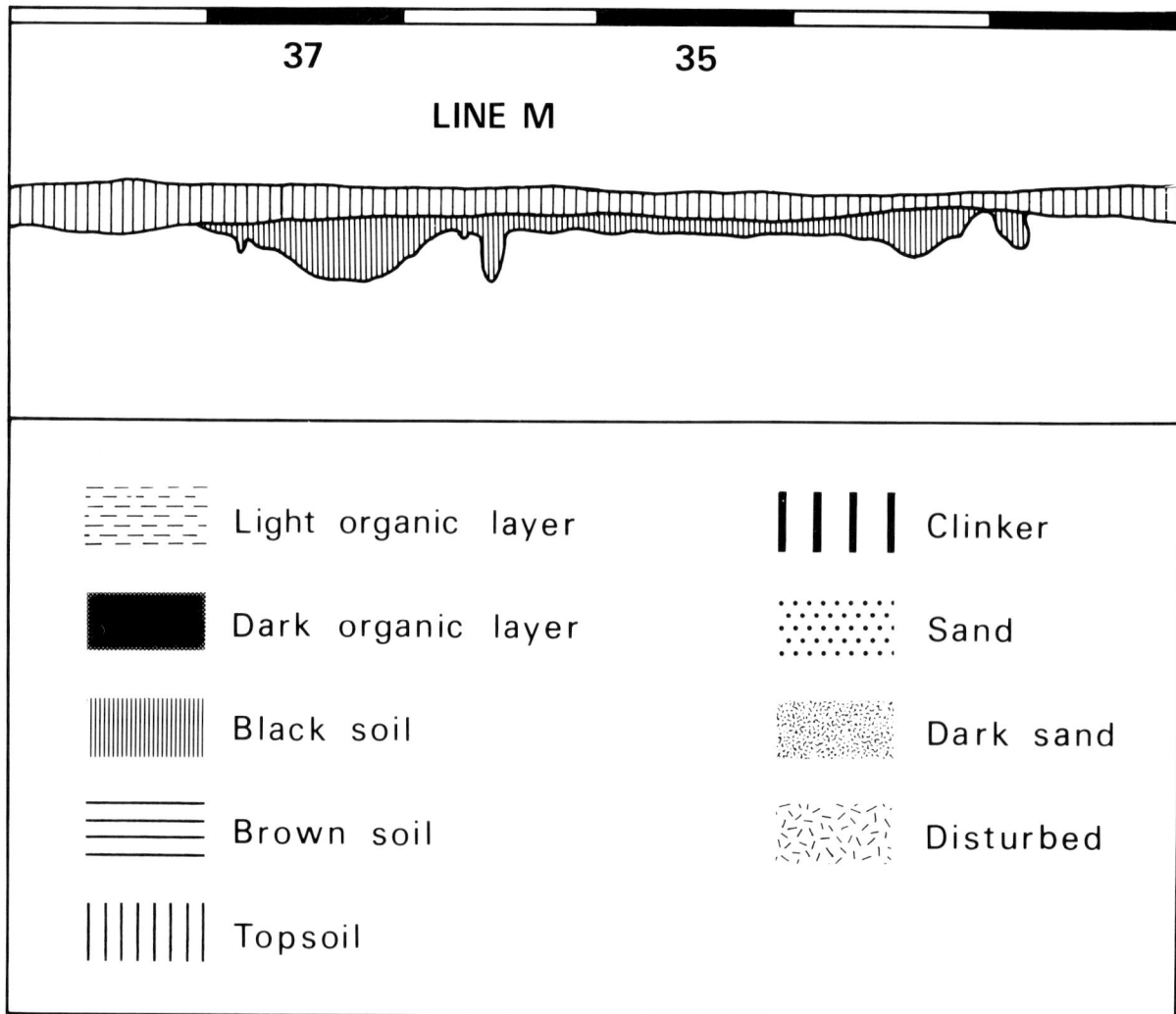

Fig 6   Section through main hut hollow along line M, with key to conventions for sections

underlying the occupation layer. The archaeological material was found throughout the whole depth of the occupation soil and this, together with the relative flatness of the subsoil, would suggest that the original pre-occupation soil had been cleared from the area. The significance of the vertical distribution of the archaeological material can be seen by comparing representative squares from this dwelling area with those from the industrial area further west, where there is virtually nothing from the bottom half of the sequence (Fig 7).

While the archaeological material and its spatial distribution will be considered in some detail later (Chapter 11), here one must note that a significant proportion of the blades, cores and microliths were concentrated in the north-eastern quadrant of the dwelling hollow, while the scatter of the heavier artefacts in the south-eastern quadrant was greater than could be accounted for solely by the differentially more extensive erosion of that area.

Various other elements were not spread evenly across the dwelling hollow. Some will, like the artefacts, be examined in the broader context of the whole site, for example the spread of organic materials. There were, however, a few notable scatters of comminuted bone fragments, often in a slightly lighter context (Fig 8), and occasionally concentrations of burnt earth or hazel nut shells which marked the uppermost portions of pits and hearths. This indicated that some features at least were contemporary with, or later than, the bottom part of the occupation soil. The clearest examples were spreads of burnt hazel nut shells which were found in squares L/37 (related to hearth 56/5) and K/38 (related to F22). There was also some evidence in the form of blade declination that some of these pits post-dated the main layer of occupation soil (discussed in detail in Chapter 11).

The two most obvious features of the dwelling hollow were the arc of post-holes running along its lip

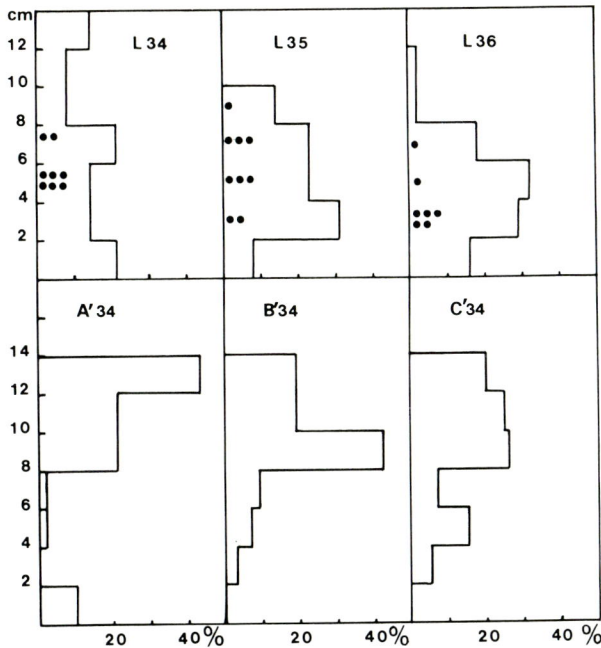

Fig 7 Vertical distribution of blades by metre square and individual microliths (dots) through selected squares in the hut and western area

from approximately true east to true north, and the complex of pits in the centre of the hollow (Fig 9* and Pl 3). The arc of post-holes appeared as a very simple curved line at its eastern end but became more complex to the north where a second, less easily defined arc, which subtended to a point slightly to the south and west of the former, abutted onto it. A source of added confusion was the presence in this area of post-holes which may have belonged to a hut built to the north of the main dwelling hollow. To the south-east the arc had been obliterated by later activity such as tree-falls and hearths, while the eventual tailing-out of the escarpment on the north-west made it much more difficult to trace an arc of post-holes with any confidence.

At its simplest the arc appeared to consist of substantial post-holes placed about 800 mm apart, with occasional runs of stake-holes in between. The post-holes were relatively narrow, up to 250 mm across, and many were less than 200 mm. They were, in spite of their narrowness, quite deep (Pl 4): for example ph 217 (J/35) was 330 mm deep, 301 (L/34, Fig 10) was 270 mm deep, 321 (M/34, Fig 10) was 330 mm deep and 337 (N/35) was 250 mm deep. Their diameters tended to vary according to the

---

*In Figs 9, 15, 17, 18 and 21 unfilled hachures denote significantly later activity.

nature of the subsoil: in areas where the softer sand had been preserved the edges had collapsed, resulting in a larger post-hole.

Occasionally chocking stones were found round the edges of posts, though none were found in this arc. None of the post-holes contained clear evidence that the posts had been allowed to rot in place. While some contained flecks of charcoal, none had sufficient to warrant the suggestion that a hut had been burnt down. Doggart (Chapter 8) has found some evidence in the magnetic susceptibility readings that posts may have been left in place. Many of the larger post-holes were set at up to 30° away from the vertical (eg phs 327 and 328 in Fig 10). Their placing was not random as they tended to face towards the point on which the arc was centred. The fill was remarkably similar in most post-holes: usually the top contained a lens of black occupation soil, while underneath the charcoal content was significantly less. This lower, browner, soil was usually 7.5 YR 3/2, a slightly different shade of brown from some of the later post-holes. Occasionally lenses of lighter-coloured soil were found containing comminuted bone fragments. The complexity of the post-hole pattern in squares L–M/33–34 can be seen in the sections (Fig 10) as well as in plan. In two instances post-holes overlapped: 301, the more northerly, cut 300, while 321, the more southerly hole, cut 319.

Around ph 217 (K/35) there were several small stake-holes that usually did not exceed 60 mm in depth. A second run of stake-holes was found between post-holes 178 and 301 (L/34), but this was less clear, partly because the larger, more substantial, post-holes were closer together in this area, possibly indicating several building phases. However, these stake-holes were so shallow that it was difficult to be certain of anything more than their presence: thus ph 302 and ph 303 (L/34), containing black soil, could not really be separated from ph 301 (Fig 10). There may have been many other runs of stake-holes which, cut into black soil but not penetrating the B horizon and filled with the same black soil, were not noticed during excavation.

Dominating the centre of the hollow was a series of pits and hearths (Fig 12). The most substantial was F56/1 on the north-western edge of this group, about 600 mm deep. The pit was filled with occupation soil which showed some slight evidence of internal layering and it may have been recut (Fig 11A). It was relatively straight-sided and had several slight depressions in its base. The fill contained numerous flint artefacts and an unusually large quantity of charcoal but not a substantial amount of animal bone. Besides cutting through the edge of F56/4, F56/1 cut through a small heap of flint flakes (F25 in Fig I). In contrast, 100/0–2 was found to be a group of pits with two small pits (100/0 and 100/1) cutting the fill of

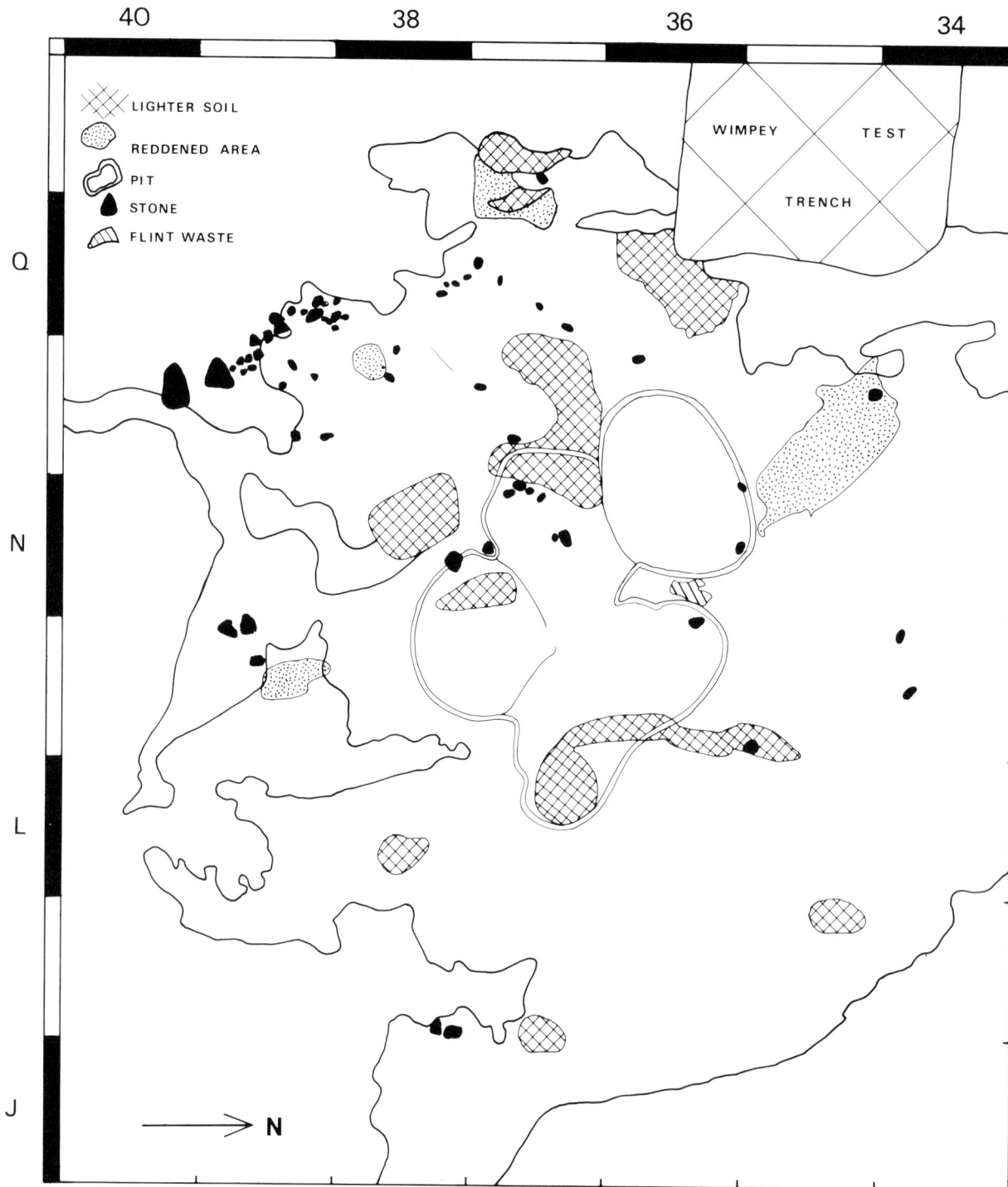

Fig 8   Plan of lighter soil, stones and other features in hut area (single line indicates extent of occupation soil)

100/2 (Fig 64). The two smaller pits were under 600 mm in diameter and only about 200 mm deep. They cut a larger, deeper pit (F100/2) which was just over 400 mm deep. This contained a series of layers alternating between light soil, rich in burnt bone fragments, and dark layers which contained burnt

hazel nut shells as well as burnt bone fragments. Another possible pit was cut into the fill of F100/2. On either side of F100/2 were other small pits which contained in some instances lenses of soil with burnt bone fragments. These features (100/3–5 and 100/6) were approximately the same size as those which cut

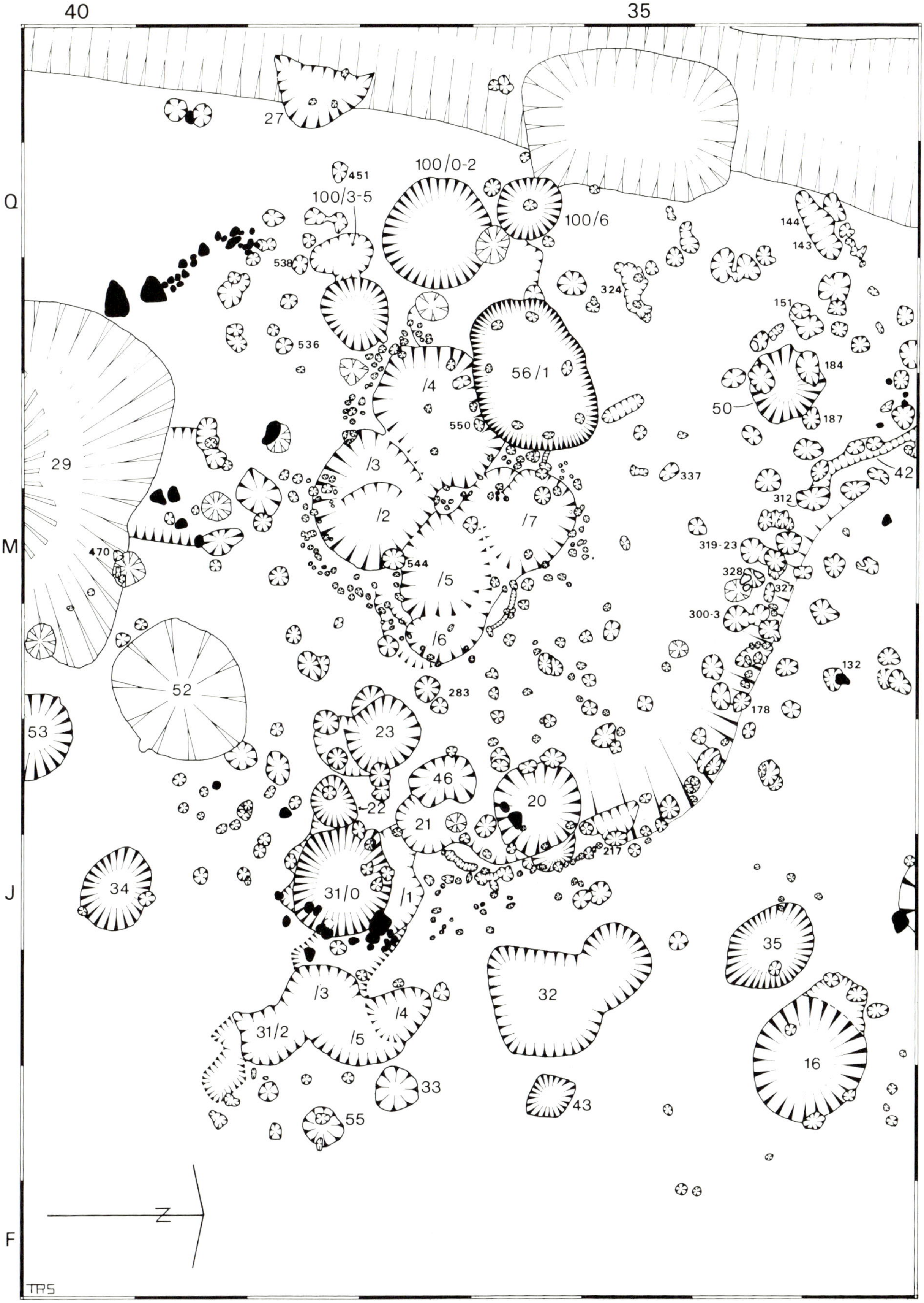

Fig 9   Plan of hut area

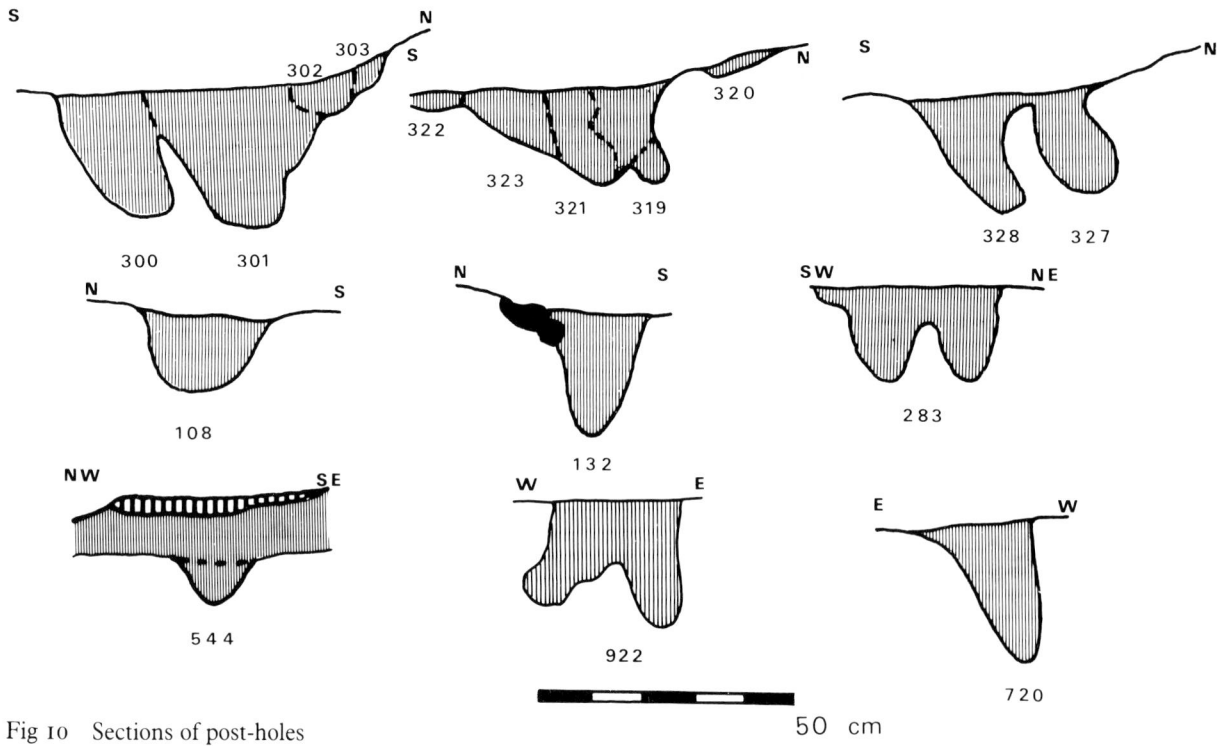

Fig 10   Sections of post-holes

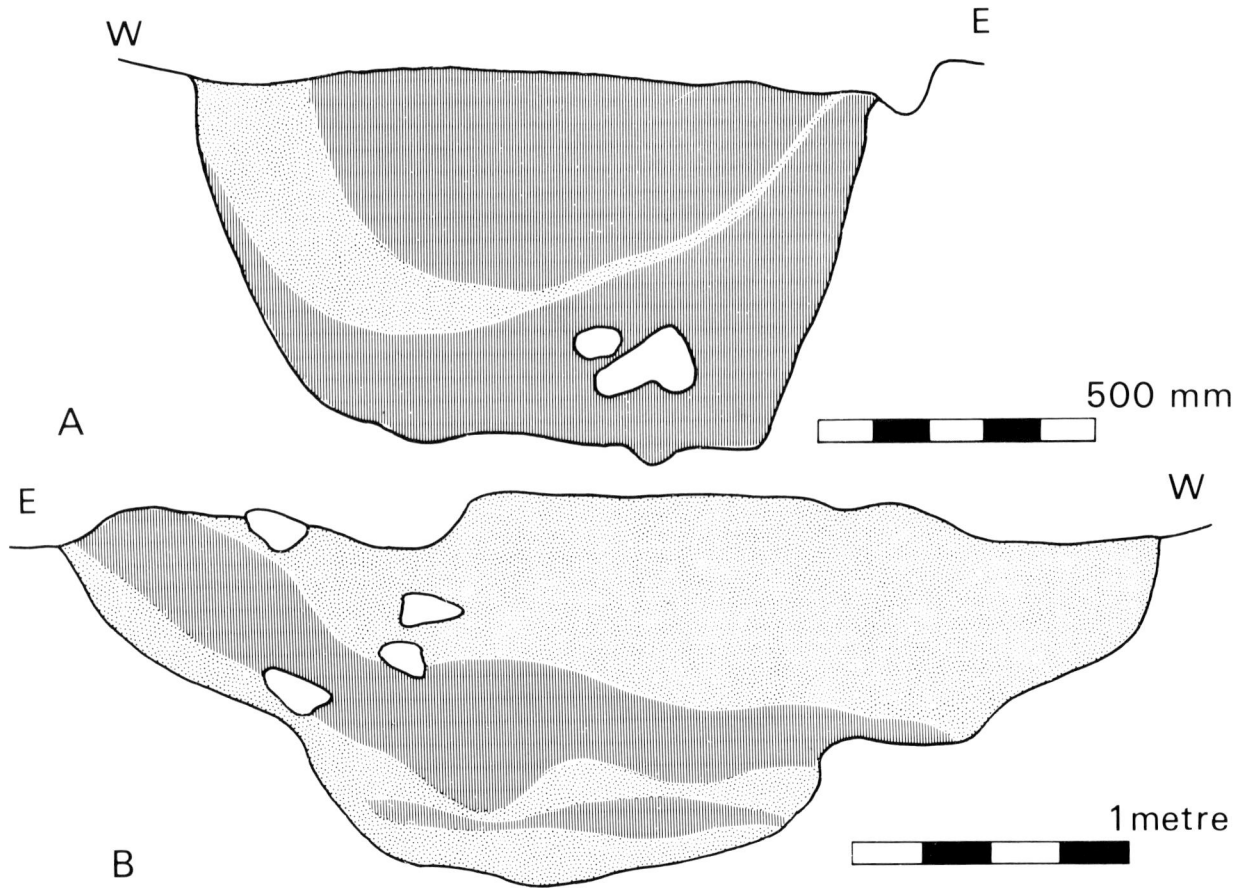

50 cm

A

500 mm

B

1 metre

Fig 11   Sections of (A) F56/1 and (B) F29

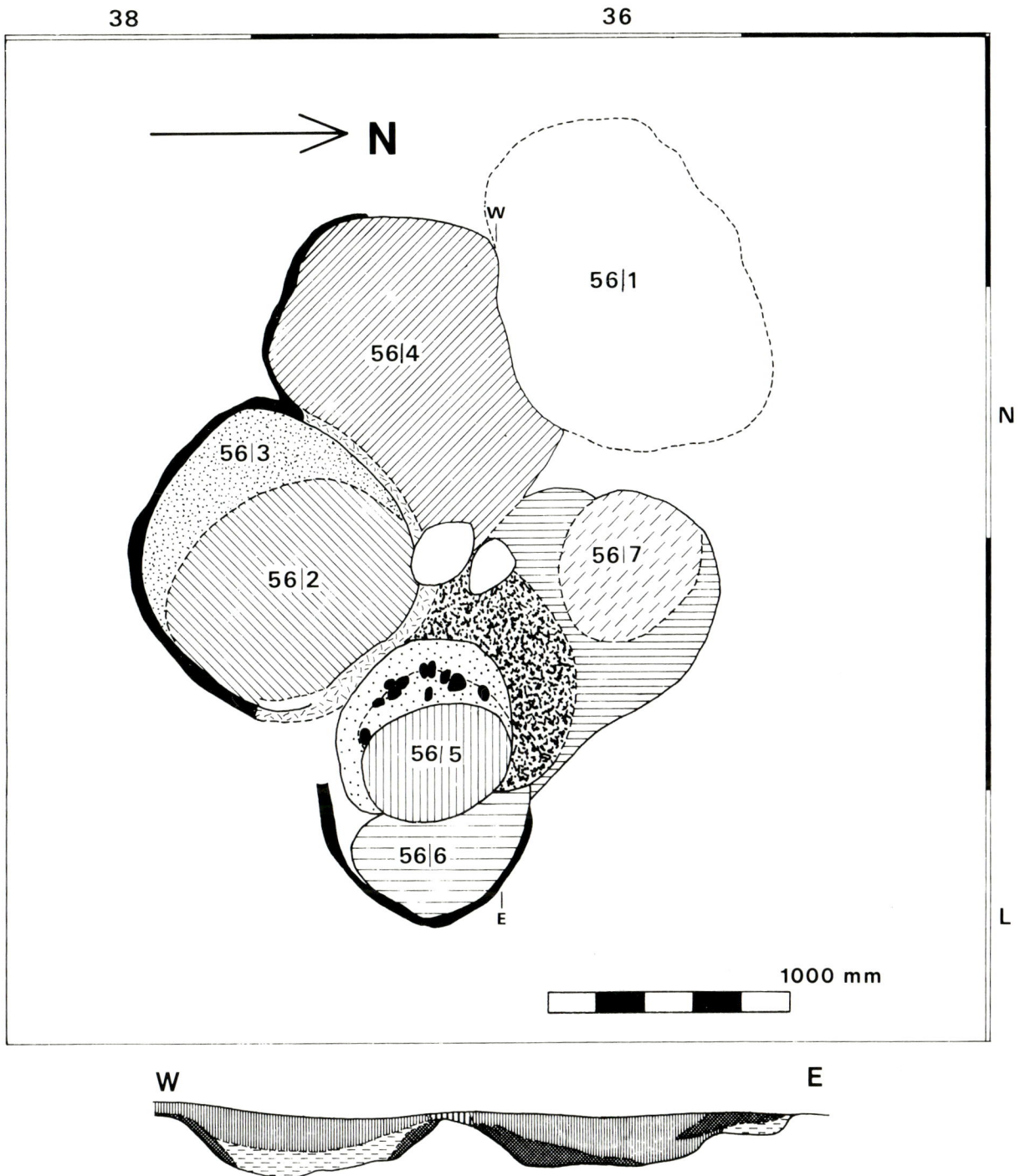

Fig 12 Central hearth area: plan and section (shading denotes individual pits, not particular fills; solid black edge indicates clinker)

100/2 (a section of 100/6 appears in Fig 13 and further details of the F100 complex are in Appendix 1a with Fig 92, in microfiche).

The main part of this complex was a group of hearths (Fig 12). There were four main hearths, two of which (56/5 and 56/2) had been recut. They did not overlap to any substantial degree, although F56/5 appeared to cut F56/7 and F56/2 may have cut F56/4. It could be argued that they were deliberately placed in an area where they could be cut into the sandy subsoil rather than the fill of another pit; in fact it is noticeable that the recutting of 56/2 seems to have entailed the filling in with sand of an earlier hearth, 56/3. The shape of the hearths was similar, roughly curvilinear, about 1 m in diameter, and their depths varied between 200 and 300 mm. While many of the other pits were straight-sided, these were much more curved with the profile of an inverted bowl.

It is instructive to examine the contents of these four hearths. There was no uniformity in their filling. In F56/2 (Pl 6) and F56/4 the sequence of fill was black soil underlain by a discontinuous layer of soil containing burnt hazel nut shells. Below that was a layer of lighter soil containing a large quantity of burnt bone fragments. At the base was sometimes a thin lens of black soil. The surface of the basal subsoil was stained red, which may be a pedogenic phenomenon. In contrast, F56/7 contained only occupation soil. The most complex hearth was 56/5. The final form was partly lined with stones which separated a greasy black fill from an inner core containing occupation soil. This pit cut through an earlier, shallow version (F56/6) whose centre lay further to the east, which contained a layer of burnt hazel nut shells and some burnt bone. The upper part of the fill of F56/6 was not contained in the bowl of the pit: it was first encountered during removal of the overlying occupation soil.

Much of the southern edge of this group of hearths was lined with a hard black clinker. On removal numerous small stake-holes were found (shown in Fig 9). These were up to 60 mm deep and were filled with a black occupation soil. It was assumed that many other stake-holes had been destroyed by the cutting of hearths so close to each other. Although they were numerous they did appear to be confined to certain specific areas of the edge of the hearths rather than to go completely round them. Other post-holes were found in the hearth complex (Fig 9). Some, such as ph 550, were cut into the surface of the bone-rich layer in F56/2, but these were relatively slight compared with the line of substantial post-holes which cut across 56/5 and 56/7. One post-hole, 544, underlay the clinker (Fig 10) whilst the others may also have pre-dated the hearths. Unlike the large post-holes round the lip of the dwelling hollow, these were vertical and had flat bottoms. The largest was over 200 mm across and, cut from a higher old ground surface, their depth must originally have been over 200 mm (Fig 10).

Essentially all the other features found in this southern part of the eastern area have to be examined in the light of their position in relation to the dwelling hollow, the arc of post-holes and the central complex of pits and hearths. Many of these other features, both man-made and natural, unfortunately obscured the possibility of obtaining a complete plan of an individual hut.

The rest of the post-holes formed an almost meaningless pattern whose detailed interpretation will be left until later (Chapter 11), but several general observations can be made at this stage (Fig 9). Nowhere were there as many post-holes as on the north-east edge of the hollow and in the area adjacent to it. In certain areas their relative scarcity could not be explained by differential survival, as much of the area was covered by Mesolithic occupation soil. The absence of smaller stake-holes could have been due to their failure to penetrate from the original surface through the occupation layer into the subsoil. Therefore it can be argued that the relative scarcity of the post-holes on the southern edge of the hollow resulted from the nature of the construction of the huts. In parts of the south-eastern quadrant of the hut hollow the old ground surface had been partly eroded, as well as, in certain places, having been totally destroyed by tree-falls. Some post-holes were therefore slighter and in many instances it was impossible to be certain if the post-hole had been originally angled. In the south-western quadrant there were occasional deeper post-holes, for example 538 (360 mm deep) and 536 (210 mm deep), though most were again rather small. Here there was also a group of large stones which appeared to have been deliberately placed in a line (shown in Figs 8 and 9). Some of them fragmented after exposure.

The post-holes in the north-west quadrant of the hollow were notable for their larger diameter. This almost certainly resulted from the softer sandy subsoil which allowed a much greater degree of collapse. This creates the problem that few are known with certainty to have been angled post-holes. Another problem in this area was the more extensive presence of roots. In certain instances, such as ph 324, it was impossible to know whether there was a complex of posts or fewer, larger, though shallower, post-holes which had been disturbed by roots.

Some other post-holes formed arcs, such as the group within the north-eastern quadrant, but not all examples could be related to structures round the central complex of hearths. Thus while most could be seen to be angled towards the central hearth complex, others, such as 451 (Q/38) and 151 (P/34), were angled away from it.

The most destructive features were the two tree-falls that lay on the southern edge of the area (Fig 9). The larger was F29 which took the form of a large, pear-shaped depression, measuring approximately 4 by 2 metres. The bottom, as can be seen in Fig 9, was rather irregular, as was the southern edge. Its maximum depth was 800 mm. This feature was first observed as an incomplete ring of black soil cut into the subsoil (visible in Fig 5), superficially like a circular foundation trench, but on excavation it was found to be a large irregular depression, mostly filled with redeposited sand. Below this, however, were two layers. The lower was a rapid silt of soft sand and above was a thick black layer containing lenses of sand and occasionally stones over 300 mm across. While the black layer was relatively thin on the northern edge and even at the deepest part of the depression, to the south was a considerably thicker layer and a substantial area where the black soil was not sealed under the redeposited natural (Fig 11B).

Obviously the main effect of this tree-fall was to destroy a large area on the edge of the dwelling hollow. The occasional groups of post-holes to the east and west and those, such as ph 470 (M/40), which partly survived on its upper edge, showed how destructive this tree-fall had been. It may however be the case that, as this part of the site had all its occupation soil stripped by ploughing, this and other tree-falls *preserved* samples of the material adjacent to them, albeit in a disturbed context. These tree-falls appeared to be of some antiquity in their own right. In this instance the occupation soil had not disappeared before the tree-fall, while in other cases, such as F304 (Fig 18), the demesne ditch cut through them. The other feature which related to F29 was the line of more recent post-holes already shown in Fig 5, two of which cut the annular ring of black soil.

A second, rather smaller, possible tree-fall, F52, lay south-east of the hearth complex. This had the same characteristics as F29. It was first noted as an incomplete ring of black soil, and on excavation showed the same sequence, of redeposited sand, lenses of occupation soil, and sand. The most noticeable difference between this and F29 was that for its diameter F52 was relatively deep—550 mm. It lay on the harder, compact sandy gravel.

The edge of the dwelling hollow was further obscured by a group of pits and hearths in the area H–K/36–40. The most destructive of these was the hearth F31/0 which had cut through several post-holes. It was clear from the absence of a black fill in the top of many post-holes in this area, and from the profile of F31/0, that the top of the subsoil had been eroded. F31/0 was rather shallow, so that although in most pits the upper part of the fill usually consisted of occupation soil, in F31/0 we have a hearth about 1 m across with only two substantial layers: (1) was a dark layer containing large quantities of burnt hazel nut shells and bone, while (2) was the lighter-coloured layer which contained only bone fragments. This hearth was, unlike those in the central complex, partly cut into other features and was delimited by a line of stone. There may have been at least one earlier hearth to the east.

Apparently post-dating F31/0, and also the main spread of occupation soil, was a complex of pits (Figs 9 and 64). One cut through F31/0 while two others cut the occupation soil (this has been shown by blade declination). Many were relatively small, straight-sided pits: for example F22, F33 (Fig 13) and F55 were all less than 500 mm in diameter though quite deep. At the other extreme were F20 (over 800 mm in diameter) and F53 (700 mm across, Fig 13). Some of them were complex pits which cut each other, like F34 and the most complex, F31/3–5, where there appeared to be several pits (Fig 13). As in the central complex there was no consistency in fill: F31/3–5 had layers containing bone and burnt hazel nut shells in varying quantities while others contained only occupation soil. The complexity of this area is best illustrated by F23 where in a relatively small area there were three small pits, one of which was cut by a post-hole (Fig 13). One aspect of this group of pits which varied was their depth, partly because of the removal of some of the subsoil in areas such as F33 (Fig 13) and F55.

Scattered around the immediate vicinity of the dwelling hollow were numerous other pits. Usually these were under 1 m in diameter and contained only occupation soil, though in the case of F27 (R/38), which had been partly obliterated by the ditch system, more organically rich layers were present. One feature—F16 (H/33)—may have been a hearth although again, like F31/0, it had been truncated. It contained only a single thin lens of light, organically rich soil.

The main problem with the eastern edge of the eastern area was that agricultural activity had removed the tops of numerous post-holes and so it was impossible to assign them to any particular period of occupation. However, as certainly later post-holes were relatively scarce in the area adjacent to the eastern edge of the site, it was assumed that most of the post-holes here were likely to be Mesolithic. The erosion was at its most extensive in the north-eastern corner of the area where no features or post-holes were found. Here perhaps up to 200 mm had been removed from the original old ground surface, while along the rest of the eastern edge perhaps 100 mm of a sandy gravel had been removed. Therefore apart from F74 (G/27, Fig 15), a large pit filled with layers of occupation soil and sand, this area contained only the rather battered remnants of features, and in the case of F108 (D–E/34) it was impossible to be certain whether this was a small pit or a pair of post-holes. Similarly F97 (G/29) had been extensively damaged and was less than 100 mm deep. The bases of other, later, features were also found in the vicinity of F108.

The area between the dwelling hollow and the east–west ditch was also badly damaged (Fig 15). The proportion where the old ground surface could be argued to be preserved was tiny, again represented by the spread of occupation soil. The features and post-holes formed no clear pattern, lacking the key to their elucidation which the edge of the dwelling

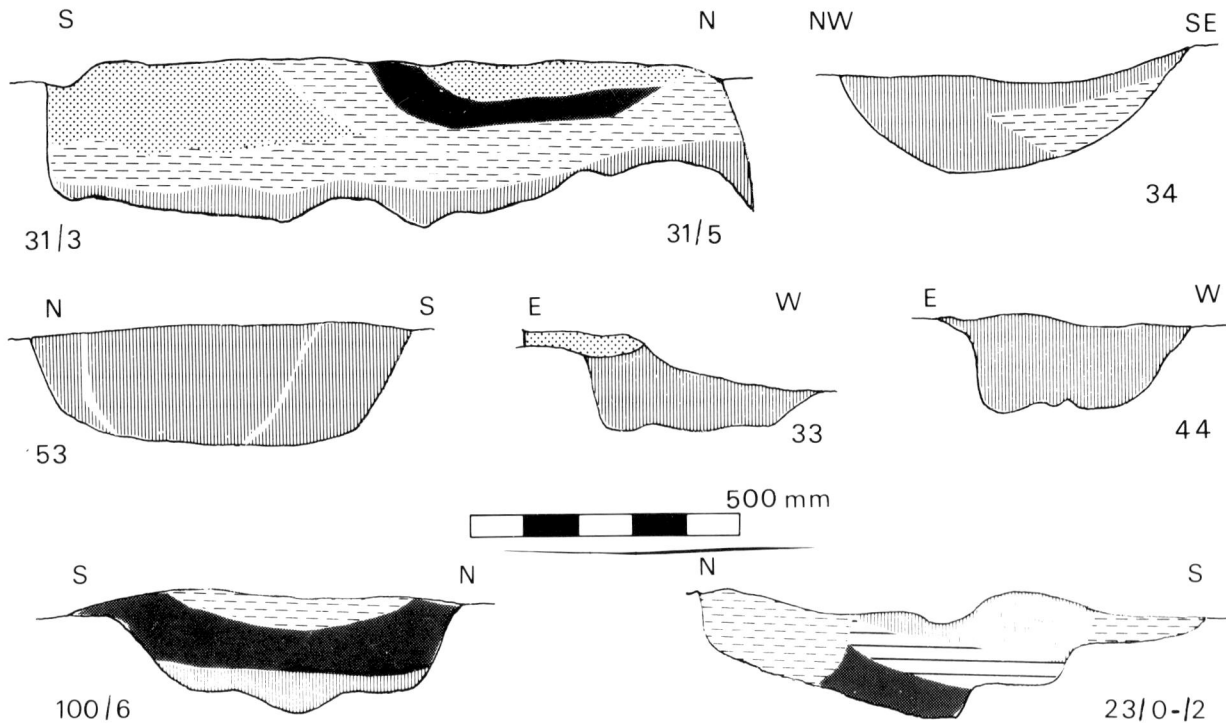

Fig 13   Sections of pits

hollow provided further south. The plan shows that there could have been at least one structure built in this area. The centre was represented by F83 and F91 (M–N/30). The latter, though surprisingly deep, may have been a hearth as it had the clinker-like ring of occupation soil around it, though again the fill did not reflect its function; in fact its rather deep, straight-sided profile (Fig 14) suggested that it may have been deliberately deepened and used as a rubbish pit. F83 was rather more enigmatic. It appeared to be a shallow, recut, two-phase pit which truncated three substantial post-holes. The fact that stake-holes were found round both these pits suggests that they may be in the same category as the hearths in the centre of the dwelling hollow to the south.

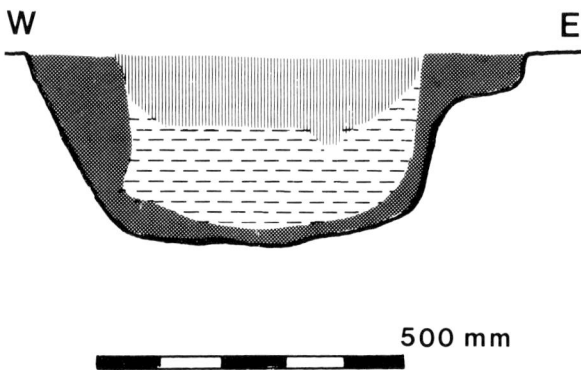

Fig 14   Section of F91

It was possible to distinguish part of the outline of a hut centred on these hearths. This ran from ph 755 (J/29) in a north-westerly direction towards ph 843 (M/27) and south-westerly to ph 842 (P/28). Other possible lines of post-holes were found on the southern side of these features, apparently abutting onto the main dwelling hollow. The structure in this area seems to have been ovoid (for a fuller discussion of the shapes of the huts see below, Chapter 11).

As the eastern edge of the area had been heavily eroded, many of the post-holes had been partly destroyed and there was no evidence of stake-holes between larger post-holes. Another result was that many of the post-holes on the eastern edge were significantly shallower than those on the west. As the lower part of most of the post-holes on the site contained a rather similar light brown fill (irrespective of their upper fill) it was almost impossible to ascertain here which were intrusive and later. However, many were of a similar size to those found in the dwelling hollow area, for example ph 761 (K/28) and ph 817 (M/27) (Fig 15). Again many of these post-holes were angled towards the possible central hearths.

Once these remnants of putative structures are taken out of consideration we are left with a random scatter of features and post-holes. At this stage of the site description only the more important elements will be enumerated. In the area N–Q/32–33 was a short narrow gully up to 200 mm deep, F42, filled

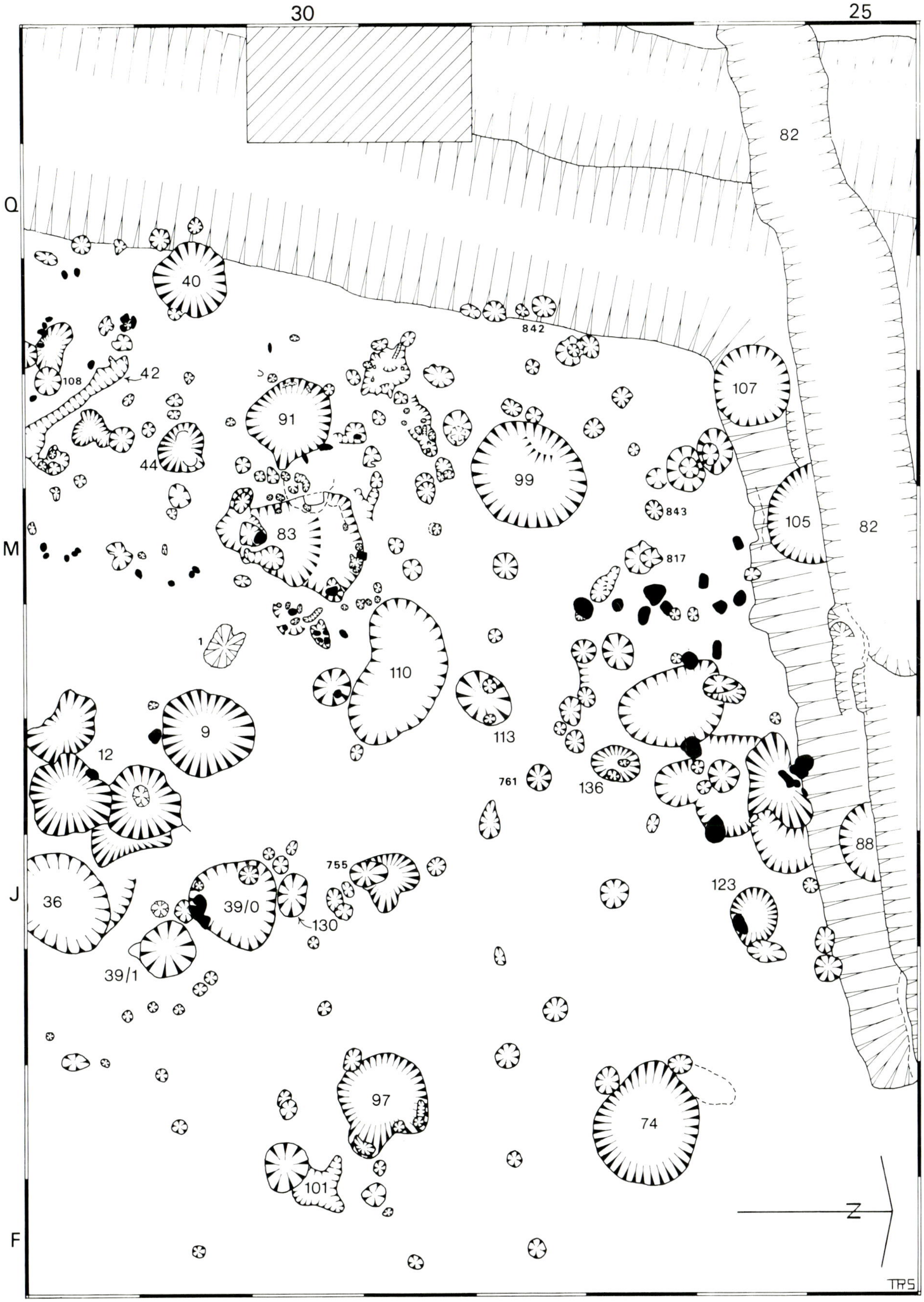

Fig 15   Northern part of eastern area: plan

with occupation soil. Most of the post-holes in this area were filled with the same soil as the gully and were impossible to separate into examples pre-dating, contemporary with, or post-dating it. The one exception was ph 312 (M/33, Fig 9) which cut the slot.

To the north and east of the hut hollow was a group of pits which had been partly obliterated by lazy beds (Figs 9 and 15). Several were approximately 1 m across, including F36 (J/32), F16 (G–H/33–34), F110/0 (L/29) and F99 (M–N/28). Some had lenses of organically rich soil, like F16 and F36, but they usually contained only occupation soil. There were also smaller pits, such as 39/1 (H/31), less than 500 mm across. F40 (P–Q/31), F44 (N/31: Fig 13) and, tentatively, the F12 complex (K/31) could belong to this group. In the case of F12/1–3 it was concluded that these had collapsed as they were cut into soft sand. The most enigmatic group was made up of F110/1 (K/29), F123 (J/26), F136 (K/27), F113 (L/28–29) and possibly F130 (J/30). These were small oval pits less than 500 mm across. Unlike F39/1 they were rather shallow and contained a brown fill rather than the darker fill which was usual where the Mesolithic occupation soil had filled a pit. As 110/1 cut through a Mesolithic feature (F110/2) it is by no means certain that this group of features was Mesolithic in date.

Along the lip of the east–west ditch, F82, the old ground surface was apparently better preserved because of the presence of a hedge. The scatter of stones embedded in the sandy subsoil of this area

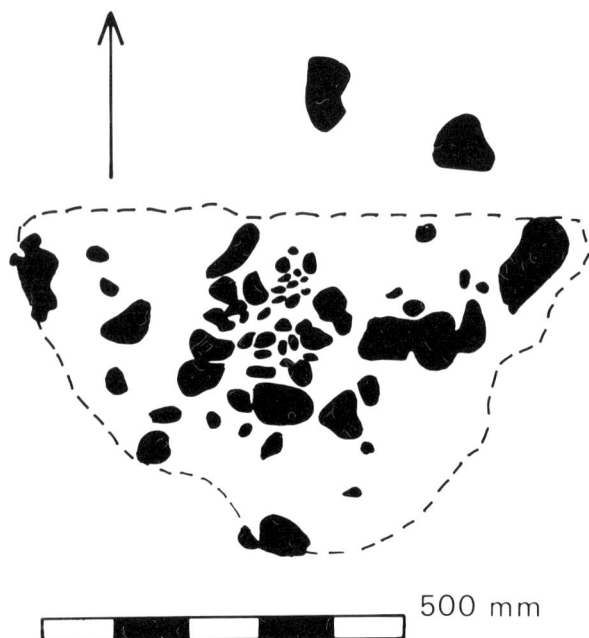

Fig 16   Plan of F88

(shown in black on Figs 1 and 15) was a relatively rare phenomenon for this part of the site. Several quite deep pits, including F105, had been partly destroyed by F82, the east–west ditch. Two examples, F107 (N–Q/26) and F105 (M–N/25–26), were over 300 mm deep. F88 (J–K/25) differed from these in that it contained a number of burnt stones (Fig 16) and was relatively narrow in comparison to its depth.

Northern Area

This area was conveniently divided off from the rest of the site by the two late ditch systems and the limits of the excavation (Fig 17). It was a hollow, formed by a ridge running east–west along the edge of the excavated area. This hollow had been deep enough to warrant the dumping of up to 500 mm of soil to level up the field, and this had provided some protection to the site.

At the base of the topsoil was a lens of relatively sterile yellow sand. The extent of this layer (Fig 60) appears to have been conditioned by the configuration of the subsoil: it was confined within the bottom of the hollow, while round its edges the modern soil lay directly on a truncated sandy subsoil. During excavation a few shallow gullies were noted cutting across this sandy layer from north-east to south-west, whilst at a later stage several other pits were found to contain a light, very sandy soil of similar colour to the yellow sand. Therefore it can be suggested that many pits, including F114 (G/19) and F127 (J/22), were not necessarily sealed below this sand. The most reasonable explanation for the layer is that at some point an old ground surface was denuded of its humus and, without protection, elements of the sandy subsoil were washed into the hollow. This area produced a significant quantity of hand-made pottery. While some was found within the sandy layer, it mostly came from its top and from the base of the topsoil. Much of the pottery was found in areas adjacent to pits which were notable for their sandy fill. Therefore in spite of the occasional sherd found below the sandy layer, it seems that much of the pottery, which was mostly Neolithic but also included souterrain ware, was found on an old ground surface stratified above the sandy layer, and the pottery indicates that a number of pits were cut through this old ground surface into the subsoil (Fig 17).

Usually it proved very difficult to ascertain where the yellow sandy layer ended and the subsoil began. The only area where the two were clearly separated was in the vicinity of F109 (J/23). Here the black occupation soil was not present, but an area of sand round this pit was stained a dark brown. The pit contained numerous stones, was relatively narrow and deep, and had a clinker-like ring of black soil

Fig 17 Northern area: plan

round part of its edge. The brown sand area around the pit contained some industrial waste and artefacts that could be presumed to be *in situ*. Besides this a dense scatter of small stones was found, mostly to the east and north of the pit (see below, Chapter 11, Fig 68).

Many of the pits on the eastern and southern edge of the northern area were rather enigmatic shallow features which contained little apart from the light brown sandy fill. To the south-west, however, there was some evidence of two phases of occupation. Here a small circular structure was traced (Fig 17 and Pl 7), consisting of a series of short gullies up to 150 mm deep, filled with the usual dark occupation soil. There was no clear evidence that substantial individual posts ever stood in them. The one exception is the possible post-hole 700 at the eastern end of F94. The two southern slots (F94 and F116) were found to be rather intermittent, as the sand covering them was indistinguishable from the subsoil and this created the impression of a run of post-hole slots, each about 200 mm long. These would, however, be very substantial for such a series of shallow trenches. It could simply be that the sand dug out of the trenches was used to hold down the edges of a small tent. This complex of narrow slots had been partly destroyed on its northern edge. A large, shallow, irregular pit (F137) cut across two earlier gullies, F135 and F128: its lighter brown fill was clearly superimposed on the dark fill of F135 and F128.

The post-holes were again scattered in an apparently random fashion in this area. Those to the east had been partly truncated and were therefore undatable, while many further west can be assigned to either the Mesolithic or later periods. It is tempting to interpret some in K/22–23 as forming a porch belonging to the little curvilinear structure, but this leaves all the other post-holes unexplained. At this stage one can only observe that many of the post-holes were rather large.

Central Area

Before excavation the demesne bank ran north–south across the central area (shaded in Fig 2). A trial trench was cut through it in 1974 on lines 31–32, and the rest of the bank was removed, mostly in 1976. The bank in places was up to 2 m high, but in the excavated area was usually little more than 1 m high. It consisted of the local forest brown earth and lacked any clear evidence of layering (Fig 11). The only distinctive area within it was a patch of lighter sandy soil which underlay the brown earth, unfortunately disturbed by a large tree root. The southern end of the bank had been used extensively as a rabbit warren, so there was no trace of surviving stratification or structures. Nothing of significance was found

under the bank. The only *in situ* feature was a small pile of stones which contained a sherd of a tyg.

East of the bank was F5, the flat-bottomed ditch already described (above, page 10), and along the bank's west edge was another flat-bottomed ditch, F202, also rather shallow (Fig 18). A small extension trench along lines 22–23 revealed the remains of a stone wall in the bottom of this ditch, a relatively slight structure, two stones thick and high. There was no evidence for a collapsed higher wall. The only dating evidence associated with the F4–5 ditch complex was some late and post-medieval pottery found in an area towards the northern end of the ditch system. While much of it was found in the brown earth filling the ditch, some was associated with a mortar slick in the base of F4. The pottery was almost all recovered between lines 20 and 25. The two flat-bottomed ditches, F5 and F202, were probably of recent date, 18th-century or later.

In spite of the destruction caused by the north–south ditch systems it was hoped that the area under the demesne bank might preserve a virtually undisturbed record of the Mesolithic occupation. The 1974 trial trench located only a small area of occupation soil but the top of the B horizon appeared to be more or less *in situ*. Full excavation did, however, reveal a surface that had suffered more damage than the dwelling hollow area or the Mesolithic old ground surface within the forest. Apart from three small areas, the Mesolithic palaeosol had been destroyed. At the southern end of the bank it had been destroyed by the rabbit warren, while to the north the area may have been truncated during post-medieval bank-building operations. The main features preserved were two large pits on the northern edge of the bank, a chipping-floor (F214) near the southern edge, and a scatter of post-holes and pits, including several on the ridge between the two eastern ditches (F4 and F5).

The description of the excavated remains will proceed from north to south (Fig 18). Excavation below a modern gap in the demesne bank revealed a complex of post-holes which overlay a large pit, F126 (Q–S/22–23). The post-holes could not be distinguished by size, but some had a darker fill reminiscent of those in the dwelling hollow area (7.5 YR 3/2) while others had a lighter brown fill (5 YR 3/3). The post-holes with the lighter fill appeared to form a straight line running at right angles between the ditch systems (Fig 60). While no extensive black occupation soil was found in this area, some of the post-holes did cut across an area of dark soil which was the upper filling of F126, a large pit filled with black occupation soil and lenses of brown soil. Sections through the pit showed that it had been recut (Fig 19). The earlier pit contained black soil in a lighter brown fill, while the second contained

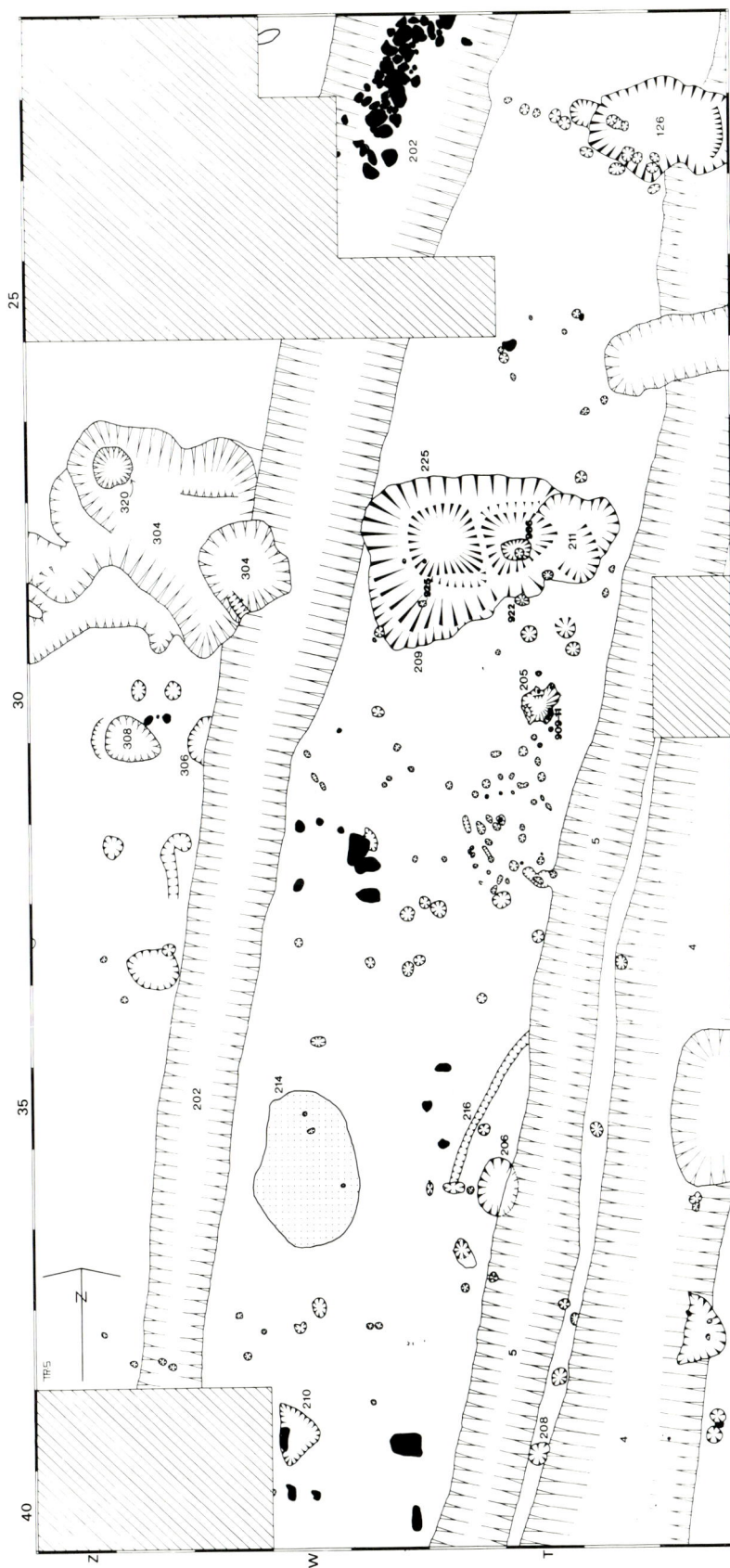

Fig 18   Central area: plan

EAST   WEST

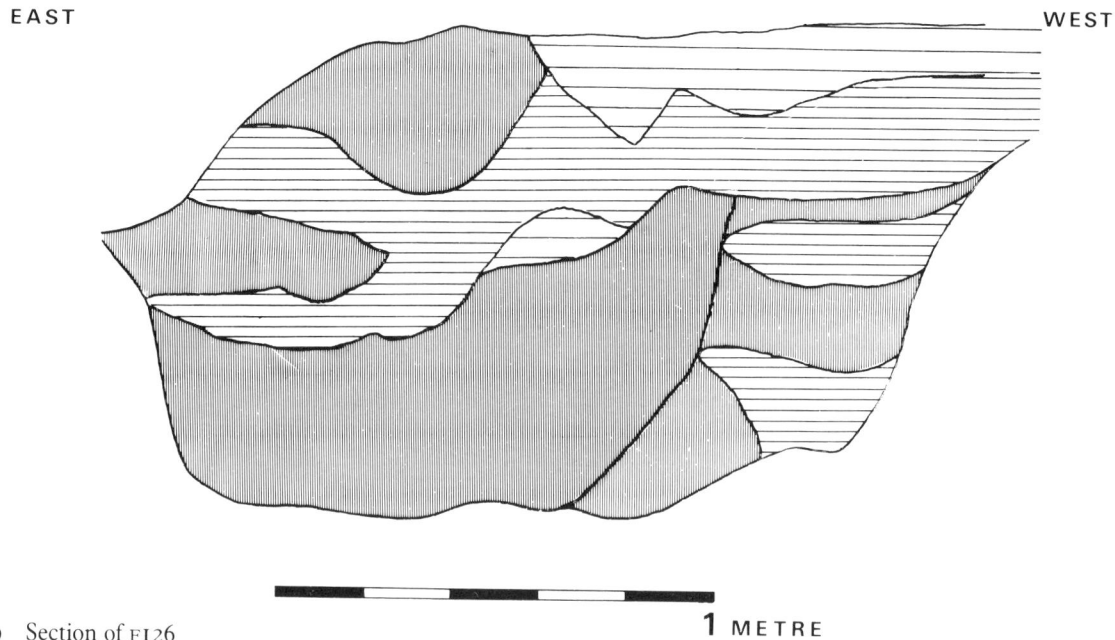

Fig 19   Section of F126   **1** METRE

mostly black soil. They were roughly 1 m deep and about 1 m wide. The overall length of this complex was only 1600 mm. A smaller pit on the western edge appears to have been largely obliterated. Neither of the F126 pits contained any significant concentration of organic material.

The area south of this feature appeared to have been levelled, and again no real trace of occupation soil was preserved. The area was dominated by the complex F209/211 (Fig 18) which on excavation turned out to be similar to F126. The refilling of part of it with sand created the superficial impression that F209 was a group of rather small pits adjacent to F211. Only during excavation was it realized that this area had been truncated by a large pit filled with sand, F225. The result was that the area was not sectioned along the most strategic points, but the available sections are illustrated (Fig 20). Root disturbances had badly damaged the top of these features. F209 was made up of a complex of pits which may have been over 600 mm deep, partly destroyed by the sand-filled pit, F225, and a small pit (209/0) overlay 209/1 on its western edge. The original section did not show clearly how many pits were present and so it was recut, revealing three pits, 209/1, /2 and /3, filled with lenses of black soil, some containing bone fragments, others relatively sterile (Fig 20A and C). Other lenses were brown and some were layers of slumped sand. F209/1 was observed to be cut by /2 and both were cut by /3. Several small patches of clinker helped to mark the edge of a small pit, which unfortunately lay between sections and so was only noted in plan. Other small pits (again

disturbed) may have existed further to the east, and one substantial post-hole (ph 986, Fig 18) cut through the uppermost part of these deposits. On the other hand ph 925 was cut by F209. The post-holes could be substantial, for example ph 922 (Figs 10 and 18). The pits were unusual in that the southern edges had rather irregular shapes and their fill included lenses of slumped sand. Two more pits lay east of 209, filled with black occupation soil. F211/2 cut through the edge of F209/2, and was in turn cut by F211/1 (Fig 20C). The fill of these F211 pits, in comparison with the 209 complex, was relatively homogeneous.

The pits had been truncated by a large depression filled with sand, F225 (Fig 20B), and near the base of the sand were two depressions filled with black soil. In places the black soil was found on the sides of the pit, and it was its appearance on the surface which indicated that the sand was not *in situ*. Two post-holes were cut into the top of the sand.

There was a scatter of post- and stake-holes south of the F209/211 complex, mainly concentrated west of ditch F5. Perhaps the levelling of the old ground surface under the demesne bank had removed some post-holes further west and so exaggerated their tendency to cluster in a small area. A pit, F205 in T/30, lay on the edge of this group, cutting several post-holes including 908–911. The pit itself was less than 600 mm across and funnelled down to a narrow bottom. The total depth was 390 mm. Within the black, almost greasy, fill was a layer with numerous burnt stones, while some flint flakes and burnt bone fragments underlay them.

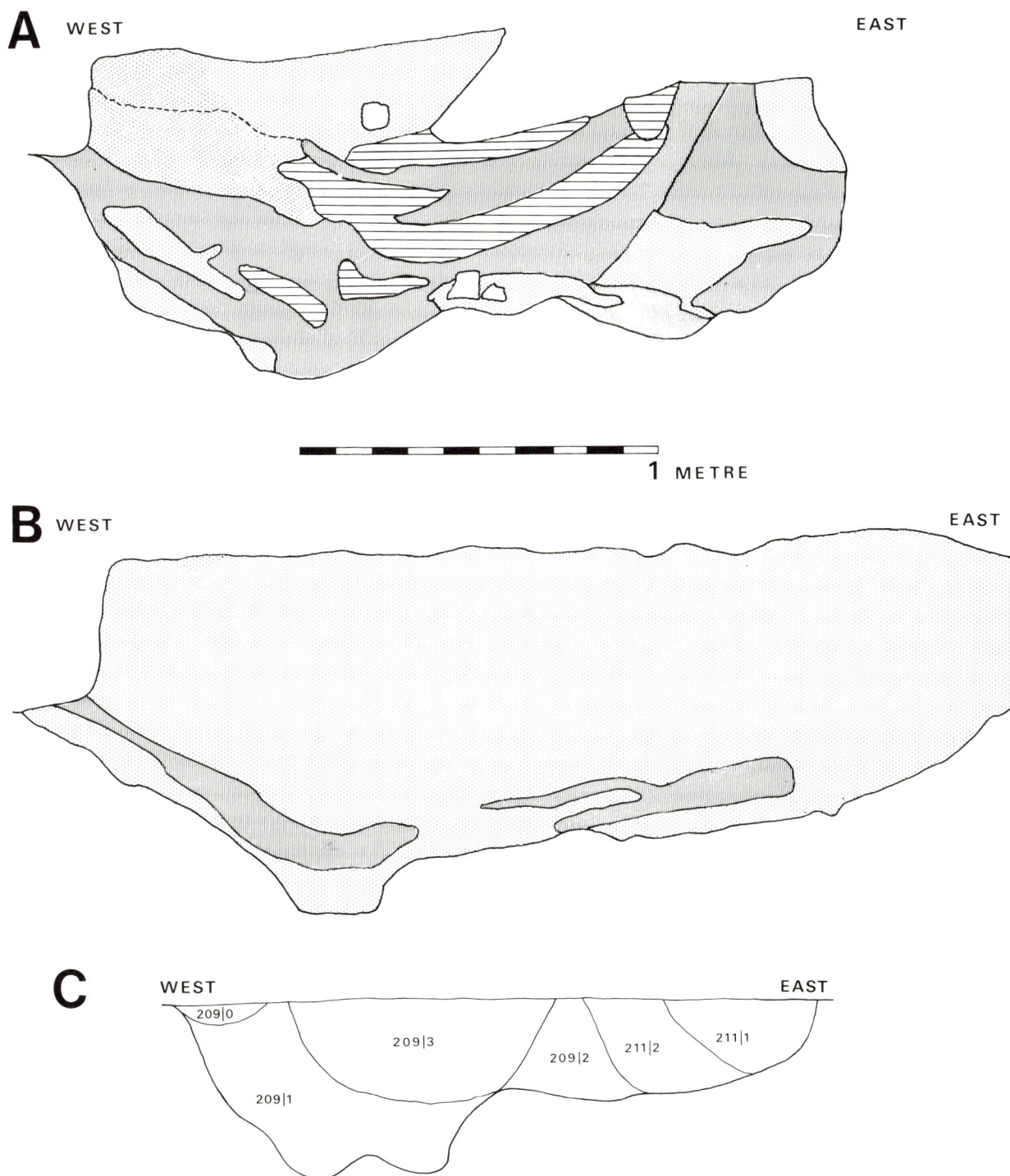

Fig 20   Sections of (A) F209/1–3, (B) F225 and (C) schematic key section across FS209 and 211

Further south, from line 32 to 40, was an area where the surface had been destroyed by rabbit burrows. Large numbers of stones were scattered over the surface, but relatively few areas of occupation were preserved. Many of the stones may have belonged to the period of bank construction rather than having been present before the Mesolithic occupation. Therefore apart from the remnants of a chipping floor, F214, this area consisted of an eroded old ground surface in which were found a variety of post-holes as well as three pits, FS206, 208 and 210. Only F210 contained any significant concentration of organic material. The chipping floor, F214, covered an area of approximately 4 square metres and on its northern edge was a small patch of red ochre. It seems likely that this floor, which was up to 100 mm thick, represented only the densest area and that the rest had been destroyed by rabbit burrows. A shallow gully, F216, containing only brown soil, was a rather slight feature, perhaps later than the others.

Western Area

Up to 600 mm of soil had accumulated in this area in recent centuries, and in most parts this was a homogeneous brown layer, disturbed by tree roots and rabbit holes. Though recently planted trees were beginning to cause disturbance, much of the worst damage had been done by trees which had already died and disappeared. This brown layer contained occasional sherds of post-medieval pottery.

In a trial trench, later absorbed in a larger area excavation, the brown soil or humus was almost non-existent, and two ridges of rather more sandy soil were found to run across the trench from north-east to south-west. These contained sherds of tyg, salt-glazed ware and a sherd of Bellarmine. Below these ridges was a darker layer which was also quite sandy, again different from the humus layer found elsewhere. As this trial trench was placed in an optimum location to avoid tree roots, it is hardly surprising that it proved impossible to trace these sandy layers elsewhere because of root disturbance.

This area was not under threat from development and so the limits of the excavation were set to determine the extent of preservation of the Mesolithic settlement. To the west and north, therefore, the limit was set several metres beyond the apparent limit of the Mesolithic features or occupation soil, and on the northern edge this coincided with a slight rise in the subsoil. To the south a test trench (marked in Fig 2) revealed that roots and rabbit burrows had destroyed any trace of occupation and, as only two small post-holes cut into the subsoil were found and excavation of adjacent areas in the field had produced nothing, it was decided that little of significance would be likely to occur south of line 40.

On clearing the humus down to the top of the black occupation soil it was clear that there had been a great deal of disturbance (Fig 21). Not only were there many later features, but tree roots had caused some mixing of deposits. In spite of these problems, however, an area of occupation soil was still preserved, cut into by two recent root systems. One, F305, had left a visible depression, while another root system in area Y–Z/37–35 had from a higher level totally destroyed the black occupation soil.

Although disturbed by roots, the occupation soil was quite thick and was not cut by lazy bedding, but

because of later occupation it was impossible to be certain how much of its upper portion had been removed. While no sherds of post-medieval pottery were found embedded in the soil layer or just above it, they were found within 100 mm of it. Sherds of Neolithic pottery and souterrain ware were found in it. On the western edge (F'/33) at least one post-hole (ph 1020) was cut into the lower sandy dark layer from only 50 mm above the subsoil, and this layer clearly post-dated the Mesolithic occupation layer. Therefore, as there was no substantial layer of soil between the Mesolithic and many later reoccupations, the former cannot be presumed to have been intact. Indeed, significant quantities of Mesolithic material found in the lower part of the overlying soil were presumed to be locally derived rather than to have been brought in from elsewhere through later activities.

The spread of Mesolithic occupation soil was very irregular in outline, but was roughly 9 m north–south by 6 m east–west and 160 mm thick at its maximum (marked in Fig 2). This occupation soil had probably extended over a much larger area but had been destroyed. The two tree root holes already described illustrate one method of its destruction. The Mesolithic layer was twofold. Its upper part was quite black and contained most of the archaeological material, while the lower part was rather grey and lacked any significant concentration of flint. This division can be seen in section (Fig II) and in the record of archaeological material found in each layer. Much larger quantities of archaeological material were found in this area than in the hut hollow but consisted mostly of industrial waste. Many stones were scattered through the layer (Fig 22), but except for F335 (B'/31–32) none appeared to have been deliberately placed. F335 was a small pit edged with stones, found when the upper part of the occupation soil was removed.

While Mesolithic features were relatively sparse there were other traces of human activity. Along the southern edge of the area was a series of shallow, flat-bottomed trenches running north–south. None was over 150 mm deep. Although they all ran parallel, they differed in length and breadth, F318 being rather more irregular than the others. All contained brown soil but no diagnostic archaeological material. Immediately north of this area lay the edge of the occupation soil. Here a series of small pits cut into it, almost rectilinear in outline, no more than 600 mm long and between 150 and 200 mm deep. Good examples are F314 and F315, while a slightly irregular possible example is F328/0, which cut an earlier feature filled with black soil (F328/1).

There were other clearly later features in this area, such as pit F313 (E'–F'/30) which contained two glass beads, and a rather intermittent gully, F326/220,

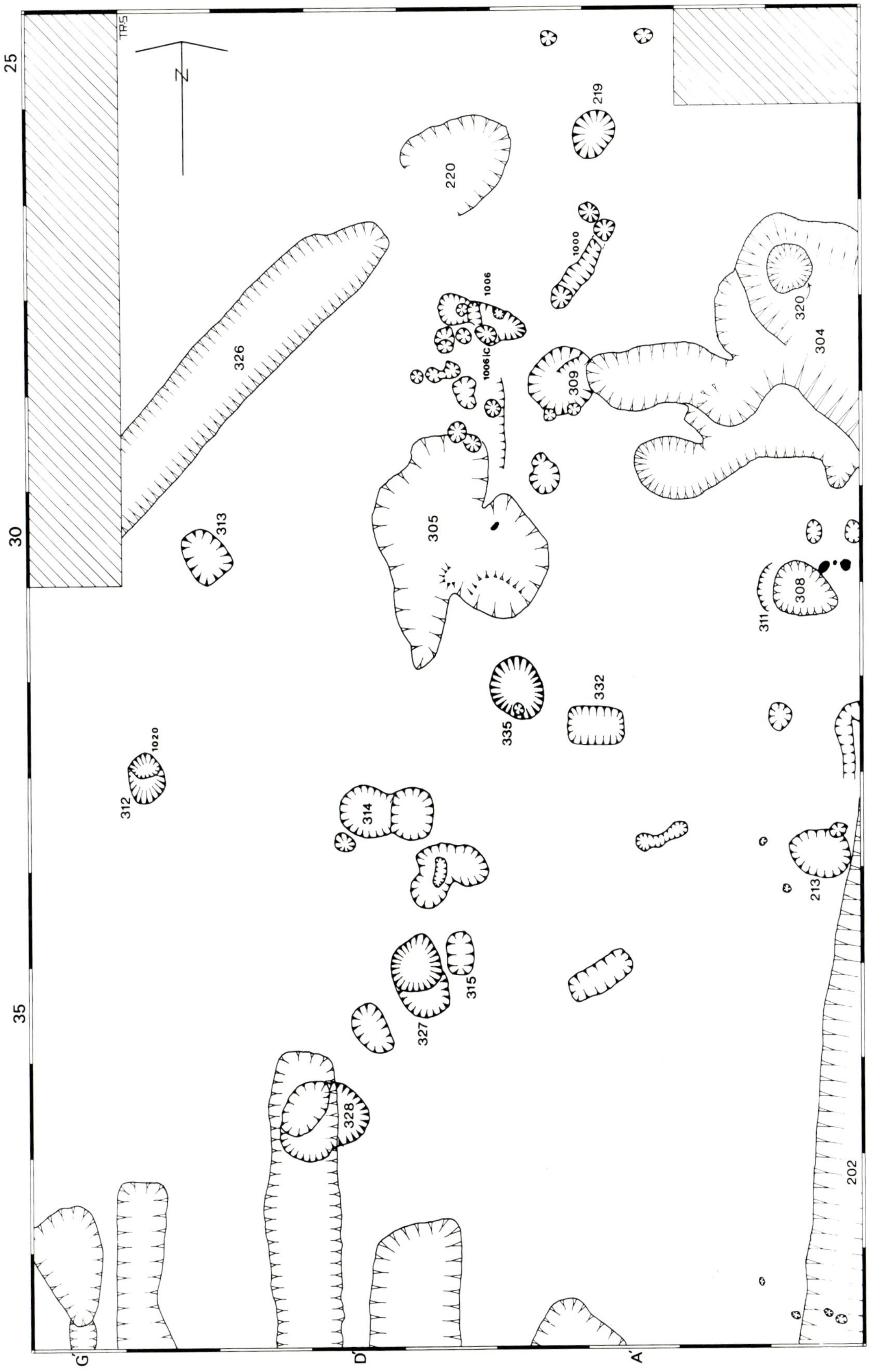

Fig 2I   Western area: plan

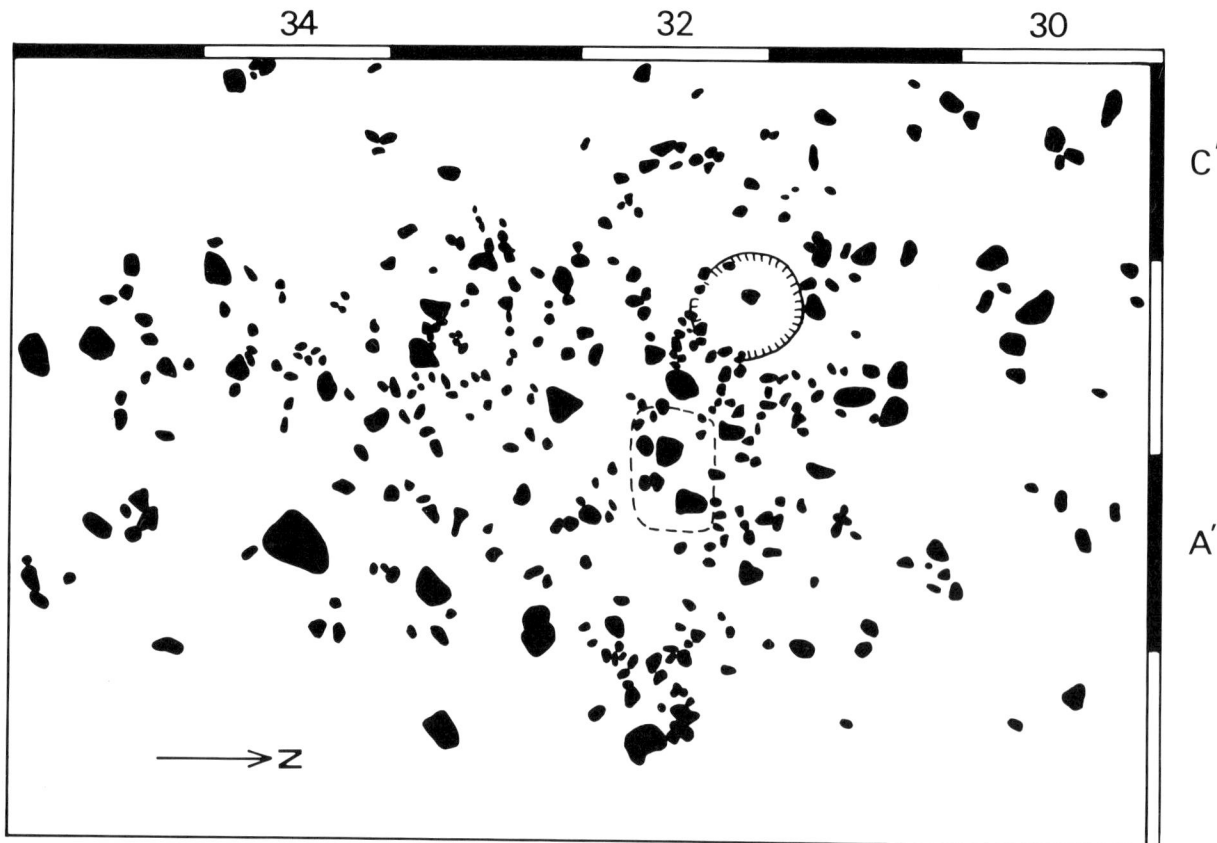

Fig 22   Distribution of stones under western scatter of flints

found in the north-eastern corner of the excavation. F326 contained a brown soil while its probable continuation, F220, produced two sherds of souter-rain ware. The pit, F313. was filled with large lumps of charcoal which produced a ^{14}C date of 218 ± 40 bc (Appendix 4).

Apart from the occupation soil and later features, one is immediately struck by the substantial area in which relatively little was found. The whole southern part of the area contained virtually no post-holes and very few pits. Extensive erosion cannot explain their absence since much of the area was covered by the Mesolithic soil and there was no significant alteration in the level of subsoil in adjacent areas. Therefore, while partial destruction is possible, the absence of pits and post-holes must be considered as genuine. Numerous small depressions were found, but these were shallow, irregular and usually filled with a grey soil and were presumed to be the natural hollows in the old pre-Mesolithic ground surface. Numerous small examples found in Y–Z/38–32, for example, were so shallow that it was concluded that they were simply stone hollows. These irregularities of surface, and the numerous stones and the grey horizon, indicated that a natural soil had survived in this area.

The few pits in the southern part of the area were

shallow, often only 100 mm in depth, and rather indistinct: examples included F328/1 and F327/1. Other more distinct pits found in the north-eastern corner of the area were often damaged. F306 was a small pit about 500 mm across (X/31–32, Fig 18), cut by a post-medieval ditch, F202, while F311 was a small pit, possibly 500 mm in diameter (Z/31–32), destroyed by a modern pit, F308. F309 (B'/29), a small pit 700 mm across, partly disturbed by a tree-fall (F304), contained fragments of burnt bone, and finally F219 (A'–B'/26) contained numerous fragments of burnt mammal bones.

Much of this area was disturbed by a recent root system and so much of the occupation soil in the area X–Z/31–32 was destroyed. There was also a large tree-fall hollow, F304. Though one small area of F304 may have disturbed a possible large pit, F304/1 (Fig 18), it was almost entirely a natural hollow which had filled up with a brown soil and redeposited natural. One intriguing aspect of this tree-fall was the presence of F320, a small pit filled with brown soil, cut into the redeposited natural filling of the hollow. It was never clear whether F320 post-dated the tree-fall or whether it had been lifted bodily in the roots of the tree and then collapsed back into the hollow more or less intact!

The post-holes were similarly sparse, with only one concentration in the northern area. Some were definitely post-Mesolithic: ph 1020, for example, was cut down from a higher, post-Mesolithic level, while ph 1006/C(1) was filled with brown soil and cut clearly Mesolithic post-holes. Some of these later post-holes may have run parallel to the line of the gully, F326. The Mesolithic post-holes were often angled, and at least two distinct groups were noted, ph 1000 and ph 1006/7. These post-holes were often over 150 mm deep and were rather narrow, similar to those found in the occupation area. However, they did not form a consistent pattern, and the placing of so many substantial posts close together, combined with the fact that some adjacent post-holes faced in divergent directions, suggested that they may not all have been contemporary. The other post-holes in the western area were too scattered to be meaningful and often could not be confidently assigned to either the Mesolithic or later periods.

The description of the western area can be concluded by noting that though the thick soil cover had not provided total protection for the underlying remains, disturbance resulting from the later phases of occupation had not been as serious as had at first been feared.

CHAPTER 3

Description of the archaeological material

Introduction

This chapter has been divided into two main sections. The first, on the Mesolithic material, refers to the *in situ* Mesolithic deposits as well as some material in tree-falls. Other distinctive stray finds from the disturbed deposits will occasionally be referred to. The second deals with the later excavated material. The later stone industries mostly consist of the few diagnostic artefacts which are recognizable as either Neolithic or Early Bronze Age. The hand-made pottery includes a heterogeneous collection of sherds which may range in date from the later Neolithic through to Early Christian and medieval. As few of the sherds show any diagnostic features they are often impossible to assign to any specific period. The medieval and post-medieval wheel-thrown pottery is described by M L Simpson. A short final note deals with the surface collection made before excavation in 1972.

Mesolithic Material

The Mesolithic material has been divided into retouched and unretouched pieces, though this division does not imply that all unretouched pieces were simply discarded or unused. The significance of the distribution of the artefacts is discussed in Chapter 11, while a preliminary examination of the functions of some of the tools is presented in Chapter 4. The present chapter offers a descriptive typology of the material. Detailed descriptions of the quantities and types found in various layers and areas are provided in Appendix 1b (microfiche). Table 1 lists only the total quantities of each type found.

RAW MATERIAL

Over 99% of the extant material from Mount Sandel is flint. Although occasional nodules could have been derived from the local Armoy Ice Sheet (Creighton 1974), most of the material was probably brought to the site. North Antrim flint, particularly that found in the Portrush area, is rather poor, of uneven quality and with many impurities. The flint found during the excavation shows many variations: dark glossy, matt white, blue-grey and a slightly cherty variety. While many nodules contain inclusions, none have the cavities which typify much of the Portrush area flint.

The cortex varies in condition, but a substantial quantity of the flint appears to have been collected from a shingle beach or river bed as it has the heavy damage typical of these environments. Smaller quantities must have been collected from screes at the foot of the chalk cliffs, and there are a few nodules which may have been removed from the chalk itself, as their cortex is so soft. While some cortex is so heavily damaged that the nodule must be from a shingle beach, it is difficult to be certain whether some of the less damaged cortex indicates a beach or riverine environment.

While occasional banded nodules might indicate that some flint came from outside the north-east area, the rest of the variations in character could be explained by the stratigraphic variations in the flint within the cretaceous deposits. The glossy flint, for example, would come from the upper part of the sequence. Therefore, as will also be shown below, most of the flint could have been procured within 10 km of the site, perhaps in one locality.

Materials other than flint occasionally occur, most noticeably chert. Several microliths and one possible composite implement of chert were recovered, but unfortunately because many of the microliths were burnt it is impossible to quantify how many were made from chert. There are several other small flakes of a rather more poorly silicified stone, but none of these have been made into implements. Amongst the surface finds was one piece of a heavily weathered core axe made from chert.

PROBLEMS OF CONDITION

The main problem of condition arises from burning. The proportion of burnt pieces has been noted for all material in terms of absolute numbers, and the proportion of burnt cores, flakes and other types has also been calculated by weight. This was essential as burning is liable to increase dramatically the number of individual fragments and weight therefore gives a more accurate assessment.

THE INDUSTRY

This description of the industry at Mount Sandel assumes that the material recovered came from a number of different stages in manufacturing processes and perhaps included by-products from the manufacturing of several different implements. There is no doubt, however, that while the main emphasis at this site was on the production of blades, a certain amount of the waste is likely to be from the manufacture of axes. The rather restricted range of retouched tools, in particular burins, means that there is little chance that burin spalls will be present. The material has been divided into three groups, blades, flakes and debitage.

Blades
These are flakes which have relatively parallel sides and have a length/breadth ratio of more than 2:1. Length is measured as the longest distance at right angles to the striking platform, while the width is the maximum width at right angles to the main axis. As blades are subject to a high rate of fracture—a potential source of bias in relation to other pieces—a minimum number index is often used. This is a count

of the number of pieces retaining striking platforms, which avoids the problem of counting the same blade twice. It is a method which allows a relative comparison between categories rather than providing absolute numbers; thus a blade mostly complete but without striking platform is excluded while a smaller fragment with platform is included. Any piece less than 20 mm long is regarded as an accidental by-product and is included in the waste category.

The blade size on this site was relatively small: the mean length of samples from both the hut area and the industrial area was 43 mm. The author (Woodman 1977) has shown that the size of blade is not a product of flint availability and that the most important attribute is the size of striking platform (Fig 23A). The consistently small platform suggests the use of a controlled knapping technique, perhaps a punch technique. The blades lack that regularity which is usually associated with pressure flaking. There has been no attempt to subdivide the blades into microblades and blades as the Mount Sandel material probably represents the normal range from small to large blades. No group of blades such as those produced from Scandinavian Mesolithic 'handle' cores can be identified.

Flakes
This group consists of pieces which have a length/breadth ratio of less than 2:1. The minimum

Industry		Retouched tools	
		Axes and related forms	
Cores	262	Core axes	21
Core by-products	67	Flake axes	13
Decortical flakes	358	Picks and borers	8
Blades	6166 + *(1640)	Miscellaneous	4
Flakes	3492	Sharpening flakes	45
Debitage	32401		
Total weight	101,586 gm	Scrapers	7
		Spokeshaves	2
		Burins	5
* Fragments without striking platforms		Microliths	
		Scalene triangles	523
		Rods	315
		Obliquely trimmed	50
		Needle points	100
		Double	30
		Miscellaneous	45
		Micro-burins	92
		Lamelles à cran	24
		Micro-awls	40
		Stained blades	48
		Retouched blades	37
		Miscellaneous worked	42

Table 1   List of *in situ* Mesolithic material

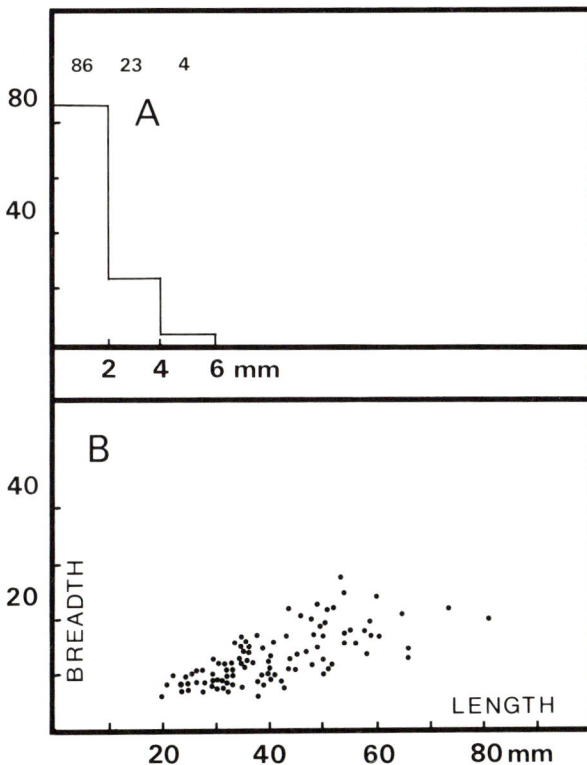

Fig 23 (A) Histogram of depth of striking platforms, (B) length/breadth scatter diagram of a sample of blades from hut area

size of the flake has been set at 300 mm. The group includes many pieces which can be placed in sub-categories.

i) DECORTICAL FLAKES These are flakes which have more than 50% of their surface covered in cortex. This provides an indication of how much preparing of flint nodules has taken place. The amount of cortex does not mean that these flakes were all unusable, but it would indicate the level of flint knapping.

ii) PLATFORM REJUVENATION FLAKES These are a product of removing a portion of the striking platform on a core. They are usually used to correct the angle between platform edge and core surface.

iii) CORE PLUNGING FLAKES These are flakes which have removed the distal end of the core. Obviously many flakes could run to the end of the core, and so to distinguish the plunging flakes a minimum requirement is that the flake has removed more than 20% of the opposing face of the core.

iv) AXE-MANUFACTURING FLAKES These must be distinguished from the axe-sharpening flakes (see below under Axes). The manufacturing flakes are rather broad, thin flakes which often have flake scars running from two directions. One series will be the

distal portion of truncated flake scars running from the opposite side of the axe. In section the dorsal surface often mirrors in part the lenticular cross-section of the axe. These were noted occasionally during sorting of the material but no detailed record of them was kept.

The first three sub-categories can be considered as core by-products while group iv should be included with the axe-sharpening flakes as axe by-products.

Debitage
This consists of those pieces below the minimum size of blades and flakes. There may appear to be a slight inconsistency in that the minimum size of a blade is 20 mm, but for a flake it is 30 mm. While a consistent definition at 30 mm might seem preferable, it was felt that blades less than 30 mm long could have been used, for example as parts of composite tools, whilst flakes smaller than 30 mm were probably unusable. Therefore the inconsistency caused fewer problems than it solved. Much of the material in this category consists of very small pieces of flint which can hardly be considered as parts of anything diagnostic.

Cores
Previous discussions of Mount Sandel industrial techniques (Woodman 1978) were based on the examination of the cores from the hut area, but when all the material was examined some variations in the quality of flint-working could be seen, and the material from the hut hollow emerged as amongst the poorest.

The cores are often made from small portions of flint nodules, many of which have started as decortical flakes which have in turn been worked along one edge in a fashion reminiscent of the Scandinavian 'handle' cores (Henricksen 1976, fig 4). Because of the scarcity of flint in the immediate vicinity of the site, many of the cores have been worked to a point of exhaustion. Large cores are very rare.

As Table 2 shows, the single-platformed cores were the dominant type in every part of the site. No distinction has been made between potential sub-types (cylindrical, pyramidal and so on) as in this type of assemblage they grade into one another. Because many were made on decortical flakes, a large number retain cortex for part of their circumference. Multi-platformed cores were very rare and were for flake production. The dual-platformed cores are normally opposed-platform cores worked on the one plane rather than the dual-plane type of dual-platformed cores.

As has already been noted (Woodman 1978) the main characteristics of this industry are a product of the use of a controlled percussion technique, probably with the aid of a punch. This is reflected in

	I	II	III	IV
Single-platformed	23	8	16	66
Dual-platformed	3	1	1	5
Multi-platformed	1	—	—	4
Miscellaneous	3	—	2	8

I Eastern hut area	III Feature 214
II Northern area	IV Western industrial area

Table 2   Types of cores from selected areas of the site

the cores by an almost complete absence of examples where the angle between the striking platform and the core face is 90° or more. Few of the cores have numerous narrow parallel blade facets, and the result is that the mean facet width (see Woodman 1978) on the cores from Mount Sandel is 10.5 ± 2.3 mm. This can be compared with 10.9 ± 2.4 mm from Glynn, while from Poilvaish on the Isle of Man a better blade production technique has left the cores with a mean facet width of 6.5 ± 0.8 mm. The few fine, almost prismatic, cores must be seen within the context of the full range of cores and are as atypical as the occasional very crude examples. Flint-working must be seen as covering a broad spectrum, varying according to the skill of the worker and the quality of the individual core.

RETOUCHED TOOLS

Axe group
This group can be divided into four classes: core axes (21), flake axes (13), pointed implements (8) and miscellaneous pieces (4). In previous studies (Woodman 1978) most of the axes examined were from surface collections in which, owing to the lack of context, only examples retaining major characteristics could be considered as Mesolithic. At Mount Sandel, however, axes found in clearly Mesolithic contexts also included a few poorer specimens. The term fragment has been reserved for those specimens which lack most of the attributes of any individual class.

CORE AXES (15 complete, 6 fragments)   This term has been chosen instead of the commonly used 'tranchet', which is wrongly borrowed from the French. Core axes are usually characterized by one or more transversely struck flakes being removed from the functional edge of the axe. These axes can, however, be used without the removal of a transverse flake and they can also be made from large flakes. Therefore they can be best described as having a symmetrically placed cutting edge which is rounded and usually formed by secondary retouch. The transversely sharpened axes represent the most clear-cut examples of this type. The word 'core' should be understood as referring to the method of production of the edge, not their manufacture from cores. (For a detailed

discussion of the typology of these axes see Woodman 1978, chapter III (3)e.)

With the exception of one rather badly burnt axe, which may be rectilinear-sectioned, all the core axes appear to be face-trimmed. A total of nine axes have retained their cutting edges. These are mostly the rather narrow-edged type of the Early Mesolithic (Fig 24). Occasionally the flakes removed are tiny and the edge can be quite thin, and some also have such thin butts that it can be difficult to be certain which is the butt and which the cutting edge (Fig 24.8).

One example (Fig 24.1) shows clearly how these implements were made. This is a large flake which still retains most of its striking platform. While this could be regarded as an unfinished example—it has a very irregular denticulated edge—attempts were made to form a narrow cutting edge, significantly narrower than the remainder of the implement. Attempts to finish the axe may have been abandoned because of the intractable shape of the flake.

Few of the axes appear to be made from large cores as they are often rather flat with a lenticular rather than a diamond section. Some have retained a small area of an original bulbar face, showing that they have been made on flakes. They rarely have any context and have often been very carefully retouched, though the more diamond-sectioned axes can be worked in a somewhat cruder fashion. The largest example is less than 110 mm in length. Their shape varies from a narrow cylinder to a form which can taper to a narrow butt (Fig 24.2); in one instance the butt is almost pointed (Fig 24.4). These tapered forms usually have their point of maximum width closer to the cutting edge than to the butt.

Some of the fragmentary specimens show signs of being used as cores (Fig 24.6). There is little evidence that this was done in order to fit the axe as an inset into a sleeve as in some instances the cutting edge was not preserved, and the only case of a complete axe with core-like retouch on the butt was one of the largest.

The importance of the Mount Sandel axe assemblage is further enhanced by the recovery of forms such as Figs 24.3 and 24.7. Types such as these exist in museum collections but there was no way in which they could be described, purely on morphological grounds, as Mesolithic core axes. Their recovery from the Mount Sandel excavations does, however, indicate that they are a type of Early Mesolithic core axe.

FLAKE AXES (10 complete, 3 fragments)   The flake axe is made on a deliberately prepared flake which has a relatively high angle, usually over 40°, created by the two surfaces forming an edge. This large flat flake is then retouched into the shape of an axe with part of the high-angled edge being retained as the functional

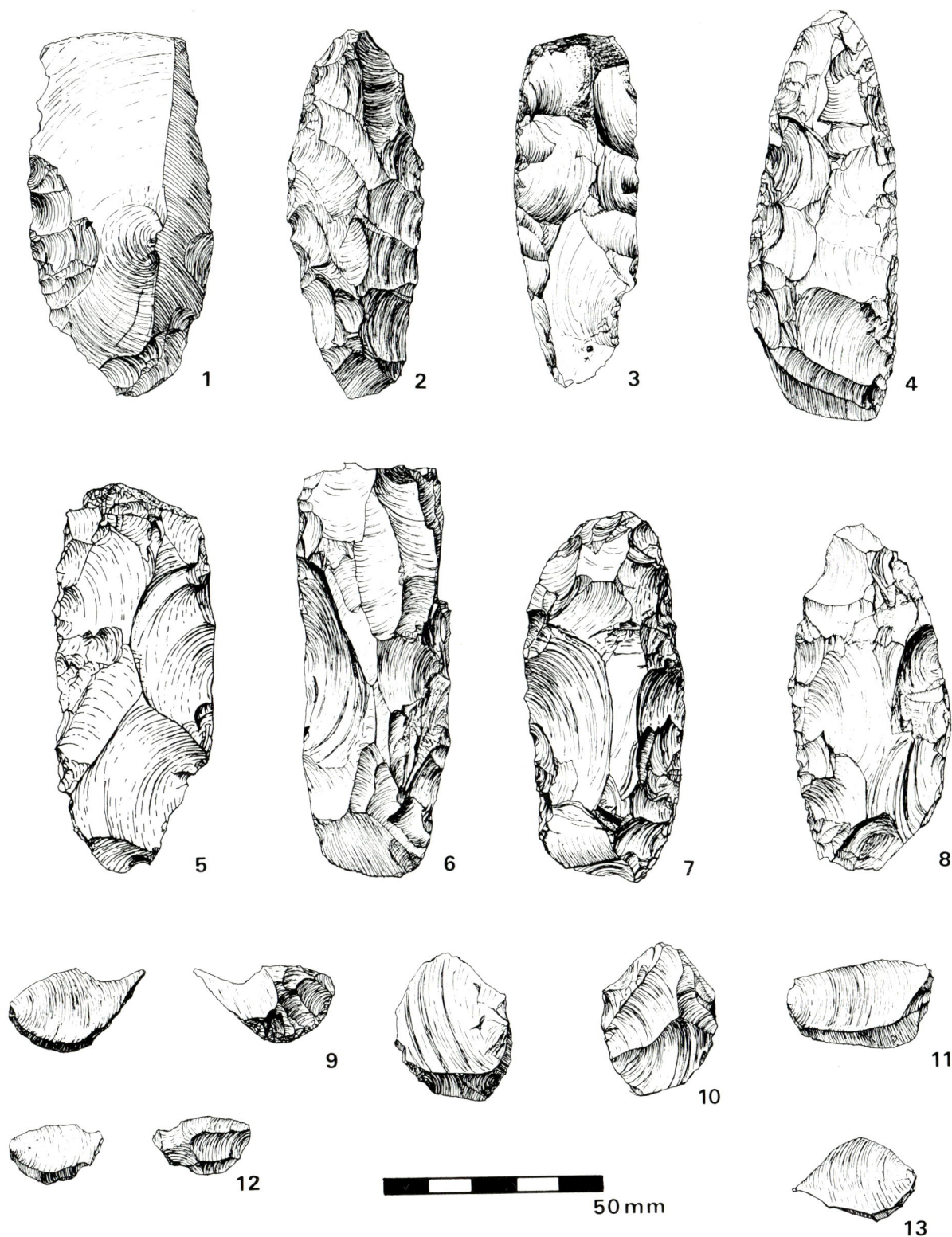

Fig 24 1–8, core axes; 9–13, axe-sharpening flakes

edge. These axes will usually have a splayed outline with the broadest point being close to the functional edge. The portion of its leading edge which is left usually forms a straight line.

The fragmentary and incomplete specimens which have been assigned to this class exhibit a broad splayed profile and the existence of only peripheral retouch on the bulbar face. As with the core axes, specimens from surface collections which might not have been included, as they did not fit the concepts of the classic flake axe, can now be assigned to this group. Thus most of the flake axes have a broad, flat cutting edge with a high angle on the dorsal face, and they are more heavily retouched over the dorsal face than the bulbar. Most have a flat or convex bulbar face which usually has only peripheral retouch.

While there are some classic examples, such as Figs 25.2, 4 and 5, others are slightly anomalous: Fig 25.1, for example, is rather square and has only peripheral retouch on both faces, while Fig 39 has a bulb of percussion at the butt rather than the side of the axe. Fig 25.3 is unusual in that its bulbar face is concave rather than convex and it has an irregular thin butt. Two show signs of attempted conversions into other implement types: Fig 25.7, for example, shows a fragment of a flake axe retrimmed for another use, perhaps as a chisel. Fig 25.6 shows a rather unusual little implement which may have started as a flake axe but has been trimmed down to a chisel. The original asymmetrical flake edge is still preserved, but the implement has been retouched overall on both faces and turned into a narrow, face-trimmed chisel.

POINTED IMPLEMENTS *Single-pointed borer* (1) (Fig 26.1) One rather large flake has been trimmed to a crude point in the fashion of the core borers, which occur more frequently in the Later than the Early Mesolithic. The point is trihedral, relatively obtuse, and it has a rather broad heavy butt.
Single-pointed pick (1) (Fig 26.2) This is a rather more elongated specimen than that described above. It again has been made from a large flake and has a relatively broad retouched butt. While the body is quadrangular the point tends to be triangular in section.
Narrow and double-pointed picks (6) While there are no complete examples of this group, they can be compared with the double-pointed picks defined by the author (Woodman 1978, IV). The term 'narrow' has been added, since examples such as Fig 26.3 and 4 may have had only one pointed end but can be considered as part of the same group. When complete these implements are narrow (less than 30 mm across) and elongated, and they taper to a point. Their section varies from quadrangular to triangular, and in some instances they have triple *arrête* retouch (Fig 26.5). Unfortunately these implements are repre-

sented mainly by fragments with few functional ends preserved.

MISCELLANEOUS (4) These are bifacially-flaked pieces which cannot be assigned with any confidence to one of the three major groups. Three have a large unworked area which was a bulbar face, and so they may be fragments of flake axes. The fourth piece is a small bifacially-worked flake which is almost leaf-shaped in outline. While it is rather too thick to be considered as a later laurel leaf (Flanagan 1970), it is not quite the correct shape for a core axe. Its slightly irregular edge suggests that it may have been discarded before it was finished.

AXES: DISCUSSION There appears to be no distinction in raw material between types of axe: the flint used varies from a mottled blue-grey to a glossy dark flint. With the exception of the reworked flake axe made of banded flint, which has an almost scree-fresh area of cortex, the axes were made from nodules of flint which had formed part of a gravel; some were almost certainly derived from a beach shingle.

In general these implements can be described as small and carefully made. They are so small and, as already noted (Woodman 1978, III), the butts are treated so carefully that it is a reasonable assumption that they were hafted. There is unfortunately no evidence of Mesolithic antler sleeves in these islands, though there is every possibility that wooden sleeves such as those found at Vedbaek (Brinch-Petersen *et al* 1979) could have been used.

The writer has suggested that the flake axes from Mount Sandel were in the process of development as an implement type (Woodman 1978). This was based on the presence of several atypical forms, one of them from a pit (F109) which has subsequently been ^{14}C-dated to after 6000 bc. In this case, as so often, crudeness is therefore not an indicator of an early stage of typological development. This specimen examined by Dumont in Chapter 4 (Fig 39) had been used extensively and thus its crudeness is not due to its being an unfinished specimen.

It is interesting that the distinction drawn between broad-edged flake axes and narrow-edged core axes, which was based on samples drawn from surface collections (Woodman 1978), seems to be equally valid for the implements from this particular site (Table 3).*

Microwear analysis would seem to confirm that the core axes are essentially chopping tools while the flake axes are more likely to be planes and chisels (see below, Chapter 4). Unfortunately the pointed

---

* Because of a misunderstanding British Archaeological Reports failed to correct the probability statements on pages 49 and 51 of Woodman 1978. They should read 'less than 0.1%'.

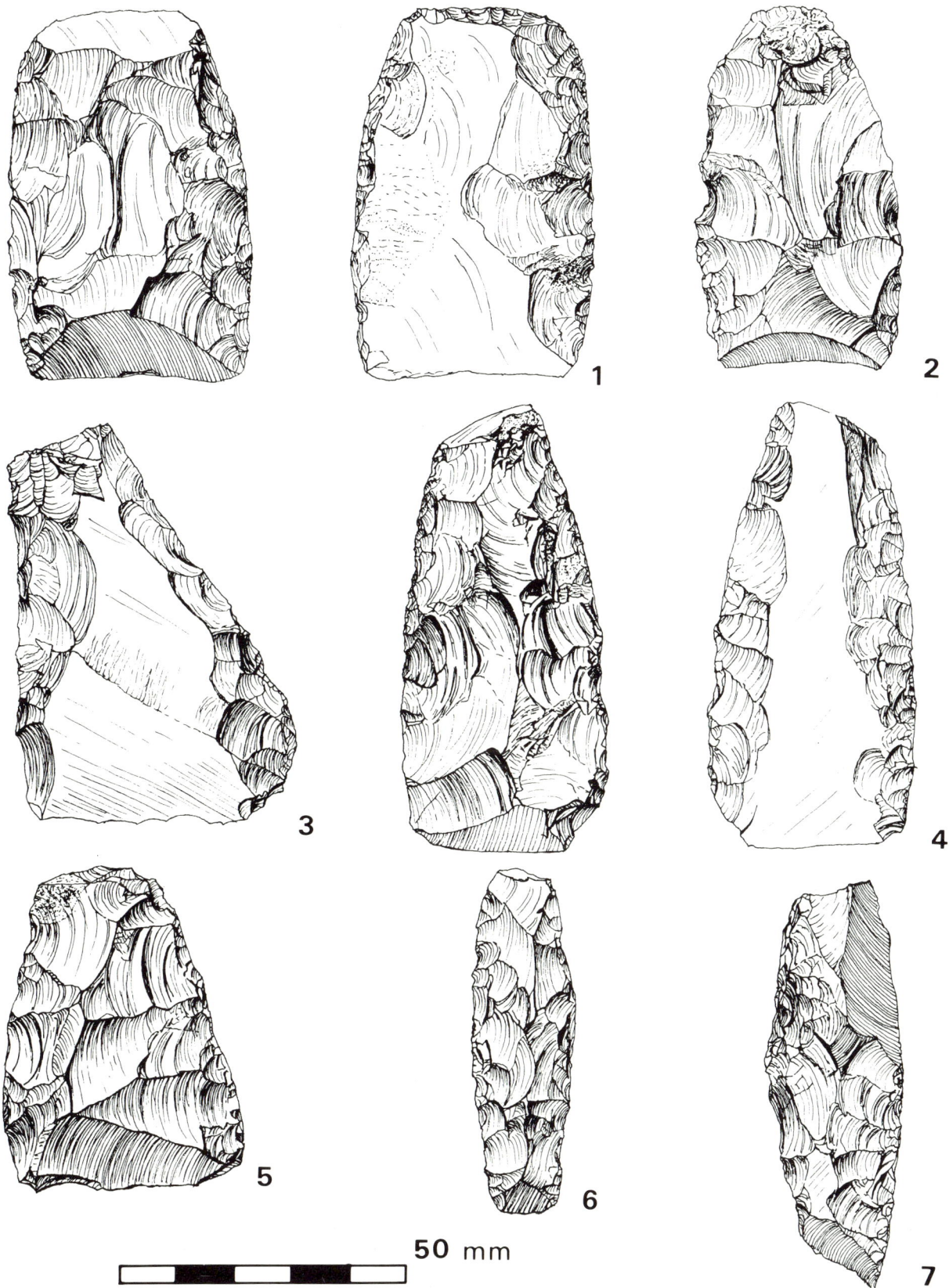

Fig 25   Flake axes

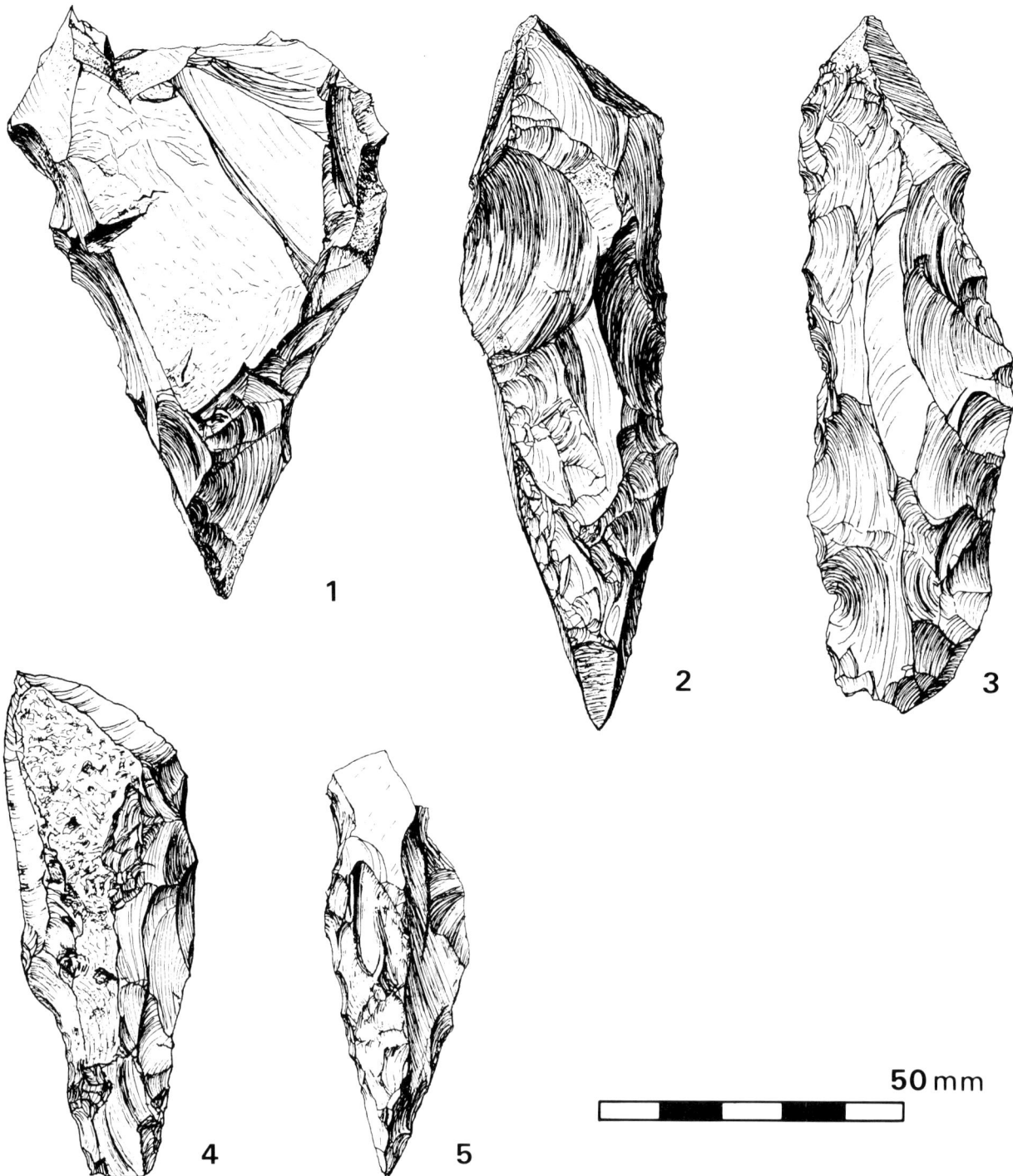

Fig 26   Pointed implements: 1 single-pointed; 2–3 double-pointed; 4–5 fragments of pointed implements

implements were so rare and in such a poor state that they have provided relatively little useful information.

AXE-SHARPENING FLAKES (43)   These confirm that the core axes used on the site were very narrow, and in fact when apparently broad examples are examined it usually becomes clear that the cutting edge forms a

very small portion of the flake. In some instances (Fig 24.9) there is evidence of very intensive retouch along the adjacent edge, the purpose of which is to narrow the functional edge. Therefore the apparent breadth of the sharpening flake can be caused by its removing a longer portion of the opposite edge. When the small size of the surviving transverse flake scars on the axes

More than	Axe-sharpening flakes	Core axes	Flake axes
15 mm	13	6	
20 mm	10	2	
25 mm	6		2
30 mm	1		
35 mm			3
40 mm			1

Table 3   Width of functional edges of axes

is considered, it seems quite possible that the commonest sharpening flake would be similar to Fig 24.12, but these are not necessarily easy to identify from amongst the large quantities of flintwork. The number of axe-sharpening flakes identified may therefore be too low.

One minor problem arises from the presence of forms such as Fig 24.12. These are so narrow that it must remain a possibility that they are a product of reworking the butt. If this were a Later Mesolithic assemblage they could be explained as the cutting edges of the narrow transverse picks (Woodman 1978, IV).

Scrapers (7 + 2?)
Except for Fig 27.1 and 2 the selection of scrapers is very poor, much poorer, in fact, than in many of the surface collections from other sites in this area. Only Fig. 27.1 is a clear example of a scraper: a large implement made from a flake, with slightly irregular edges. Two small examples (Fig 27.2) can be regarded as terminally retouched blades. The others vary from carefully retouched fragments to a small flake fragment with crude retouch on one edge which might be a scraper. The other doubtful specimen is a large, irregular flake which has been steeply trimmed, described elsewhere as a nucleiform scraper (Woodman 1978). It is difficult to be sure whether the leading edge was prepared for use as a scraping edge, or whether it was a regularizing process carried out to remove the ridges left by the removal of a previous series of blades. It must be noted that the only sites to have produced these large, heavy, nucleiform scrapers are those which are some distance from a flint source, that is the Mount Sandel sites and the Cushendun lower gravels (Movius 1940), where the cores might be more likely to be made on large flakes than from nodules. The removal of blades from such a large flake could leave a core which would resemble a scraper (see also Clark 1954).

Spokeshaves (4)
These are large flakes with one or more notches on an edge. They often show signs of use in or around the notch, but none of the edges are as heavily used as those on the pieces from Newferry (Woodman 1977a).

Burins (4 + 2?)
As noted elsewhere (Woodman 1978) these form the most enigmatic group within the Irish Mesolithic and all examples must be regarded with a certain degree of scepticism. In the case of the Mount Sandel material there is the added complication that some of the cores started out as large flakes which were worked from both lateral edges towards the centre, resulting in a tendency for these cores to resemble burins; it can therefore be very difficult to decide when these pieces became burins. Only two of the Mount Sandel examples show signs of the removal of several burinal flakes from the supposed burinal edge. Four examples can be described as angle burins which, in three instances, have been made from a flake with a retouched edge. This, at least, indicates that they have been struck off a surface after the flake has been removed from the core. In all but one instance (Fig 27.3 apparently exhibits two edges) the burinal edge is formed by a large blade facet running down the edge of the flake. This forms a rather broad burinal edge which, in at least two cases, does not appear to have a very effective shape.

Two examples, perhaps dubious, could be described as dihedral burins. One example is made from an angular break across the proximal end of a blade. The second is also made from a blade, though in this instance there is damage to an *arrête* at its distal end (Fig 27.4).

Microliths
As roughly 1100 microliths were found, they form by far the largest group of retouched pieces from the site. The typology used here is essentially that already published by the author (Woodman 1978). It is a relatively simple typology in which only a few major types are distinguished. This approach was adopted because, as the Mount Sandel sites have produced such a large proportion of the known microliths in Ireland, distinctive variations may turn out to be peculiar to this area alone rather than having any broader typological significance for the Irish Mesolithic as a whole. Therefore distinctive forms within the major classes will be noted and described but will often not be formally divided into sub-types.

One major problem arising at Mount Sandel is that a relatively small proportion of the microliths are complete. Obviously careful sieving increases the number of fragments and, as the organically rich layers which produced so many of the microliths

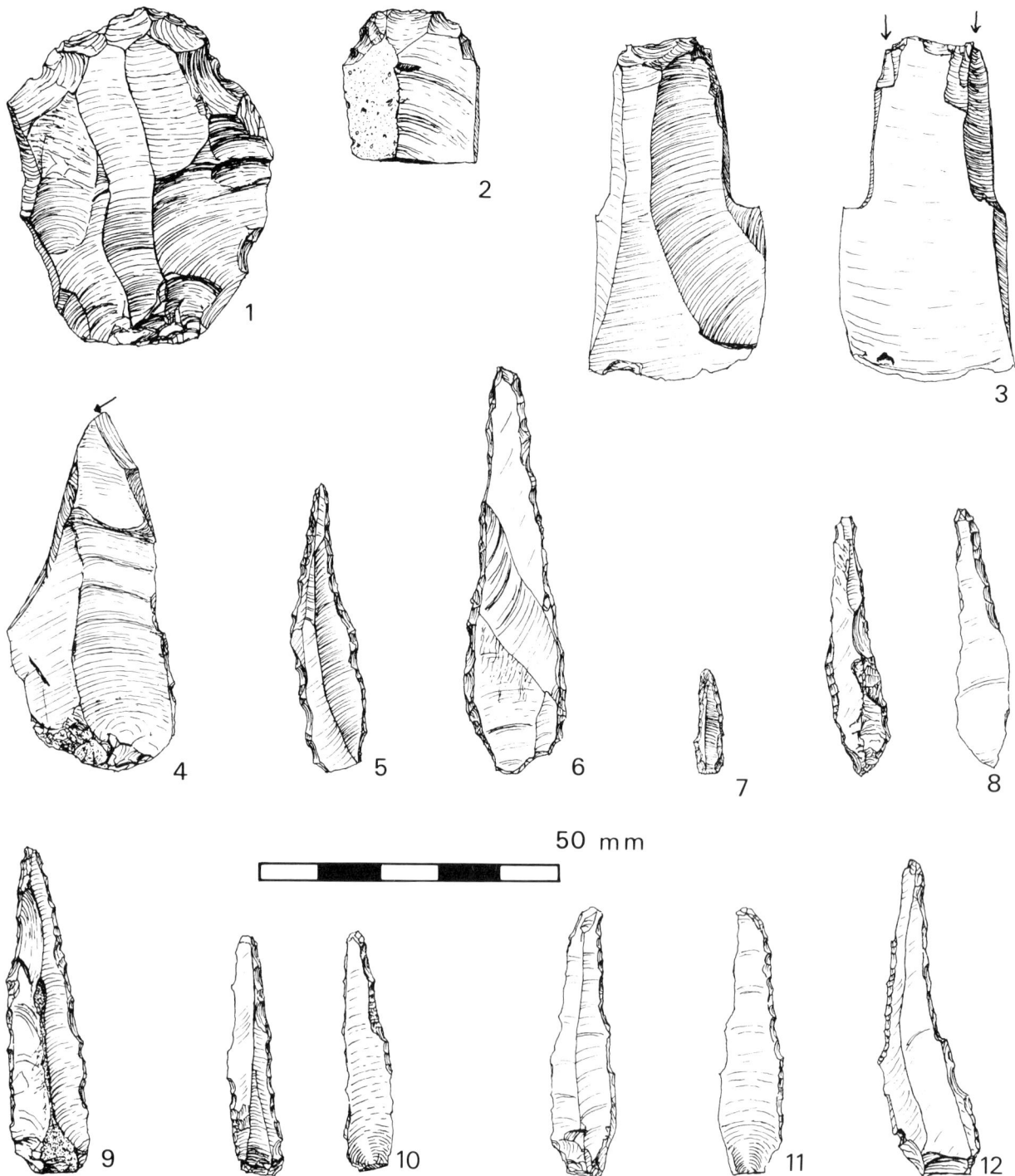

Fig 27   1–2 scrapers; 3 angle burin; 4 dihedral burin (?); 5–12 awls

contained mainly burnt specimens, it is hardly surprising that they are mostly incomplete.

The distribution of the microliths will be considered in some detail in the discussion section (Chapter 11) but major concentrations of these forms can be noted here. Most of the microliths came from the eastern part of the site. There is also no doubt that the features in and around the edge of the huts had many more microliths than elsewhere, whilst the industrial area on the western edge of the site, where there was a greater expanse of occupation soil, produced relatively few microliths.

OBLIQUELY TRIMMED This is a relatively rare form of microlith. The type has been divided into two groups. In the first (A) the retouch is simply carried at an oblique angle across the blade (Fig 28.1–3). Both distal and proximal ends of the blade can be removed in this group, and among those found in the occupation soil distal and proximal retouched examples exist in almost equal numbers. The second group (B) consists of forms retouched across the blade and along one edge (Fig 28.4). Because they are usually rather short, less than 20 mm, they cannot be considered as backed bladelets or rods (Figs 28.1–4). The normal form at Mount Sandel appears to be rather narrow, with retouch running at either an oblique angle or transversely to the body of the blade; the few rather broad examples so typical of assemblages such as Star Carr (Fig 28.2) (Clark 1954) are the exception. Their small size reflects the available blade size of the Mount Sandel industry. Few of them have the opposed retouch which occurs on many of the forms found in the Pennines (Radley and Mellars 1964). It is tempting to dismiss these pieces as unfinished scalene triangles, and some of those found in the occupation soil can be considered as such, particularly those which have retained their striking platform. There was, however, one instance where several specimens were found together in one layer of a pit (F100/5). The association of several in one layer implies a possible composite implement, as they are so rare that it would be unusual for several to be found by accident in one small pit. (This point will be examined in more detail below (page 46), where it will be demonstrated that the association of retouched pieces in certain pits cannot be described as random.)

RODS Rods have been distinguished from backed blades by the simple and arbitrary use of 10 mm as the maximum width of the rods. Rods are retouched for more than 50% of their total length along a line parallel to the main axis of the blade. The distinction between blades and bladelets may eventually be shown to be unreal, but the use of this distinction allows an estimate to be made of the numbers of macro- and microlithic backed forms. The rod group must be divided into two sub-types. There is a definite distinction between the very narrow forms, such as Fig 28.5, and broader examples, such as Fig 28.10. Unfortunately as these forms are so simple it is necessary to divide narrow from broad forms by the use of a second arbitrary measurement: those less than 5 mm in width are described as narrow rods. As can be seen from Table 4, there is no obvious dividing line between the broad and narrow forms.

The narrow rods are distinguished by their extensive use of the *enclume* or anvil retouch, which results in flakes being removed from the dorsal and bulbar face simultaneously. This produces vertical

2 mm	2	6 mm	7
3 mm	22	7 mm	5
4 mm	20	8 mm	3
5 mm	9	9 mm	2

Table 4 Width of microlithic rods from main hut hollow

retouch which is often along a very straight edge. One end can come to a point, sometimes formed by a slight use of retouch on the opposed edge, and the other end usually runs out in a narrow thin edge. Retouch or damage can be found on the other edge, but this is usually much lighter than the *enclume* retouch which generally runs the total length of the microlith. One of the problems with these forms is that they are so narrow that they rarely survive intact.

The broader rods, which Table 4 shows to be rarer than their narrow counterparts, are also rather more fragmentary than the narrow forms. Usually they are not made with the *enclume* technique and tend not to be pointed, though there is a possible small group which are pointed at both ends (Fig 28.11).

SCALENE TRIANGLES These are, of course, the dominant type of microlith, and in certain pits they occurred in overwhelming numbers (Appendix 1b). As can be seen from Fig 28.12–22, there is a wide range within this group, yet none of the differences are so distinctive as to separate them from the main group. Essentially the dominant type of triangle is a relatively narrow elongated form, which is usually less than 10 mm across and often over 30 mm long. Figs 28.22 and 29.13 illustrate the size variation within this group. A common attribute is that the short edge of the triangle can be concave (Fig 29.14). The angle between the two retouched edges can vary from almost a right angle to a very obtuse angle. While it is tempting to consider this form as a type of hollow-based point, the retouch in the hollow is usually on the dorsal face and it can be abrupt, in contrast to the thinning retouch on the bulbar face usually associated with hollow-based points. No distinction is made between triangles which run out to a point and those which do not (sub-triangles, *pace* Mellars 1974). Not only does the angle vary, but in some instances there is a concavity on both edges adjacent to this angle, and where this occurs, as in Fig. 28.21, a slight spur can exist.

The retouch used on these triangles is by no means as regular as that on the rods, though occasionally an example can be found which has *enclume* retouch. Similarly, particularly in the hut area, some of the more complete triangles are extensively retouched along their leading edge.

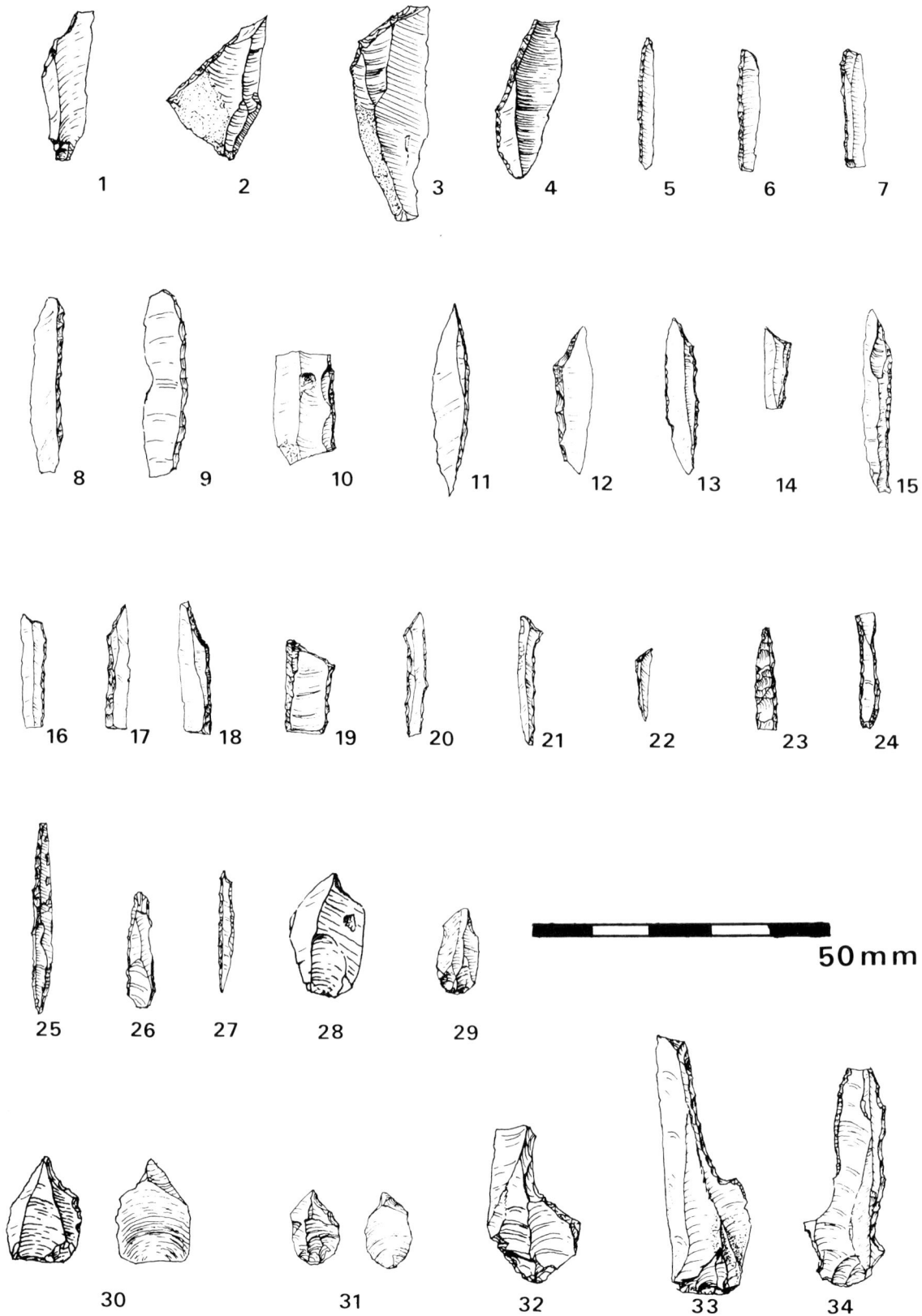

Fig 28   Microliths from occupation soil: 1–4 obliquely blunted points; 5–11 rods; 12–22 scalene triangles; 23–27 needle points; 28–31 micro-burins; 32–34 *lamelles à cran*

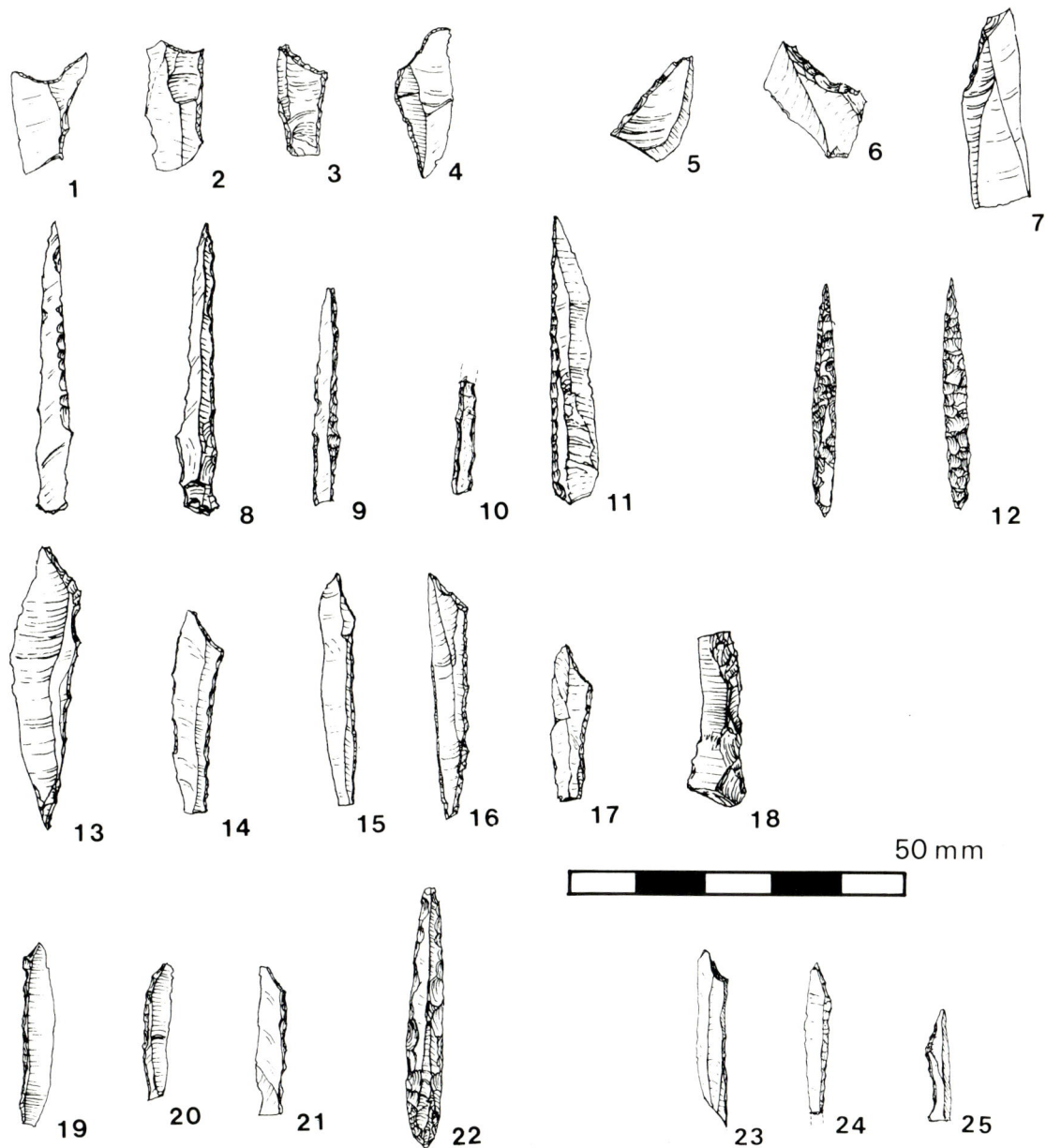

Fig 29   Microliths from features: 1–4 F31/3; 5–7 F100/5; 8–11 F22; 12–18 F56/1; 19–22 F31/0; 23–25 F31/5

While there is a large variation even in size, it will be shown below that many of the variations in the types of triangles are not totally random, and that in certain pits there was a high level of stylistic similarity between groups of triangles.

POINTS (NEEDLE POINTS)   There are sufficient differences within this group to allow a division into three sub-types.

Type A is the most common form of point. They are exceptionally elongated, usually less than 4 mm in width, and can be more than 30 mm long. In their most sophisticated form these implements are retouched, abruptly, along both edges though one can be retouched rather more heavily than the other. This could be used to form the point and achieve the overall shape of the implement. Many specimens have a certain amount of surface retouch which helps to form the point and reduce the butt (Figs 28.23 and 29.12). The points made on these pieces are exceptionally sharp and, because of their thickness, are stronger than is usual on most microliths. Some rather simpler examples, such as Fig 28.25, have also been included in this group.

Type B points form a more distinctive group. While they are of a similar length to type A points, they are rather broader and are made with extensive use of invasive retouch which can also form the outline of the implement. The invasive retouch tends to be on the bulbar surface. The other characteristics of this group are that the point is slightly more obtuse and the butt is rather broader than in the type A points (Fig 29.22).

Type C are small piriform pieces which are usually trimmed to a point with abrupt retouch and have a slightly retouched butt. These points are shorter than the other forms and have a minimum of invasive retouch (Fig 28.26).

SCALE-FLAKED POINTS   This form has been separated from the needle point (Type D in Woodman 1978). These points exist as rather broad forms which have a certain amount of surface retouch but which can by no means be considered to be needle points. Although the excavated examples are fragmentary, their existence at both Tullywiggan (Woodman 1978, site 19 (Area 1b); Briggs and Bamford, personal communication) and Mount Sandel seems to confirm that they did exist as a specific implement type (Fig 29.18).

DOUBLE-EDGED   It can only be emphasized that this group may represent the detritus of a number of other groups as some could be fragmentary needle points while others may be small examples of micro-awls (Fig 28.24, 27).

COMPOSITION OF ARTEFACTS   The presence of microliths in the organically rich layers within discrete units like pits offered the possibility of studying small closed groups of material. Where microliths occurred in the organically rich layers they were not only more frequent than expected (Chapter 11) but there was a marked tendency towards mutual exclusion of triangles and rods. There appears to be a clear correlation between triangles and mammal bones, and there is also some evidence that some of the microliths formed parts of large composite implements.

The scatter of fish bones across the site was so extensive and their size was so small that a ratio of importance of fish to mammals was achieved by dividing the number of fish bones by ten. Table 5 has been divided into three groups, A, B and C. The first includes layers where scalene triangles dominate and are in fact more than twice as common as rods. Here pig is usually dominant. The only exception is F31/3 where fish and pig are of equal importance. In the second group triangles and rods occur in roughly similar numbers, though in the case of F100/2 where pig bones are more important the triangles also predominate. In F210, where fish bones only are present, the rods are almost as common as triangles. In the third group fish bones are patently more important and rods are also more common. It is therefore tempting to correlate triangles with mammals and rods with fish bones, but a closer examination of the data suggests alternative explanations. In Chapter 11 it is noted that many of the pits containing fish bones are the larger central hearths, and so the concentrations of rods could have a locational explanation rather than a simple correlation with a certain type of food-procurement strategy. Also in Table 6 it will be observed that some of the groups of rods are not associated with the bone-rich layers while the triangles are usually spread between both charcoal- and bone-rich layers. As F56/2 contains the largest concentration of water-lily and pond-weed seeds, it could be argued that some of the rods were used in camp site implements for plant processing (Clarke 1976; and see below, Chapter 6). It is unfortunate that the microliths from these layers

Group	Feature	Layer	Fish bones	Pig	Triangles	Rods B	N	Oblique	Needles
A	31/0	(1)–(3)	15	70	36	2	7	1	6
A	31/4	(2)–(4)	16	16	13	—	—	—	1
A	31/5	(2)–(4)	59	13	19	—	2	—	—
A	31/3		6	7	7	—	1	—	—
A	F27	(2) + (3)	14	69	9	—	—	1	1
A	F23		5	6	14	—	2	—	4
A	F16	(2)	—	3	11	—	—	—	—
				(Lepus)					
B	100/2		105	25	27	4	14	2	3
B	210		161	—	6	—	5	—	—
C	56/4	(2)–(4)	544	—	7	2	17	3	3
C	56/2	(2)–(4)	149	—	2	1	11	—	1
C	91	(2)–(4)	136	3	1	1	7	—	1

Table 5   Association between microliths and fauna in selected features

Feature	Layer	Character	Triangles	Rods	Approx ratio charcoal to bone
31/0	1	Charcoal	17	3	100%
	2	Pig	16	3	
31/4	2	Charcoal	2	—	100%
	3	Pig	10	—	
31/5	2	Charcoal	4	2	100%
	3	Pig	13	2	
56/4	2	Charcoal	4	10	20%
	3	Fish	3	4	
56/2	2	Charcoal	2	7	40%
	3	Fish	—	5	
91	2	Fish	—	8	
	3	Charcoal	1	—	50%

Table 6 Layer type against microlith type from certain selected features

were usually burnt and were therefore not suitable for microwear analysis.

Other associations of microlith types are relatively poor. The author has suggested (Woodman 1978) that the needle points were the tips of projectiles which used scalene triangles. The fact that the points are often unburnt when the triangles are burnt, and that in certain instances groups of points were found without other forms, does however suggest that they were used on their own. The obliquely trimmed forms were usually scattered across the site but in one instance, F100/5, six were found together in one layer. Therefore some of the particularly broad examples, such as Fig 29.5–7, could be parts of composite implements in their own right, as has been suggested by Pitts and Jacobi (1979). It is tempting to see these forms as associated with bird bones since both they and bird bones were found in F100/5, but the evidence from just one pit is insufficient for general conclusions to be drawn.

The fact that microliths were generally used as parts of composite implements is an accepted truism within Mesolithic studies, but there is little clear evidence as to how they were used. Certain groups have been observed on the Pennines (Jacobi 1978, fig 3) though no detailed publication is available. At one extreme the Lilla Loshult arrowhead contained only two microliths—different types (scalene triangle and obliquely trimmed) (Malmer 1969)—while Clarke (1976) has suggested that very large numbers could have been used as part of plant-processing equipment. Therefore in evaluating the role of microliths one has to consider not only how many functionally distinct implement types were present, but also how many individual pieces went into creating one composite implement.

Perhaps the most distinctive type is the scalene triangle. The more complete examples were originally examined for evidence of stylistic variation which it was hoped might show chronological change. There is no clear shift through time to narrower, more elongated, forms as suggested for the south Scandinavian examples (Henricksen 1976; Larsson 1978). Instead, the results of the analysis indicate that individual stylistic variations were more likely than a chronological progression, as stylistically similar triangles were often found together in the same pit. Since this could be a random occurrence, a summary has been provided of those triangles in the occupation soil and F56/I which are presumed to reflect the normal population of forms on the site.

The attributes recorded (Fig 30) were (I) breadth at the angle of the two shorter edges measured at point A in Fig 30, (2) height from the angle to the end of the short edge, (3) ratio of height to width, (4) whether the short edge was concave, straight or convex, and (5) the presence of extensive anvil retouch. Relatively few microliths from Mount Sandel were complete and the advantage of these attributes was that they could be applied to fragmentary specimens. Many layers did not have sufficient microliths to warrant testing for stylistic similarities, and therefore only pits producing three or more diagnostic fragments were considered. When the individual groups are examined the following trends emerge (see Appendix 1c (microfiche) for details).

F31/3 Four examples, all concave ends (two almost hollow based), mean width 8 mm (Fig 29.1–4).

F31/5, (2) + (3) Ten examples in two possible groups: (a) five examples, medium angle, straight short edge and anvil retouch; (b) 0.4 to 0.7, five examples, all concave edge, no anvil retouch.

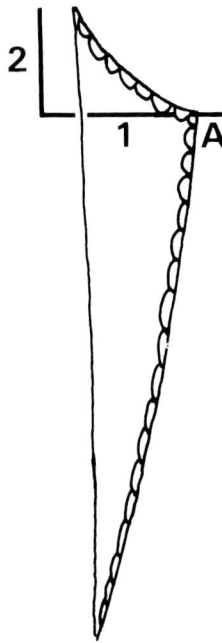

Fig 30   Schematic representation of measurements taken for Table 7

(mm) (1) Breadth	No	(2) Height	No	(3) Ratio	No
2	2	−2		−0.4	5
3	7	−1		−0.2	10
4	15	0		0	26
5	16	1		0.2	11
6	5	2	12	0.4	4
7	2	3	13		
8	2	4	7		
9	1	5	6		
10		6	8		
		7	8		
		8	3		

(4) Concave	Straight	Convex
21	26	3

(5) Anvil Retouch 12 out of 50

Table 7   Attributes of scalene triangles from F56/1 and main hut hollow occupation soil

F23   Six examples, all narrow, medium angle, one convex edge, two with anvil retouch.

F52   Not an organically rich layer, containing eight examples, of which four are burnt and are medium to broad in width, with a low angle and concave short edges.

F100/2, upper fill   Five narrow examples with medium angles, four with concave short edges.

There are other groups in which it is not as easy to distinguish potential components of the same composite implement. The material from F31/0 is a good example. Here there could be 1) a small group of narrow microliths with convex short ends (Fig 29.20) and two other implements, 2) a group of narrow microliths with high angles and a straight edge, and perhaps 3) a group with a broader, lower-angled concave edge. It is also difficult to distinguish a group within F31/4.*

A comparison of the figures in Table 7 with those listed above suggests that the groupings of attributes cannot be best explained as random clumping. Thus the concave short edge present on four occasions out of four, as in F31/3, has a probability of P = 0.16, but all four are rather broad and this has a probability of P = 0.0001. Similarly in F31/5 (2) and (3) the narrower examples are associated with anvil retouch

and a straight edge, while a slightly broader group have a concave edge and no anvil retouch. More often the groups are rather more difficult to define. As many of the differences are relatively slight it is likely that a single artefact would have been made up of components which were relatively similar rather than identical.

Since the triangles are burnt and often rather fragmentary it is unfortunately difficult to assess how many triangles were in one artefact. However, it is probable that there were never more than ten triangles in one projectile head. Similarly if we assume that the bulbar face was always placed in the same direction, the presence of both left and right hand forms suggests that at least some projectile heads had bi-serial rows of microliths (Fig 31).

The writer has suggested (Woodman 1978) that the needle points were used to tip projectile heads which had triangles as barbs. This was based on the observation that several pits contained triangles and needle points in a rough ratio of 4:1 to 6:1. However, a fuller examination of material suggests that this explanation may have been over-simplified. In several pits the needle points were unburnt while the triangles were burnt. While various explanations can be offered which would still allow both these forms to be part of the same composite implements, they usually involve special pleading. The possibility that needle points were parts of totally different implements must therefore be considered.

There are insufficient attributes to attempt a similar analysis of the rods or obliquely trimmed points. There is also a much poorer correlation between these types of microliths and a specific type of deposit, and so it is impossible to suggest how these forms were used.

_____

*Wiessner (personal communication) has noted similar individual stylistic variations amongst certain San Bushmen projectile points. She also notes that not all manufacturers are capable of consistency.

Fig 31   Possible reconstruction of use of scalene triangles

MICRO-BURINS (94) NOTCHED (4) These occurred relatively rarely. They are usually the snapped-off ends of rather small blades which reflect in size the complete blades found during the excavation. They were made in a consistent fashion by notching the right side of the blade near the butt and then removing its proximal end. Fewer than 10% were made by removing the distal end of the blade or by notching the left edge.

The high proportion of right-hand-notched examples was a uniform feature across the site, yet as shown in Appendix 1c there is no trend towards either left- or right-handed triangles. This could either imply that the micro-burins and microliths found on the site related to entirely different phases of occupation, or that micro-burins were not necessarily a by-product from the manufacture of microliths.

Besides the micro-burins there are some rather small pieces in which the blade has snapped transversely outside the notch. These are so slight that they could easily have been broken without a notch. Two other small blades with notches were recovered which may have been pieces which had been notched before being snapped.

LAMELLES À CRAN (16) These are much rarer than micro-burins and are usually much larger (Fig 28.32–34). They appear to represent a stage in the manufacture of scalene triangles in which the long

backed edge is worked before the snapping off of the proximal end of the blade (Brinch-Petersen 1966). A comparison of the width of the butts of this form with the micro-burins suggests that many of the larger micro-burins could be the snapped-off proximal ends of *lamelles à cran*. One slightly anomalous form is Fig 28.34. Usually the *lamelles à cran* are retouched only along one edge while this specimen has been worked along both edges, has retained its proximal end and has two shoulders.

Retouched blades
As noted earlier, no distinction has been made between blades and bladelets. An arbitrary distinction has been made between certain forms of transversely retouched blades and laterally retouched examples.

TRANSVERSELY RETOUCHED (17 + 1 misc) Previously this group has been divided into Type A, those with slight retouch, and Type B, those where the shape of the blade has been modified (Woodman 1978). The examination of a larger sample suggests that the Type A forms could be regarded as anomalous examples of the one main class. Therefore this distinction has been abolished. The essential characteristic of this form is that it is retouched across one end at an angle of more than 45° to the axis of the blade (Fig 32.1).

Usually it is the distal ends of the blades which have been retouched, though several have either been worked on a fractured proximal end or the striking platform has been removed. The retouch on these pieces is mostly distinguished by its irregularity. The worked end is often denticulated and varies from concave to convex. In some instances it is even lopsided, while other examples almost resemble end scrapers. Other attributes which vary are the thickness of the worked edge and the size of the blade.

The one miscellaneous form has been retouched on both ends. In fact Fig 32.2 would appear to have been snapped from the middle of a substantial small blade and then retouched into a very slightly trapezoidal shape.

OBLIQUE AND PARTIALLY RETOUCHED BLADES (8) Examples of this group are retouched on the distal end of the blade for less than 50% of their length (Fig 32.3,4). This retouch is often at an oblique angle across the blade. The angle created between the retouched edge and the axis of the blade is less than 45°. Most of the examples in this group are made on very light though elongated blades (Fig 32.4). All are retouched on the distal end and none appear substantially to alter the shape of the blade.

BACKED BLADES (8: heavily retouched 4, lightly retouched 4) The backed blades fall into two groups. There are some rather small, light examples,

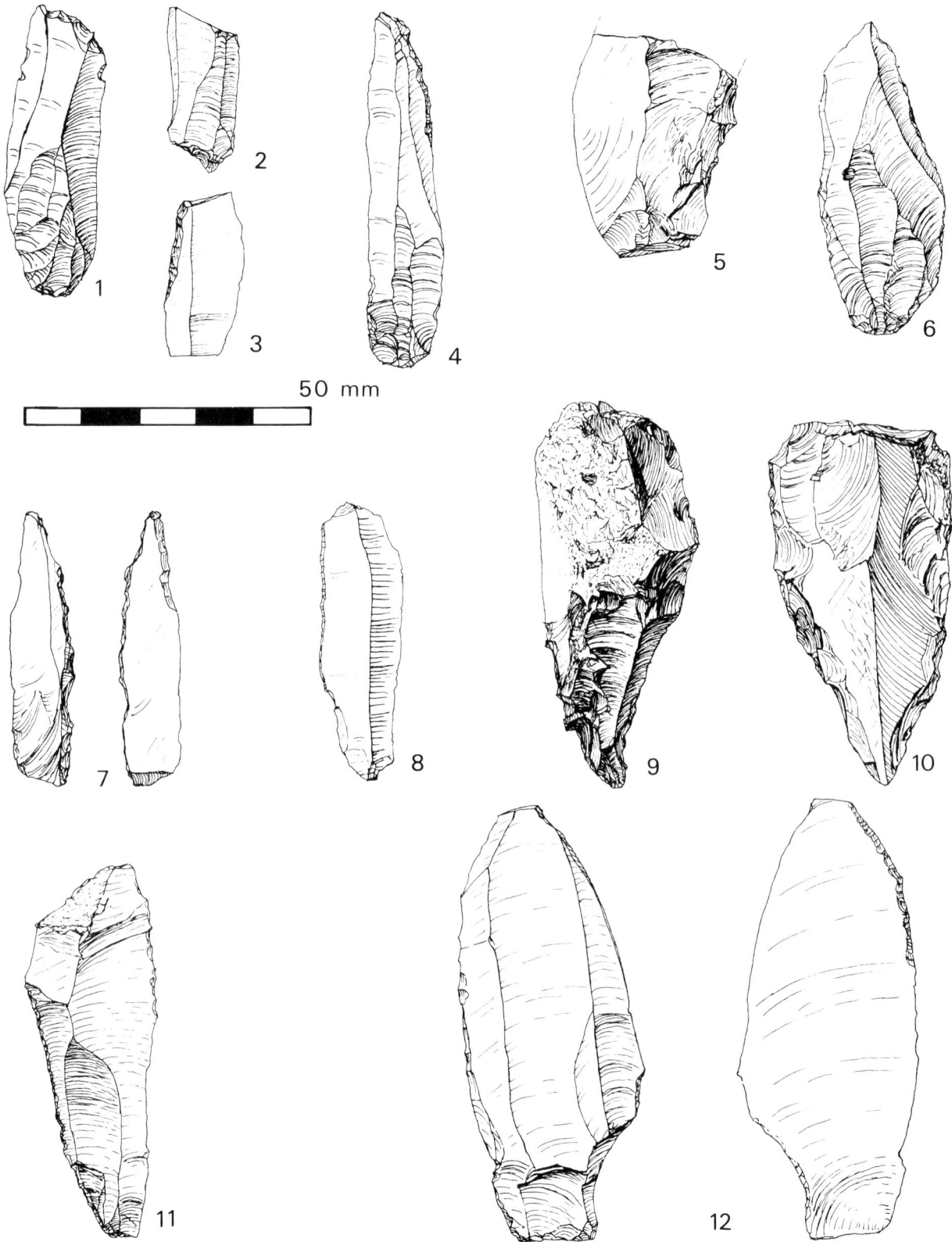

50 mm

Fig 32   1–2 transversely retouched blades; 3–4 obliquely retouched blades; 5–8 backed blades; 9–10 miscellaneous
pointed implements; 11–12 stained blades

such as Fig 32.7 (which might be an unfinished awl) and there are those with rather heavier retouch, such as Fig 32.5, which could be regarded as small backed knives. In this second group the retouch is not only heavier but it can be slightly invasive. The retouch is also not confined to the periphery of the flake. Only one of these pieces could be described as being made on a large blade or flake (Fig 32.6), though Fig 32.5 could possibly be a fragmentary example.

It is at first sight tempting to regard Fig 32.3, 4 as unfinished microliths, but while microliths can occasionally be as large as this, they rarely combine the width and thickness characteristics of these pieces: one is over 50 mm thick while most are in excess of 30 mm. Dumont (Chapter 4) has noted use damage on several pieces within this group.

Micro-awls
These implements are usually made on blades. They are trimmed to a narrow point which often exhibits signs of damage that are visible to the naked eye. The point can be made with either dorsal or alternate retouch, though it is noticeable that those with alternate retouch usually have heavier traces of damage. These blade-like implements vary considerably in size from examples such as Fig 27.6 to Fig 27.7. The one characteristic they share is that within approximately 20 mm of the tip the blade is trimmed to a very narrow acute point. Many of these pieces are made on quite thick blades with the result that the point is usually rather robust. In some instances the point has been narrowed and strengthened by anvil retouch. This has created an equilateral triangular section near the point. This type of retouch can be found on those pieces which have dorsal retouch. While it is usual for the point to be made on the distal end of the blade this is not an absolute rule. The rest of the outline of these pieces is rather varied. Some are retouched for their total length (Fig 27.9) while others are left unworked. All the complete examples are, however, very narrow and, with two exceptions, thin enough to be hafted. The irrelevance of the shape of the rest of the blade is best illustrated by one having been converted from a large backed blade.

Several blades have been retouched on both lateral edges but not retouched to an actual point. As an acute robust point seems to be the main characteristic for this group, these have been excluded.

Miscellaneous (42)
These pieces are mostly blades and flakes on which there is some irregular retouch and/or extensive damage caused by utilization. Several examples were retouched in a way which might be regarded as a conscious attempt to produce a specific implement type, but because of the variety of these pieces and their irregularity they have been retained with the miscellaneous group.

HEAVY NOTCHED FLAKES (2) There is only one large flake in this category. It has two notches which have been regularized into steep concavities. A second smaller fragment has one notch.

POINTS (2 + 2 frag?) Both points are made on large flakes. Unlike the later blade points (Woodman 1977a) these are by no means symmetrically retouched, and both show signs of being retouched on the bulbar face (Fig 32.9 and 10). One is made from a portion of a decortical flake.

Utilized
A small number of utilized blades was recovered from the hut area. These were pieces which bore easily identifiable traces of edge damage (Fig 32.11).

Ochre-stained pieces (48)
A series of flakes and blades of different sizes and shapes stained with ochre was recovered. These vary from small flakes to large blades, though there is a distinct trend towards narrow elongated blades. The positioning of the ochre staining is also irregular: it has been found on distal, mid and proximal portions of the flakes. Some are burnt, though this is assumed to have happened after the flakes had been used. Usually the ochre is ground onto the edge which is often so extensively damaged that the damage is visible to the naked eye. It is possible that many other specimens had ochre staining, but it may have weathered off while the flint lay in the soil or, if the ochre was not extensive or ground onto the flint, it could inadvertently have been washed off. On some flints there is only the slightest trace of ochre, while on others the whole edge is stained red. In the first case great care is needed to distinguish between ochre-stained blades and pieces which can have a slight red fleck within the flint.

Two large blades have staining on their surface as well as on their edges. In one instance this appeared to be ground onto the surface (Fig 32.12), while in another the ochre consisted of a layer applied to the surface of the flake. This plastering of the surface of the blade would leave little trace after the bulk of the ochre had weathered off.

Stone axes (2 + 1?)
Only two axes were found in a stratified context, one in a late context within the Mesolithic sequence. The only complete example is Fig 33.2, a relatively small axe which has an asymmetrically placed cutting edge. One face is polished overall while the other is polished extensively only near the cutting edge. The material is soft enough to have polishing grooves left on the surface and the raw material, like many of the axes found at Newferry (Woodman 1977a), is rather light in weight.

The second axe, recovered from F56/5, lacks its cutting edge (Fig 33.1). It is made of a banded rock

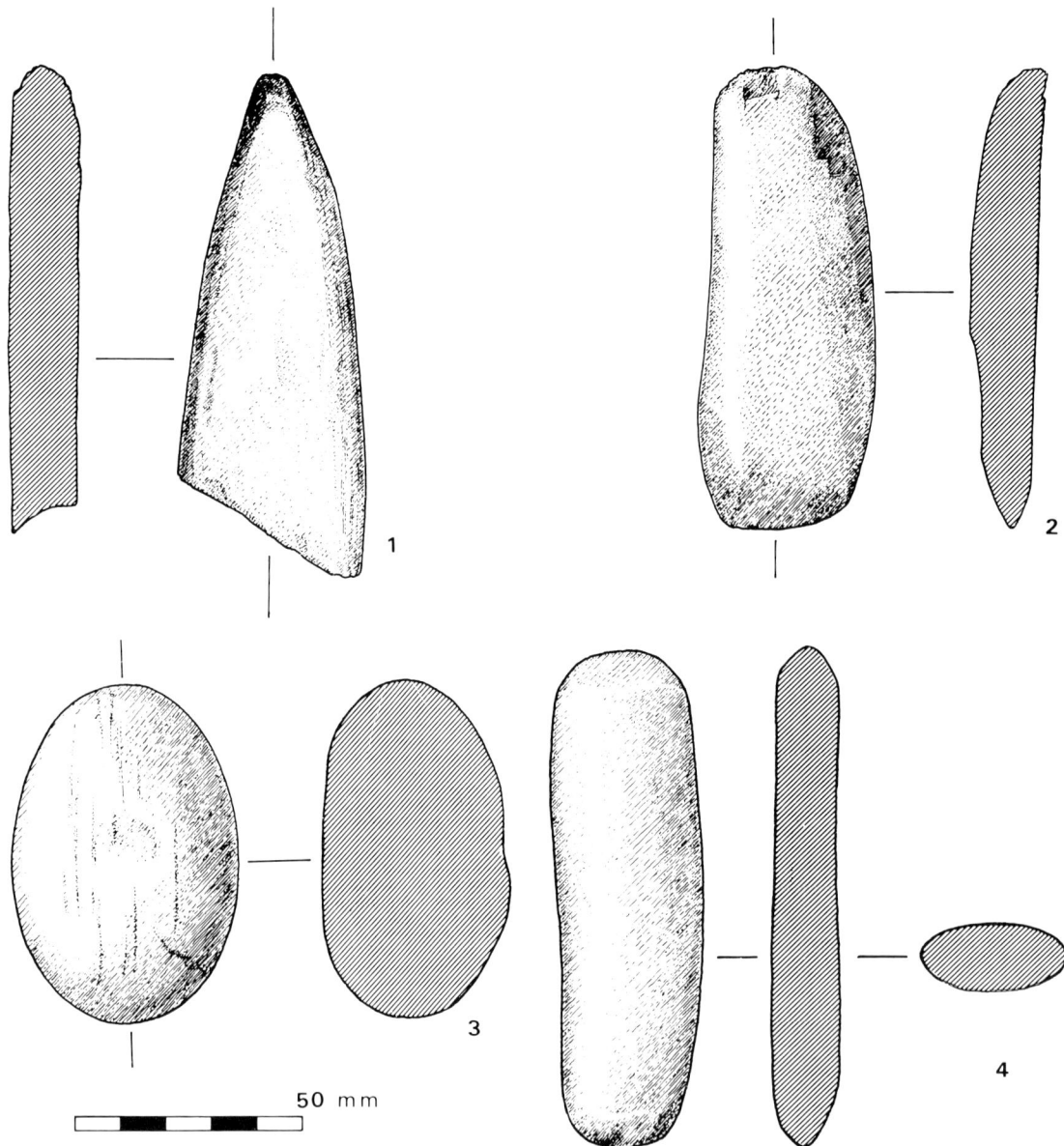

Fig 33   1–2 stone axes; 3 anvil stone; 4 bevel-ended pebble

which, like many of the axes from the Bann valley, has lent itself to a triangular outline and rectilinear section. In this instance the pointed butt has survived (see Appendix 2c).

A third axe has been tentatively included with this group. Usually the inclusion of examples in the tentative category results from the implement not quite conforming to the typological requirements. In this instance, however, there is no doubt that this is an axe; it is the context that is uncertain. The axe was found in a rabbit burrow beside the chipping floor (W/36) and it cannot absolutely certainly be regarded as Mesolithic. This example is a rather small but

thick axe which has been polished overall. The slight irregularity of the section could derive from the shape of the original pebble. The cutting edge is broad and symmetrically placed.

Bevel-ended pebble (1)
One example of this type was recovered. It was made on an elongated pebble, and both ends had been chipped and then ground to a narrow bevel. The remainder of the surface was smooth. This was probably a water-smoothed pebble which was chosen from a river bed as it had the correct shape (Fig 33.4).

Hammerstones (5 + 1?)
In spite of the large quantities of discarded waste, quartzite hammerstones are relatively rare: only three were found. These, as on so many prehistoric sites, are water-smoothed pebbles. Only one complete example occurs at Mount Sandel. One piece from F13 might be better regarded as a deliberately produced flake as it is made of quartz. Two small flint nodules show signs of extensive damage on their edges and would appear also to have been used as hammerstones.

Elongated pebbles
A selection of small elongated pebbles was collected during the excavation. These were made from a variety of schistose rocks and none showed any evidence of being deliberately altered. The main problem arising with these is that a certain subjective element entered into their retention, based on the presence of similar forms at sites such as Newferry (Woodman 1977a). A particularly worrying aspect of this group is that all but one were found in large pits (with one exception tree-falls) and for this reason no specific numbers are quoted for the group.

A similar difficulty is encountered with several large rounded pebbles. These were probably noted because of their shape, but they may represent only the more regular extreme of a range which would be expected on a site situated on a fluvio-glacial gravel ridge. One pebble showed slight traces of damage and pitting as if it had been used as an anvil stone (Fig 33.3).

Later Excavated Material

While later prehistoric implements were occasionally found during surface collection and topsoil removal, few were found during the careful removal of the soil immediately overlying Mesolithic occupation layers. One implement was found in F77 (a tree-fall hole) along with some potsherds. Most of the recognizable artefacts were found along the northern edge of the site where a later level of occupation was stratified above the Mesolithic layers (see above). The occasional item found embedded in the western area of occupation soil was probably a product of disturbance by roots. The rather sparse selection of later material results, at least in part, from the

	Northern upper	Hut area	Western industrial
Single	12	23	66
Dual	2	3	5
Multi-platformed	4	1	4

Table 8   Types of cores found in (2) northern compared with those from certain selected areas of occupation soil

stripping of the topsoil. A sufficient proportion of the topsoil in the hut hollow area was however trowelled and sieved, so the virtual absence of later implements from that area is probably genuine.

FLINT INDUSTRY
Unfortunately there is no way in which much of the industrial waste from the topsoil can be separated into Mesolithic and later assemblages, as the distinctions are quantitative and the Neolithic of this area would also appear to have been based on a light blade industry. In the northern area, however, it was possible to show that a slightly different industrial tradition was present. When the cores from layers (2) and (3) were examined, a slightly higher proportion of multi-platformed cores was noted than elsewhere (Table 8). The condition of these implements varied from fresh to heavily patinated, presumably due to the length of time they had been in the topsoil.

Hollow scrapers (3)
The only complete example was found embedded in the top of the occupation soil on the west of the site (Fig 34.5). This is made on a slightly lopsided blade, steeply retouched on its left edge. The other two specimens are only fragments (Fig 34.6).

Notched blades (2)
One example was found in a tree-fall, F77. They are not large classic examples and neither is waisted.

End scrapers (6)
These vary from large, well-made scrapers such as Fig 34.1 and 2, which are almost certainly Neolithic, through to small scrapers, one very invasively trimmed, which could be rather later in date.

Plano-convex form (1)
This is a small fragment of a flake which has been invasively retouched over the dorsal face and has slight retouch at one end on the bulbar face.

Barbed and tanged arrowhead (1)
This appears to be a small Beaker-style arrowhead which has lost both its barbs and the tang (Fig 34.7).

STONE IMPLEMENTS
Several stone implements were found out of context. One is a fragmentary axe made from baked mudstone, recovered from the upper fill of the post-medieval ditch (F5). The other item was a miniature chisel of the type found at Newferry (Smith and Collins 1971; Woodman 1977a) (Fig 35.2). It is impossible to be certain whether these are later than the main phase of Mesolithic settlement or are Early Mesolithic items out of context. The possible net-sinker (Fig 35.3) is a rather more enigmatic artefact. This was also found in the upper level of the ditch system. It is made from chalk and is similar to

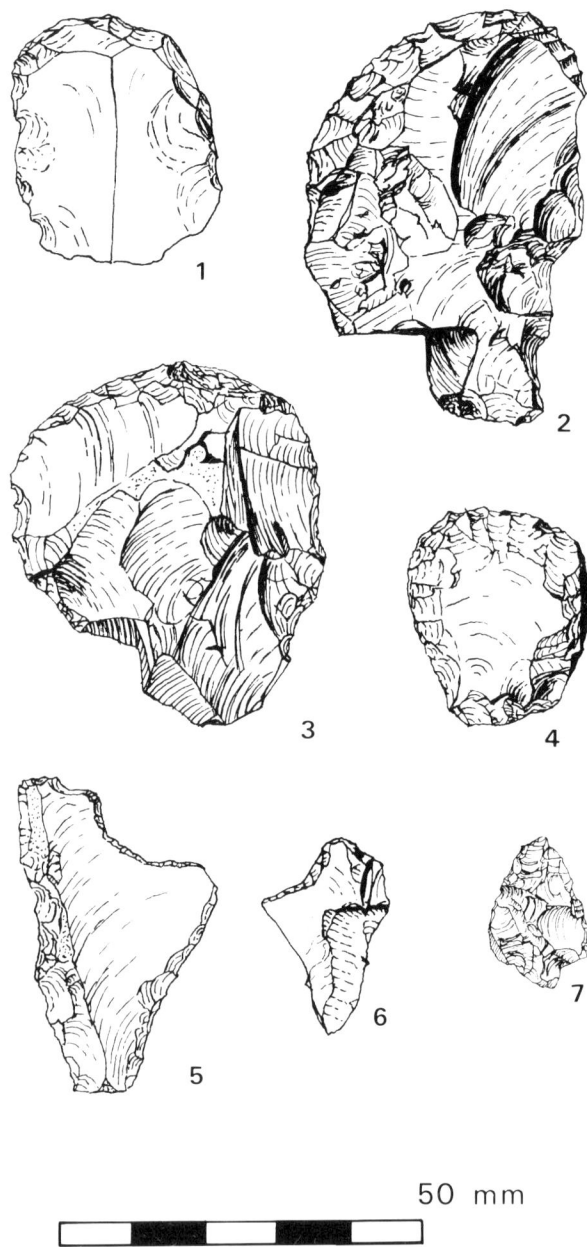

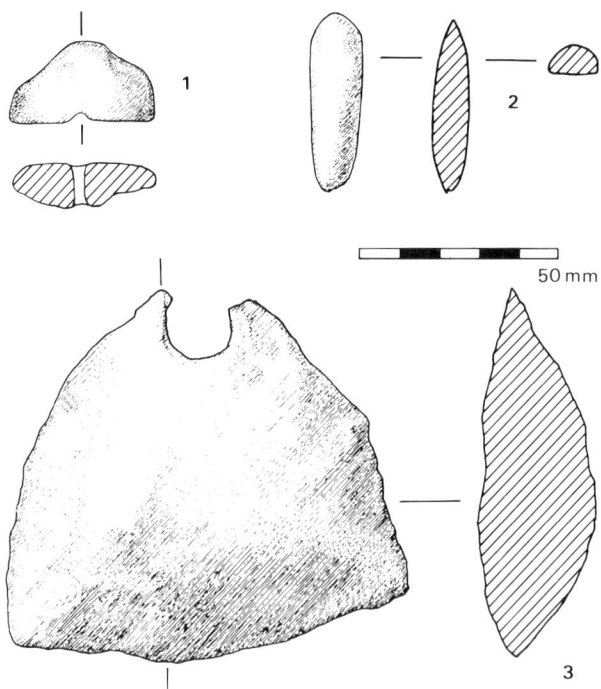

Fig 35   Miscellaneous later artefacts: 1 spindle-whorl
         fragment; 2 miniature stone chisel; 3 stone
         net-sinker (?)

POTTERY

Spindle-whorl

Only half of this remains. Unlike most spindle-whorls
it is made from a potsherd. While the break is
relatively fresh, the original edge is rather worn (Fig
35.1).

Hand-made pottery

In total 160 sherds of hand-made pottery were
recovered, mostly during excavation of the northern
and western edges of the site, although occasional
sherds were found on the southern edge. Obviously

50 mm

Fig 34   Later flint artefacts: 1–4 scrapers; 5–6 hollow
         scrapers; 7 barbed and tanged arrowhead

several other triangular net-sinkers found during the
Bann drainage scheme, but these items are unfortunately undatable.

GLASS

Two small *glass beads* were found in F313. One (Fig
36) is a small, perforated, blue glass bead while the
other is a dumb-bell bead. The significance of these
and the ^{14}C date from F313 are discussed in
Appendix 4.

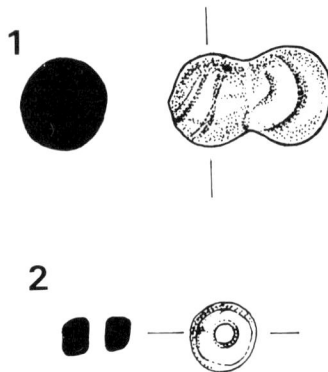

Fig 36   Glass beads from F313: 1 at twice life-size; 2 at
         four times life-size

this material was usually found in upper post-Mesolithic layers, although some was found in the western area where root disturbance was extensive. The pottery survived in the northern and western areas because the sherds were usually protected by an extra thickness of humus (western area) or by a combination of extra humus and redeposited soil (northern area). In most other areas ploughing had totally removed later levels of occupation and in most instances had destroyed the uppermost levels of the subsoil. Friable pottery could not survive in horizons that were being subjected to a continual series of changes in moisture content and temperature, as well as being disturbed by agricultural activity. In fact the only sherd of hand-made pottery found in the ploughzone in the central area was from an everted-rim medieval cooking pot, a type of pottery of rather better quality than most of the sherds found. On the southern edge of the site the only concentration of potsherds came from a tree-fall.

Unfortunately, because of the small quantity of pottery recovered, there were relatively few diagnostic sherds. Few were of any size: the largest sherd had a maximum width of 80 mm. They rarely came from areas such as base angles, shoulders, necks or rims of pots. However, considering that few were found in features (most being derived) and none were complete pots, the condition of most of the pottery was surprisingly good. A visual inspection showed that its fabric was varied, with inclusions of chalk, sand, mica and flint, and grano-diorite (?). Considering the direction of ice movement in this area, the Armoy advance would have brought flint, mica and chalk into this area (Creighton 1974), and there is nothing to indicate that this pottery is of anything other than local origin. Miss Alison Sheridan (New Hall, Cambridge) has undertaken a chemical analysis of the clays of prehistoric pottery and as this work includes a selection of sherds from Mount Sandel it may eventually shed further light on the origins of the pottery.

The types of hand-made pottery identified from the site include Western Neolithic, Sandhills ware, Coarse Ware(?), souterrain ware(?), and medieval everted-rim ware. The wheel-thrown medieval and post-medieval pottery will be described below by M L Simpson.

PREHISTORIC POTTERY The bulk of the pottery is presumed to be prehistoric and mostly Neolithic in date. There are several rim and shoulder sherds from plain Western Neolithic pottery (Fig 37.4) as well as one highly decorated sherd from a Western Neolithic bowl (Fig 37.1). The few rim sherds indicated that these were deep pots with flat rims of Case's Lyles Hill style (1961), as well as bowls with outward-flaring rims. Some of the burnished sherds could also

be attributed to Western Neolithic pottery. These included sherds with every type of grit except the grano-diorite(?) group. It is only possible to state that on the basis of rim shape and inclusions at least four different pots are represented in this group.

Of the remainder, one sherd at least is part of the rim of a small, cord-decorated, globular Sandhills bowl (Fig 37.5), while another sherd (also from a Sandhills bowl) has cord maggot impressions (Fig 37.3). Another decorated sherd is rather more enigmatic (Fig 37.2) and appears to have a darker, grittier fabric than the rest (several undecorated sherds were also found). It appears to be from either a smaller, cord-decorated, beaker-derived pot, or from a food vessel. However, it is unusual in that the decoration is limited to the area adjacent to the rim and Herity (personal communication) suggests that it is a form of Sandhills ware.

The rest of the prehistoric sherds are less diagnostic and vary in condition, firing and thickness. Many are certainly from Neolithic bowls. The ^{14}C dates from F313 and F10 might indicate either a Late Bronze Age or Early Iron Age occupation of the site, though the age lapse on the wood charcoal used would increase the likelihood that this date belongs to a phase of occupation during the Early Iron Age (Warner 1976). In spite of the evidence of Freestone Hill (Raftery 1969), there is no unequivocal evidence that coarse pottery was used during the Early Iron Age. Some of the pottery is so coarse that it could well belong to Late Bronze Age Coarse Ware pots. The absence of base sherds is not an argument against the presence of Coarse Ware, as these are also absent at sites such as Clogher (R B Warner, personal communication). The absence of diagnostic rim sherds could be explained by the small size of the samples.

SOUTERRAIN OR EVERTED-RIM WARES There is one small group of fourteen sherds which date either to the Later Iron Age (Early Christian) or medieval periods. These sherds have a hard sandy fabric, red and black in colour. Besides these there are parts of an exceptionally crude ring-built, everted-rim pot which were recovered from the mortar at the base of the ditch in N-P/22-24 (F4). In places the surface is not smoothed over so that the structure of rings is easily visible. There is also a rim sherd from another everted-rim medieval pot (Fig 37.7). It is much more difficult to attribute the rest of the sherds to either the Later Iron Age or the medieval period. On a rather subjective basis, the one base sherd (Fig 37.8) is heavy while the rim sherd (Fig 37.6) flares out in a fashion not usually associated with medieval pottery, so that some at least of this group of pottery could be souterrain ware.

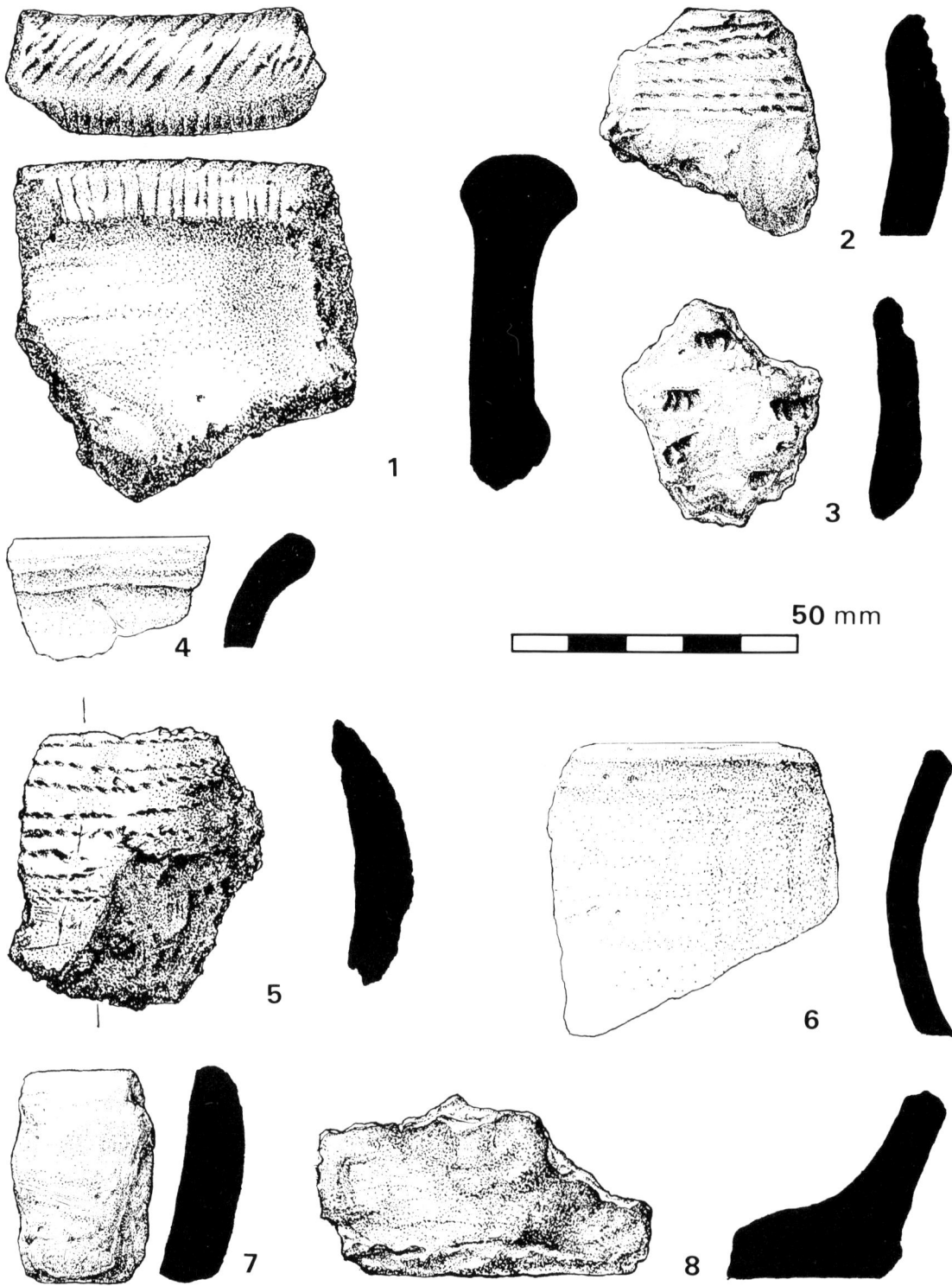

Fig 37   1–5 Neolithic pottery; 6–8 souterrain or everted-rim wares

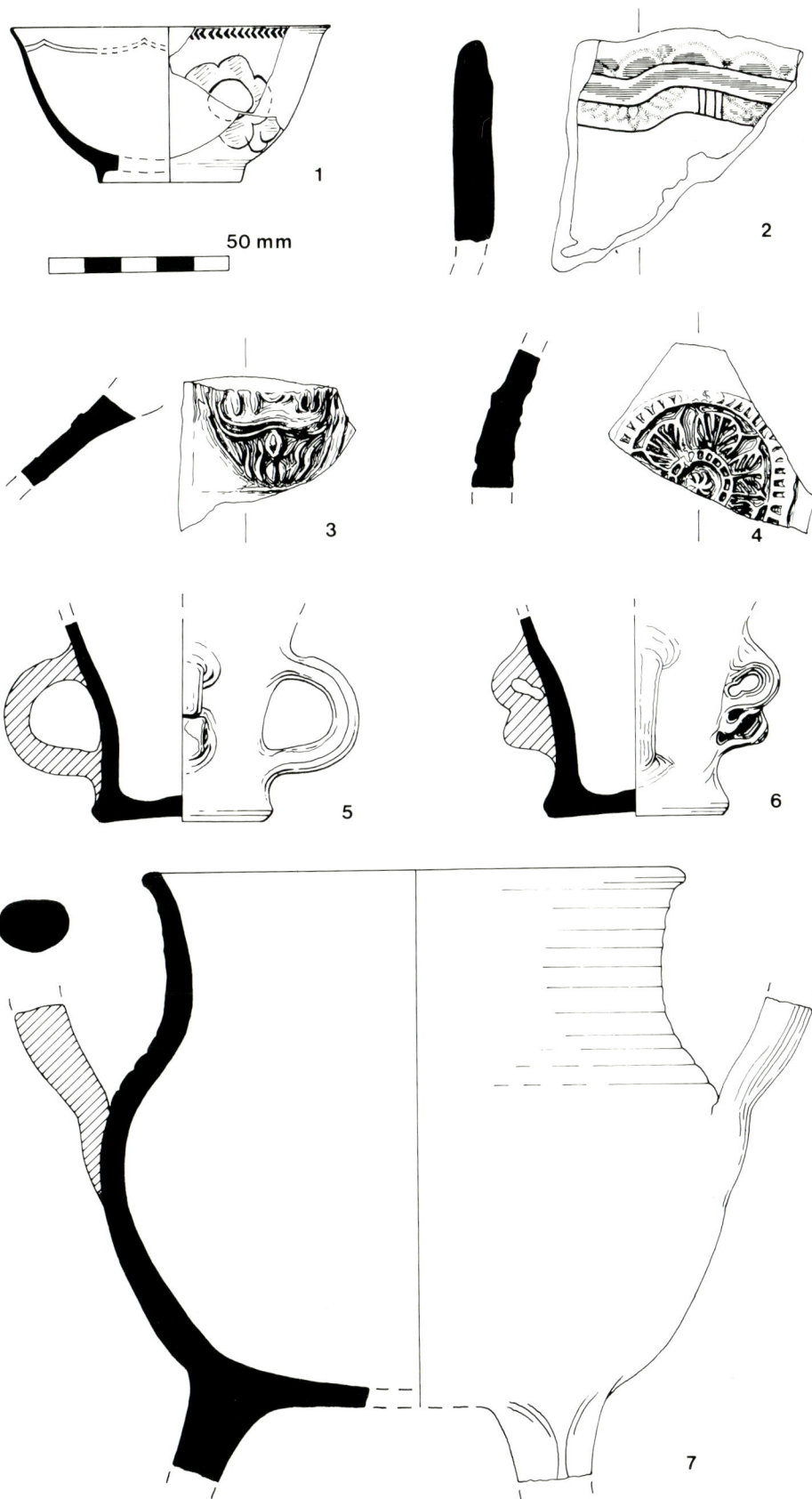

Fig 38 Medieval and post-medieval pottery (colours represented by standard DOE conventions)

Medieval and later pottery, including clay pipes
by M L Simpson

POTTERY On the whole, the medieval and post-medieval pottery considered here reflects the kind of material one would expect to find during field-walking in an area of rural settlement. In an urban environment one would expect a wider range, a higher proportion than is represented here of earlier pottery and finer vessels and, from a port, more Continental imports. The sherds range in date from (probably) the 13th to the 20th century (catalogued in Appendix 1e).

The medieval sherds are probably all from wheel-thrown English style jugs. Although some coarse ware sherds may be from hand-built, locally-made cooking pots (everted-rim pottery) they are too small for certainty that they are in fact medieval, and have therefore already been discussed with souterrain ware. The lack of proper contexts for the medieval material, however, makes it difficult to interpret and it does not, unfortunately, help with the problem of identification of Mount Sandel as de Courcy's castle of *Kil Santain* (see Appendix 4).

The majority of the post-medieval sherds are from vessels in common use in the kitchen or dairy in the 18th and 19th centuries, such as the familiar coarse black and brown lead-glazed wares which are difficult, at least at present, to pin down to a particular region, even where kilns are known, and, of course, transfer-printed and other 19th-century wares. Other types represented are tin-glazed earthenware, stoneware and a variety of slipwares. Of particular note, because they are finer, are the two sherds of polychrome tin-glazed ware, probably French in origin, a fine Bellarmine mask and medallion, from Cologne/Frechen and a Staffordshire scratch blue tea bowl (Fig 38.1–4). The tripod-footed earthenware vessel illustrated may well be of local origin (Fig 38.7). Two partly reconstructed tygs are also shown in Fig 38 (5–6). Prominent by its absence is lead-glazed earthenware from the south Lancashire potteries and North Devon pottery, both of which were found at excavations in Londonderry and Carrickfergus. The sgraffito sherds may well have been made locally and have more in common with the South Somerset than the North Devon types in terms of fabric and firing.

Many of the sherds, both medieval and post-medieval, were worn, and sherds from the same vessel often came from different parts of the site. The only true contexts from which post-medieval pottery was recovered were the following features: F4 (a ditch), F32 (a modern pit), F200 (the base of a bank), F201 (a bank), F202 (a ditch), F206 (a Mesolithic surface cut by a ditch), F220 (a gully) and F228 (a ditch). Even within these contexts, however, there was evidence of disturbed or derived material. In some cases, of course, it appears to be the medieval or post-medieval pottery disturbing an earlier feature. The rest of the pottery was found scattered throughout the site in the upper levels (separated by the excavator into upper and lower topsoil). The grid squares within which finds were excavated were recorded, should a distribution pattern become evident. In the case of the pottery such a pattern could not be seen but these details have been retained in the catalogue for the more important groups to facilitate any future work. A number of sherds were unprovenanced but have been included for the sake of completeness.

CLAY PIPES The majority of the clay pipes from Mount Sandel are from topsoil, the only exceptions being three 17th-century bowls from the second level of a bank (F200) and six stems from three different features (F200, F202 and F203). They would thus seem to have little significance for the interpretation of the site. The relatively high proportion of 17th-century pipes is, however, interesting: elsewhere in Ulster very few 17th-century pipes have turned up in field-walking groups so that a concentration at Mount Sandel of at least fourteen pipes of this date suggests occupation of the site at that time, even if the evidence has since been disturbed. The small proportion of 18th-century pipes is consistent with the evidence of most other groups found in Northern Ireland. Dating has been based on the bowl size and shape, following Oswald's typology as far as possible (catalogued in Appendix 1e).

As far as the marks are concerned, the AD stamp is not known from any other site in Northern Ireland, while the 'mulberry' mark is rare; nor is the early 18th-century pipe with decorated heel a common type, occurring elsewhere only in Carrickfergus. The particular variant of the 'COCK OF THE NORTH' pipe from this site is different from those recorded from other locations and the distribution of the type generally is mainly limited to the Coleraine area, with isolated examples from Dungiven and Ballycastle. The common mark of a cross-hatched heart is combined here with a diamond (more usually found with a hand) while the ubiquitous 'DERRY' stamp (not necessarily made in Londonderry, of course) occurs twice in this group.

Surface Collections

Very little can be said about the surface collections. They were carried out in 1972 when the site was rediscovered and before it was decided that an excavation would be carried out. Unfortunately no control grid was used to monitor variations in surface concentrations of material.

Cores 500+	Core axes	10	Microliths	12
Blades and Flakes 5000+	Flake axes	6	Awls	2
	Picks	2	Retouched blades	2
	Scrapers	10	Stone chisel	1

The most obvious difference between this material and that found *in situ* during the excavation is in condition. The surface collection material is patinated and many implements, including the axes and the blades, are very fragmentary. There is also a noticeable difference in the amount of notching and edge damage on blades if the topsoil and *in situ* material are compared. Much of what had at first been considered use damage on the topsoil material must in fact result from plough damage.

Amongst other differences, it was noteworthy that the ratio of axe to microlith in the occupation soil was 1:13 but in the topsoil material it was less than 1:1. Excavation of the topsoil showed that microliths were indeed present in relatively large numbers and the contrast obviously results from the method of recovery. The scrapers appear to be more common but many, like those found during the excavation of the upper deposits, are of a later Neolithic or Bronze Age type, and Mesolithic scrapers were by no means common in the topsoil.

Four copper and bronze *coins* were found during surface collecting. They range in date from a possible copper penny of Elizabeth I, issued in 1601 and 1602, to a Queen Victoria bronze halfpenny (1860–1894). These are listed and discussed in Appendix 1f.

CHAPTER 4

A preliminary report on the Mount Sandel microwear study

John V Dumont

Introduction*

This report presents the conclusions concerning the function of particular artefact types derived from the use of the medium magnification microwear method (see Keeley 1980 and also Cook and Dumont in press). No attempt has been made here either to formulate statements about the activities represented at the site by the use-episodes found on the tools, or to assess the typological composition of activity tool-kits (such as hideworking or woodworking tools). These topics, in addition to the supporting individual microwear interpretations, will be addressed in the author's dissertation (Dumont in preparation). The limits of space have prevented discussion of the methodology employed in this study and the theoretical foundation of the functional interpretations. With respect to the methodology, I have stressed the importance of the recognition, identification and distribution of microwear polishes and linear features, with the evidence of the edge-damage being utilized in only a very restricted manner (see Dumont in press, Dumont in preparation and Cook and Dumont in press). The theoretical basis of the functional interpretations can be found in Dumont 1982, Dumont in preparation and Cook and Dumont in press. This paper supplants and makes redundant the preliminary comments made in Dumont in press.

A total of 273 artefacts was examined during this study. Eighty-four of these exhibited functional and/or potential hafting traces, while 65 exhibited technological traces. The number of artefacts with microwear traces (including functional, hafting and technological traces) is 127. The functional and potential hafting traces are summarily presented, in units of artefacts within each type, in Tables 9 and 10. Table 11 provides a summary of the functional interpretations relating to each type, though now the data is presented in units of use-episodes. Plates 9–16 show examples of the types of microwear polishes found on the Mount Sandel artefacts. With the exception of the type 'edge-damaged/retouched flakes and blades', I have followed Woodman's 1978 typology (Woodman 1978, 33–40).

The Artefacts

CORE AXES, CORE AXE-SHARPENING FLAKES AND FLAKE AXES

Twenty-eight sharpening flakes were examined and fourteen exhibited functional and/or technological traces. Of the fourteen flakes with traces, twelve exhibit functional traces while the remaining two appear to exhibit traces (stone-on-stone polish, linear arrangements of 'stone' polish, striations and scattered areas of wood polish) related to the initial manufacture of the axes. The functional traces consist of wood polish, hide polish, linear arrangements of wood polish, edge-damage, and edge-/arrête-rounding. Wood polish was the most common trace, occurring on eleven of the twelve utilized flakes, followed by edge-damage (present on nine), linear arrangements of wood polish (on seven), striations (on four), and edge-/arrête-rounding that was restricted to the only flake exhibiting hide polish. Of the eleven flakes with functional wood polish, seven (about 64%) also had linear arrangements of this trace and nine (about 82%) exhibited edge-damage. The presence of hide polish on the working edge of one sharpening flake (Mu 2124)* is surprising. Of the three core axes examined, only one exhibited traces: wood polish, striations, linear arrangements of wood

* The references for Chapter 4 will be found on page 70.

*Mu here and elsewhere refers to the Mount Sandel finds catalogue.

Artefact type / Class of trace	Polishes or deposits								Linear traces		Edge alterations			
	wood	bone	antler	hide	meat	functional haematite deposits	stone on stone	?	LAP	striae	damage[1]	rounding	crushing	IF
Core axe-sharpening flakes														
functional	11	0	0	1	0	0	0	0	7	4	9	1	0	0
technological	0	0	0	0	0	—	1	0	1	1	0	0	0	0
Core axes														
functional	1	0	0	0	0	0	0	0	1	1	1	0	0	0
Flake axes														
functional	6	0	0	0	0	0	0	0	1	2	4	0	0	0
technological	0	0	0	0	0	—	2	0	0	0	0	0	0	0
Borers														
functional	1	3	0	2	0	1	0	2	1	6	4	5	4	0
technological	0	0	0	0	0	—	3	0	3	0	0	0	0	0
Edge-damaged/retouched flakes and blades														
functional	2	4	0	0	2	12	0	0	3	10	17	10	0	0
Variously backed blades														
functional	0	1	0	1	0	2	0	1	0	4	4	3	0	0
technological	0	0	0	0	0	—	1	0	0	0	0	0	0	0
Truncated blades														
functional	1	0	1	1	0	0	0	1	1	3	3	0	0	0
technological	0	0	0	0	0	—	1	0	1	0	0	0	0	0
Scrapers														
functional	0	1	0	0	0	0	0	0	0	0	1	0	0	0
Picks														
technological	0	0	0	0	0	—	1	0	0	0	0	0	0	0
Burins														
technological	0	0	0	0	0	—	0	0	0	1	0	0	0	0
Needles														
functional	0	2	0	1	1	0	0	0	2	0	0	0	0	0
technological	0	0	0	0	0	—	1	0	0	0	0	0	0	0
Triangles														
functional	0	1	0	2	0	0	0	0	0	0	2	1	0	0
technological	0	0	0	0	0	—	3	0	0	0	0	0	0	0
Obliquely blunted points														
technological	0	0	0	0	0	0	3	0	0	0	0	0	0	0
Misc microliths														
technological	0	0	0	0	0	0	2	0	0	0	0	0	0	0
Rods														
functional	0	2–4	0–1	2–3	0–1	0	1	0	3	2	11	2	0	3–5
technological	0	0	0	0	0	—	47	0	0	0	0	0	0	0

[1] Only the edge-damage that can be confidently related to other microwear traces, on the affected edge, is listed here

Table 9   Summary of functional and technological microwear traces recognized on each tool type (in units of artefacts) (LAP = linear arrangements of polish or deposits; IF impact fractures; ? unidentified polishes or deposits; — not applicable)

polish and edge-damage. Both ends of this core axe appear to have been used for woodworking.

All of the flake axes examined (six in number) exhibit traces that are considered to be related to their use. These include wood polish, linear arrangements of wood polish, striations and edge-damage. Although stone-on-stone polish was present on the surfaces of two axes, its distribution suggests a technological rather than functional origin. Two flake axes (Mu 2264 and Mu 2287) exhibit areas of wood polish across both surfaces (dorsal and ventral) in a distribution that is more easily explained by inferring

the former presence of a wooden haft than by 'woodworking' (Fig 39). Of the functionally significant traces, wood polish was the most common and occurred at the working edge of each of the six axes. Edge-damage, of an apparent functional origin and primarily consisting of snap-like fractures (Keeley's half-moon breakages (1980, 25)), was also present at the working edges of at least four of the axes. Linear features were surprisingly uncommon and occurred on only two of the six axes. Only one axe exhibited linear polish arrangements, while two exhibited striations. This frequency of occurrence is less than

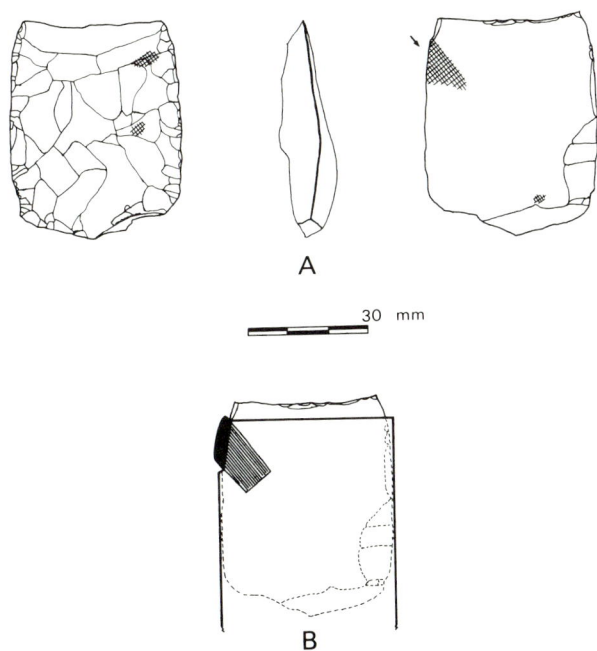

30 mm

Fig 39   Flake axe Mu2287: (A) schematic drawing showing extensive and well-developed areas of wood polish (cross-hatched); (B) suggested method of formation, by use of a wooden, sleeve-like haft, periodically tightened with a wooden wedge (solid and hatched)

half (about 44%) of the frequency of linear features found on the demonstrably utilized core axe-sharpening flakes: eight of the eleven sharpening flakes used on wood (about 74%) exhibited striations and/or linear polish arrangements. This difference in frequency is only apparent at the typological level of analysis (sharpening flakes against flake axes) but disappears when one examines the frequency of linear features with respect to the manner of tool use: seven of the working edges used for chopping wood exhibit linear features, while five of those used for planing/adzing wood also exhibit linear features. The difference in frequency in relation to each tool type is likely to be merely an artefact of the small size of the sample examined.

A total of 21 distinct use-episodes have been identified on 20 working edges of the nineteen demonstrably utilized core axes, sharpening flakes and flake axes. With the exception of a single use-episode on a sharpening flake, all the functions are related to woodworking; the exception, Mu 2124, was used to work hide. Two principal manners of tool use have been identified on the basis of the distribution and orientation of the available traces: chopping and planing/adzing. The distinction between the two manners is one of tool orientation and the nature of the contact between tool and wood. Chopping involves a low to oblique orientation of first

one, and then the opposing, edge-aspect towards the wood. The roughly alternate contact of the two edge-aspects at similar orientations should produce a roughly similar distribution of traces corresponding to the similar areas and direction of tool/wood contact on both aspects. Chopping also involves the use of impact: the edge strikes the wood after a swing of varying length and strength. Although the use of a haft would no doubt improve the efficiency of 'chopping', there is no *a priori* reason to assume the necessary presence of such an aid. The microwear analysis has unfortunately shed no light on the question of the hafting of core axes.

Planing and adzing have been conflated into a single category because of the difficulty of defining criteria that could confidently discriminate one action from the other, on the basis of the distribution and orientation of the microwear traces. In both instances the tool is orientated at a low to oblique angle to the wood, with respect predominantly to a single face. This orientation causes a greater area of surface contact of one face against the wood compared with the other. The distribution of the traces across both faces reflects the differential tool/wood contact. The difference between adzing and planing rests on the initial contact or entry of the edge into the wood. Like chopping, adzing requires that the edge enters the wood after a swing of varying length and strength. Planing has no such requirement; the edge can be pushed through the wood from an initial state of rest. In a sense, then, chopping and adzing are related in that the contact between the wood and the edge causes a rapid deceleration of the tool, while planing (also whittling and scraping) involves an acceleration of the edge or tool through the wood. In both cases a portion of the kinetic energy is dissipated by producing work against the wood, damage to the edge (including microwear polishes) and heat.

Of the fifteen use-episodes on the core axe-sharpening flakes and one core axe, nine are 'chopping' (60%) while six are 'planing/adzing' (40%). All of the use-episodes represented on the flake axes, six in number, are of planing/adzing. With regard to the manner of tool use, all nine of the chopping use-episodes are associated with core axe-sharpening flakes, while the twelve planing/adzing use-episodes are evenly divided between the core axe-sharpening flakes (including the core axe) and the flake axes. In more simple terms, the core axes (represented by the sharpening flakes) were used for both chopping and planing/adzing, with chopping being exclusively associated with this type of axe; the flake axes were exclusively used for planing/adzing, but this same function was also performed by the core axes (represented by the sharpening flakes). There is, then, a direct correlation between tool type and function: within the limits of this sample, all flake axes were used for planing/adzing while chopping was restricted to the core axes. It is also clear that the ancient tool users considered core axes suitable for planing/adzing. There are no significant differences in either the spine or edge angles of those edges used for chopping as opposed to those used for planing/adzing (see Dumont in preparation).

If the haft reconstructed for flake axe Mu 2287 is accurate (Fig 39) and common to all or most of the flake axes, then the proximity of the hafting sleeve to the working edge may well have made the hafted tool totally unsuitable for chopping. One could argue that the haft would impede the entry of the working edge into the wood and, in so doing, cause damage to the haft itself. If the core axes were hafted then it is likely that the haft would have been designed to avoid any interference with the worked material. A core axe that is suitably hafted for 'chopping' could, of course, be used for planing/adzing as well.

BORERS

Thirty-two borers (micro-awls) were examined as part of this study. Twelve of these exhibited traces but only nine had functionally significant microwear. Two further artefacts exhibited traces that may have been caused by hafting, while another merely exhibited technological traces. The possible hafting traces consist of wood polish and striations on Mu 109, and an unidentified deposit (perhaps a hafting adhesive) on Mu (Y61). The technological traces consist of linear arrangements of stone-on-stone polish which occur at the edges of three artefacts where their orientation and position, on the edge-aspects opposite those that show retouch scars, strongly suggest that they were caused by hard hammer retouch (Keeley's hammerstone smears: 1980, *28*; see also Pl 16). The functional traces consist of polishes, deposits, linear arrangements of deposits, striations, edge-/*arrête*-rounding and edge-damage/crushing. Of the polishes, bone polish was the most common and occurred on the working tips of three

borers. Wood polish was present on two borers, though only one is thought to be derived from the use of the tool; the polish on the other (Mu 109) is more likely to result from hafting (see the discussion of Mu 109 in Dumont in preparation). Hide polish was also observed on the working tips of two borers. Two more artefacts exhibit haematite deposits that by their distribution and form suggest an origin other than through natural causes. Striations were found on six artefacts in apparent association with wood polish (two instances), hide polish (one), bone polish (one), linear arrangements of haematite deposits (one) and with edge-damage/crushing and haematite deposits (one). Edge- and/or *arrête*-rounding occurred with both hide (two instances) and wood (one) polishes. Rounding also affected the edges and/or *arrêtes* of two other artefacts that exhibited no polish. Edge-damage or crushing was observed on the working tips of at least four and up to eight borers, the uncertainty being caused by the difficulty of resolving damage from retouch scars. Of the certain instances of edge-damage, only two were 'associated' with polish (bone). Three of the possible cases of edge-damage occurred with hide, bone and wood polishes. The remaining uncertain instance and the two certain examples occurred in 'association' with no polish.

Nine use-episodes have been identified on the nine utilized borers. From the evidence of the polishes, bone, wood, hide, haematite and an unidentified material were worked by the borers. Although the working of bone, wood and hide with this tool type is not surprising or counter-intuitive, the rationale of working haematite with a borer is not clear. It is of course possible that lumps of haematite were perforated for beads, but such artefacts were not found at the site so the suggestion remains unsupported. It is perhaps more likely that at least one of the borers exhibiting haematite may have acquired this trace by working a material, such as hide, that had been treated with haematite for the purposes of coloration or preservation. In the absence

Artefact type	Polish or deposit					Linear traces	
	wood	bone	antler	unidentified deposits[1]	biased distribution of pedogenic iron[2]	LAP	striae
Flake axes	2	0	0	0	0	0	0
Borers	1	0	0	1	0	0	1
Picks	1	0	0	0	0	0	1
Needles	1	0	0	0	0	0	0
Rods	2	1–2	1	1	2	1	0

[1] perhaps a hafting adhesive
[2] perhaps reflecting the distribution of a former adhesive

Table 10   Summary of potential hafting traces on particular tool types (in units of artefacts) (LAP = linear arrangements of polish)

of hides recovered from the site, this uncommon suggestion must also remain speculative. The working of the other materials (bone, hide and wood) is less difficult to assert in the absence of the final product.

With respect to the manners-of-use of the borers, two methods have been inferred from the orientation and distribution of the observed traces: boring and piercing (conflated into one category in Table 11). The manner-of-use of one artefact, however, remains entirely unknown. Boring, a rotary motion around the long axis of the tool, was the most common manner-of-use and is represented by six or seven of the nine use-episodes. Piercing, a motion parallel to the long axis of the tool, is represented by at least one of the use-episodes. The distribution of the traces has allowed a resolution of the rotary boring action into clockwise and anti-clockwise motions in four instances (clockwise: three examples; anti-clockwise: one example); the remaining three boring use-episodes are either undifferentiated or represent a reciprocal action.

The longitudinal extent of the traces back from the working tip of each borer, and the greatest cross-sectional dimension of the tip at the limit of their extent, provide an approximation of the size of the holes produced in the worked materials. The inferred diameter of the holes represents the minimum value of the true greatest diameter of each hole produced by the tool at the stated depth of penetration. The smallest potential diameter of the holes, then, ranged from 1.7 mm to 5.7 mm with a mean diameter of 3.84 mm (standard deviation: 1.26 mm).

The microwear analysis has not shed much light on the hafting of the Mount Sandel borers. Only two tools exhibit traces that may relate to the former presence of a haft, but the evidence is far from compelling. On the one hand there is certainly no *a priori* reason to assume that the tools were necessarily hafted, for they are quite easily manipulated by hand. On the other hand the absence of conclusive, and the paucity of suggestive, hafting traces does not, of course, indicate that hafts were not employed.

EDGE-DAMAGED/RETOUCHED FLAKES AND BLADES
Thirty-one edge-damaged or casually retouched flakes and blades were examined as part of this study. A total of 39 utilized edges or edge-segments were identified on 20 of the artefacts. The microwear traces found consist of polishes, haematite deposits, linear arrangements of polish/deposits, striations, edge-/*arrête*-rounding and edge-damage. Pedogenic iron compounds were also found on six of the artefacts exhibiting functional traces. For the purposes of the present discussion, the haematite deposits will be considered a 'polish' because although it is a deposit,

its presence conveys the same sort of information as the true polishes, that is the partial identity of the worked material. The polishes (including the haematite deposits) were the most common of the microwear traces and occurred on 38 of the 39 utilized edges/edge-segments (hereafter abbreviated to edge-segments). The vast majority of this group consists of edge-segments exhibiting the functional haematite deposits: 31 of the 38 edge-segments with polish showed this trace (about 82%).

Bone polish occurred on four of the edge-segments with one in apparent 'association' with meat polish. Meat polish also occurred on another edge-segment giving a total of two occurrences. Wood polish was found on the remaining two edge-segments exhibiting polish. Edge-damage occurred on 36 to 38 of the utilized edge-segments. Of the 22 examples exhibiting edge-/*arrête*-rounding, all but one also exhibited functional haematite deposits, the exception being 'associated' with only edge-damage. Although virtually all of the rounding instances were 'associated' with the functional haematite deposits, only about 68% of the edge-segments exhibiting haematite (21 of the 31 segments) were affected by rounding. With respect to the edge-damaged/retouched flakes and blades, then, edge-/*arrête*-rounding is virtually exclusively 'associated' with the working of haematite (or a material bearing this mineral), but it is not a necessary effect of such use.

Striations occurred on fifteen edge-segments. Of these, twelve were 'associated' with functional haematite deposits, one with wood polish, one with bone polish and the remaining instance on an edge with both bone and meat polishes. All of the edge-segments exhibiting both functional haematite deposits and striations were also affected by edge-/*arrête*-rounding. Linear polish arrangements were observed on only three edge-segments: two of bone polish and one of haematite.

Forty-one use-episodes have been identified on the 39 edge-segments of the 20 utilized artefacts. The majority of these use-episodes (33 of the 41, about 80%) were concerned with the working of either haematite directly or the working of a material bearing this mineral. Of these 33 'haematite-working' use-episodes, 19 to 20 consisted of scraping/planing (about 58–61%), six to seven of sawing/cutting (about 18–21%), one of boring (about 3%) and six of an unidentified manner(s)-of-use (about 18%). The remaining eight use-episodes are evenly divided amongst wood-, bone- and meat-working, and an unidentified worked material. With respect to woodworking, sawing/cutting and planing/whittling are each represented by a single use-episode, while boneworking is represented by two scraping/planing episodes. Although meat-working or butchering is only represented by two episodes of sawing/cutting, I would not be surprised if this figure is under-representative of the true frequency of meat-cutting with these artefacts. With respect to the unidentified worked materials, one episode of either sawing/cutting or scraping/planing is represented while another completely unidentified manner-of-use is also represented. Considering all the use-episodes, then, the frequency of the various functions can be ranked as follows: scraping/planing haematite* (about 46–49%), sawing/cutting haematite (about 15–17%), unidentified uses against haematite (about 15%), scraping/planing bone (about 5%), sawing/cutting meat (about 5%), sawing/cutting wood (about 2.4%), planing/whittling wood (about 2.4%), boring haematite (about 2.4%), either sawing/cutting or scraping/planing an unidentified material (about 2.4%) and, finally, an unidentified use against an 'unknown' material (about 2.4%). It is interesting to note that the majority of the use-episodes (21 to 23 of the 41, about 51 to 56%) were concerned with scraping/planing, a frequency that is perhaps unexpected of artefacts of this type.

In order to investigate the potential morphological/functional differences within this group of tools, I have divided the artefacts (or edge-segments) into several groups and compared the newly derived mean values of their metrical attributes (see Dumont in preparation). Potential differences were tested for significance through the use of the Fisher Exact Probability Test (FEPT) and the Mann–Whitney U Test (MWUT). The groupings consist of (1) all the utilized artefacts, (2) all the artefacts interpreted as having been used against haematite or a material bearing this mineral, (3) all the artefacts utilized on materials other than haematite, (4) all the examined artefacts except those used on haematite, (5) all the artefacts devoid of traces and, finally, (6) all the examined artefacts. The attributes that were compared consist of length, maximum width, maximum thickness, length/width ratio, thickness/width ratio, weight, and the spine and edge angles of the lateral edges. After applying the above statistical tests to the metrical attributes of the different groups, it became clear that significant differences only exist between the width, thickness and weight of 'all the utilized artefacts' and of the apparently 'non-utilized' groups.

With respect to the width of these two groups, the demonstrably utilized artefacts tend to have higher values than those with no functional traces (mean width of 17.5 mm compared with 13.0 mm, respectively). The FEPT confirmed this apparent tendency by giving the result that the probability of this distinction being present within a single uniform

population would be 2.51%: that is the probability of the presence of two distinct but overlapping groups is 97.49% ($p = 0.0251$, $n = 30 + 1$ median value). The MWUT provides a similar probability of greater than 97.83% ($n_1 = 20$, $n_2 = 11$, Standard Normal Deviate (SND) = 2.02). Similarly, the thickness of the demonstrably utilized artefacts is also greater than the apparently non-utilized artefacts (mean thickness of 5.3 mm compared with 4.2 mm, respectively). Both the FEPT and MWUT confirm that the difference is significant. The FEPT gives a probability of 2.75% that a single population is represented: that is the probability that two distinct though overlapping groups are actually represented is 97.25% ($p = 0.0275$, $n = 31$). The MWUT gives a similar probability of greater than 95.64% ($n_1 = 20$, $n_2 = 11$, SND = 1.71) for the presence of two distinct groups. With respect to the weight of the two groups, the demonstrably utilized artefacts tend to be heavier than those without functional traces (a mean weight of 5.3 gm compared with 3.2 gm, respectively). The FEPT and MWUT both confirm this apparent difference with the probabilities of 97.05% (FEPT: $p = 0.0295$, $n = 31$) and greater than 96.56% (MWUT: $n_1 = 20$, $n_2 = 11$, SND = 1.82).

These results indicate that the ancient tool-users at Mount Sandel were selecting the wider, thicker and heavier blades and flakes, per given length, for use against the materials represented by the polishes and deposits. The absence of observable microwear traces, apart from edge-damage, on the apparently non-utilized flakes and blades does not, of course, necessarily indicate that these artefacts were not utilized. All or some of them may have been used against materials, such as meat, that produce a slowly forming and unobtrusive polish or they may have been used against other materials for too short a time to produce an observable polish. These speculative comments should not be read as an argument for the presence of unrepresented activities, but rather as a caution against the *a priori* dismissal of their possible former presence.

VARIOUSLY BACKED BLADES

Eight variously backed blades (three naturally backed, two partially backed and three fully backed) were examined during this study. Five utilized edges were identified on four of the eight artefacts. The traces found on these tools consist of polishes/deposits, striations, edge-/*arrête*-rounding, edge-damage and stone-on-stone polish. Polish/deposits were observed on all five identified working edges: two instances of hide polish (on a single artefact), two of functional haematite deposits, one of bone polish and one of an unidentified deposit. Striations were observed on four of the five working edges, the exception being the edge exhibiting hide polish.

---

* In this list the reader is asked to understand 'haematite' as including 'or a material bearing this mineral'.

Edge-/*arrête*-rounding also affected all but one of the working edges; no rounding was observed in 'association' with the bone polish. Edge-damage occurred on all five working edges while stone-on-stone polish was restricted to the edge exhibiting the unidentified deposit.

The five use-episodes represented on the five working edges were concerned with the working of hide, bone, haematite (or a material bearing this mineral) and an unidentified material. One artefact (Mu 2203) may well have been used to work haematite-impregnated hide, thus giving rise to the observed juxtaposition of hide polish and haematite deposits along one edge. Of the two hide-working use-episodes, one consisted of scraping/planing while the other was a sawing/cutting action. The remaining two scraping/planing episodes were against bone and haematite (or a material bearing this mineral). The remaining sawing/cutting episode was directed against the unidentified material. It is interesting to note that the majority (three of the five) manners-of-use are of scraping/planing, a frequency that is, at least to this writer, somewhat unexpected in the light of their typology.

Although I am reluctant to make any generalizations based on statistics, because of the small size of this sample, about the utilized and apparently non-utilized backed blades, the following informal comments can be made based on the metrical attributes of each individual tool. Each of the utilized artefacts is longer, wider, heavier and, with one exception, thicker than the apparently non-utilized artefacts: that is, they are simply larger. Furthermore each of the utilized artefacts has a lesser length/width ratio value than the 'non-utilized' artefacts: in other words the demonstrably utilized artefacts are less 'blade-like' in final form than the others. The absence of observed microwear traces on the apparently non-utilized, though intentionally manufactured, artefacts does not necessarily indicate that they experienced no use. It is possible, but not demonstrable, that they were used against softer materials, such as meat, that are not conducive to rapid and obtrusive polish development, or perhaps they were used for too short a period for a polish (or other traces) to be recognizable on their surfaces.

TRUNCATED BLADES

Four truncated blades were examined during the course of this study. Four demonstrably utilized edges were identified on three of the four artefacts. The traces found on these tools consist of polishes, linear arrangements of polish, striations, edge-damage and stone-on-stone polish. Neither edge- nor *arrête*-rounding was observed on these tools. Polishes were found on each of the four identified working edges: one instance each of antler, wood, hide and an unidentified polish. Linear arrangements of wood and stone-on-stone polish were only observed on a single working edge. Striations and edge-damage occurred on three of the edges; the remaining edge (with hide polish) was free of these traces.

Four use-episodes, corresponding to each of the four working edges, were identified on the three artefacts and were concerned with the working of antler, wood, hide and an unidentified material. Three of these use-episodes consisted of scraping/planing while the woodworking episode was of whittling. With one exception, the working edges of these artefacts were the lateral sides.

SCRAPERS, PICKS AND BURINS

Two scrapers were examined and one exhibited microwear traces: bone polish and edge-damage at the steeply retouched working edge. The function of this tool has been interpreted as 'scraping bone'. Only one pick was examined. The surface of this tool exhibited potential hafting (wood polish) and technological traces, the latter presumably caused during its manufacture. The single burin examined only exhibited traces that are thought to relate to the preparation and removal of one of the burin spalls (see Dumont in preparation for a full description of these artefacts).

NEEDLES (NEEDLE POINTS)

Of the 34 needles examined, only two exhibited functional traces while a third exhibited traces that may have been caused by a haft. The traces observed on these three artefacts consist entirely of polishes: one instance of wood polish that may be a hafting trace, a single instance each of hide and meat polishes that may well be functionally related, two instances of linear arrangements of bone polish, and probably technological stone-on-stone polish. Both the linear arrangements of bone polish appeared on the two needles with likely functional traces. The identity and distribution of the meat and hide polishes, and the location and orientation of the linear arrangements of bone polish, are consistent with the suggestion that these two tools were used as projectile tips.

The low percentage of needles with functional or hafting traces (about 8.8%) appears remarkably small when compared with the rates achieved in the other artefact types from Mount Sandel and Star Carr (with the exception of the Star Carr microliths: see Dumont 1983 and Dumont in preparation). It would be unwise to argue that the three *identifiably* utilized needles represent the only tools of this type that actually experienced use. If it is the case that all or most of the needles were used as weapon tips, the types of polishes likely to have been produced on their surfaces are exactly those that are the most difficult to recognize in their early stages of formation. The recognition of hide and meat polishes on two of the needles indicates that these particular tools were in energetic contact with meat and hide for relatively long periods. The extended duration of contact could have been achieved by the building-up of a palimpsest of repeated uses of the weapon containing the armatures, or the armatures themselves in different shafts, in successive hunting episodes. One might expect that the weapons were reused until a poorly directed impact caused contact with the prey's skeleton and damage to some component of the weapon. Such instances could be represented by the formation of the linear arrangements of bone polish visible on two of the needles. The absence of recognizable functional traces on the remaining 32 needles might therefore indicate only that these armatures experienced insufficient duration of contact (hunting episodes?) rather than the absence of use.

TRIANGLES

Microwear traces were observed on four of the nine triangles examined. Three of these artefacts exhibit stone-on-stone polish which is thought to be related to the tools' manufacture rather than to use. Functionally significant traces were observed on three artefacts: hide polish (two instances), bone polish (one), edge-rounding (one) and edge-damage (three). Although edge-damage occurred on each of the three utilized triangles, only in two cases can it be confidently described as resulting from use.

The microwear analysis has not provided unequivocal functional interpretations for these tools. In each case the functional interpretation has had to rely on the morphology of the tool and the functional preconceptions associated with this particular tool type. In a manner of speaking, then, the analysis has only served to confirm, or at least not refute, the traditional assumption that these microliths were weapon armatures without actually enabling this interpretation to be derived directly from the type and pattern of traces observed on each tool.

OBLIQUELY-BLUNTED POINTS

Seven obliquely-blunted points (obliquely-trimmed points) were examined but none exhibited functional or potential hafting traces. Three of these microliths did show traces (stone-on-stone polish) that are thought to relate to their manufacture.

MISCELLANEOUS MICROLITHS

Six variously backed and/or trimmed microliths which do not fall easily within the recognized types were also examined but none exhibited functional traces. Two of these did exhibit stone-on-stone polish at locations consistent with a technological origin.

RODS

Of the 101 rods* examined as part of this study, only nineteen had traces that could be argued to have resulted from either the use of the tool or the former presence of its haft. Eleven of the nineteen rods exhibited traces (stone-on-stone polish and striations) that could be ascribed to the hard hammer percussion used in their manufacture. In addition to these eleven rods, a further 36 exhibited only technological stone-on-stone polish at or near their abruptly retouched edge. The presence of technological stone-on-stone polish on 47 of the 101 rods (about 46%) thus indicates that hard hammer percussion was a common method of abruptly retouching these tools.

The traces that are thought to relate to the actual use of the rods rather than to their hafting or manufacture are composed of polishes, striations, 'impact fractures', edge-/arrête-rounding and edge-damage. Polishes (including linear arrangements) were the most common functional trace and were observed on eleven artefacts: areas of bone polish were present on two to four rods, linear arrangements of bone polish on three, hide polish on two or three, functional stone-on-stone polish on one, meat polish on perhaps one, and perhaps antler polish on another. Striations were observed on two rods: one with an impact fracture and one with functional stone-on-stone polish. Although the majority of the rods exhibit a snap at one or both ends (77, representing about 76% of the rods examined), only those breaks that are 'associated' with a pseudo-burin facet (or other 'associated' flake removal originating from the break: see Barton and Bergman 1982 for a discussion of experimentally produced impact fractures) and also other corroborative functional and/or potential hafting traces are here considered as impact fractures. Impact fractures were observed on three rods: two along with potential hafting traces and one with striations. Impact fractures may also be present on two other rods but no other corroborative traces were observed on their surfaces. Edge-/arrête-rounding affected the leading edge of two rods and in both cases hide polish was present as well.

Traces that are, by virtue of their distribution, more easily interpreted as having resulted from hafting, either from contact against the haft itself or from the former presence of a hafting adhesive, were observed on nine rods. These traces were found either along the backed edge or differentially across the surface(s) at one end of the rods. The following polishes and deposits have been interpreted as evidence of hafting: areas of bone polish on one or

---

* It should be noted that the category 'rods' here embraces fragments which in Chapter 3 have been suggested to be the broken tips of triangles, lacking the important diagnostic right angle.

Artefact type / Worked material	Manner-of-use								Totals[2]	Totals[3]
	chopping	planing adzing	scraping planing	boring or piercing	sawing cutting	whittling	projectile components	unidentified		
Core axe-sharpening flakes										
wood	9	3	0	0	0	0	0	0	12	
hide	0	1 or	1	0	0	0	0	0	1	13
Core axes										
wood	0	2	0	0	0	0	0	0	2	2
Flake axes										
wood	0	6	0	0	0	0	0	0	6	6
Borers										
bone	0	0	0	3	0	0	0	0	3	
hide	0	0	0	2	0	0	0	0	2	
wood	0	0	0	1	0	0	0	0	1	
haematite[1]	0	0	0	1	0	0	0	1	2	
unidentified	0	0	0	1	0	0	0	0	1	9
Edge-damaged/retouched flakes and blades										
wood	0	0	0	0	1	1	0	0	2	
bone	0	0	2	0	0	0	0	0	2	
meat	0	0	0	0	2	0	0	0	2	
haematite[1]	0	0	19–20	1	6–7	0	0	6	33	
unidentified	0	0	0–1	0	0–1	0	0	1	2	41
Variously backed blades										
bone	0	0	1	0	0	0	0	0	1	
hide	0	0	1	0	0	0	0	0	1	
hide & haematite	0	0	0	0	1	0	0	0	1	
haematite[1]	0	0	1	0	0	0	0	0	1	
unidentified	0	0	0	0	1	0	0	0	1	5
Truncated blades										
wood	0	0	0	0	0	1	0	0	1	
antler	0	0	1	0	0	0	0	0	1	
hide	0	0	1	0	0	0	0	0	1	
unidentified	0	0	1	0	0	0	0	0	1	4
Scrapers										
bone	0	0	1	0	0	0	0	0	1	1
Needles										
---	0	0	0	0	0	0	2	0	2	2
Triangles										
---	0	0	0	0	0	0	3	0	3	3
Rods										
stone	0	0	0	1	0	0	0	0	1	
hide	0	0	0	0	1	0	0	0	1	
wood	0	0	0	0	1	0	0	0	1	
---	0	0	0	0	0	0	10	0	10	13

[1] Or a material bearing this mineral
[2] Per worked material per artefact type
[3] All use-episodes per artefact type

Table 11   Summary of functional interpretations by tool type (in units of recognized use-episodes)

two rods, linear arrangements of bone polish on one, wood polish on two, antler polish on one, suggestively-biased distributions of pedogenic iron compounds (perhaps reflecting the distribution of a former hafting adhesive) on two, and an unidentified deposit on one rod.

Of the nineteen rods with functional or hafting traces, thirteen have been assigned functional interpretations with varying but mostly diminished confidence. The remaining six rods exhibited either no functional traces or traces that were too ambiguous to allow even speculation. In the interpretation of the microwear traces, two different methods were required: first, the comparison of the observed traces with a model of the *presumed* function of the tools and, secondly, the more cautious and stronger argument from the nature, distribution and orientation of the observed traces themselves. The latter method was only possible with three rods which in my opinion exhibited sufficient microwear data: boring holes in stone, cutting hide, and sawing/cutting wood. Although this approach was not allowed by the traces on the other ten tools, the nature and location of the available traces (including the impact fractures and hafting traces) were, in each case and as a group, consistent with the assumption of their use as projectile tips (three instances), barbs (six), or a tip or barb (a single example).

With respect to the hafting of the presumed projectile components, only three rods (two tips and one barb) exhibited relevant traces. Both of the inferred projectile tips showed a biased distribution of pedogenic iron that has been interpreted as reflecting the extent of a former hafting adhesive, while the barb exhibited antler polish at its backed edge. This suggests that the barbs were set into slotted antler shafts while the tips were mounted at the fore end of the shaft and were nearly entirely encased within some type of adhesive. Of the three rods that have been interpreted as *not* being projectile components, two exhibited traces that are thought to relate to wooden hafts, and no hafting traces were found on the third. Of the four other rods whose functions remain unclear, three appear to have been mounted within slotted bone hafts and one perhaps exhibits traces of a hafting adhesive. If these four rods were in fact projectile components, then clearly bone as well as antler shafts were used. As already emphasized, the demonstrably utilized rods need not and are not likely to be the only utilized rods within the collection of artefacts examined. The absence of functional and/or hafting traces on the other 82 rods may merely reflect the fortune or skill in either or both the hafting or use of the presumed projectile components or other forms of tools.

Conclusions
The remarks presented above indicate that many of the Mount Sandel artefacts were subjected to a variety of uses and do not simply represent the waste and/or final products of a stone artefact production area. Although the presence of particular activities at this site, as elucidated by the microwear analysis, has not been addressed in this paper, it would certainly be perverse to believe that all of the use-episodes found on the tools represent off-site activities. It has, however, still to be determined by this study whether spatially distinct areas within the site contain artefacts of related function that could, in turn, define specific activity areas. These points and others, such as the relative frequency of particular functions and the intriguing use of haematite, will be fully discussed in the final report of the microwear study (Dumont in preparation).

References

Barton, R N E and Bergman, C A (1982): 'Hunters at Hengistbury: some evidence from experimental archaeology', in *World Archaeol* 14 (1982), *237–248*.

Cook, J and Dumont, J V (in press): 'The development and application of microwear analysis since 1964', in *The human uses of flint and chert: papers from the fourth international flint symposium*, eds G de G Sieveking and M H Newcomer (Cambridge, forthcoming).

Dumont, J V (1982): 'The quantification of microwear traces: a new use for interferometry', in *World Archaeol* 14 (1982), *200–217*.

—— (1983): 'An interim report of the Star Carr microwear study', in *Oxford J Archaeol* 2 (1983), *127–145*.

—— (in press): 'Mount Sandel microwear: a preliminary report', in *The human uses of flint and chert: papers from the fourth international flint symposium*, eds G de G Sieveking and M H Newcomer (Cambridge, forthcoming).

—— (in preparation): *A microwear analysis of selected British Mesolithic sites*, thesis to be submitted to the University of Oxford.

Keeley, L H (1980): *Experimental determination of stone tool uses: a microwear analysis* (Chicago, 1980).

Woodman, P C (1978): *The Mesolithic in Ireland* (Brit Archaeol Reports 58, Oxford, 1978).

CHAPTER 5

The faunal remains

Louise H van Wijngaarden-Bakker

Introduction*

An intensive sieving programme was carried out to retrieve the faunal remains from the occupation area of the site. Features that were recognized on site as containing layers rich in bone material were sieved through mesh sizes of 3, 1.5 and 0.85 mm. The remaining features and the occupation soil were sieved through a 3 mm mesh (Woodman 1978 and above, p 4). The faunal remains thus retrieved consisted exclusively of burnt bone fragments of a whitish to light greyish colour. It was evident that all bone material that had not been subject to conditions of heavy calcination had disappeared because of the acid nature of the local soil (pH c 5). It cannot be assessed to what extent the surviving sample is representative of early hunting strategies. Taphonomic processes such as food processing and storage techniques may present a severe bias. A total of 2192 fragments could be identified (Table 12).

	Features	Occupation soil	Total
Mammals	308 (16%)	21 (8%)	329 (15%)
Birds	70 (4%)	9 (3%)	79 (4%)
Fish	1540 (80%)	244 (89%)	1784 (81%)

Table 12   Total number and relative frequency of identified bone fragments

Mammals

The mammal remains were all very small, the largest fragments not exceeding 2 cm. The remains could be identified with certainty to *genus* level: *Sus* (322 fragments), *Lepus* (6 fragments) and *Canis* (1 fragment) (see Table 13). On zoogeographical grounds the *species* involved are presumably the wild pig, *Sus scrofa* L, and the mountain or varying hare, *Lepus timidus* L. As to the canid bone (a proximal radius), this could be either from a wolf, *Canis lupus*,

or a dog, *Canis familiaris*. Dogs are known in western Europe from the Preboreal onwards (Degerbøl 1961) so their presence at Mount Sandel would not be surprising. One small fragment of the enamel covering of a (pre)molar of possibly a ruminant was found. Its size indicates a deer but the identification is by no means certain.

Table 13 shows that about 98% of the mammal remains consist of pig bones. The restricted nature of Ireland's post-glacial mammal fauna is well known.

	Sus	Lepus	Canis
cranium	27(1)		
dentes	47(1)	3	
atlas	1		
axis	2		
vertebrae	4(4)		
costae	4		
scapula	3	1	
humerus	1	1	
radius	4		1
ulna	3		
carpalia	3		
metacarpus	9		
pelvis	1		
femur	4	1	
tibia	2		
fibula	6		
astragalus	3		
calcaneum	2		
other tarsalia	3	(1)	
metatarsus	7		
metapodia	29	(2)	
phalanx I	47		
phalanx II	44		
phalanx III	29		
sesamoidea	14		
phalanx I/II	23		
Total	322(6)	6(3)	1

( ) identification uncertain

Table 13   Identification of mammal remains

---

* The references for Chapter 5 will be found on page 75.

Large herbivores such as aurochs (*Bos primigenius*), elk (*Alces alces*) and roe deer (*Capreolus capreolus*) are entirely lacking and, rather unexpectedly, the evidence for the presence of red deer (*Cervus elaphus*) is so far limited to a surprisingly small number of sites (van Wijngaarden-Bakker 1974; Woodman 1978 and 1978a). One may thus expect a concentration on wild pigs.

Among the pig bones all skeletal elements are present, but there is a marked over-representation of foot bones, metapodials and phalanges. Of the remaining appendicular skeleton, a small number of epiphyseal fragments could be recognized, while of the cranial skeleton a fairly large number of fragments of cheekteeth and of the petrosum were recovered. When all the fragments are taken together they represent only two to three individuals, but if a 'maximum distinction' approach (Grayson 1973) is used and each feature is treated separately, over 30 individuals may have been present. Taking into account the taphonomic loss of uncalcined bone, already mentioned, a further attempt at quantification does not seem appropriate in this case. Measurements of the pig bones have not been taken, nor could the sex ratio be established. There were, however, 97 epiphyseal fragments that could be used to study the age distribution (Table 14). Unfortunately detailed epiphyseal fusion data for wild pig are not available and the data for domestic pigs had to be used, but these have been adjusted by 25% to allow for the presumably slower growth of wild stock. From Table 14 have been excluded a total of seven foetal bones. The aging data presented here indicate a selection of young pigs with nearly half the animals killed consisting of juveniles. In many cases the phalanges were found complete; the general size of the unfused ones indicates that they were approaching fusion. Assuming that births took place in April/May, this suggests that the animals were mainly hunted during winter. The presence of foetal bones points in the same direction.

Adjusted age at fusion (yrs)	Skeletal element	No	% Unfused	% Fused
1.25	prox radius prox phalanx II	34	47	53
2.5	distal tibia distal metapodial prox phalanx I	54	57	43
3.1	prox humerus prox femur distal femur distal fibula prox calcaneum	9	100	0

Table 14   Epiphyseal fusion data of wild pig

Birds

A total number of 79 fragments of birds have been identified. The families and the species involved are listed below (Table 15) and the frequency of the skeletal elements for the different families can be found in Table 16.

Family/Order	No	Species
Gaviidae	3 (1)	*Gavia stellata*—red-throated diver
Anatidae	19	*Anas platyrhynchos*—mallard; *A. crecca/A. querquedula*—teal/garganey; *A. penelope*—wigeon
Accipitridae	8	*Accipiter gentilis*—goshawk; *Aquila chrysaetos/Haliaeetus albicilla*—golden/white-tailed eagle
Tetraonidae	8	*Lagopus lagopus*—red grouse; *Tetrao urogallus*—capercaillie
Rallidae	1	*Fulica atra*—coot
Scolopacidae	8	*Gallinago gallinago/Scolopax rusticola*—snipe/woodcock
Columbidae	24	*Columba livia*—rock-dove *C. palumbus*—wood-pigeon
Passeriformes	8	*Turdus philomelos*—song thrush; small song birds

Table 15   Identification of bird remains: families and species

With the exception of the red-throated diver, all the species listed above are of birds that are or have been residents in Northern Ireland. Deane (1979) recently expressed the belief that the capercaillie was never an indigenous Irish species in post-glacial times. The record from Mount Sandel provides evidence that the species was present at least in Boreal times. The goshawk is now a very rare vagrant (Deane 1954; Ruttledge 1966), but bones have been found at several prehistoric sites: Late Mesolithic at Dalkey Island (Hatting 1968) and Beaker period at Newgrange (van Wijngaarden-Bakker 1974; 1980). It is a typical woodland bird. Two phalanges come from a large bird of prey, possibly either a golden or a white-tailed eagle. Both species nowadays are rare vagrants but they bred in Northern Ireland until the last century. The remaining species are all members of the recent resident Irish avifauna, but all are also winter visitors. In particular the mallard, teal, pigeon, coot, snipe, woodcock and wood-pigeon immigrate in large numbers in autumn and winter (Deane 1954). The red-throated diver only occurs from October to April on the Irish coasts (Ruttledge 1966). During winter all these species tend to aggregate in suitable habitats, and hunting them at that time would certainly reduce the level of effort expenditure. At a time when the diet consisted mainly of wild pig with a little hare, and with

	Gaviid.	Anat.	Accip.	Tetraon.	Rall.	Scolop.	Columb.	Passerif.
axis	1							
vertebrae						1		
sternum		2						
coracoïd		8	1			1	3	
scapula		1				1	3	
humerus		1		1				1
radius		1		1		2	7	
ulna							5	
carpometacarpus		3		1	1	3	5	
femur		1						1
tibiotarsal	(1)			4				2
tarsometatarsus	2	2					1	4
phalanx			8					
Total	3(1)	19	8	8	1	8	24	8

( ) identification uncertain

Table 16   Identification of bird remains: skeletal elements (see Table 15 for full family names)

vegetable foods being scarce, birds would also provide the desired variety in the diet. The list of species suggests that not only the woodlands (wood-pigeon, woodcock, goshawk, capercaillie) but also the inshore waters (red-throated diver) and the estuarine and river environments (ducks, coot, snipe) were exploited.

Fish

A total number of 1784 fish bones, mainly vertebrae, have been identified (Table 17).

	S. salar	S. trutta	S. spec	D. labrax	A. ang	Pleuron.
skull	2		2			
basioccipitale				1		
articulare	6		4			
dentale	9		4	5		
hyomandibulare	3					
gillskeleton			1			
premaxillare			4			
maxillare			1			
vertebrae	868	568	43	125	116(2)	13
fin spine	3					
lepidotriche	1					
urostyl			1			
teeth	2					
Total	894	568	43	144	122(2)	13

( ) identification uncertain

Table 17   Identification of fish remains

The fish remains consist of *c* 84% salmonids, *c* 8% bass (*Dicentrarchus labrax*), 7% eel (*Anguilla anguilla*) and 1% either plaice or flounder (*Pleuronectes platessa*/*Platichthys flesus*). The salmonid vertebrae are of two distinct sizes, of which the larger have been attributed to salmon, *Salmo salar*, and the smaller to trout, *S. trutta*, and the few intermediate ones to

Salmo spec, but it should be stressed that there are no morphological differences between the two groups of vertebrae.

The salmonids and the eel both are migratory euryhaline species, while the bass and flounder are sea fish found regularly in freshwater or under estuarine conditions (Wheeler 1977). Purely freshwater species in Ireland are, with the exception of the glacial relict populations of charr (*Salvelinus alpinus*) and pollan (*Coregonus albula*) in some of its lakes, all recent introductions (Wheeler 1977). The absence of stenohaline species at Mount Sandel confirms this notion.

Salmon are anadromous fish. In Co Antrim the 'run' of the salmon generally begins by the end of April or beginning of May and continues to the middle of August (Dubourdieu 1812). Recent counts at Portna on the river Bann (Fig 40) and 19th-century sales records from the Netherlands (Boddeke 1974)

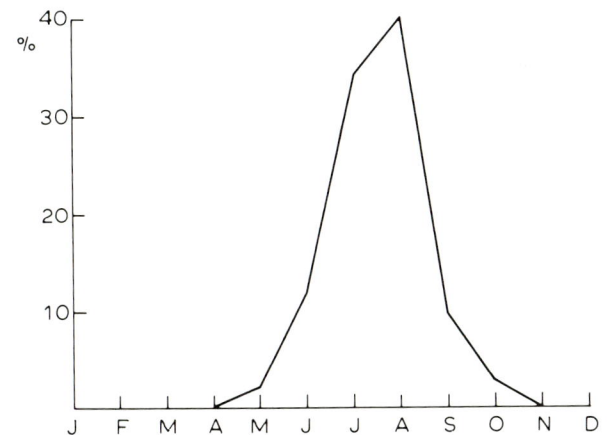

Fig 40   Frequency of salmon at Portna on the River Bann in 1979–80

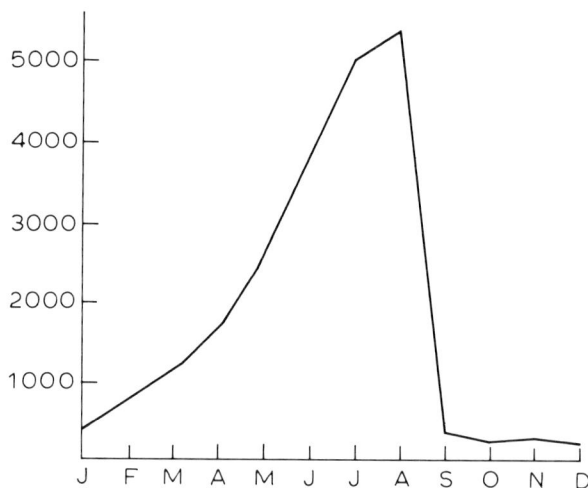

Fig 41   Monthly sales of salmon at Kralingse Veer,
Netherlands, in 1870–74 (from Boddeke 1974)

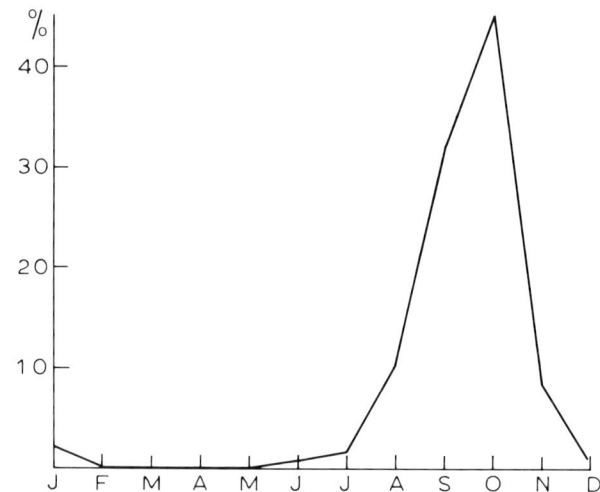

Fig 42   Frequency of eels at Toome on the River Bann
(from Frost 1950)

show the highest densities in July and August (Fig 41). These data suggest that salmon constitute a highly predictable and productive resource. Their exploitation at Mount Sandel would be centered on the summer months when the least effort was needed to catch the fish.

At the moment salmon fishing takes place at the Cutts, which lie about 800 m south of Mount Sandel (Figs 1 and 54), and at the Cranagh about 2.5 km north of the site. The Cutts lie at a point where the river used to form a number of small natural rapids. In the 17th century a cut through the rock was used to establish a complex series of salmon weirs. Before then fishing was carried out with dip nets or loopers (Mitchel 1965). During Mesolithic times these rapids, where the salmon have to make a jump to continue their journey upstream, would have been eminently suitable for fishing.

The trout contains two subspecies. The lake trout typically inhabits the upper reaches of rivers and lakes but also sometimes the lowland reaches; its different forms exhibit a variety of migratory patterns. The sea trout is distinctly anadromous, but during its stay in the sea it often penetrates into estuaries (Wheeler 1969). Trout spawn in autumn like salmon, mainly in the upper reaches of rivers. Migrating trout can be caught in summer.

Little is known of the ecology of the bass. The species occurs commonly in inshore and estuarine waters from April to October. It probably spawns in inshore waters in May. In the autumn an offshore migration takes place (Wheeler 1969).

The ecology of the eel is fairly well known. The species is catadromous, the adult eel migrating to sea to spawn. Counts at the Toome eel weir at Lough Neagh (Frost 1950) show that migration takes place mainly in September and October (Fig 42). Eels can easily be trapped at rapids.

Flounder can penetrate well into estuaries and can even live in freshwater for short periods. They spawn offshore in March and April and then migrate inshore in summer and may at that time also enter into freshwater. In autumn and winter they return to deeper water (Wheeler 1969).

Plaice live in relatively shallow water. They are far less tolerant of freshwater than the flounder and only the younger specimens are usually found in the inshore waters; they rarely penetrate into estuaries.

The available data all suggest the summer as the season for fishing at Mount Sandel. In fact none of the species mentioned would be available in winter. The salmon and trout could be taken in July and August, followed by the eels in September and October. The data also suggest that fishing may have taken place both at the rapids (where nowadays the Cutts are situated) for salmon, trout and eel, and further north in the estuary of the river Bann for bass and flounder. The diatom analysis (below, p 116) has shown that a saline wedge may have reached as far as Sandelford in Boreal times. If that were so the Mount Sandel site would be ideally located, just between the freshwater and estuarine environments.

Discussion

The faunal remains from Mount Sandel can be used to examine the seasonality of the occupation. In the preceding paragraphs evidence has been presented that the site was occupied during two distinct seasons, a winter occupation and a summer occupation. During the winter occupation the activities may have centred mainly on the hunting of wild pigs. Pigs are solitary animals occupying a territory of 20 to 200 ha per animal (Bay-Petersen 1978). In winter, however, both their territory and their mobility are reduced (Oloff 1951; Jochim 1976). Rutting takes place during winter (December/January) and at this time the young males are often driven away by the older boars and thus would constitute fairly easy prey for hunting. The epiphyseal fusion data (Table 14) show that nearly half of the animals killed were juveniles and it is possible that this group mainly consisted of young males. As pigs are characterized by a high reproduction rate (50–60% in good years: Oloff 1951), this concentration on young animals would presumably have little effect on the density of the pig population. Pigs are also characterized by a rapid growth: at 8 to 10 months old, pigs of the Dutch Landrace attain a weight equal to about 50% of their adult weight (Walstra 1980) and the same figures may also apply to wild pigs.

Hunting may have continued throughout the winter as is shown by the presence of foetal bones, but the strategy seems to have been to leave the settlement when the piglets were born. This same pattern was observed at the Ertebølle site of Ringkloster in Denmark, where pigs were killed at 8 to 12 months and 17 to 24 months (Andersen 1974). A high percentage of juvenile pigs was also found at several other Danish Mesolithic sites such as Ertebølle, Vedbaek and Svaerdborg (Bay-Petersen 1978). Hares may also have been caught in winter, when their fur is thickest. It is possible that during the hunting expeditions for wild pigs traps were set in the woods for catching birds. This may be inferred from the finds of bones of the goshawk, a typical woodland bird which could have been caught because it was attracted by the traps.

Besides the woodlands, the river area was also exploited where water birds, wintering there in great numbers, could easily be caught. The list of bird species indicates that possibly both riverine and estuarine environments were exploited. During the summer occupation these same environments, woodland, riverine and estuarine, were exploited. In July and August salmon and trout could be caught at the rapids, and bass and flounder in the estuary. One may assume that water-related plant communities along the river were also exploited (below, Chapter 6, and Clarke 1978). A little later in the season (September/October) eels could be trapped at the rapids on their run downstream while in August in the woods the hazel nuts would start ripening. Large quantities of hazel nut shells were recovered at Mount Sandel. It is even conceivable that the nuts were stored in the deep storage pits to be used during the reoccupation of the site in winter. Some form of storage may also have been used for the salmon and trout, as both species can be easily smoked. In the hearth F56/4 over 500 vertebrae of salmon were found, and these could be taken to suggest that the hut was used for smoking purposes.

The fishing, autumn gathering and storage of food would presumably involve a fairly large number of people, and this might be reflected in the great number of storage pits at the site. The scattered distribution of wild pigs, also in winter, means that these animals can best be hunted by small units of one or at most two hunters. It is conceivable from a zoological viewpoint that the number of people occupying the site in winter was smaller than in summer, although this is contrary to the general opinion about winter camps.

The fact that all the bones have been subject to high temperatures for a fairly long time remains rather puzzling. One explanation could be that this is the result of food-processing methods. After the meat had been eaten all the available scraps, including the bones, could have been boiled to make some kind of broth. A leather container may have been used (Ryder 1966). After the broth was eaten the remnants could have been thrown directly on the fire where the bones would automatically undergo a process of calcination. The fish bones probably did not undergo this process as boiling usually renders them so soft that they will not survive in a recognizable form.

Acknowledgments

I am grateful to Rik Maliepaard who weighed the faunal samples and identified the bird remains, Pauline Kelk who identified the fish remains, Bob Donker (IPP) who made the drawings, and Professor Lew Binford, Professor Willy Groenman-van Waateringe and Dr Klaus Ransborg for their valuable comments.

References

Andersen, S H (1974): 'Ringkloster: en jysk inlandsboplads med Ertebøllekultur', in *Kuml* (1973–74), *10–108*.

Bay-Petersen, J L (1978): 'Animal exploitation in Mesolithic Denmark', in P Mellars (ed), *The early post-glacial settlement of northern Europe* (London, 1978), *115–145*.

Boddeke, R (1974): *Vissen en vissen* (Amsterdam, 1974).

Clarke, D (1978): *Mesolithic Europe: the economic basis* (London, 1978).

Deane, C D (1954): 'Handbook of the birds of Northern Ireland', in *Belfast Museum and Art Gallery Bulletin* I, no 6 (1954).

—— (1979): 'The capercaillie as an Irish species', in *Irish Birds* I (3) (1979), *364–369*.

Degerbøl, M (1961): 'On a find of a Preboreal domestic dog (Canis familiaris L) from Star Carr, Yorkshire, with remarks on other Mesolithic dogs', in *Proc Prehist Soc* 27 (1961), *35–55*.

Dubourdieu, J (1812): *Statistical survey of the County of Antrim* (Dublin, 1812).

Frost, W E (1950): 'The eel fisheries of the River Bann,

Northern Ireland, and observations on the age of the silver eels', in *J Cons Intern pour l'explor de la mer* 16 (3) (1950), *358–383*.

Grayson, D K (1973): 'On the methodology of faunal analysis', in *American Antiquity* 38 (4) (1973), *432–439*.

Hatting, T (1968): 'Animal bones from the basal middens', in G D Liversage, 'Excavations at Dalkey Island, Co Dublin, 1956–1959', in *Proc Roy Ir Acad* 66 c (1968), *172–174*.

Jochim, M A (1976): *Hunter-gatherer subsistence and settlement: a predictive model* (New York, 1976).

Mitchel, N C (1965): 'The Lower Bann Fisheries', in *Ulster Folklife* 11 (1965), *1–32*.

Oloff, H-B (1951): 'Zur Biologie und Ökologie des Wildschweines', in *Beiträge zur Tierkunde und Tierzucht* 2 (1951).

Ruttledge, R F (1966): *Ireland's birds* (London, 1966).

Ryder, M J (1966): 'Can one cook in a skin?', in *Antiquity* 41 (1966), *225–227*.

—— (1969): 'Paunch cooking', in *Antiquity* 43 (1969), *218–220*.

van Wijngaarden-Bakker, L H (1974): 'The animal remains from the Beaker settlement at Newgrange, Co Meath: first report', in *Proc Roy Ir Acad* 74 C (1974), *313–383*.

—— (1980): *An archaeozoological study of the Beaker settlement at Newgrange, Ireland* (thesis, Amsterdam, 1980).

Walstra, P (1980): *Growth and carcass composition from birth to maturity in relation to feeding level and sex in Dutch Landrace pigs* (thesis, Wageningen, 1980).

Wheeler, A (1969): *The fishes of the British Isles and north-west Europe* (London, 1969).

—— (1977): 'The origin and distribution of the freshwater fishes of the British Isles', in *J Biogeography* 4 (1977), *1–24*.

Woodman, P C (1978): 'The chronology and economy of the Irish Mesolithic: some working hypotheses', in P Mellars (ed), *The early post-glacial settlement of northern Europe* (London, 1978), *333–369*.

—— (1978a): *The Mesolithic in Ireland* (Brit Archaeol Reports 58, Oxford, 1978).

CHAPTER 6

The botanical remains

A Hamilton, D Bannon, M A Monk and J P Pals

PART 1: POLLEN ANALYSIS (A Hamilton and D Bannon)*

Nine samples collected from Mesolithic occupation soil have been examined for their pollen contents. The collection codes for the samples are shown in Table 18. The samples were prepared for examination by the usual procedure (Faegri and Iversen 1975), involving removal of alkali-soluble humic acids by boiling in 10% KOH, sieving, digestion of silicates in HF, and acetolysis in a 9:1 mixture of anhydric CH_3COOH and concentrated H_2SO_4. The residues were stained with safranin and mounted on slides in silicone oil. For comparison with modern pollen spectra, four surface soil samples were collected within 10 m of the Mesolithic site from beneath a modern conifer/hardwood plantation (mainly *Larix*, *Pinus* and young *Fagus*). These samples and no 9 from the Mesolithic occupation soil were examined by D Bannon; the remainder were studied by A Hamilton.

Under the microscope the preparations were seen to consist predominantly of numerous dark-coloured plant fragments. Pollen grains were infrequent in most preparations, but on the whole were sufficiently well preserved to allow confident identification.

It can be seen from Table 19 that the pollen spectra of samples from the occupation soil have very high herb/tree pollen ratios. Considering all samples together, herbaceous pollen accounts for 84.3% of total identifiable pollen, the equivalent figure for tree and shrub pollen being only 11.2%. The most abundant pollen type is Gramineae (60.6%), other common herbaceous types being *Plantago lanceolata* (8.9%), Tubiflorae (6.1%), Cyperaceae (2.3%) and Liguliflorae (1.7%). Among trees and shrubs, *Corylus*-type is most abundant (3.9%), followed by *Quercus* (2.3%) and *Alnus* (1.4%).

There are two reasons for doubting whether the pollen in these samples is of Mesolithic age. First,

previous palynological investigations in Ireland indicate that the country was, in general, thickly wooded from before 9000 bp (7050 bc) to the onset of forest clearance during the Neolithic (Mitchell 1976). Studies of modern pollen deposition, both in Northern Ireland (Goddard 1971) and elsewhere (Faegri and Iversen 1975), show that an arboreal pollen percentage of only 11.2, as at Mount Sandel, indicates open vegetation with few or no trees. In the absence of further evidence, it would seem unwarranted to postulate, solely on the basis of the pollen spectra, that Mesolithic man would have had such a devastating effect on the woody vegetation.

The second reason for doubting the contemporaneity of these samples with Mesolithic occupation stems from a consideration of the relative arboreal percentages. According to ^{14}C determinations, the Mesolithic site was occupied from about 9000 to 8500 bp (7050 to 6550 bc). Pollen diagrams from Northern Ireland show high values of *Corylus* at this time and *Alnus* is virtually absent (eg Pilcher 1973). The arboreal spectra from Mount Sandel seem irreconcilable with our general information about forest composition in Ireland at the time of the occupation.

Some insight into the origin of the pollen in these samples comes from consideration of the surface pollen spectra collected from the nearby plantation

---

* The references for Part 1 will be found on page 79.

Sample no	Situation	
1	F56 (2)	1–9 from Mesolithic
2	F100/2 (4)	occupation soil
3	F56/5 (4)	
4	F100/2 (3)	
5	F31/5 (1)	
6	F31/5 (3)	10–13 Surface soil samples
7	F31/5 (4)	from beneath modern *Fagus*/Conifer
8	F100/2 (5)	plantation—all collected within
9	F100/2 (2)	10 m of Mesolithic site

Table 18 Collection codes for pollen samples

Sample number (see code in Table 18)	Samples 1–9: Mesolithic occupation soil											Samples 10–13: surface soil samples						
	1	2	3	4	5	6	7	8	9	1–9 Total	1–9 %	10	11	12	13	10–13 Total	10–13 %	10–13 %—*Pinus*
TREES AND SHRUBS																		
Alnus				4	2	5	1	2	5	19	1.4	6	2	9	2	19	1.6	2.1
Betula	3	1	1	1	1	2	1	3	4	17	1.2	7	12	5	4	28	2.4	3.1
Corylus-type	10		5	11	1	1	7	5	13	53	3.9	10	3	4	10	27	2.3	3.0
Cupressaceae	2		1							4	0.3							
Fagus													2	1	1	4	0.3	0.4
Fraxinus								1		1	0.1			1		1	0.1	0.1
Ilex								1		1	0.1							
Pinaceae	7		1	4				1	1	14	1.0	90	28	110	32	260	22.5	—
Quercus	4		5		4	9	3	6		31	2.3	1	2	1	1	5	0.4	0.6
Salix	2		4		3		1		2	12	0.9	1	1	2	6	10	0.9	1.1
Ulmus	1		1							2	0.1		2	3	4	9	0.8	1.0
Total trees & shrubs:	29	1	13	25	11	17	14	17	27	154	11.2	115	52	136	60	363	31.4	11.5
HERBS																		
Alchemilla	4		1	1		1	2			9	0.7							
Artemisia	4									4	0.3							
Calluna				3	1	1		1		6	0.4	2	3	3	2	10	0.9	1.1
Caryophyllaceae			2	1						3	0.2							
Chenopodiaceae	3		2	1				2	3	11	0.8		2	1		3	0.3	0.3
Cruciferae					1					1	0.1							
Cyperaceae	3		6	4		1	2	1	15	32	2.3	19	17	20	20	76	6.6	8.5
Erica-type	3					1				4	0.3	1				1	0.1	0.1
Filipendula	4			1	2		1		1	9	0.7		1	6	2	9	0.8	1.0
Gramineae	94	4	106	98	125	117	120	110	55	829	60.6	161	140	132	174	607	52.6	67.8
Liguliflorae	5		1	2	3	1	8	3		23	1.7							
Myriophyllum														1		1	0.1	0.1
Plantago lanceolata	20	3	15	25	8	10	23	10	8	122	8.9	3	1	2	5	11	1.0	1.2
Ranunculus	1				1					2	0.1							
Rosaceae								4		4	0.3	4		4	4	12	1.0	1.3
Tubiflorae	11		10	12	5	5	12	5	23	83	6.1	1	5	27	12	45	3.9	5.0
Umbelliferae	3		1		1		1	1		7	0.5	1		2	2	5	0.4	0.6
Urtica					1			3	1	5	0.4	1		1		2	0.2	0.2
Total herbs:	155	7	144	148	146	137	171	136	110	1154	84.3	193	169	199	221	782	67.7	87.4
SPORES																		
Monolete spores	1		1	2			2	2		8	0.6	3	1	2	2	8	0.7	0.9
Polypodium					1	1				2	0.1	1				1	0.1	0.1
Trilete spores	16		1	2	1		6	4		30	2.2							
Total spores:	17	1	3	4	1		8	6		40	2.9	4	1	2	2	9	0.8	1.0
UNKNOWN	6		2	4			7	2		21	1.5		1			1	0.1	0.1
Total identifiable:	207	8	160	180	161	155	200	161	137	1369	100	312	223	337	383	1155	100	100
Unidentifiable:	14		13	8	13	4	12	3	★			★	★	★	★	★		

★ = not counted

Table 19   Pollen counts

(Table 19). Pinaceae pollen is abundant, no doubt because of local over-representation from planted trees. If Pinaceae values are excluded from the pollen sums, then the proportions of arboreal and non-arboreal pollen in all four samples, considered together, are 11.5% and 87.4% respectively, remarkably close to the values obtained for the occupation horizon samples. Examination of Table 19 shows that similarities are maintained in most cases at the level of the pollen type. Some of the discrepancies which do occur, for instance the lower values of *Plantago lanceolata* and of some other herbs in the plantation samples, could well be a consequence of the exact collection locality of these samples, that is within the forest.

The low *Fagus* and Pinaceae values in the occupation soil samples suggest that the pollen spectra of these samples represent *relatively* recent, but not *very* recent pollen deposition at the site. No doubt there is a lag of a few years in through-flow of pollen grains from the surface to the underlying occupation layers.

In conclusion, it is considered that pollen spectra from the occupation soil contain no information useful for the reconstruction of vegetation during the Mesolithic period.

Acknowledgments

We are grateful to John Shaw for drawing the diagrams and Isobel McClelland for typing the manuscript.

References

Faegri, K and Iversen, J (1975): *Textbook of pollen analysis* (Oxford, 1975).

Goddard, A (1971): *Studies of the vegetational changes associated with initiation of blanket peat accumulation in north-east Ireland* (unpublished thesis, Queen's University, Belfast, 1971).

Mitchell, F (1976): *The Irish landscape* (London, 1976).

Pilcher, J R (1973): 'Pollen analysis and radiocarbon dating of a peat on Slieve Gallion, Co Tyrone, N Ireland', in *New Phytol* 72 (1973), 681–689.

PART 2: CHARRED PLANT REMAINS
(M A Monk and J P Pals)*

During the course of the excavations soil samples were taken for environmental study including the extraction of charred plant remains. Nine of these samples were water-sieved on site through a series of meshes and the resulting charred remains were sent to J P Pals for identification. A further 29 soil samples of varying sizes (average volume 650 cc) from 21 contexts were later submitted to M A Monk for laboratory extraction of the plant remains and their identification.† This report combines the results from both studies.

In the case of the second group of samples, processing involved simple hand flotation in water followed by the water-sieving of the residue. Plant remains were separated from the residue by eye and with the aid of a low-powered binocular microscope from the flot. Of the 29 samples dealt with, four produced no identifiable remains. The other 25 produced shell fragments of hazel nuts, varying in representation from one sample to another. This may in part be a true reflection of the actual representation per sample, but the frequency of shell fragments recovered may also be affected by problems encountered in their recovery. Because hazel nut shells have a relatively dense cellular structure, and thus contain

little if any trapped air in their cells following charring, they cannot be extracted by simple water flotation methods. In many cases, therefore, it was necessary to extract shell fragments by eye from the sieved residues after flotation. Inevitably many smaller fragments would have been missed, and for those samples with a high degree of fragmentation, the figures for number and/or volume of fragments extracted may give no more than a broad indication of the representation of hazel nut shells in those samples. However, even given a fairly wide latitude of error, at least the extremes of shell fragment representation will show up.

The samples that produced the largest quantity of hazel nut shells were as follows: F100/6 (3), F100/1, F56/2 (2), F56/4 (4), and F31/5.

The second author extracted a number of modern seeds from the samples with which he dealt, and similarly the incidence of modern uncharred seeds was high in the samples submitted to the first author, with almost half the samples producing such seeds. As the Mesolithic occupation layer was so close to the present day surface, the occurrence of these seeds should come as no surprise. The most frequent modern seeds were of the *Atriplex* and *Chenopodium* genera, the plants of which are commonly found in disturbed ground. Other modern seeds found included *Polygonum persicaria*, *Carex* sp and *Fumaria* sp. The occurrence of intrusive modern seeds in the samples is, however, worrying because it could be taken to suggest that possible cross-contamination of ancient plant remains may also have occurred. There is unfortunately no real way of assessing the extent of this cross-contamination or indeed whether it was significant at all.

Although the majority of plant remains were hazel nuts, a few other identifiable items were found by both of us, including seeds of *Vicia* sp (vetches), *Galium* sp (goosegrass group), *Carex* sp (the sedges), *Pyrus* sp/*Malus* sp (wild pear/crab apple) and *Nymphaea* cf *alba* (white water-lily). The charred nutlets of *Nymphaea* were particularly prevalent in the samples from F56/2 (2), (3) and (5). The concentration of this material in a hearth pit would suggest that not only was it contemporary with the Mesolithic deposits but that the remains had accumulated as a result of human activity. Water-lily seeds have been found in the past on several sites of Mesolithic and later date, including the Maglemosian site of Holmegaard in north Germany (*Nuphar lutea*) and the Bronze Age Swiss lake villages (Clark 1952, *48*, after Broholm 1931, *2*, and Hatt 1937, *14*; Heer 1966, *350*). The closest parallel is Derravaragh, a Larnian lakeside site in Co Westmeath, where Mitchell found a number of charred as well as uncharred yellow water-lily seeds, *Nuphar lutea* (Mitchell 1972, *165*). Although the water-lilies would

---

* The references for Part 2 will be found on page 81.

† The excavator thought this necessary both to test the efficiency of the field recovery methods and to extract more remains.

have been growing in the shallows around the lake in any case, Mitchell quoting Bois (1927) felt that the Mesolithic occupants of this site had possibly collected the water-lilies to supplement their diet, as both the seeds and rhizomes, particularly the latter, are recorded as being edible. Indeed further references can be made in this connection: for example Assiniwi's work, referred to by Erichson-Brown (1979, *211*), based on observations made of North American Indians, suggests that the seeds of the yellow water-lily make a good gruel when boiled and if fried in fat make a kind of popcorn.★ Although there was no independent evidence to suggest this type of food processing was occurring at Mount Sandel, it is not difficult to envisage that the water-lily seeds were being eaten or being discarded in the food processing of some other part of the plant, especially given their presence on the site in the first place, their charred state and their occurrence in a hearth pit along with other food waste.

Of the other plants listed, *Pyrus* sp/*Malus* sp (wild pear/crab apple) are edible and *Malus* sp at least has been commonly found on early prehistoric sites in Europe. In addition various species of *Galium* sp (cleavers, goosegrass) have been exploited for food in the recent past: the leaves of *Galium aparine*, for example, can be boiled and eaten as spinach (Mabey 1972, *106*) although the seeds of cleavers could of course all too easily have found their way on to the site accidentally, for example caught up in clothing. The berries of barberry are also edible, if a little sharp to the taste, and have been exploited in the past (Pierpoint Johnson 1862, *15*). It is not possible to demonstrate that these charred remains certainly represent the residue of food preparation, but the possibility remains strong, especially in the case of the water-lily seeds. The dominance of hazel nuts in all the samples undoubtedly indicates their dietary importance in the Mesolithic economy practised at Mount Sandel. This dominance is not, however, peculiar to Mount Sandel since many other Mesolithic sites in both Britain and Ireland have produced numerous hazel nuts, for example Oakhanger in Sussex (Rankine, Rankine and Dimbleby 1960, *246*). Mellars (1976) therefore states with some justification than hazel nuts are likely to have been a staple in the Mesolithic diet. This assertion is not only supported by the evidence but also strengthened by the food potential of hazel nuts. They are a very concentrated dietary resource, being low in water content but high in protein and starch, sugar and various trace elements. On nutritional evidence it

would seem that hazel nuts contain, per weight, up to 50% more protein, seven times more fat and five times more carbohydrates that eggs. They also contain five times more calories than eggs and are four times richer in calcium and almost twice as rich in phosphorus. In addition, although they do not have vitamins A and D, they contain five times as much vitamin B$_1$ and a similar amount of vitamin C, which is not present in eggs at all (Loewenfeld 1957, *43, 283*). They are also easily digestible and, what may perhaps have been more important in the Mesolithic period, they can be stored and do not require any complex processing technology.★ All these factors, particularly their ease of storage and portability, would have enhanced their attraction as a fundamental food resource for man in the early post-glacial. If we are to accept the palynological evidence for Britain and more particularly Ireland, hazel was one of the most significant arboreal plant species present between 8000 and 5000 bc, even taking into consideration the usual over-representation of hazel in the pollen rain (Godwin 1975, *269*; Moore and Webb 1978, *110*). Some workers have attributed its frequency in the later post-glacial flora to man's actions, through manipulating the vegetation by burning selected areas to encourage the growth of this and other fast-growing nutritious plants (Waterbolk 1968, *1101*; Dimbleby 1978, *34*). Hazel, unlike many other broad-leaved trees, is not affected by excessive grazing—indeed its foliage is unpalatable to cattle—and it will regenerate far more quickly than other tree species following a forest fire (Smith and Willis 1962, *269*). It is possible that the expansion in hazel was a by-product of a deliberate practice, fire setting, which may have begun in Mesolithic times (Smith 1970, *82–3*; Simmons and Tooley 1981, *103–4, 284*).

Whether this was the case or not, and the balance of evidence points to the former, the dominance of hazel in the Irish pollen diagrams and the presence of charred nut shells at such Mesolithic sites as Mount Sandel and Carnlough (Monk, in progress) serve to underline further the significance of the plant and the recognition of its food potential at that time.

Acknowledgment
We are indebted to Gordon Hillman for confirming the identification of remains to species, albeit tentatively.

★ Also, according to Phillips (1977, 132), seeds of the white water-lily were eaten in a broth in Elizabethan times to cool the passions!

★ Storage of hazel nuts in recent times usually requires that they be put into a container with a tight-fitting lid and buried 2 to 3 ft into the ground. In this way, the nuts will be safe from frosts and pests (Loewenfeld 1957, *40*).

References

Bois, D (1927): 'Plantes alimentaires', in *Encyclopédie Biologique* vol I (Paris, 1927).

Broholm, H C (1931): 'Nouvelles trouvailles du plus ancien âge de la pierre. Les trouvailles de Holmegaard et de Svaerdborg', in *Mémoires de la Societé Royale d'Anti-quaires du Nord* 1926–31, *1–128*.

Clark, J G D (1952): *Prehistoric Europe: the economic basis* (London, 1952).

Dimbleby, G W (1978): *Plants and archaeology* (London, 1978).

Erichson-Brown, C (1979): *Use of plants for the past 500 years* (Ontario, 1979).

Godwin, H (1975): *History of the British flora* (Cambridge, 1975).

Hatt, G (1937): *Landbrug i Danmarks Oldtid* (Copenhagen, 1937).

Heer, O (1966): 'Treatise on the plants of the lake villages', in Keller, F (trans Lee, J E), *The lake dwellings of Switzerland and other parts of Europe* (London, 1966).

Loewenfeld, C (1957): *Nuts* (London, 1957).

Mabey, R (1972): *Food for free* (London, 1972).

Mellars, P (1976): 'Fire ecology, animal populations and man: a study of some ecological relationships in prehistory', in *Proc Prehist Soc* 42 (1976), *15–45*.

Mitchell, F (1972): 'Some Ultimate Larnian sites at Derravaragh, Co Westmeath', in *J Roy Soc Antiq Ireland* 102 (1972), *160–73*.

Moore, P D and Webb, J A (1978): *An illustrated guide to pollen analysis* (London, 1978).

Phillips, R (1977): *Wild flowers of Britain* (London, 1977).

Pierpoint Johnson, C (1862): *The useful plants of Great Britain* (London, 1862).

Rankine, R W, Rankine, W M and Dimbleby, G W (1960): 'Further investigations at a Mesolithic site at Oakhanger, Selborne, Hants', in *Proc Prehist Soc* 26 (1960), *246–302*.

Simmons, I and Tooley, M (1981): *The environment in British prehistory* (London, 1981).

Smith, A G (1970): 'The influence of Mesolithic and Neolithic man on British vegetation: a discussion', in Walker, D and West, R W, *The vegetational history of the British Isles* (Cambridge, 1970).

—— and Willis, E H (1962): 'Radiocarbon dating of the Fallahogy landnam phase', in *Ulster J Archaeol* 24–5 (1962), *16–24*.

Waterbolk, H T (1968): 'Food production in prehistoric Europe', in *Science* 162 (1968), *1093–1102*.

CHAPTER 7

Chemical analysis of soils

F W Hamond

Introduction*

Past human activity is often recognized in the form of upstanding monuments, surface concentrations of artefacts, and in some instances by localized vegetational changes. This last characteristic reflects a less obvious, but no less significant, anthropogenic effect, namely upon the soil's chemical composition. Depending on the type of activity pursued, such as food processing and storage, rubbish disposal, defecation and interment, and the intensity and duration of these activities, certain of the soil's constituent elements may be appreciably enhanced in and around the activity area.

Phosphorus, in the form of phosphate, is of particular value to archaeologists. Not only does it accumulate rapidly in the vicinity of such activity, but also remains stable in the soil over many thousands of years, unlike many other elements. Its permanence may be attributed to its strong fixation by aluminium, calcium and iron ions present in the soil, a process which minimizes losses through leaching, plant uptake and so on (Proudfoot 1976). Using an appropriate soil sampling strategy and relevant chemical test, enhanced phosphate levels may be detected, and so the overall extent and variability of past human activity in and around sites can be delineated.

The cost-effectiveness of phosphate analysis has been recognized by archaeologists for over half a century (Arrhenius 1934; Bakkevig 1980; Cook and Heizer 1965; Dauncey 1952; Eidt 1977; Lorsch 1940; Provan 1971). In Ireland the technique has been employed mainly in the investigation of buried soil horizons uncovered during archaeological excavations (Gardiner and Walsh 1966; Gay 1964; Proudfoot 1957 and 1959; Proudfoot and Simmons 1958). More recently it has been applied to the investigation of sites as a whole (Burenhult 1980; Edwards *et al* 1983; Hamond 1983; Proudfoot 1976).

Having highlighted areas of high phosphate production, the question arises as to its source. For example, human burial and animal stalling may both create high phosphate levels, the former on account of its high concentration in the skeleton, the latter because of the high rate of dung production. Trace-element analysis provides a straightforward means by which such sources might be distinguished. Although this technique has only infrequently been applied to archaeological sediments, its potential is nonetheless clear. Thus high calcium and manganese levels may indicate soils having a high bone content, whether from human burial or the processing and disposal of foodstuffs (Biek 1957; Keeley *et al* 1977). Copper and zinc levels are especially high in certain shellfish and animal, fish and bird viscera, such as the liver, and may again suggest specialist food-related activities (Broadbent 1979; Paul and Southgate 1978; Sokoloff and Carter 1952). Although carbon is not a trace element as such, its determination may indicate the presence of hearths (high in elemental C), plant and animal residues, and buried soil horizons (rich in organic C).

With this theoretical background in mind, two main lines of investigation were pursued at Mount Sandel. The first was concerned with the sub-surface variability of phosphate levels around the Mesolithic site. Its aim was to determine whether soils in the immediate vicinity of the site, and indeed elsewhere in its locality, contained appreciably higher phosphate levels than surrounding soils. This aspect is discussed in the next two sections.

The second line of investigation concerned the chemical properties of sediments revealed by excavation. Many of these were clearly distinguishable by obvious physical properties such as texture, colour and content. Moreover, most could be related to specific archaeological contexts, such as pit or post-hole fills, and specific layers within features. A number of questions thus arise. Are physical

---

* The references for Chapter 7 will be found on page 97.

differences in sediments reflected chemically? Conversely, to what extent do seemingly homogeneous sediments differ chemically? More generally, can different archaeological contexts be characterized by specific chemical attributes? Finally, can the source materials from which specific sediments were formed be inferred on the basis of particular chemical properties? These questions will be considered in the remaining sections of the chapter.

Sub-Surface Phosphate Variability: Methodology

To delineate a suspected archaeological site, it is obviously necessary to collect samples both from the site and from the natural soil around it. Several factors did, however, preclude the full realization of this strategy at Mount Sandel. Because soil investigations were instigated only after the excavation was complete, the area of known occupation could not be sampled because of the disturbed nature of the backfilled topsoil. Moreover, the construction of a housing estate precluded sampling to the north and east of the site. Lastly, the accumulation of 500 to 1000 mm of forest soil to the west of the site prevented the ready sampling of soils near the level of prehistoric settlement. Sampling was thus confined to the pastureland lying to the south-east.

Up to 100 m from the site sampling locations were determined, where possible, following a 20 m grid. Beyond this, a variety of topographical locations—slope top, side and bottom—were sampled. Soil specimens were taken from the A horizon, at 200 to 250 mm depth, a constancy of depth minimizing natural variations of phosphate (below, p 88). At this depth, moreover, the masking effects of recently applied phosphates (such as fertilizer and dung) are considerably reduced. That prehistoric phosphate may be found, despite soil erosion, at this depth is due to the long-term action of earthworms and leaching.

In all, 29 samples were collected (Fig 43). Before analysis the samples were dried (below 50°C), then sieved to 106 μm, thus minimizing variability that might have arisen from the processing of potentially unrepresentative soil particles.

Phosphate concentrations were determined following the ashing-acid digestion method of Andersen (1976). Briefly, 0.20 gm of soil is ignited at 550°C for 1 hour; the ashed residue is then boiled with 25 ml 1N hydrochloric acid for 30 minutes, filtered, and made up to 100 ml. A 10 ml aliquot is then developed with 10 ml vanadomolybdate, the resultant yellow colour being read at 470 nm on a Pye-Unicam SP6-500 Spectrophotometer. Results are set out in Table 20.

No	ppm	No	ppm	No	ppm	No	ppm
1	2550	9	1900	17	2150	25	1600
2	2450	10	1400	18	1550	26	1500
3	950	11	1050	19	2050	27	950
4	2300	12	1750	20	1950	28	1350
5	2100	13	1650	21	2400	29	1650
6	1800	14	1550	22	2250		
7	1900	15	1650	23	1400	precision	
8	2100	16	1700	24	2250	±100	

Table 20   Sub-surface phosphate variability

One in five samples was re-analysed to check the internal consistency of this procedure, and to determine the precision to which the results could be specified. Imprecision arises from slight differences in the experimental procedure to which each sample is subjected, such as in weighing the soil and intensity of boiling in HCl. It can be shown (Vermeulen 1953, *269*) that the overall precision of the method is given by

$$\left(\frac{\sum_{i=1}^{N} \left(d_i^2 \right)}{2N} \right)^{0.5}$$

where d_i is the difference between the ith of N replicate pairs. In this case, precision was found to be ±100 ppm.

It can be shown (Chambers 1964, *42*) that two results, V_1 and V_2, having an overall precision s, are only likely to differ significantly (at a 90% confidence level) if

$$|V_1 - V_2| \geqslant 4.13s.$$

Here, $s = 100$ where V_1, s_1 and V_2, s_2 are the mean and standard deviation (precision) of each result. Here, $s_1 = s_2 = 100$; thus phosphate values differing by more than 500 ppm are extremely unlikely to be explicable in terms of experimental error. They may thus be attributed to actual chemical differences inherent in the samples.

Sub-Surface Phosphate Variability: Discussion of Results

Mapping of sub-surface phosphate concentrations indicates considerable local variability (Fig 44). Two areas of appreciably higher P levels can, however, be discerned: one in the immediate vicinity of known occupation, and the other on the side of a small rise 150 m to the south-east.

The magnitude of these concentrations—above 1750 ppm P—suggests an anthropogenic rather than a natural origin, and would coincide with presumed areas of past human activity in the vicinity of the Mesolithic site and nearby mound. Given this

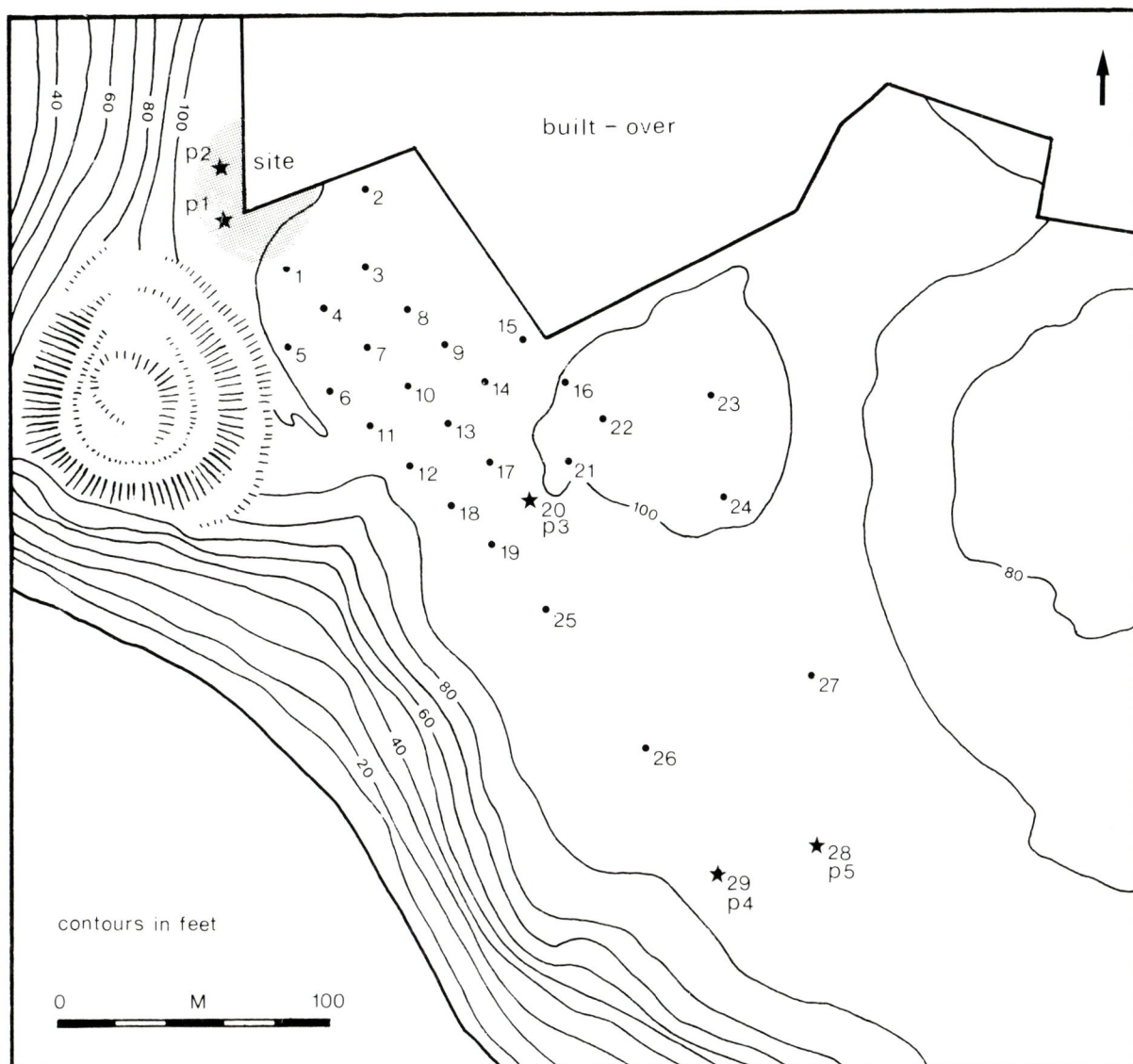

Fig 43   Location of soil profiles (p1–5) and sub-surface phosphate samples (1–29)

correlation, a further activity area to the south-east is also probable, particularly as Mesolithic artefacts have been found here. Indeed, such activity may have been still more extensive, given that erosion is likely to have severely depleted both phosphate and artefact concentrations on the summit of this rise.

To conclude, enhanced P levels were found around the Mesolithic site, though whether this reflects a natural movement of phosphate-rich soil from the site or an *in situ* occupation is as yet unclear. An area of occupation to the south-east is also suggested but again must await further investigation.

Intra-Site Variability: Methodology

Since excavation and the collection of related samples were largely completed before the author's investiga-

tion, fieldwork in March 1980 was restricted to supplementing the samples with natural soil profiles for comparative purposes. Samples were also taken from several features excavated at that time.

The natural soils around Mount Sandel comprise reasonably well drained acid brown earths derived from basaltic glacial tills. Certain differences are discernible between soils from the forest west of the site, and from the pastureland around the remainder of the site. The former are more friable, darker brown, and less stony than the latter. The depth at which B and C horizons commenced varied greatly with topographical location in the forest, whereas their depth in the pastureland was fairly constant, averaging 300 mm and 700 mm respectively. More-over, the forest soils were some 500 to 1000 mm

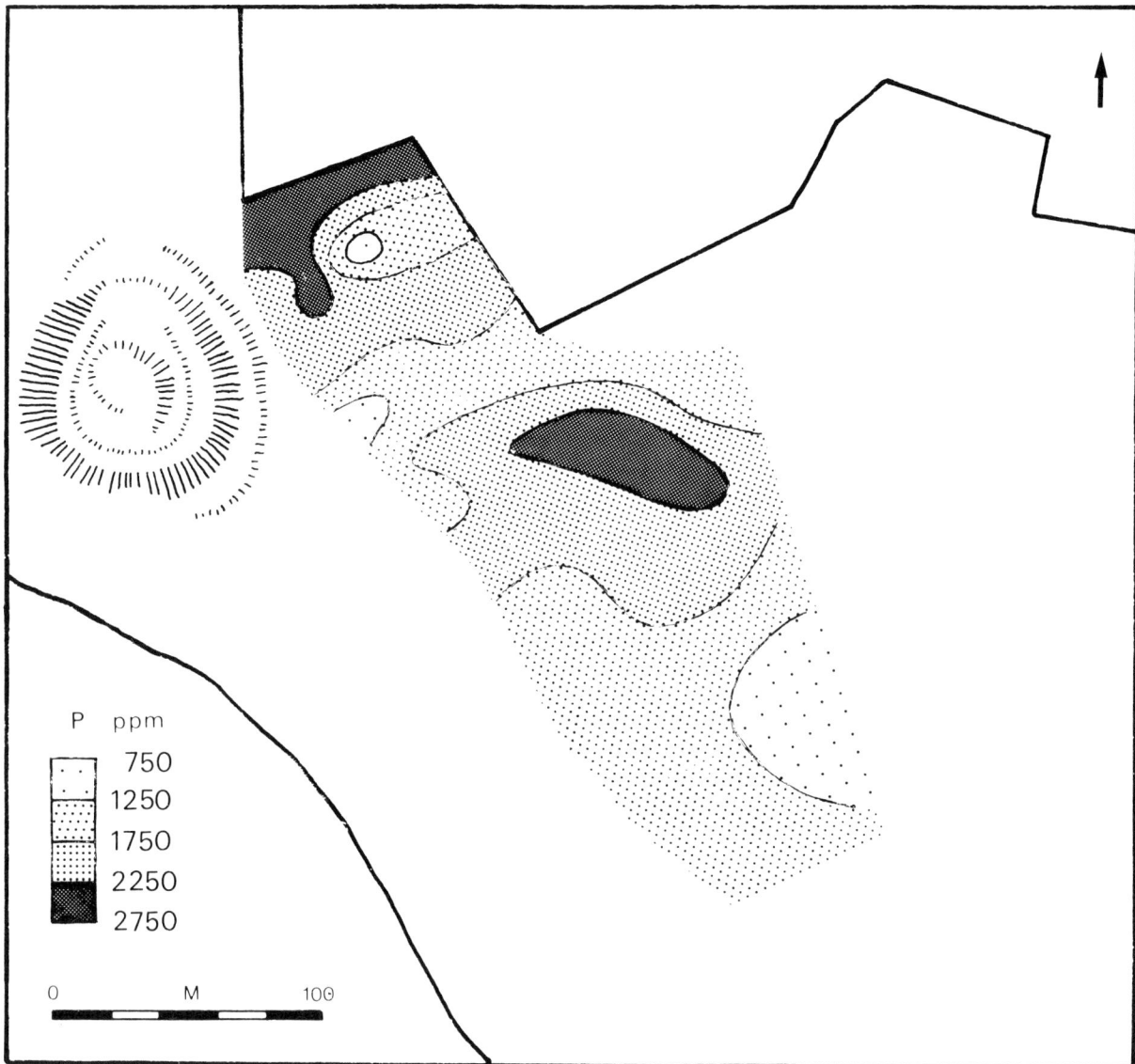

Fig 44   Sub-surface phosphate variability

above the pastureland, reflecting a greater degree of erosion outside the forest and/or a greater accumulation of forest litter. Indeed, the presence of medieval pottery in the forest soil, often at considerable depth, suggests a degree of human influence before recent times.

To gauge the difference between forest and pasture soils, and to compare them with archaeological sediments, two forest and three pastureland soil profiles, some distance from the site, were sampled (Fig 43). In addition, samples were taken from the natural B horizon below areas of known Mesolithic occupation to determine whether they had been chemically altered by past activity (Fig 45).

As regards archaeological sediments, samples from a number of contexts were analysed: fills of, and apparently natural soils below, post-holes and other features, and recognizable layers within the general occupation soil and certain features (Fig 45). The contextual distribution of all analysed samples is summarized in Table 21, each sample being fully described in Table 22 (microfiche).

As before, samples were air-dried and sieved before analysis. Total phosphate determinations are as already described (above, p 84). Organic carbon was assessed following Walkley and Black (1934). To 0.25 gm of soil is added 10 ml M/6 potassium dichromate and 20 ml concentrated sulphuric acid.

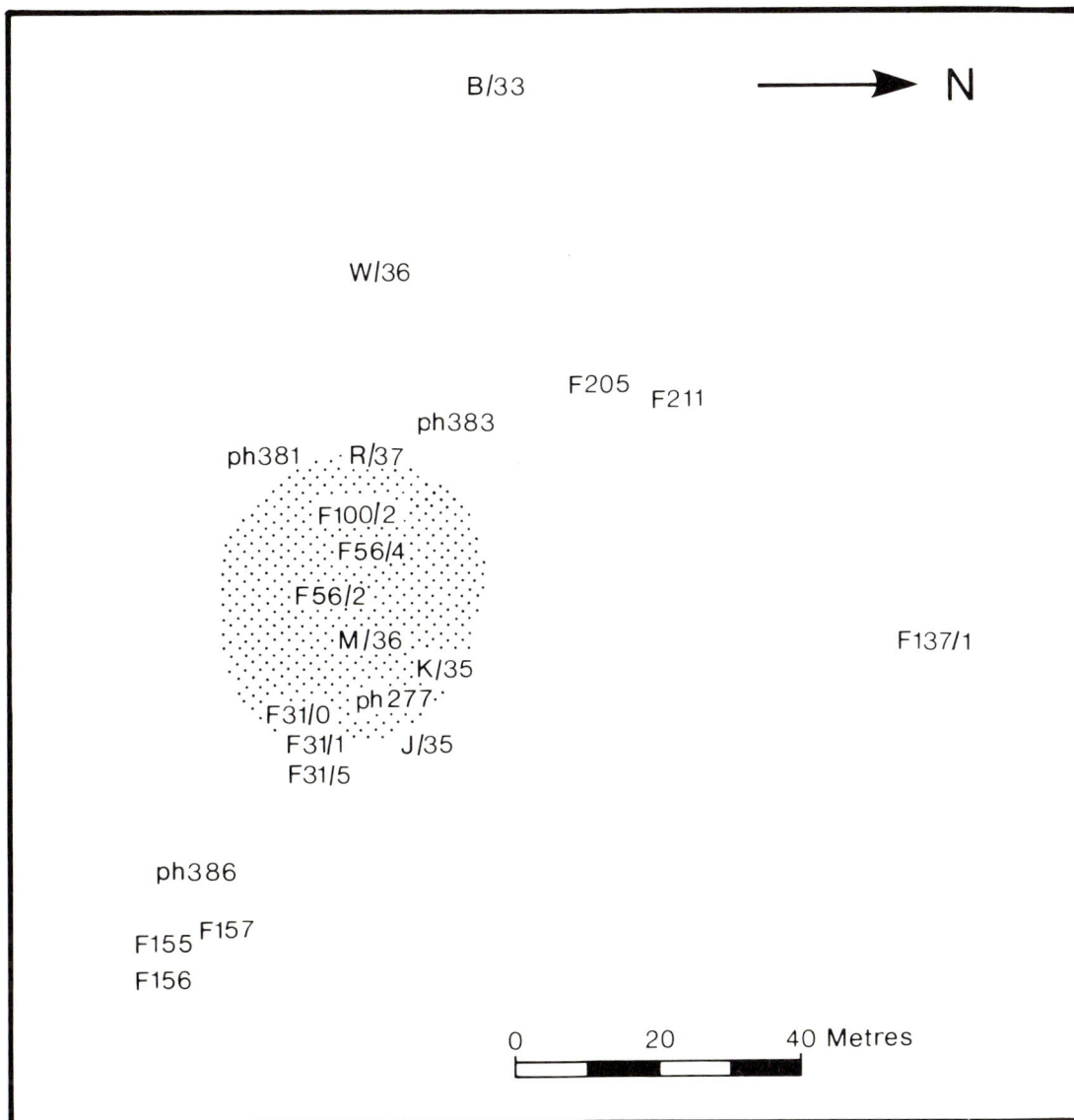

Fig 45   Location of soil samples in vicinity of hut area (shaded)

After 30 minutes, 170 ml deionized water and 10 ml 85% orthophosphoric acid are also added, the mixture then being titrated against 0.5 M ammonium

1	Natural A horizon	10
2	Natural B horizon	14
3	B horizon under site	10
4	B horizon under post-holes	3
5	B horizon under features	2
6	Post-hole fill	5
7	Feature fill	15
8	Specific layers in occupation soil	2
9	Specific layers in feature fill	12
		Total 73

Table 21   Distribution of samples by context

ferrous sulphate, using a diphanylamine indicator. Comparison with blanks enables the sample's percentage oxidizable organic carbon content to be calculated; multiplication by 1.33 converts this figure to the sample's total organic carbon content. In non-calcareous soils, moreover, one can assume the sample's inorganic carbon content (in the form of carbonates, etc) to be negligible (Hesse 1971, *205*). In most Mount Sandel soils, therefore, the total organic content can be equated with their total carbon content; only in the case of bone-rich sediments will this estimate be lower than is actually the case.

Trace-element concentrations were measured by Atomic Absorption (Ward *et al* 1969) using a Perkin–Elmer 306 Spectrophotometer. A variety of methods have been developed to extract such elements from the soil, bringing them into solution for subsequent measurement. That of Krishnamurty *et al* (1976) was followed here, primarily on account of its relative safety, simplicity and low cost. Briefly, 0.50 gm of soil is slurried with 0.5 ml deionized water, to which 10 ml concentrated nitric acid is added. The mixture is then boiled for several hours. After cooling, 3 ml 30% hydrogen peroxide is added, heating being continued for a further hour. Finally the mixture is filtered and made up to 50 ml. This is used directly in the AA machine, or with appropriate dilution; in the case of Ca and Mg, strontium chloride is employed to reduce interference from phosphorus and aluminium.

Initially analysis was confined to 48 sediments, from a variety of contexts, to determine which trace elements best differentiated between them. Nine elements were investigated: aluminium (Al), calcium (Ca), copper (Cu), iron (Fe), magnesium (Mg), manganese (Mn), potassium (K), sodium (Na) and zinc (Zn); the lead (Pb) contents of 29 samples were also determined. Analysis of the results of these determinations showed Ca, Cu, Mn and Zn to be the most useful in the discrimination of sediments (see next section). Accordingly, trace-element analysis of the remaining 25 samples was confined to these elements. All results are presented in Table 22 (microfiche).

The Characteristics of Archaeological Sediments

In this section the variability of sediments with respect to their P, C, and trace-element contents will be examined. However, rather than consider each individual sediment in detail, attention will be directed towards the relationship between the sediments' archaeological context and their respective elemental attributes. In this way, it is hoped to highlight the applicability of each element to the discrimination of certain types of archaeological context.

PHOSPHATE
The ability of an element to distinguish between sediments depends on those sediments' inherent chemical difference, and also the precision to which they can be measured (see above, p 84). Extending this argument, if the range of elemental concentrations encompassed by all samples is commensurate with their respective precisions, few sediments are likely to be discriminated. Of all the elements considered in this study, P has the lowest ratio of precision to range (Table 23). It thus differentiates best of all between sediments, this being reflected in the differentiation of archaeological contexts with respect to P concentrations (Fig 46).

Element	Precision	Range	Precision/range	
Al	7000	32000		0.22
Ca	1000	63350	0.02	
Cu	10	136	0.07	
Fe	2500	11250		0.22
K	400	2260		0.18
Mg	3000	9200		0.33
Mn	100	1900	0.05	
Na	300	900		0.33
Zn	20	435	0.05	
C	0.2	11.6		0.02
P	100	25100		0.002

(excepting C, in %, all precisions and ranges in ppm)

Table 23 Precision and overall range of 48 samples analysed initially

Considering natural profiles first, all have a relatively low P content. As expected, P decreases with increasing depth, this being particularly pronounced in the transition from A to B horizons. Interestingly, profile 1 from the forest adjacent to the Mesolithic site has considerably higher P levels than other natural profiles; this is especially marked in its A horizon. Given that the Mesolithic level is some 500–1000 mm below this, upward movement of P-rich prehistoric sediment through earthworm action is unlikely. More probably it reflects medieval activities, medieval pottery having been found there. That no such enhancement is to be found in the pastureland soils is probably due to subsequent topsoil erosion.

The B horizons below the occupation area in general, and post-holes and features in particular, also exhibit a degree of P enhancement compared with natural B levels. Evidently some degree of downward movement has occurred, through earthworm action and long-term percolation.

Although the majority of feature fills are not dissimilar to the natural soils' P range, a number of post-hole and feature fills contain appreciably higher P levels than natural soils, encompassing the range 4550–8550 ppm P.

Recognizable layers both within the occupation soil and in specific features exhibit, as one might expect, yet higher and more variable P levels than other sediments. Samples from square R/37 and features 31/0 (2), 31/5 (2) to (4), and 100/2 (1) and (6) are particularly rich in P, having a concentration of above 20,000 ppm P; not surprisingly these appeared as dark organic and/or bone-rich layers in the course of excavation. However, although recognizable layers may have clearly different P contents, so have some apparently homogeneous feature fills, such as F157.

To highlight more clearly the relationship between context and P content, the sediments were grouped in such a way that those within each group had a greater

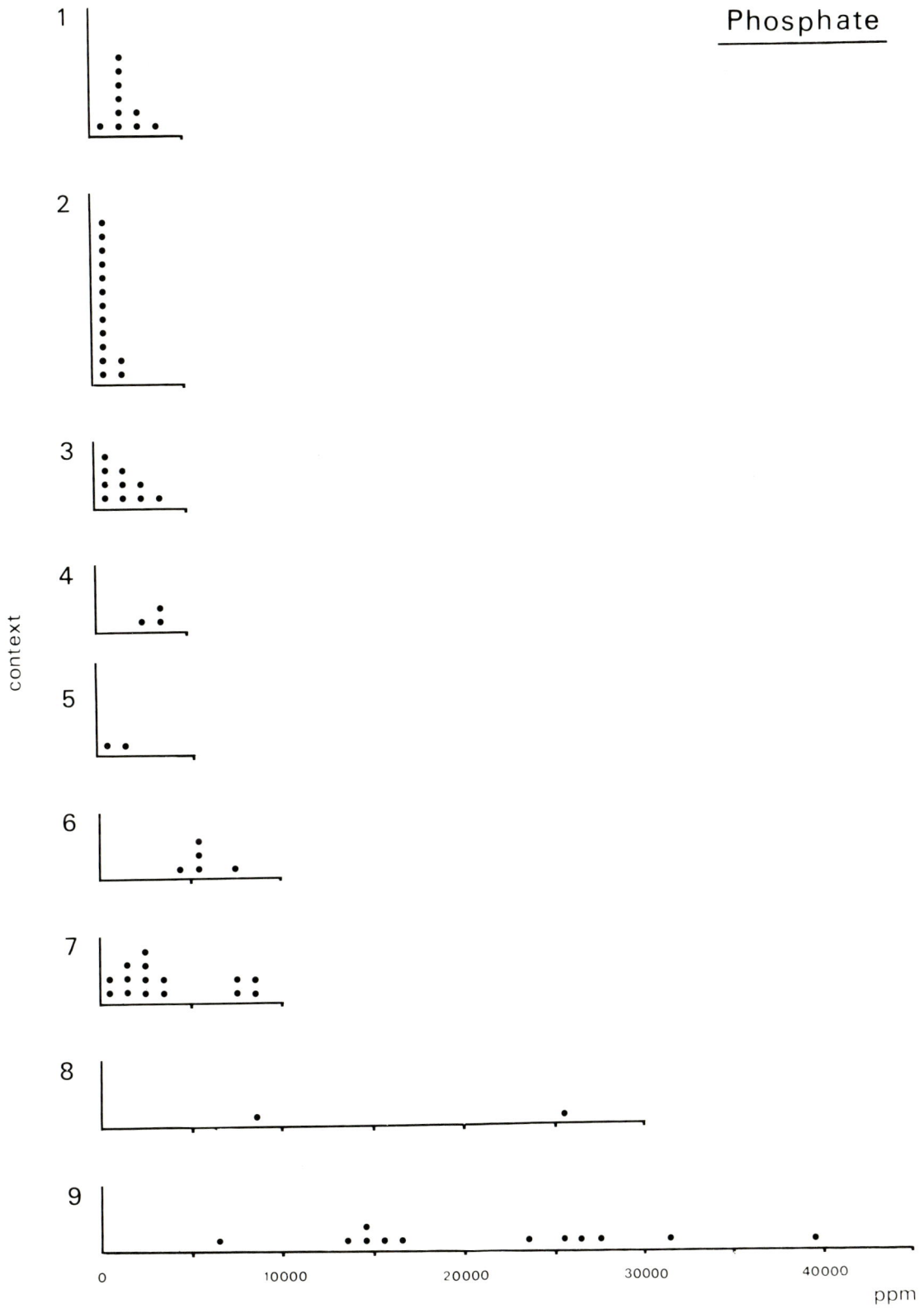

Fig 46   Contextual distribution of sediments with respect to phosphate content (see Table 21 for key to contexts)

	Phosphate concentration		
	low	medium	high
Total range (ppm)	350–3700	4550–16000	23000–39500
Interquartile range (ppm)	700–2350	6850–13000	25500–31500
Natural A horizon	100	—	—
Natural B horizon	100	—	—
B horizon under site	100	—	—
B horizon under post-holes	100	—	—
B horizon under features	100	—	—
Post-hole fill	—	100	—
Feature fill	73	27	—
Specific layers in occ soil	—	50	50
Specific layers in feature fill	—	50	50

Table 24   Percentage distribution of samples by context and phosphate content

	Carbon concentration		
	low	medium	high
Total range (%)	0.1–1.4	1.5–4.7	5.1–11.7
Interquartile range (%)	0.2–0.8	2.5–3.7	5.5– 6.7
Natural A horizon	—	90	10
Natural B horizon	93	7	—
B horizon under site	100	—	—
B horizon under post-holes	100	—	—
B horizon under features	100	—	—
Post-hole fill	—	100	—
Feature fill	33	60	7
Specific layers in occ soil	—	100	—
Specific layers in feature fill	—	25	75

Table 25   Percentage distribution of samples by context and carbon content

similarity of P content to others in that group than to samples from other groups. A CLUSTAN analysis was performed on the data (standardized) using Ward's method (Trasi 1975). The resultant dendrogram (Fig 47: microfiche) indicates the existence of three main groups which, when translated into P values, fall into well defined groups of low, medium and high P content. Tabulated against context (Table 24), the ability of P to discriminate essentially natural soils, of low P content, from anthropogenic soils, generally of medium and high P content, is clear. Whilst many feature fills are of low P content, suggesting a non-anthropogenic origin (see below), all post-hole fills are of medium content, specific layers being of medium and high content.

CARBON
Although the precision:range ratio of C is higher than P (being 0.02, Table 23), some discrimination of sediment context is nevertheless apparent (Fig 48). As with P, there is a diminution of C with depth in natural profiles, this being greatest, as one would expect, between A and B horizons. For the same reasons as were cited for P, profile 1 has significantly higher C levels. Unlike P, however, B horizons within the occupation area, and under post-holes and features, do not exhibit any appreciable enhancement of C.

Post-hole and feature fills exhibit higher C levels, again specific layers having highest and most variable elemental levels. Two samples in particular stand out: a charcoal-rich sediment from F205 (11.7% C), and a dark organic sediment containing burnt hazel nut shell from F56/2 (2) (8.5% C). Interestingly, burnt soil from the north edge of F56/4 contains relatively little C, suggesting its formation by heat transmission, rather than by direct contact with fire.

CLUSTAN analysis indicates that the sediments fall into three well defined groups, of low, medium and

high C content (Fig 49: microfiche; Table 25). Clearly C does not discriminate as well between natural and anthropogenic soils as P: natural A horizon and many feature and layer sediments all have medium C contents. Not surprisingly, those five samples seen to contain C, in the form of charcoal flecks and burnt hazel nut shell (47, 50, 51, 68, 69), and a further four of dark organic appearance (48, 49, 53, 73) all belong in the group of high C content.

TRACE ELEMENTS
As already explained, 48 samples were initially analysed with respect to ten elements. Two factors suggest that Ca, Cu, Mn and Zn best discriminate between sediments. First, a Principal Components Analysis was applied to these results (standardized, and excluding Pb), using the PA1 facility of the SPSS computer package (Nie *et al* 1975, *479*). This showed that Ca, Cu, Mn, and Zn accounted for most of the data's variability; in other words, sediments might best be differentiated with respect to these four trace elements. Second, the overall ranges of these 48 samples were ascertained, together with their precision of measurement (Table 23). Comparing precision with range, the elements fall into two discrete groups: first, high precision relative to range—Ca, Cu, Mn, Zn, and second, low precision relative to range—Al, Fe, K, Mg, Na. Elements of group 2 are thus less likely to discriminate sediments than are those of group 1. Indeed, no differentiation between archaeological contexts is apparent in any group 2 elements (and, in those cases analysed, Pb).

Given that Ca, Cu, Mn and Zn most usefully discriminate those sediments, the question arises as to why the other elements are unsuitable. In answering this, one must consider four factors: the concentration of these elements present in the anthropogenic matter relative to their levels in the natural soil, the

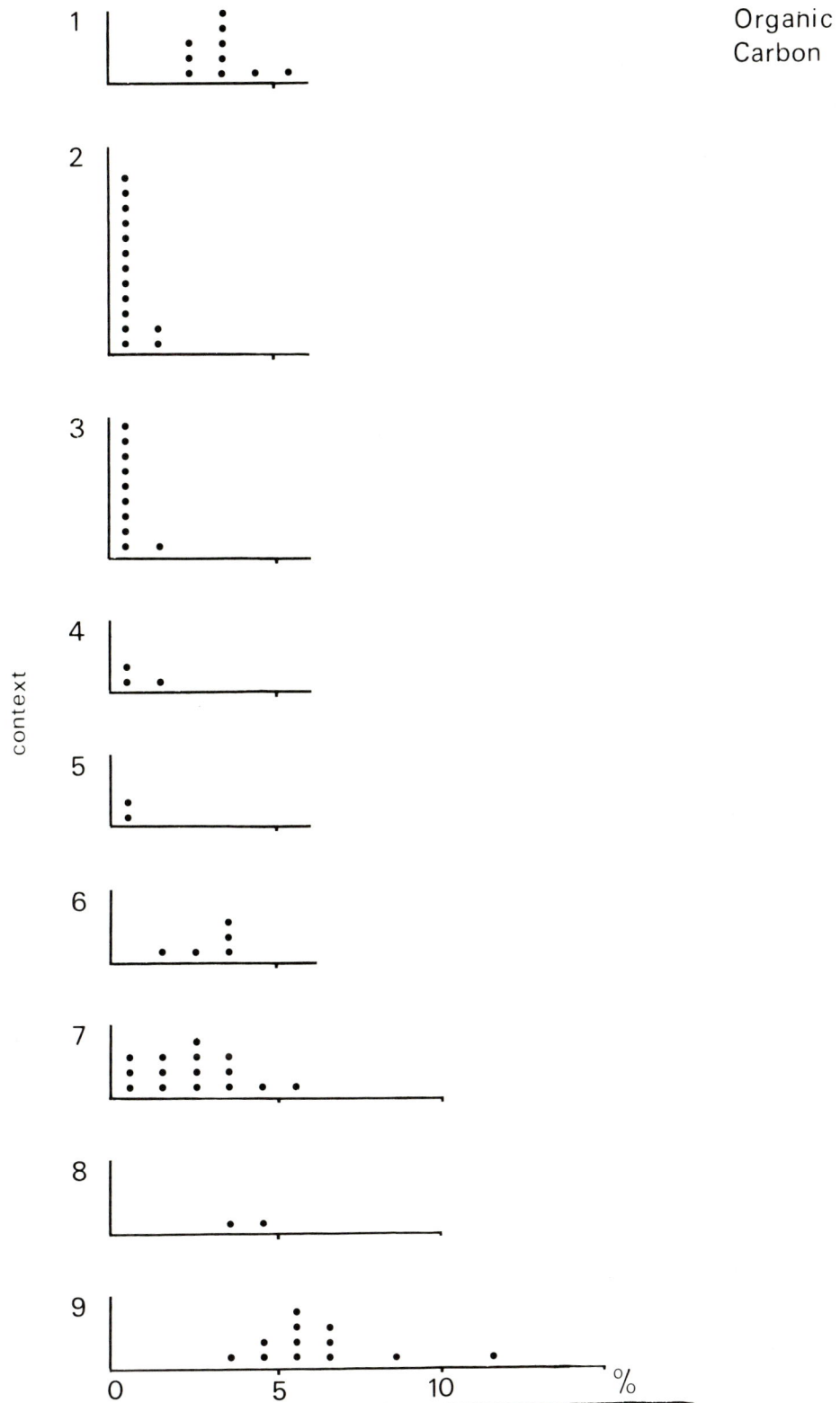

Fig 48   Contextual distribution of sediments with respect to carbon content
(see Table 21 for key to contexts)

extent of their 'dilution' by natural soil, the stability of these elements over time, and the precision to which they can be measured. Thus, highly diluted matter whose elements are of similar concentrations to those found in the soil, and which are determinable to a high imprecision only, is unlikely to be differentiated from the natural soil. Even if it were distinguishable, a high susceptibility to leaching may lead to the dispersion of elements into contiguous sediments, thus making them appear more homogeneous than is actually the case.

Certainly the base elements Ca, K, Mg and Na are highly susceptible to leaching, especially in the acid soils of Mount Sandel (pH 5–6, Table 22: microfiche; Kurtz and Melsted 1973). Although the absence of iron pan suggests that little weathering has taken place, there are indications that some downward mobilization of Ca and Mg has occurred in natural profiles. Calcium has, nevertheless, proved useful in the study, but only in the discrimination of sediments containing burnt bone: despite leaching these have remained relatively high in calcium. Potassium and sodium are also likely to have been leached. This is reflected in their inability to discriminate the wood ash from F205 (no 68, Table 22: microfiche), which would otherwise contain appreciable amounts of these elements (Cornwall 1958, 67). Despite the acid conditions, all the other elements considered in this study are less prone to leaching (Thompson and Troeh 1973).

Regarding the concentration of other elements in anthropogenic plant and animal material, further inquiry indicated that Al and Fe are not especially high compared with natural soil levels. All group I elements, on the other hand, are highly concentrated in certain materials. Calcium and manganese are found especially in bone, whereas copper and zinc are concentrated in shellfish and certain animal, fish and bird viscera, particularly the kidney and liver (Paul and Southgate 1978). Further discussion will accordingly be restricted to these four elements.

CALCIUM, MANGANESE, COPPER, ZINC

Considering calcium first, there appears to be little variability between contexts, save for specific layers, some of which have higher concentrations (Fig 50). Four samples are especially noteworthy, having a Ca content greater than 4%: R/37, F56/2 (2) and (3), and F100/2 (1). Not surprisingly, the bone content of these samples was readily apparent upon excavation (Table 22: microfiche).

Manganese also displays little significant variability between natural soils of whatever context (Fig 50). Although anthropogenic soils tend towards a higher Mn content, only four samples have noticeably higher concentrations: F31/5 (2), (3), (4), and F100/2 (1).

		Concentration	
		low	high
Ca	Total range (ppm)	1050–13400	18400–64000
	Interquartile range (ppm)	2840–4620	27500–42400
Mn	Total range (ppm)	420–2360	1470–4540
	Interquartile range (ppm)	1000–1365	2560–3940
Natural A horizon		100	—
Natural B horizon		100	—
B horizon under site		100	—
B horizon under post-holes		100	—
B horizon under features		100	—
Post-hole fill		100	—
Feature fill		100	—
Specific layers in occ soil		50	50
Specific layers in feature fill		42	58

Table 26   Percentage distribution of samples by context and Ca, Mn contents

Again, the bone content of these samples is directly observable (Table 22: microfiche).

Copper and zinc are similar in that all natural sediments, of whatever context, have low elemental concentrations (Fig 50). Again, only specific layers have appreciably higher contents. Of these, F31/5 (4) is highest in Cu (300 ppm), and F100/2 (1) in Zn (620 ppm). Interestingly, both these sediments have observable bone contents (Table 22: microfiche).

Considering the overall structure of the data, CLUSTAN analysis was carried out on the (standardized) values of Ca and Mn, taken together. Two major groupings emerged, but tabulated against their elemental content and context (Table 26) they do not discriminate effectively between natural and anthropogenic soils. Only in the case of specific layers within fills are high concentrations found: R/37; F31/5 (2)–(4); F56/2 (2), (3); F100/2 (1), (6). Not surprisingly, bone was found in all these sediments (Table 22: microfiche; Appendix 1d). That bone-containing sediments F31/5 (1) and F211 do not also fall into this category can be explained by their greater dilution with material of lower Ca content, probably natural soil (Woodman, personal communication).

CLUSTAN analysis applied to the (standardized) values of Cu and Zn, taken together, also indicates the presence of two distinct elemental groupings. Those of high concentrations (49–53, 57–8, 68–73) comprise anthropogenic soils: specific layers in occupation soil sediment and feature fills (Table 27). Interestingly, nine of these sediments contained visible bone.

In summary, analysis of the relative elemental contents of 73 samples clearly shows the presence of distinct groupings with respect to each element. Such groupings, moreover, appear to be related to specific

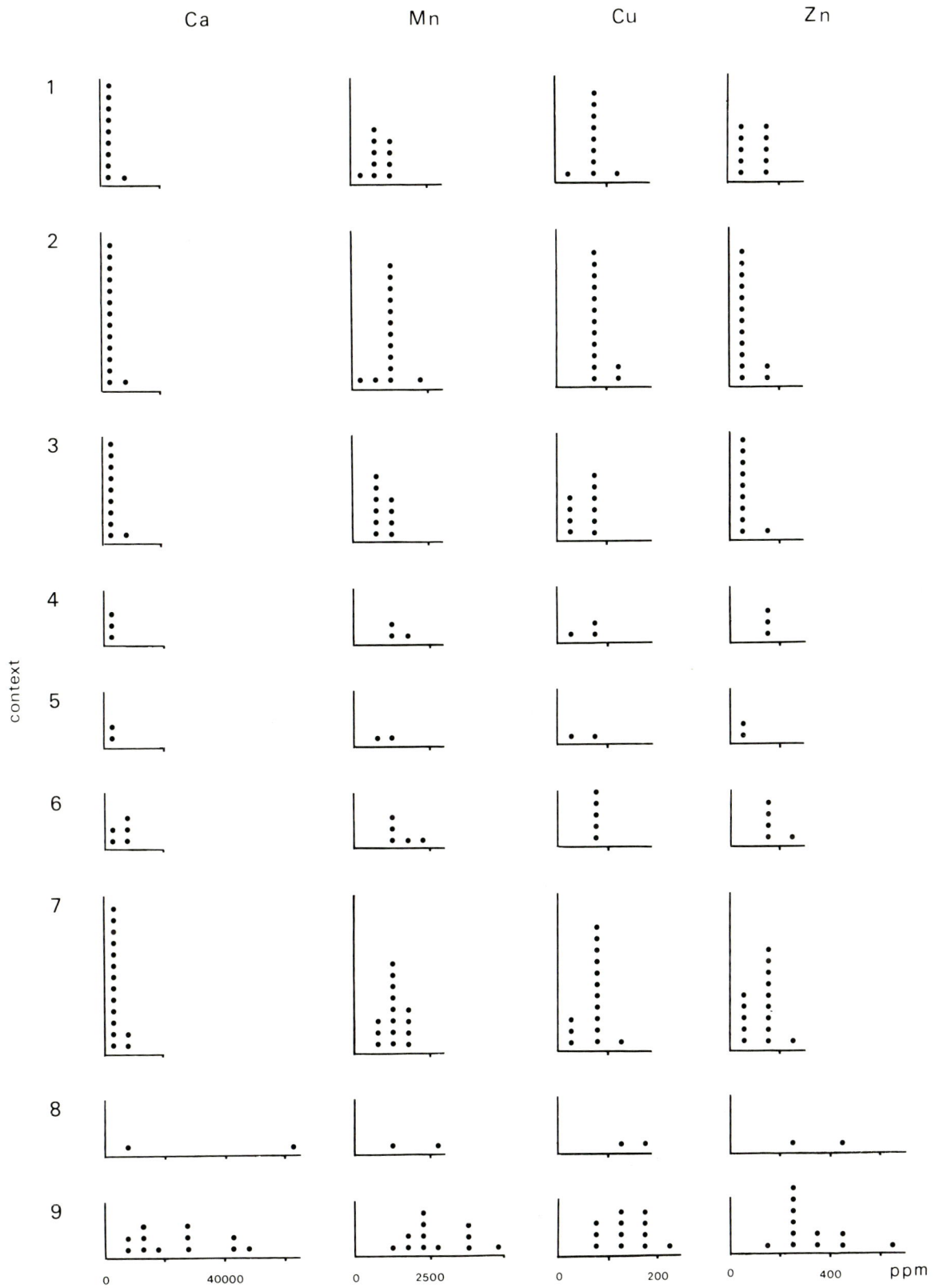

Fig 50 Contextual distribution of elements with respect to trace elements (see Table 21 for key to contexts)

		Concentration	
		low	high
Cu	Total range (ppm)	40–138	92–238
	Interquartile range (ppm)	52– 77	123–180
Zn	Total range (ppm)	20–260	200–620
	Interquartile range (ppm)	65–140	220–400
Natural A horizon		100	—
Natural B horizon		100	—
B horizon under site		100	—
B horizon under post-holes		100	—
B horizon under features		100	—
Post-hole fill		100	—
Feature fill		100	—
Specific layers in occ soil		—	100
Specific layers in feature fill		9	91

Table 27   Percentage distribution of samples by context and Cu, Zn contents

archaeological contexts. Thus P discriminates most effectively between natural soils, even those within the occupation area, of low P content, and anthropogenic soils, of medium and high content. As regards C, many anthropogenic soils are similar to the natural soils' A horizon, although both these contexts have higher C contents than B horizons. In contrast, Ca, Cu, Mn and Zn only effectively discriminate specific layers within the occupation soil and feature fills, reflecting the concentration of material rich in these elements, and which has not been diluted with natural soil to any extent.

The Derivation of Archaeological Sediments

The close relationship of certain archaeological contexts to specific elements suggests that they may be derived from different types of material. To identify the mode of origin of this material, it is necessary to extend the preceding analysis to the overall composition of each sediment. For example, a sediment high in C may be derived from charcoal or organically rich material. Only if it is found to have low P and trace-element contents is the former derivation implied. CLUSTAN analysis applied to the (standardized) values of all elements, taken together, indicates the presence of four distinct groups (Fig 51: microfiche; Table 28), each of which will now be considered.

GROUP I

Compared with sediments in other groups, those in group I are lowest in all element concentrations. This suggests that, of all the sediments analysed, these are most akin to natural soil, probably the B horizon on account of their low C content (above, p 90). This suspicion is confirmed on arranging them according to their contexts (Table 29).

Context	Sample no	Location
Natural A horizon	—	—
Natural B horizon	3– 5	p 1
	9–15	2
	18	3
	21	4
	23–24	5
B horizon under site	25–27	sq B′/33
	28	M/36
	29–31	J/35
	32–34	K/35
B horizon under post-holes	61	ph 381
	66	386
B horizon under features	42	F 156
	46	157
Post-hole fill	—	—
Feature fill	37	F 155 (bottom)
	41	156 (350 mm)
	43–45	157
Specific layers in occ soil	—	—
Specific layers in feature fill	—	—

Table 29   Distribution of group 1 sediments by context (p = profile; sq = square; ph = post-hole; F = feature)

All sediments from the natural B horizon fall into this category, clearly reflecting the absence of any human influence upon them. Moreover, all B horizon sediments from within the occupation area, under post-holes (except no 63) and under features, also lie in this group. Although their P content has been shown to be higher than natural B soils, their similar categorization shows them to be more akin to natural than to anthropogenic sediments.

Of particular interest is the presence of five sediments from feature fills in this category, especially those from F157. The excavator's interpretation that this feature resulted from the natural infilling of a root cavity formed by a tree-fall is thus

Group	P ppm	C %	Cu ppm	Zn ppm	Ca ppm	Mn ppm
1	600– 1400	0.2–0.7	52– 74	60– 85	2840– 4400	935–1185
2	1700– 5640	2.4–3.8	59– 78	100–175	2750– 5080	995–1370
3	13000–14500	5.6–6.5	96–134	220–240	8200–11600	1940–2160
4	16000–36500	4.3–6.7	123–186	240–480	25400–49500	2255–3940

Table 28   Interquartile range of elements encompassed by CLUSTAN-derived groups

confirmed. The other two sediments are from the base of F155 and F156, both apparently pits. Their chemical composition thus suggests some degree of natural infilling after their construction, probably from wall collapse (B horizon soil), rather than from topsoil influx.

GROUP 2

In several respects sediments of group 2 are not dissimilar to those of group 1. Although their P content is higher, the contrast is not as great as with group 3 soils. Their trace-element contents are also broadly similar, particularly if one also takes into consideration their precision. What chiefly characterizes this group is its markedly higher C content. This implies that such sediments are most akin to the natural topsoil, this being relatively high in C, but not appreciably so in P or trace-element levels.

Context	Sample no	Location
Natural A horizon	1– 2	p 1
	6– 8	2
	16–17	3
	19–20	4
	22	5
Natural B horizon	—	—
B horizon under site	—	—
B horizon under post-holes	63	ph 383
B horizon under features	—	—
Post-hole fill	60	ph 381
	62	383
	64–65	386
	67	277
Feature fill	35–36	F155 (top, mid)
	38–40	F156 (50–250 mm)
	54–56	F211
	59	F137/1
	71	F56/4
Specific layers in occ soil	58	sq W/36
Specific layers in feature fill	—	—

Table 30   Distribution of group 2 sediments by context

Arranging these sediments according to their context confirms this suggestion: all natural A horizon soils fall within this class (Table 30). Post-hole fills are also most akin to the natural topsoil. Given that wooden posts do not in themselves have appreciably higher P levels, such fills were probably largely derived from the influx of topsoil (upon removal or rotting of the wood), which would have contained some admixture of P-rich material, particularly in the vicinity of the hut area. This is evident in ph 277 which contains traces of bone, presumably from adjacent food-processing/disposal areas (Fig 45, and below).

All the analysed fills from the occupation soil in W/36, F211 and F137/1, and from the upper layers of

F155 and F156, are also most akin to the natural A soil. The fact that these are situated some distance from the hut area, where a variety of activities appear to have occurred, may explain the absence of appreciable P levels in the topsoil around them (Fig 45). Soil from the north edge of F56/4 also belongs to this category. Although affected by heat, its essentially natural character is clearly demonstrated.

To conclude, it can be said that the occupation soil found across the site, in post-hole fills, and sometimes in feature fills, is clearly distinguishable from sediments of more specific composition. Although to some extent enriched in P, resulting from human activities, it derives largely from the topsoil present at the time of those activities.

GROUP 3

Sediments of this group have not only substantially higher P and trace-element levels than previous groups, but also a higher C content (total range 5.5–11.7%) than those of group 4 (range 3.7–8.5%). Their anthropogenic origin is clearly demonstrated in their being derived entirely from specific layers within features (Table 31).

Context	Sample no	Location
Natural A horizon	—	—
Natural B horizon	—	—
B horizon under site	—	—
B horizon under post-holes	—	—
B horizon under features	—	—
Post-hole fill	—	—
Feature fill	—	—
Specific layers in occ soil	—	—
Specific layers in feature fill	47–48	F31/0
	49	F31/1
	50	F31/5 (1)
	68	F205

Table 31   Distribution of group 3 sediments by context

As already stated, high C levels may derive from elemental C, in the form of charcoal, and/or organic C from humus, plants and animals. Of the five samples in this group (47–50, 68), three contain clear evidence of elemental C, in the form of charcoal flecks (50, 68) and burnt hazel nut shell (47). That such C may be attributable to the burning of these sediments, rather than its influx into an otherwise unburnt horizon, is demonstrated by the magnetic susceptibility of these particular sediments (Chapter 8, below). Of the sediments analysed, those containing elemental C are of medium susceptibility and belong to groups 3 and 4 (Table 32). Not unexpectedly sediments of group 2 are of low susceptibility. Moreover, although F31/0 (2) (sample 48) and F31/1 (3) (sample 49) do not unequivocally

	Susceptibility	
	low	medium
Group 2	54–6, 58–9, 67, 71	
3		48–9, 50*
4	57, 70	51*, 52, 69*

* = contains charcoal

Table 32 Magnetic susceptibility of sediment groupings (based on Chapter 8)

indicate burning, a degree of burning is nevertheless implied by their medium susceptibility. In short, all sediments of this group appear to have been burnt.

Although rich in elemental C, these samples may also contain organic C. Certainly the presence of plant-derived organic matter is suggested by the hazel nut content of F31/0 (1). However, the high P and reasonably high trace-element content of these samples (especially Cu and Zn) suggests a derivation from the processing and disposal of animal-derived matter. Such material is indeed evident, in the form of bone, in F31/0 (1) and (2) and F31/5 (1). (That such material is not higher in Ca and Mn must be attributed to the lower concentration of bone in these sediments.) Given that only burnt bone will have survived, as the pH of most sediments is less than 6.0 (Table 22), and that these sediments have been burnt to some extent, any bone formerly present should have survived. It is thus unlikely that F31/0 (2) and F205 ever contained unburnt bone, now leached away. Probably the bulk of animal-derived matter contained in these sediments was bone-free, probably originating in viscera.

GROUP 4

In contrast to group 3 sediments, those of group 4 have higher P and trace-element contents, particularly with regard to Ca. Again, their anthropogenic origin is reflected in their derivation from specific layers within occupation soil and features (Table 33). Moreover, their high elemental contents directly

Context	Sample no	Location
Natural A horizon	—	—
Natural B horizon	—	—
B horizon under site	—	—
B horizon under post-holes	—	—
B horizon under features	—	—
Post-hole fill	—	—
Feature fill	—	—
Specific layers in occ soil	57	sq R/37
Specific layers in feature fill	51–53	F31/5(2)–(4)
	69–70	F56/2
	72–73	F100/2

Table 33 Distribution of group 4 sediments by context

reflect the P- and Ca-rich calcined bone present in all these sediments (Appendix 1d).

Although this group's C content is slightly lower than in group 3, the deposition of bone along with its probable medium of burning is clear in F31/5 (2) and (3), and F56/2 (2): all have a medium susceptibility, two also containing visible charcoal (Table 32). In contrast, R/37 and F56/2 (3) are of low susceptibility and contain no visible charcoal. It would thus appear that bone, and probably related organic matter, has been deposited in otherwise unburnt occupation soil in R/37. A similar depositional process is implied with F56/2 (3). Unfortunately it is impossible to state, without further susceptibility determinations, whether the bone-containing matrix of F31/5 (4) and F100/2 (1) and (6) have also been burnt.

To conclude this discussion of the derivation of sediments, it remains to consider the overall composition of particular features. Of the four features containing recognizable layers, two or more of which have been analysed, one contains sediments belonging to group 3 (F31/0) and two contain sediments of group 4 (F56/2 and F100/2). Given the physical dissimilarity between layers, their chemical homogeneity might suggest some movement of chemicals between layers within features. One might thus expect to find higher elemental concentrations towards the bottom of each feature, but no such trend can be demonstrated. This implies that the distribution of layers was such that, even if there was leaching, higher concentrations of elements remained in the upper layers. Alternatively, and more likely, it suggests that no significant mobilization of elements (apart from Ca) occurred. In short, the chemical composition of each feature is more related to the material deposited in it than to the action of post-depositional processes. Their homogeneity suggests that each (analysed) feature can be related to the deposition of a specific type of food-derived material. That other types of material are not also found suggests, moreover, that specific types of food-related activity were being carried out in their vicinity.

Summary and Conclusions

In the introduction to this chapter a number of questions were posed about the usefulness of chemical analysis at Mount Sandel. The next two sections were concerned with sub-surface P variability around the area of known Mesolithic occupation. It was demonstrated that, to the south of the site at least, further extensive settlement was improbable, although some traces might exist to the south-east.

The next three sections were concerned with intra-site chemical variability, and the utility of P analysis was again demonstrated. Compared with other elements, it was particularly effective in the recognition of anthropogenic soils and, conversely, in highlighting the presence of natural soil in what appeared to be possible archaeological features. Carbon and the trace elements Ca, Cu, Mn and Zn, on the other hand, proved more useful in ascertaining the source material from which specific layers revealed by excavation were derived. Using CLUSTAN analysis, the 73 analysed sediments could be grouped into four classes, each definable on the basis of the relative combinations of their constituent elements.

Although generalized occupation soil as such was not analysed, that present in features and post-holes suggested a derivation, not unexpectedly, from the topsoil formerly present at the site. Its slight P enhancement indicated its enrichment with anthropogenic material scattered across the site, particularly around the hut area. The analysis of occupation soils over the whole site would certainly have been informative in highlighting P-rich areas, and thus probable rubbish disposal sectors.

Recognizable layers within the occupation soils and feature fills were also distinguishable on the basis of their chemical properties. Conversely, some apparently homogeneous fills did differ in certain chemical respects. In the cases examined here, however, such differences probably reflect differing admixtures of natural and occupation soil, rather than gross differences in source material. Bone-rich layers in particular could be clearly recognized, especially with regard to their Ca and Mn contents. Moreover, their high C, Cu and Zn levels indicated the former presence of other organic matter, probably of animal origin. The high Cu and Zn levels of other layers also indicated the probable presence of animal-derived, but bone-free matter, again implying the processing, possible cooking, and disposal of foodstuffs. However, the unambiguous presence of unburnt bone was not detected in the sediments analysed. Only through chemical examination of an extensive range of sediments, coupled with their magnetic susceptibility determinations, might this be achieved.

Interestingly, certain features, although having recognizably different layers, were remarkably homogeneous in their chemical composition. This indicates that broadly similar types of rubbish were being deposited within particular features, and perhaps suggests that specific types of food-related activity were being carried out in their vicinity.

Given the exploratory nature of this analysis, its aims have certainly been realized, and the usefulness of chemical analysis in the mapping of prehistoric activity patterns has been clearly demonstrated.

Acknowledgments

I should like to thank J G Cruickshank and Professor W Kirk of the Department of Geography, Queen's University, Belfast, for the provision of laboratory facilities without which this analysis would have been impossible. I am especially indebted to J J McAllister and A Edwards for their guidance and advice in the laboratory. I am also grateful to R Doggart, A Sheridan, and L van Wijngaarden-Bakker.

References

Andersen, J M (1976): 'An ignition method for determination of total phosphorus in lake sediments', in *Water Research* 10 (1976), *329–31*.

Arrhenius, O (1934): 'Fosfathalten i skånska jordar', in *Sveriges Geologiska Undersökning* 28C, iii (1934).

Bakkevig, S (1980): 'Phosphate analysis in archaeology—problems and recent progress', in *Norweg Archaeol Rev* 13 (1980), *73–100*.

Biek, L. (1957): Appendix D in Ashbee, P, 'The Great Barrow at Bishop's Waltham, Hampshire', in *Proc Prehist Soc* 23 (1957), *162–3*.

Broadbent, N (1979): *Coastal resources and settlement stability: a critical study of a Mesolithic site complex in northern Sweden* (Uppsala, 1979).

Burenhult, G (1980): *The archaeological excavations at Carrowmore, Co Sligo, Ireland: excavation seasons 1977–79* (Theses and papers in North European Archaeology, 9, Stockholm, 1980).

Chambers, E G (1964): *Statistical calculation for beginners* (Cambridge, 1964).

Cook, S F and Heizer, R F (1965): *Studies on the chemical analysis of archaeological sites* (University of California Publications in Anthropology, 2, Berkeley, 1965).

Cornwall, I W (1958): *Soils for the archaeologist* (London, 1958).

Dauncey, K D M (1952): 'Phosphate content of soils in archaeological sites', in *Advancement of Science* 9 (1952), *33–6*.

Edwards, K J, Hamond, F W and Simms, A (1983): 'The medieval settlement of Newcastle Lyons: an interdisciplinary approach', in *Proc Roy Irish Acad* 83C (1983), *351–376*.

Eidt, R C (1977): 'Detection and examination of anthrosols by phosphate analysis', in *Science* 197 (1977), *1327–33*.

Gardiner, M J and Walsh, T (1966): 'Comparison of soil materials buried since Neolithic times with those of the present day', in *Proc Roy Irish Acad* 65C (1966), *29–35*.

Gay, F W (1964): Appendix in Collins, A E P and Wilson, B C S, 'The excavation of a court cairn at Ballymacdermot, Co Armagh', in *Ulster J Archaeol* 27 (1964), *20–2*.

Hamond, F W (1983): 'Phosphate analysis of archaeological sediments', in *Landscape archaeology in Ireland*, ed T Reeves-Smyth and F W Hamond (Brit Archaeol Reports 116, Oxford, 1983), *47–80*.

Hesse, P R (1971): *A textbook of soil chemical analysis* (London, 1971).

Keeley, H C M, Hudson, G E and Evans, J (1977): 'Trace-element contents of human bones in various states of preservation', in *J Archaeol Science* 4 (1977), *19–24*.

Krishnamurty, K V, Shpirt, E and Reddy, M M (1976): 'Trace-metal extraction of soils and sediments by nitric acid—hydrogen peroxide', in *Atom Absorp Newsl* 15 (1976), *68–70*.

Kurtz, L T and Melsted, S W (1973): 'Movement of chemicals in soils by water', in *Soil Science* 115 (1973), *231–9*.

Lorsch, W (1940): 'Die siedlungsgeographische Phosphat-methode', in *Die Naturwissenschaften* 40/41 (1940), *633–8*.

Nie, N H, Hull, C H, Jenkins, J G, Steinbrenner, K and Bent, D H (1975): *SPSS: Statistical package for the social sciences* (New York, 1975).

Paul, A A and Southgate, D A T (1978): *The composition of foods* (Medical Research Council Special Report 297, London, 1978).

Proudfoot, B (1957): Appendix 1 in Collins, A E P, 'Trial excavations in a round cairn on Knockiveagh, Co Down', in *Ulster J Archaeol* 20 (1957), *20–5*.

—— (1959): Appendix 1 in Waterman, D M, 'Excavations at Lismahon, Co Down', in *Medieval Archaeol* 3 (1959), *171–3*.

—— (1976): 'The analysis and interpretation of soil phosphorus in archaeological contexts', in *Geoarchaeology: earth science and the past*, eds D A Davidson and M L Shackley (London, 1976).

—— and Simmons, I G (1958): Appendix 3 in Waterman, D M, 'Excavations at Ballyfounder rath, Co Down', in *Ulster J Archaeol* 21 (1958), *54–61*.

Provan, D M J (1971): 'Soil phosphate analysis as a tool in archaeology', in *Norweg Archaeol Rev* 4 (1971), *37–50*.

Sokoloff, V P and Carter, G F (1952): 'Time and trace metals in archaeological sites', in *Science* 116 (1952), *1–5*.

Thompson, L M and Troeh, F R (1973): *Soils and soil fertility* (New York, 1973).

Trasi, A D (1975): CLUSTAN *analysis package—*CLUSTAN *1A* (Bradford, 1975).

Vermeulen, F H B (1953): 'Control of the reproducibility and accuracy of routine analyses at the laboratory for soil and crop testing in the Netherlands', in *Plant and Soil* 4 (1953), *267–75*.

Walkley, A and Black, I A (1934): 'An examination of the Degtjareff method for determining soil organic matter, and a proposed modification of the chromic acid titration method', in *Soil Science* 37 (1934), *29–38*.

Ward, F N, Nakagawa, H M, Harms, T F and Van Sickle, G H (1969): *Atomic-absorption methods of analysis useful in geochemical exploration* (Geological Survey Bulletin, 1289, Washington, 1969).

CHAPTER 8

A magnetic susceptibility survey

R Doggart

Introduction*

The location of buried remains on archaeological sites using geophysical prospecting equipment has been carried out in most countries in the last twenty years. Magnetometers as instruments for prospecting are widely employed, using variations in the earth's magnetic field to locate the remains. These variations are caused by differences in the magnetic properties of the soil which alter the earth's field. It is these differences in the soil's magnetic properties which are the main concern of this study.

The soil contains various elements which have differing magnetic properties which can be divided into four main groups: diamagnetism, paramagnetism, ferromagnetism, and ferrimagnetism. It is only the latter two groups that are of importance to this study. The ferro- and ferri- groups are made up of minerals which have a crystalline structure with iron being the most important. The main iron minerals in the soil which have these properties are magnetite and maghaemite, both of which are ferrimagnetic. This means that within the atomic structure two out of every three domains line up in one direction, while the third aligns itself in the opposite direction. If the minerals were ferromagnetic all the domains would align themselves in the same direction.

When magnetic susceptibility studies were carried out by Le Borgne (1955; 1960a; 1960b), he discovered that topsoils generally had a higher susceptibility than the subsoil, even higher than the parent rock, magnetic susceptibility being defined as the ratio of the magnetic moment of a mineral in a given magnetic field to that field (Graham 1976). Further studies revealed that the weathering process of a rock tended to reduce the susceptibility of the minerals rather than enhance them. It was concluded, therefore, that the only plausible explanation for the enhancement was the formation *in situ* of a stable magnetic iron oxide, either magnetite or maghaemite. Work carried out by Le Borgne using Differential

Thermal Analysis revealed the presence of a stable form of maghaemite in the topsoil and he suggested the following mechanisms to explain its formation.

It appeared that the enhancement was due to the conversion of a weakly ferrimagnetic iron oxide to a strongly magnetic form. This conversion is believed to be caused by two mechanisms, both of which involve the reduction of haematite as the first step. The two mechanisms are known as fermentation and burning, and both are believed to play some part in the enhancement of soils on archaeological sites. Mullins (1974) has shown, however, that the enhancement of archaeological sediments is similar to the effect produced in the laboratory when soils are subjected to burning, and it is now believed that burning is the main mechanism of enhancement on archaeological sites, with fermentation playing a secondary role. Both processes must, however, be borne in mind when considering the sediments and their origin.

The mechanism of fermentation depends on the quantities of organic debris which are decaying around a site, and the mechanism is accelerated by periods of alternating humidity. The reduction of the haematite occurs in the anaerobic conditions provided by wet periods; this is followed by reoxidation in the aerobic conditions associated with dry periods. It is believed that this mechanism of enhancement occurs only over relatively long periods of time, and it has not yet been simulated in the laboratory.

The second mechanism, and probably the more important to the archaeologist, is burning. If organic matter is burnt it produces carbon monoxide which expels oxygen from within the fire. This creates a reducing atmosphere and so converts the haematite in the soil around the fire to magnetite. Then, as the organic matter is burnt off, oxygen re-enters the fire and reoxidation occurs in the soil causing the magnetite to convert to maghaemite. Thus the high susceptibility of a site is related to the number of domestic or industrial fires which have occurred on

---

* The references for Chapter 8 will be found on page 103.

the site. Through time the topsoil of the site will present an overall increase in the percentage of iron converted, compared with the surrounding unoccupied topsoil. This overall increase will result from the mixing of topsoils heated at various times during the site's occupation with unheated areas of topsoil on the site.

Aims of Study

The main aim of using magnetic susceptibility on the Mount Sandel soils was to test the extent to which the sediments had been burnt. By doing this it was hoped to show whether or not certain layers on the site had been burnt in themselves rather than just containing burnt material such as flint and bone. A second aim of the study was to see whether or not this method of analysis could be used to give an indication of intensity of occupation independent of the archaeological data. If the method could be used for this purpose then it would be of value on sites where the archaeological evidence for occupation was very slight.

Preparation of Soils

Very little preparation is needed for samples submitted for susceptibility measurements, and a sample can be processed every two minutes once the soil is dried. After the sample has been dried the soil is sieved using a 2 mm sieve so that any stones are removed. The samples are then weighed out to equal 50 grammes, and are placed in a plastic container. All the containers have to be the same size and shape to ensure that the magnetic field in each of the samples is uniform and equal when placed in the susceptibility bridge. The susceptibility bridge used in this study is a modified version of the one used by Scollar (1968).

Results

A susceptibility section was taken through a natural soil close to the site and this gives a standard with which to compare the archaeological sediments (Table 34). Two other soil sections were also studied, one from the edge of the forest close to the site, and the other from within the forest (Table 35). These soils gave relatively high readings when compared with the natural soils, and Hamond (Chapter 7) has found a slight variation in the phosphate levels. From this evidence it is believed that the soil in the forest may have been enhanced by a medieval occupation, traces of which were found during the excavation.

The results from the site itself can be divided into three groups based on the amount of enhancement

Sample description		Sus($\times 10^{-5}$)	Phos(ppm)	C(% wt)
Profile L/10	50 mm	9.3		
	150 mm	9.3		
	200 mm	10.0		
	250 mm	9.6		
	350 mm	10.6		
	400 mm	9.6		

Table 34 Mount Sandel natural soil: magnetic susceptibility

that has taken place. The lowest group of readings (Table 36) can be seen to range from 20 to 40 × 10^{-5} emu/g, and these samples came from the occupation levels and the hearths. The occupation sediments tend to concentrate in the 20 to 30 bracket while the hearths fall into the 30 to 40 bracket. The occupation levels have probably been enhanced by the spread of burnt soil as described above, or the process of fermentation may have played a part in the enhancement. Rather surprising are the relatively low readings of the hearths, most of the samples of which came from F56/4, which contained traces of burnt bone. An explanation for these low values will be offered later.

The second group of readings are in the range of 40 to 60 × 10^{-5} emu/g and this material appears to have been in direct contact with fire to a greater extent than the soil from the hearths (Table 37). The third group, which have the highest range of values, 60 to 80 × 10^{-5} emu/g, all come from the pits F100/2,

Sample description		Sus($\times 10^{-5}$)	Phos(ppm)	C(% wt)
Profile 1,	50 mm	18.6		
north	150 mm	22.3		
of site	200 mm	22.3		
	350 mm	23.6		
	400 mm	22.3		
	450 mm	22.6		
	550 mm	21.0		
	600 mm	21.0		
	650 mm	21.3		
	750 mm	21.0		
	800 mm	19.6		
Profile 3,	50 mm	16.6		
forest	150 mm	19.3		
	200 mm	32.6		
	250 mm	19.3		
	350 mm	21.0		
	500 mm	21.3	29500	0.3
	550 mm	22.0		
	600 mm	22.0		
	650 mm	22.3		
	700 mm	22.3	32700	0.1
	750 mm	23.0		
	800 mm	26.0		
	850 mm	24.0		

Table 35 Mount Sandel forest soils: magnetic susceptibility

Sample description	Sus($\times 10^{-5}$)	Phos(ppm)	C(% wt)
ph 998	28.0		
ph 318	25.8		
W/36	29.3	7000	3.0
F137B	21.6	2100	3.0
F56/2 (hearth)	27.5		
ph 277	31.7	7700	3.8
F65/5 (3)	34.0	16000	4.7
ph 186	25.3		
ph 49B	30.3		
F56/5 (surface)	34.6		
F56/4 (burnt soil)	32.6	8500	2.9
R/37	30.6	25500	4.3
F211 (0–50 mm)	24.0		
(50–100 mm)	26.3	8550	5.1
(100–150 mm)	28.6		
(150–200 mm)	30.0	7250	4.6
(200–250 mm)	23.7		
(250–300 mm)	21.3	7500	3.8
(300–350 mm)	21.3		
L/36	24.6		
M/34	29.3		
M/35	27.3		
N/32	22.6		
N/37	33.3		
K/36	30.0		
ph 283	32.3		
F56/2 (70–80 mm)	28.6		
F56/4 (N edge)	22.3		
F56/2 (40–60 mm)	28.2		

Table 36   Magnetic susceptibility: group 1 soils

Sample description	Sus($\times 10^{-5}$)	Phos(ppm)	C(% wt)
F31/0 (2)	56.6	26500	5.7
F56/5 (2)	40.3	15000	8.5
F56/2 (3)	54.6		
F31/5 (1)	40.6	14500	5.6
(2)	55.6	25000	5.2
(3)	52.6	31500	4.7

Table 37   Magnetic susceptibility: group 2 soils

Sample description	Sus($\times 10^{-5}$)	Phos(ppm)	C(% wt)
F100/1	78.0		
F31/1 (3)	61.0	31500	
F100/2 (1)	74.3	39500	3.7
(2)	86.7		
(4)	70.6		
(5)	66.0		

Table 38   Magnetic susceptibility: group 3 soils

F100/1, and F31/1 (3). There can be no doubt that these soils have been exposed to a great deal of burning, either a single large and very intense fire, or more probably a series of fires, each converting more

haematite to maghaemite. These pits, however, showed no evidence of having been burnt in themselves, so it appears that the burnt material was dumped into them (Table 38).

Discussion

In general, therefore, the occupation soils appear to be quite distinct from the soils in the features sampled. The surviving contents of the four large central features which are thought to be hearths (Fig 12) do not stand out in relation to the other results. The features which do appear to stand out are the pits F100/2, F100/1, and F31/1. These high readings are the result of a considerable amount of burning, yet there was no evidence of the pits having been used as hearths. Since the soil must be assumed to have been dumped into the pits, this would explain why some of the hearth layers had relatively low values (F56/4, clinker): presumably the hearths were being cleaned out, probably at irregular intervals, and the soil which had been in contact with the fire was also removed with the debris. This would create a hollow where the hearth was, and each time it was cleaned out the hollow would get deeper. Below a certain depth the fire would not burn properly, lacking an updraught of air, so a new hearth would be needed.

Another way to estimate the amount of heating a sample has been subjected to, after the original readings have been taken, is to heat the soil in a kiln and simulate the effects of a fire, first by reducing and then reoxidizing at a temperature between 450 and 550°C. This gives the susceptibility of the sample had it been fired on the site to its maximum conversion and this depends on the organic matter and amount of iron in the soil. The results are given in Table 39 and the higher the 'heating level' the more burning the sample was subjected to on the site. Out of the fourteen samples tested, only three changed in respect to their positions in the original tables. These were samples from F56/5, F31/0 (2), and ph 49B. This method of estimating the amount of burning the soils have been subjected to is possibly more reliable, in that we know both the actual and potential susceptibility. Since the amount of iron available over the site may vary along with the organic matter, we need to estimate how much the iron varies. Thus one area of the site may have a higher susceptibility because it contains large quantities of iron but it has not in fact been burnt to the degree the original readings would suggest. This does not appear to be a problem at Mount Sandel since the samples come from a relatively small area, but on a large site it could create difficulties.

In order to check the maximum susceptibility which could be achieved on the site, three samples were chosen for further study, one of low, one of medium, and one of high susceptibility, from the original group of tables. These were heated in the kiln after being enhanced with 2% flour, which is enough organic matter to convert all the iron in the samples to the magnetic form. The results of the test were 180 to 200 $\times$ 10^{-5} emu/g, which would indicate that the difference across the site is slight.

The Relationship of Susceptibility to other Evidence

The results which form the lowest group, group I (Table 36), are relatively straightforward to interpret, in that this group is made up of occupation soils both from within the huts and from the exterior. These samples have also been shown by Hamond, using phosphate and trace-element analysis, to be distinct from soil in the features (Chapter 7).

The second group of readings, which are of medium susceptibility (Table 37), all come from features rather than occupation soil. The samples in this group which were analysed by Hamond tended to have high amounts of elemental carbon, which was visible in the soil in the form of charcoal flecks and burnt hazel nut shells. However, it is not advisable to say that a soil has been burnt because it contains charcoal, which could simply be mixed in with the soil. The samples in this group also had high quantities of organic carbon as well as high concentrations of trace elements, especially copper and zinc, which suggest the processing or disposal of animal-derived matter. From this evidence I would suggest that the fires which caused the enhancement were burning animal viscera—either fish or mammal.

Group 3 has the highest levels of susceptibility (Table 38), and is also bone-rich with very little visible evidence of elemental carbon. These samples were not analysed by Hamond, but I would suggest a

Sample	Sus($\times 10^{-5}$)	Total wt (gm)	Burnt wt (gm)	%
F31/0	56.0	895	845	94
F31/5 (1)	40.6	385	40	10
(2)	55.6	455	215	47
(3)	52.6	660	480	73
F100/2 (1)	74.3	5780	2645	45
(2)	86.0	620	395	64
(4)	70.0	2300	1945	84
(5)	66.0	570	555	97
F100/1	78.0	755	415	55
L/36	24.6	6380	375	5
M/34	29.3	7495	1850	25
M/35	27.3	10395	1535	15
N/32	22.6	4720	460	10
N/37	33.3	12505	3505	28
K/36	30.0	1090	480	44

Table 40   Susceptibility against percentage of burnt flint

similar history, from what evidence there is, to the samples from group 2. The fires may have been started with materials which would leave traces of elemental carbon, but were kept burning by the addition of animal debris. It should be noted that the bone survived because it was burnt.

Another indicator which has been used by archaeologists to show burning is the amount of burnt flint in an area. In order to see how reliable an indicator this is, a correlation was worked out between susceptibility and the percentage of burnt flint to total flint within the various areas (Table 40). The correlation was insignificant and would tend to suggest that density of burnt flint is not a good indicator of burning.

Conclusions

One of the main aims of this study was to test the amount of burning on the site and the results described would seem to have fulfilled this aim. They suggest that the site was extensively occupied, reflected in the general heightening of magnetic susceptibility across the area. This is in contrast to the results achieved from preliminary work on soils from a Mesolithic site at Carnlough, Co Antrim, where the natural soils are low in iron, the topsoil giving a reading of 7 $\times$ 10^{-5} emu/g, while the subsoil is only 1 $\times$ 10^{-5} emu/g. Preliminary results suggest that the effect of the occupation on the soils was slight in comparison to Mount Sandel. This underlines the transient nature of the settlement at Carnlough in contrast to the extensive occupation at Mount Sandel where we have definite evidence that certain layers of soil were extensively burnt (Table 38). These layers perhaps suggest a long period of use, and it is noticeable that the highest readings do not come from features which can be readily interpreted as hearths.

Sample description	Pre-heated ($\times 10^{-5}$)	Heated ($\times 10^{-5}$)	Heating level %
F100/1	78.0	120.0	0.65
F56/5	40.3	101.6	0.40
F56/2 (black area)	54.6	91.3	0.60
F137B	21.6	120.0	0.18
F56/2 (hearth edge)	27.5	83.3	0.33
ph 277	31.6	130.0	0.24
ph 49B	30.3	71.3	0.42
F56/4	32.6	97.6	0.33
F56/5 (3)	34.0	83.3	0.40
ph 318	25.8	96.6	0.27
F31/0 (2)	56.6	83.3	0.68
F56/5 (surface)	34.6	71.3	0.48
F31/1 (3)	61.0	76.6	0.80

Table 39   Change in susceptibility of heated samples

These features, FI00/I, FI00/2, and F31/I, probably contain hearth material which has been dumped into them.

Acknowledgments

I am grateful to A Aspinall of the Department of Archaeological Sciences, University of Bradford, for providing the susceptibility bridge, and to M A R Monroe and F Hamond for helpful comments and assistance.

References

Graham, I (1976): 'The investigation of the magnetic properties of archaeological sediments', in *Geoarchaeology: earth science and the past*, eds D A Davidson and M L Shackley (London, 1976), *49–65*.

Le Borgne, E (1955): 'Susceptibilité magnétique anomale du sol superficial', in *Annales de Géophysique* 11 (1955), *399–419*.

—— (1960a): 'Influence du feu sur les propriétés magnétiques du sol et sur celles du schiste et du granit', in *Annales de Géophysique* 16 (1960), *159–95*.

—— (1960b): 'Étude expérimentale du traînage magnétique dans le cas d'un ensemble de grains magnétiques très fins dispersés dans une substance non-magnétique', in *Annales de Géophysique* 16 (1960), *445–93*.

Mullins, C (1974): 'The magnetic properties of the soil and their application to archaeological prospecting', in *Archaeo-Physika* 5 (1974).

Scollar, I (1968): 'A simple direct reading susceptibility bridge', in *Journal of Scientific Instruments* 1 (1968), *781–2*.

CHAPTER 9

Aspects of the environment of the Mesolithic site

Alan Hamilton*

Radiocarbon determinations for material from the occupation soil at Mount Sandel give dates lying between 9000 and 8500 bp (about 7000 and 6500 bc),† with a concentration within the first two hundred years of this period (see below, page 146).

There is much uncertainty as to the geographical extent of the area exploited by the Mount Sandel people. Some progress can be made, however, if it is assumed that Mount Sandel was permanently occupied on both a seasonal and a nightly basis and that there was no interaction with other groups. These assumptions may well be false, but they do help towards computation of a minimum area of exploitation. Fig 52 shows some features of the 10 km zone which surrounds Mount Sandel: the area defined by the 10 km radius is 314 km², nearly all of which is terrestrial. It is considered that, with the possible exception of a brief period in mid-winter, there would have been ample time for people based at Mount Sandel to have visited any part of this area during the course of a day, with plenty of time to spare for resource exploitation (Vita-Finzi and Higgs 1970).

Examination of topographical, geological and present day land-use maps, in conjunction with general knowledge of post-glacial environmental history, suggests that no fewer than six major and contrasting environmental types were represented within a 10 km radius of Mount Sandel at 9000–8500 bp. Their juxtaposition could well have been an attraction of Mount Sandel to the Mesolithic folk. The types are as follows.

1 Lowland, well drained environments. These must have covered the greater part of the area. The substrate was mostly boulder clay, but this was replaced locally by either basalt or glacial-outwash sands and gravels.

---

* The references for Chapter 9 will be found on page 109.

† The normal form for radiocarbon dates in this volume is bc, but the author's preference for bp has been respected in this chapter.

2 Highland environments. These were represented to the west by a fairly extensive area of land exceeding 700 ft (215 m) in altitude. The maximum altitude within the 10 km zone was about 950 ft (290 m).

3 Mires. Judging by the distribution of lowland bogs at the present day, mires must have been extensive, especially towards the east.

4 Riverine environments. These were represented by a long stretch of the River Bann, several tributaries of the Bann, and a short reach of the River Bush. With the lower sea levels and deeper Bann channel of the time (see Chapter 10), the waterfall below Mount Sandel would have been higher by at least 4 m and, depending on the channel gradient downstream from the waterfall and the sea level, possibly by as much as 9 m. This waterfall may well have offered exceptional opportunities for catching migratory fish.

5 Estuarine environments. The configuration and tidal characteristics of the Bann estuary would have been different from now, perhaps with discharge through several channels lying between Castlerock and Portstewart, and probably with an enhanced tidal surge (Carter, personal communication). Sea level was at least 4 m and probably about 9 m lower than now at 9000–8500 bp (see Chapter 10; also Carter, personal communication). It is uncertain whether saline conditions would have extended as far as Mount Sandel.

6 Marine environments. It is likely that both rocky and sandy shores were present within the 10 km zone.

Some information concerning the nature of the vegetation is available from studies of macrofossils and pollen. Garry Bog, lying some 7 km east of Mount Sandel, is the closest site with sediments of appropriate age which has been subjected to fairly detailed investigation. The stratigraphy of one of the peat lobes of Garry Bog has been studied by students

Fig 52   Diagram showing the variety of habitats contained within a 10 km radius of Mount Sandel at 9000–8500 bp. The
         extent of wetland habitats was probably greater than is indicated by this map

from the New University of Ulster. Two main strata were present, an upper bog peat and a lower reed peat. Two ^{14}C dates and a pollen diagram are available for a locality along this transect, and these demonstrate that the upper *Sphagnum*-rich peat layers had not started to form at the time of the occupation of Mount Sandel. This agrees with much evidence from elsewhere in Ireland that at 9000–8500 bp many of those sites which are today covered by lowland raised bog then carried more eutrophic communities

such as reed-swamp and mire-carr. For Ireland as a whole little is known in detail about the floristics of these wetland communities or the degree of variation which was present at any one site, but it is certain that they were generally more productive ecosystem types than the bog ecosystems which succeeded them. They may have offered an attractive environment for man as a hunter of birds.

Robert Larmour has also constructed a pollen diagram for Garry Bog. This diagram is relatively well dated and in some respects relatively detailed and, by kind permission of the author, part of it is reproduced here and used for further comment (Fig 53). A complication arises, however, in that the lowest of the three ^{14}C samples available for the relevant part of the pollen diagram clearly underestimates the true age of the sediments. This sample came from above the basal clay and it is possible that it has been enriched by accumulation of downward-moving humus. Here, dating of the sediments is based on the upper three of the four ^{14}C dates shown in Fig 53; the interpolated ages are those proposed by Robert Larmour.

The early post-glacial pollen diagram for Garry Bog follows the same general outline as is seen in many other pollen diagrams for Ireland. A phase of high non-arboreal pollen is succeeded by successive major rises in the following pollen types: *Juniperus*, *Salix*, *Betula*, *Corylus* (which might include some *Myrica*), *Pinus* (a poorly defined rise), *Ulmus*, *Quercus* and finally *Alnus*. Leaving aside the *Juniperus*, *Salix* and *Betula* rises, which are not well dated at Garry Bog and which in any case certainly precede the time of Mount Sandel occupation, the *Corylus* expansion seems to have begun at approximately 9000 bp (7000 bc), the *Ulmus* expansion at approximately 8500 bp (6500 bc), the *Quercus* expansion at approximately 8000 bp (6000 bc), and the *Alnus* expansion at or slightly after 7000 bp (5000 bc). These dates may be compared with those quoted in a review paper by Smith and Pilcher (1973) which discusses the ^{14}C chronology of pollen zones in the British Isles. In some cases these authors distinguish between the 'empirical' and 'rational' limits of pollen types in pollen diagrams. An empirical limit is defined as the point at which pollen of the taxon first becomes consistently present, that is for a number of consecutive samples, and a rational limit is defined as the point at which the pollen begins to rise to a sustained high level. The dates already quoted for Garry Bog refer to rational limits. According to Smith and Pilcher (1973), the dates of the rational limits of *Corylus*, *Ulmus*, *Quercus* and *Alnus* vary considerably within the British Isles. The details of the pattern and the reasons for the variation are incompletely understood, although altitudinal effects and speeds of range expansion have been mentioned as possible causal processes. Broadly speaking, however, the dates for the rational limits of *Corylus*, *Ulmus*, *Quercus* and *Alnus* at Garry Bog are similar to those found at other lowland sites in the northern part of Ireland. Obviously, it would be desirable to secure very detailed and well dated pollen diagrams for the Mount Sandel area, but meanwhile the evidence points to the first occupation of Mount Sandel as occurring at more or less the same time as the rise of the *Corylus* curve. The entire Mesolithic settlement phase at Mount Sandel apparently pre-dates the rational limits of both *Ulmus* and *Quercus* in the Garry Bog diagram.

In reconstructing vegetation from the pollen diagram for Garry Bog or, for that matter, other Irish sites, it must be remembered that the pollen can be considered as having been derived from three environmentally very different areas of vegetation. These are the local vegetation, consisting of mire or aquatic communities growing near the sample site, the adjacent vegetation, which comprises communities established on nearby well drained soils, and the long-distance vegetation, made up of more distant communities. In the present instance, it is possible that a substantial proportion of the *Pinus* pollen, which is a particularly well dispersed pollen type, may have been derived from long-distance vegetation, but in other respects the problem with the Garry Bog diagram is to ascertain the relative contributions of local and adjacent vegetation to the pollen spectra. This presents many difficulties.

Most palynologists would accept Smith's (1970) interpretation of the rise in *Corylus* pollen as being associated with an expansion of hazel trees on well drained soils. *Corylus* is not a true mire species and *Myrica*, another producer of *Corylus*-type pollen, does not grow today in those types of wetland communities which appear to have been present in the local vegetation at Garry Bog. The origin of the *Betula* and *Salix* pollen in the Garry Bog diagram is more uncertain than that of *Corylus*. Both these genera can grow in both dryland and mire communities. *Betula* is a better dispersed pollen type than *Salix* and, from a general consideration of the ecology of *Betula* and a general association in Irish pollen diagrams between a *Betula* fall and the *Corylus* rise, it is reasonable to follow Smith (1970) in attributing the *Betula* fall partly to displacement of birch woodland by hazel-dominated communities. Wood is present intermittently but often abundantly in the reed peat at Garry Bog. The stratigraphic investigation by the New University of Ulster students revealed no consistent pattern of changes in abundance with depth at the various sample points, but the association at the point sampled by Robert Larmour between wood-rich layers and relatively high values of *Betula* and *Salix* pollen (Fig 53) suggests that birches and willows were both growing in local vegetation. Briefly now considering the possible disposition of other woody plants at 9000–8500 bp, it seems unlikely that *Quercus* was present in the region at all, while both *Pinus* and *Ulmus* could have been present in adjacent vegetation but are unlikely to have been common. The New University of Ulster students recorded the persistent presence of Rhamnaceae pollen at low percentages throughout the basal reed peat stratum. The pollen type most strongly

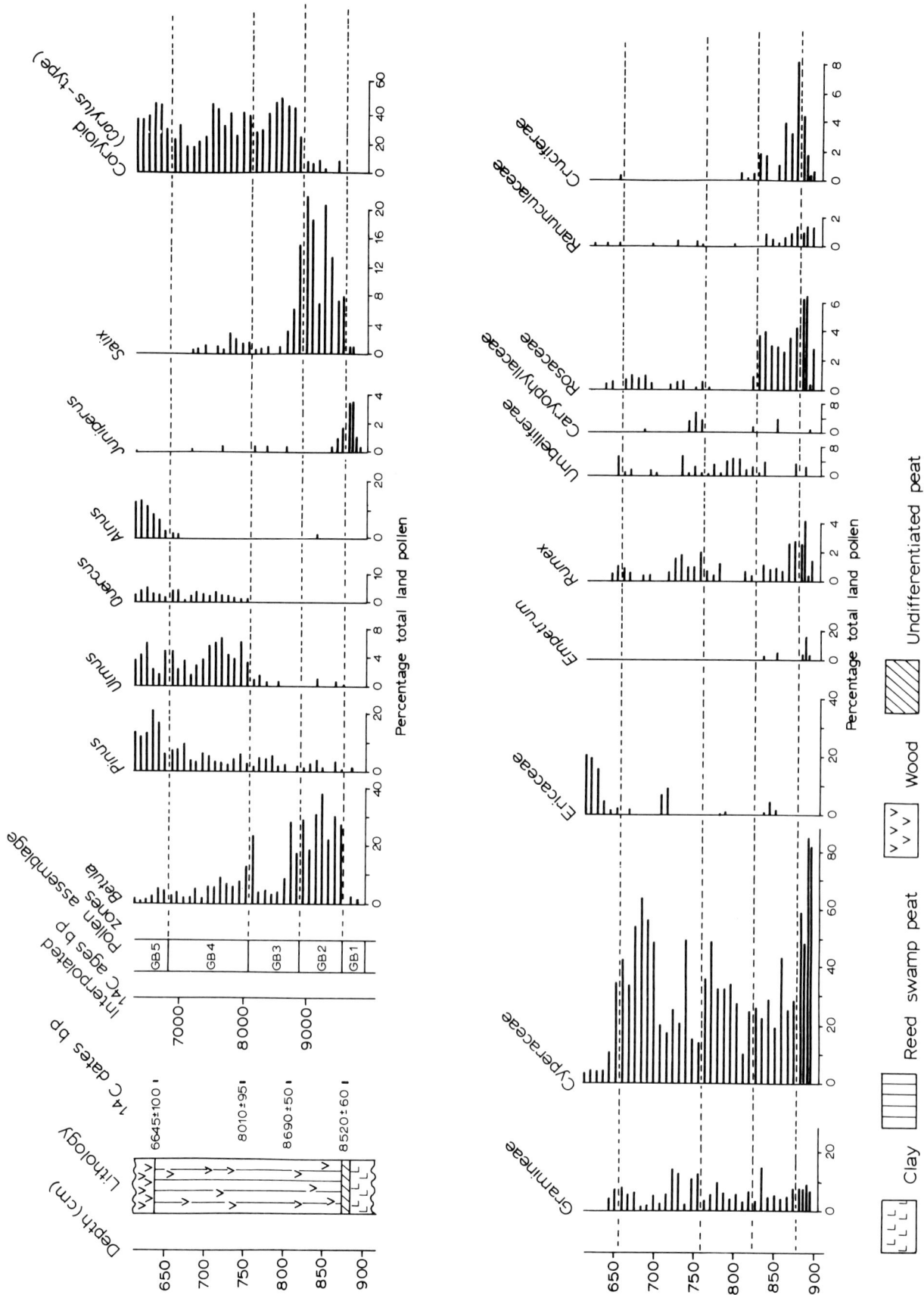

Fig 53   Pollen diagram for the basal sediments at Garry Bog, counted and zoned by Robert Larmour. The pollen sum is total pollen excluding aquatics

resembles that of *Rhamnus catharticus*, a shrub of lime-rich soils.

Most of the herbaceous pollen in the lower part of the Garry Bog diagram was probably derived from local vegetation. The high Rosaceae (a type which here includes *Potentilla* but *excludes Filipendula*) and Ranunculaceae values before about 9000 bp might be related to the presence of herbaceous fen and open water communities. Little can be said at present as to how much of the herbaceous pollen originated in dryland communities, and so the extent of open vegetation types accompanying the birch and hazel woodlands is uncertain.

Smith (1970) has discussed the possibility that Mesolithic man was an important modifier of vegetation in the British Isles. Of relevance here is the theory that widespread burning may have encouraged the spread and maintenance of hazel. It is of interest to note that, as at Mount Sandel, Mesolithic activity seems to have started at about the time of the hazel increase at some other sites in the British Isles. The Mount Sandel evidence does not help to resolve the questions raised by Smith, but it is perhaps worth pointing out that, whether burning was or was not a significant factor, hazel-dominated ecosystems might have proved attractive to Mesolithic man, providing greater quantities of food at both the primary producer (eg hazel nuts) and secondary (eg wild boar) tropic levels than the preceding birch woodland.

During the course of the investigations at Mount Sandel, Peter Woodman discovered a kettle-hole close to the excavation. The stratigraphy and pollen contents of the kettle-hole sediments were investigated by students of the New University of Ulster and are described in Appendix 3. The sediments proved to consist of a typical tripartite late-glacial sequence and a thin overlying peat. Unfortunately the period lying between about 10,000 and 7000 bp was unrepresented by sediments in the kettle-hole, thereby preventing analysis of sediment characteristics for the time of the Mount Sandel occupation. However, the hiatus in sediment accumulation is itself of some interest and it is difficult to escape the conclusion that peat initiation at about 7000 bp must

have been climatically induced. This supports the traditional interpretation of the Boreal/Atlantic transition (Jessen 1949). The climate of Mesolithic man at Mount Sandel was probably drier and in a sense more comfortable than it subsequently became. The relative contributions of decreased precipitation and increased temperature to the dryness remain uncertain; Jessen (1949) and Smith (1970) have held that temperatures during the period covered by the Mount Sandel occupation were probably at least as high as they are today and, if this was so, then rainfall was probably lower.

Unfortunately conditions have been unfavourable at Mount Sandel for the preservation of plant material, and little is known about the use of individual types of plants for food, building materials, tools and so on. The main exception is provided by hazel nuts, the abundance of which is not surprising in view of their nutritive value and the probable abundance of hazel scrub. The only other plant macrofossils recovered from the fossil soil were water-lily and apple/pear seeds. These seeds probably represent use of these plants for food (see Chapter 6).

Acknowledgments

I would like to thank John Shaw for drawing the diagrams and Isobel McClelland for typing the manuscript.

References

Jessen, K (1949): 'Studies in late Quaternary deposits and flora history of Ireland', in *Proc Roy Irish Acad* 52B (1949), *85–290*.

Smith, A G (1970): 'The influence of Mesolithic and Neolithic man on British vegetation: a discussion', in *Vegetational history of the British Isles*, eds D Walker and R G West (Cambridge, 1970), *81–96*.

—— and Pilcher, J R (1973): 'Radiocarbon dates and vegetational history of the British Isles', in *New Phytol* 72 (1973), *903–14*.

Vita-Finzi, C and Higgs, E (1970): 'Prehistoric economy in the Mount Carmel area of Palestine, site catchment analysis', in *Proc Prehist Soc* 36 (1970), *1–37*.

CHAPTER 10

Palaeoecological evidence for sea-level change in the Bann estuary in the Early Mesolithic period

Richard W Battarbee, Robert G Scaife and Stuart J Phethean

Introduction*

The large quantities of fish bones found during the Mount Sandel excavation suggest that the River Bann was an important source of food for the Early Mesolithic people of the area. Most of the bones are from the migratory species, eel and salmon. Some of the remainder, however, are from bass and flounder (see Chapter 5), species characteristic of marine and estuarine environments. One of the interesting questions to arise from the excavation is whether these fish could have been caught in the river adjacent to the site at that time. Today the Bann is estuarine at Mount Sandel and estuarine conditions extend upstream as far as the Cutts (Fig 54), but in the Early Mesolithic the sea level was considerably lower than at present and it might be expected that Mount Sandel was well above the tidal limit. On the other hand there is a strong likelihood that a deep buried channel exists below the present river bed and sea-water may have penetrated considerable distances upstream, even when sea level was quite low. This chapter, therefore, seeks to assess whether the Bann at Mount Sandel was estuarine in the Early Mesolithic. In doing so it draws on a recent review of sea-level change for the coast of Northern Ireland by Carter (1982), the early work of Jessen in the Bann estuary (Jessen 1949), and preliminary results from our own work at Sandelford, a site near Coleraine.

Sea-Level Change on the North Coast of Ireland

Relative sea level on the north coast of Ireland has varied considerably over the last 15,000 years in response to interplay between late- and post-glacial rates of eustatic and isostatic change. Carter has recently reviewed the subject and has derived a

sea-level curve for the north coast using ^{14}C-dated levels reported in the literature. His curve (Fig 55) is very tentative, partly because of the lack of dates for the early periods and partly arising from difficulties in combining data derived from differing sedimentological and geomorphological environments. As it stands the curve suggests that sea level during the early Mount Sandel occupation was about −9 m OD.

Sites Described by Jessen in the Bann Estuary

As part of a much wider survey of the vegetational history of Ireland Jessen investigated a number of sites along the river (Jessen 1949), and two of them, Somerset and the Bann Estuary (Fig 54), contained evidence for sea-level change. A further site, Spring Bridge, located a few miles upstream of the present tidal limit, showed no evidence of marine influence. None of these sites was used by Carter since they have no associated ^{14}C dates. Jessen's data, however, include lithostratigraphic descriptions and pollen diagrams, and approximate dates can be inferred by comparison with dated pollen diagrams from other sites.

The most useful of Jessen's sites is the one he ambiguously called 'the Bann Estuary' located in Farranlester townland. He describes a wood peat sequence at −5.1 to −5.9 m OD* above which occurs a muddy sand containing marine diatoms. The pollen data show that this transgression occurs at the same time as *Corylus* values represent over 400% of the total tree pollen and somewhat prior to a marked decline in *Corylus* at about −4.50 m. Jessen consequently remarks 'the invading estuarine conditions reached this part of the Bann Valley a short time before the Boreal Hazel maximum'. There is considerable variation in ^{14}C dates for the main

---

* Jessen's levels refer to the Irish (Poolbeg) Datum. Here his levels are expressed in relation to Belfast Datum, 2.9 m higher.

BANN ESTUARY & ASSOCIATED SITES

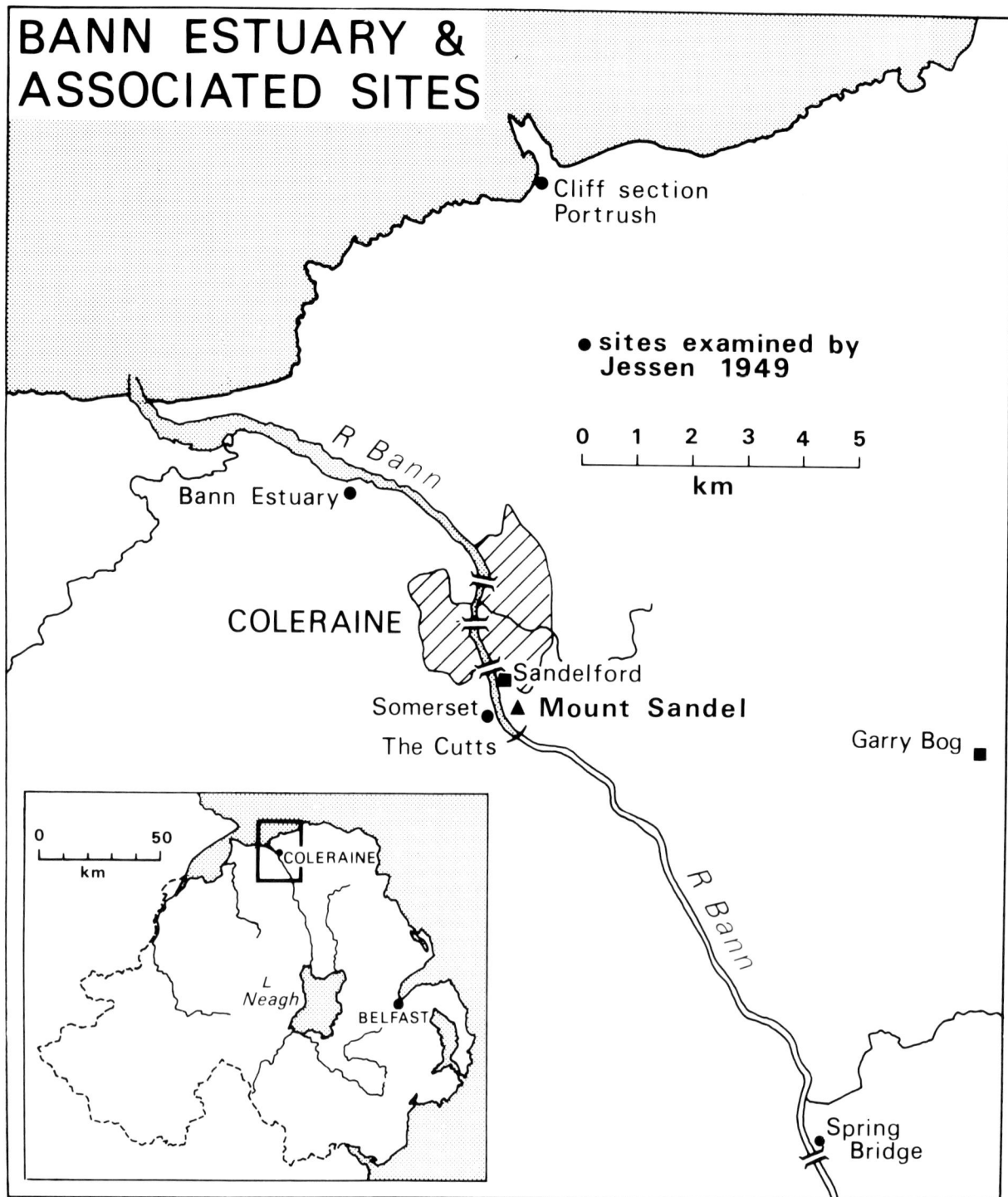

Fig 54   Map of the Bann estuary showing location of sites mentioned in text

pollen zone boundaries in the early part of the post-glacial period in the north of Ireland (cf Smith and Pilcher 1973) but some idea of the date of this *Corylus* decline can be gained from a comparison with Larmour's ¹⁴C-dated Garry Bog diagram (see above,

page 107, Fig 53).* Pollen values for Garry Bog are expressed as percentages of the total land pollen

---

* The normal form for radiocarbon dates in this volume is bc, but the authors' preference for bp has been respected in this chapter.

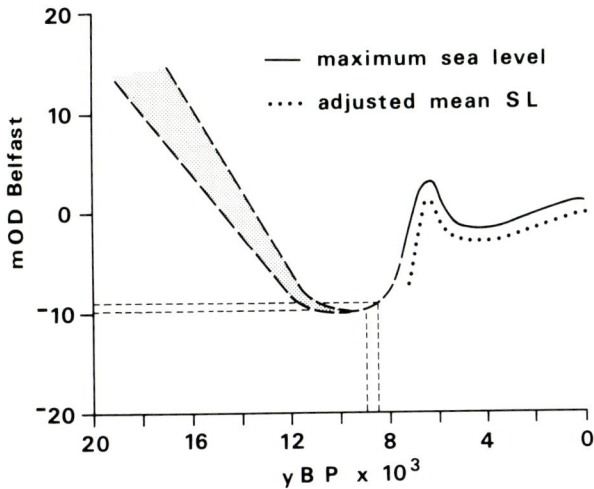

Fig 55 Sea-level curve for the north coast of Northern Ireland (redrawn from Carter 1982) showing expected position of sea level during Mount Sandel occupation

whilst Jessen uses a total tree pollen sum. If the Garry Bog values are converted to a tree pollen sum a clear *Corylus* decline can be seen to occur midway through pollen assemblage zone GB4 or, extrapolating between the ^{14}C results, at about 7500 bp (5500 bc). The later deposits at the Bann Estuary site mainly comprise estuarine muds which probably accumulated rapidly in phase with sea-level rise.

The sequence at Somerset is significant in that marine diatoms are recorded in a +1.45 m OD terrace, 0.45 m above present (1935) spring high tides. The pollen spectrum at this point is early Atlantic in age, indicating that the sea had risen to its present or to a slightly higher level by this time.

Evidence from Sandelford, near Coleraine

In a search for estuarine sediments of early post-glacial age closer to Mount Sandel than the Bann Estuary site, Peter Woodman located a site on the eastern bank of the River Bann near the new Sandelford Bridge, less than 1 km downstream from

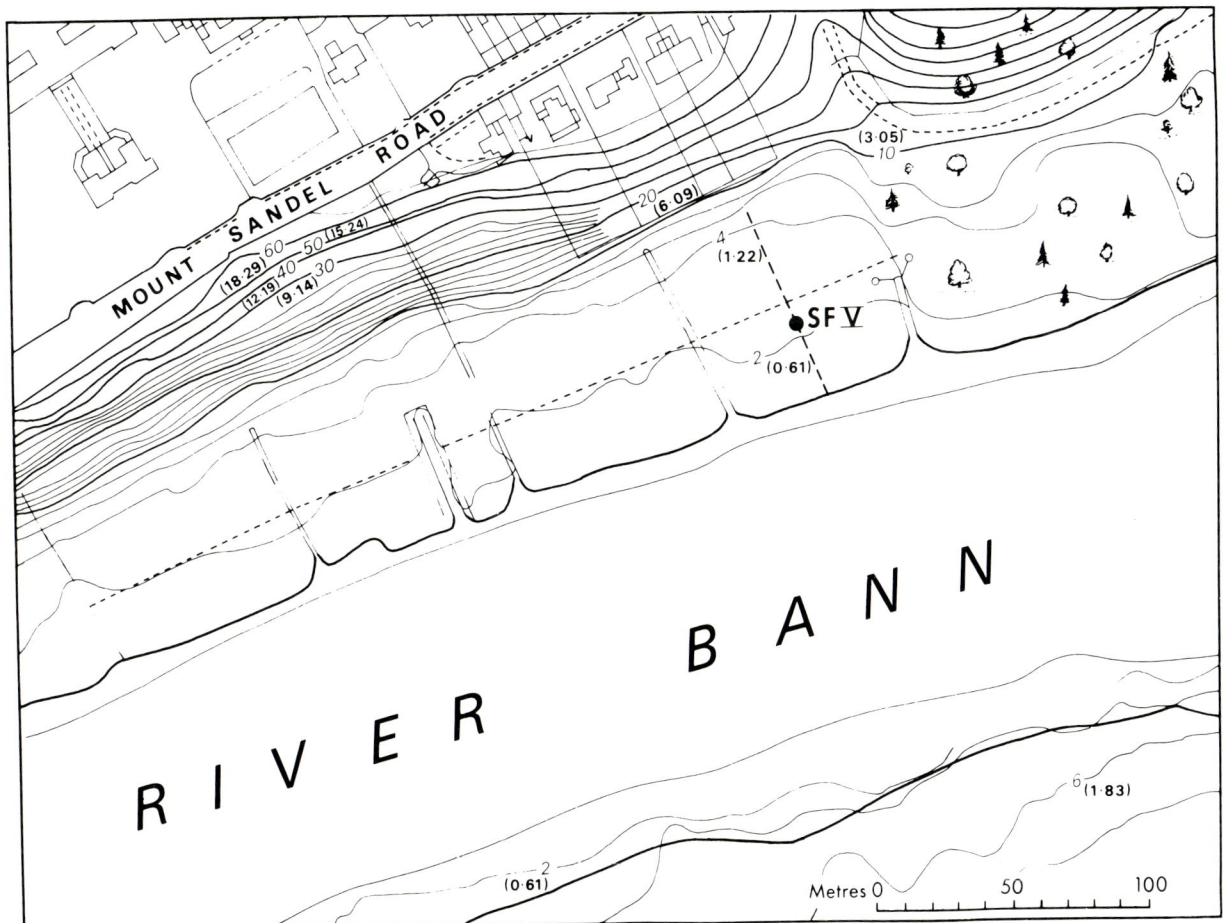

Fig 56 Detailed map of the Sandelford site showing position of stratigraphic transect (dashed line normal to the river) and location of core SF V (contour heights in both feet and metres)

distance (metres)

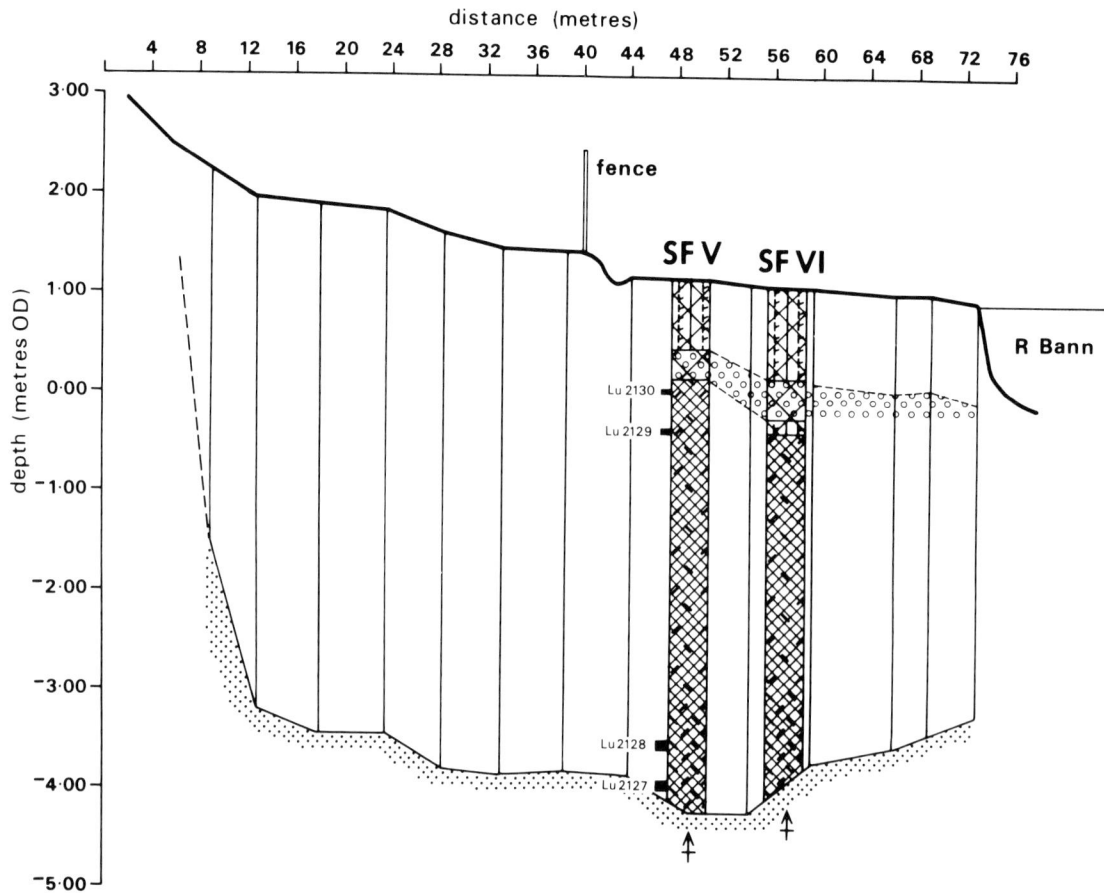

Fig 57   Stratigraphic transect for Sandelford (SF V stratigraphy described in text)

Mount Sandel (Fig 54). The site was called 'Sandelford' and it forms a rather narrow flood plain bounded by the river on the west and the steep morainic valley edge on the east.

LOCATION AND STRATIGRAPHY

A detailed map of the site is shown in Fig 56, and Fig 57 shows the stratigraphy of the site along a levelled transect. A core (SF V) was taken at the deepest point where the surface level was 1.09 m OD in an area of actively growing *Phragmites* reed-swamp. A second core (SF VI) was taken about 12 m to the west.

This stratigraphic sequence is similar to that recorded by Jessen for the Bann Estuary site, notably in relation to the relatively thick deposit of estuarine mud followed by a sand and gravel band with fresh *Phragmites* peat above. At Sandelford the sand and gravel band probably represents an erosive period at some stage after the maximum transgression and at a time when the river occupied a channel slightly to the east of its present position. Such erosion and channel movement is likely to have removed existing organic

muds, and the mud/gravel contact in the sequence probably represents a considerable hiatus. The lower muds, however, appeared undisturbed, an observation which was later confirmed by pollen analysis.

POLLEN ANALYSIS

Pollen analysis was carried out on the lower 3 metres of the sequence, from 228 to 516 cm, in order to assess the conformability of the sediment and as a means of approximate dating. Standard methods were used for concentrating the subfossil pollen and spores. Samples were counted at 8 cm intervals and each count comprised 150 arboreal pollen. Fig 58 shows a summary diagram of the results. The base of the diagram with high *Quercus*, *Ulmus*, *Pinus* and *Betula* values and relatively low *Alnus* values indicates a late Boreal spectrum, post-dating the establishment of mixed deciduous woodland but pre-dating the expansion of *Alnus* in the Atlantic period. Despite one sample with very high *Alnus* values at 428 cm, probably a case of local over-representation, the rational boundary of *Alnus* lies at about 360 cm. Shortly afterwards, at 330 cm, there is a decline in

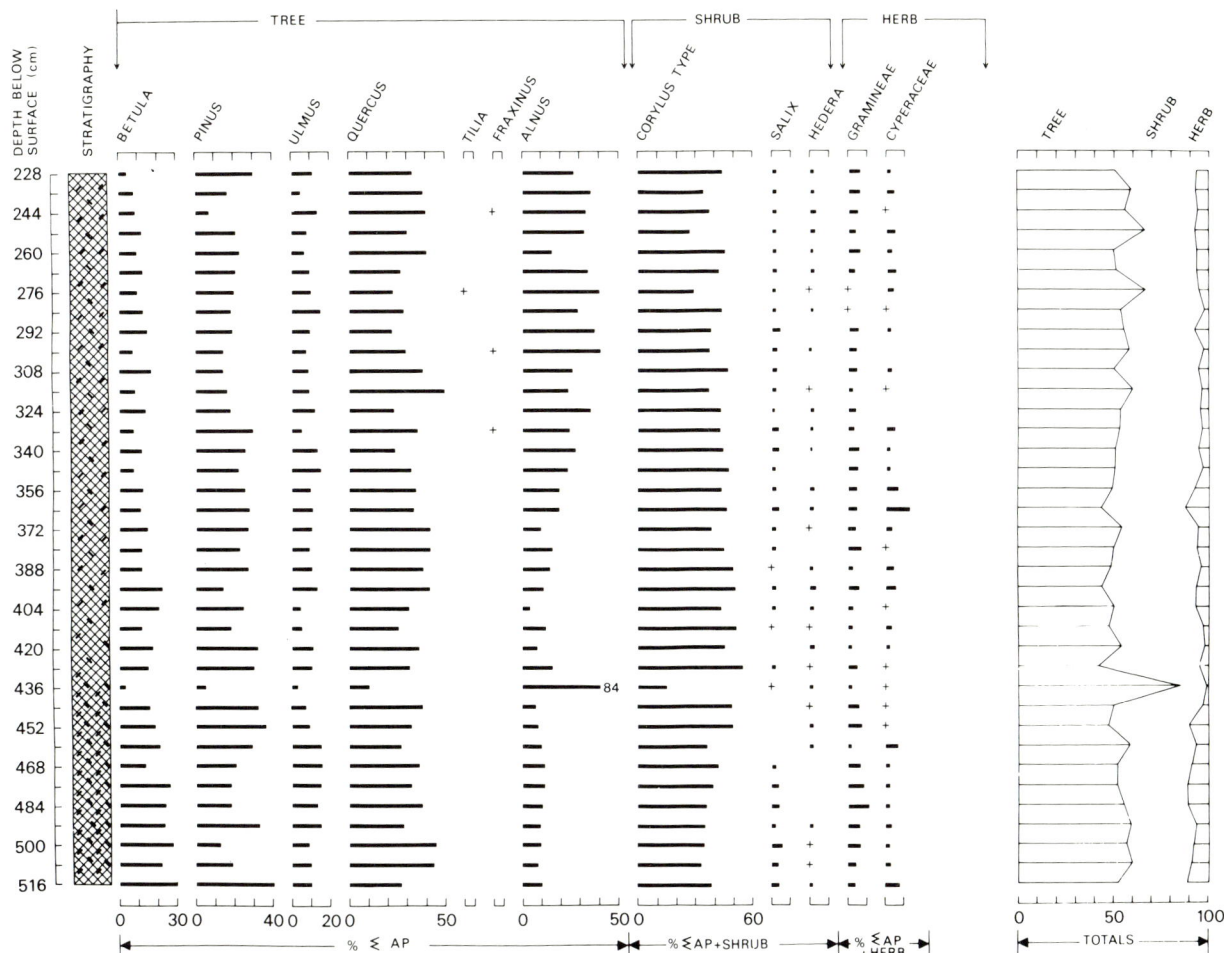

Fig 58 Sandelford V: summary pollen diagram (full list of taxa in Table 42)

m (Belfast OD)	Depth below surface (cm)*	Sediment description
+1.09–+0.40	0–69	Light brown, coarse detritus *Phragmites* peat with modern rhizomes in the top 20 cm; becoming finer and muddier below 24 cm.
+0.40–+0.09	69–100	69–83, sharp transition to a brown sandy mud. 83–90, light grey coarse sand and gravel, very little organic matter but occasionally large fragments of woody material. 90–100, dark brown muddy sand.
+0.09––4.08	100–517	100–440, grey-brown silty mud with occasional plant fragments. Sand lenses at 274 cm and 430 cm. 440–517, green-brown fine mud with abundant woody fragments and occasional hazel nut shells and charcoal.

* Although the usual unit in this volume is mm, in this chapter the author's preference for cm has been respected.

Table 41 Lithostratigraphy of Sandelford V

TREES	MARITIME	*Caltha* type
Alnus	*Armeria* 'B' line	Cyperaceae
Betula	cf *Frankenia*	*Filipendula*
Fraxinus	*Glaucium*	*Hydrocotyle*
Pinus	*Hippophae*	*Lysimachia*
Quercus	*Plantago maritima*	*Myriophyllum alterniflorum*
Tilia		*Nymphaea alba*
Ulmus	UNDIFFERENTIATED HERBS	*Polygonum amphibium*
	Bidens type	*Potamogeton*
SHRUBS	*Dianthus* type	*Sparganium* type
Corylus	*Geum* type	*Succisa*
Frangula	Gramineae	*Thalictrum*
Hedera	*Odontites* type	*Typha latifolia*
Hippophae	Papilionaceae	
Juniperus	*Ranunculus* type	PTERIDOPHYTA
Myrica	Rosaceae	*Dryopteris* type
Prunus type	Scrophulariaceae	*Equisetum*
Salix	*Sedum*	*Osmunda*
Sorbus type	*Sinapis* type	*Polypodium*
	Stachys type	*Pteridium*
DWARF SHRUBS	Umbelliferae	
Calluna		BRYOPHYTA
Empetrum	AQUATIC AND MARGINAL AQUATIC	*Sphagnum*
Vaccinium	*Alisma plantago-aquatica*	

Table 42   Pollen taxa recorded at Sandelford V

Pinus percentages. These changes indicate the transition between the Boreal and Atlantic periods. There is little further change in the diagram and the whole sequence clearly pre-dates Neolithic clearance activity. The pollen of herbaceous species which occur are mainly of taxa associated with aquatic and riverside habitats and vary little through the sequence. These are listed in Table 42.

DIATOM ANALYSIS

Diatom analysis of the lowermost samples of the Sandelford core showed that the transgression had already reached Sandelford by the time these basal sediments were deposited. The taxa encountered are listed in Table 43, and Fig 59 shows a summary diagram in which the relative proportions of the various salinity groupings (cf Hustedt 1957) are presented. All the samples examined contained a significant proportion of mesohalobous and polyhalobous taxa. The polyhalobous diatoms are dominated by epiphytic and benthic forms typical of coastal and estuarine zones, such as *Cocconeis scutellum* (and var *parva*), *Nitzschia punctata*, and *Paralia sulcata*, although a few planktonic taxa are also present,

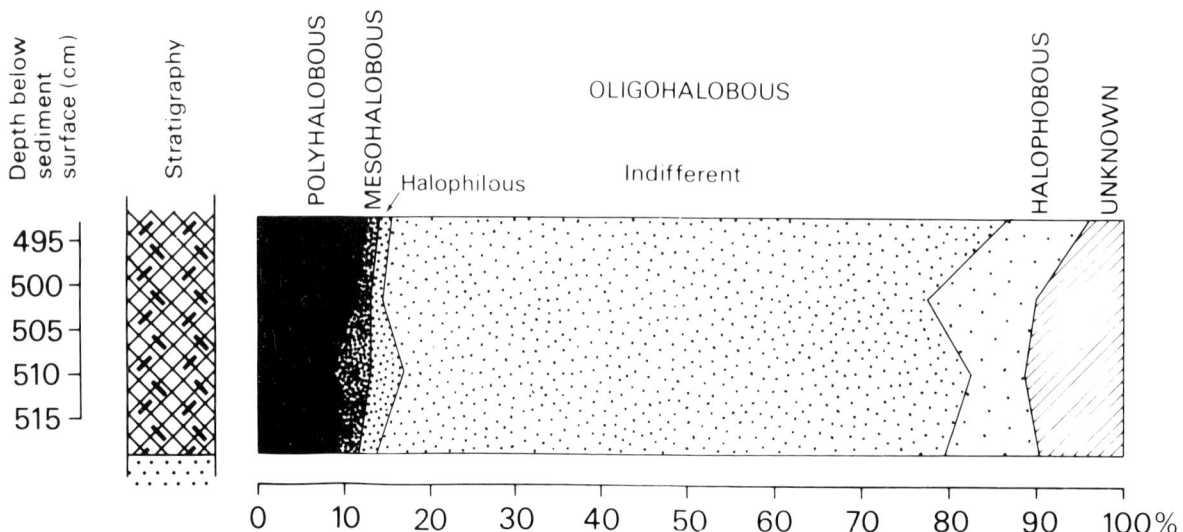

Fig 59   Sandelford V: composite diatom diagram showing presence of marine (polyhalobous) taxa in basal sediments (full list of taxa in Table 43)

TAXON	Depth below surface (cm)			
	494	502	510	518
(a) Polyhalobous				
Cocconeis scutellum Ehr	0.5	2.0	—	0.7
Cocconeis scutellum var *parva* Grun	2.5	1.0	—	0.7
Nitzschia punctata (W Smith) Grun	0.5	0.5	2.3	1.3
Nitzschia punctata var *coarctata* Grun	3.0	2.5	—	1.3
Paralia sulcata (Ehr) Cleve	3.5	1.5	4.3	3.3
Rhabdonema minutum Kütz	0.5	—	—	—
Rhabdonema sp	—	—	—	0.3
Thalassiosira decipiens (Grun) Jørg	1.5	1.0	1.3	1.7
Thalassiosira sp	—	2.0	—	—
Thalassionema nitzschioides Hust	0.5	0.5	0.3	—
(b) Mesohalobous				
Achnanthes haukiana Grun	0.5	—	2.7	—
Bacillaria paradoxa Gmelin	0.5	0.5	1.0	0.3
Cyclotella caspia Grun	0.5	0.5	0.3	0.7
Nitzschia sigma W Smith	—	0.5	0.7	1.0
Rhopalodia musculus (Kütz) O Mull	—	—	—	0.3
Synedra pulchella Kütz	—	0.5	—	0.3
(c) Oligohalobous (halophilous)				
Cocconeis pediculus Ehr	0.5	0.5	0.7	0.7
Cocconeis thumensis A Mayer	—	—	—	1.0
Cyclotella atomus Hust	—	—	—	0.3
Mastogloia smithii Thwaites	0.5	—	—	—
Mastogloia smithii var *lacustris* Grun	0.5	0.5	0.3	—
Nitzschia hungarica Grun	0.5	1.0	0.3	—
Nitzschia frustulum (Kütz) Grun	0.5	—	2.7	—
(d) Oligohalobous (indifferent)				
Achnanthes lanceolata Bréb	4.0	1.5	2.3	4.3
Achnanthes linearis (W Smith) Grun	—	—	0.3	0.3
Achnanthes lanceolata var *rostrata* Hust	—	0.5	—	0.3
Achnanthes calcar Cleve	—	—	0.3	0.3
Achnanthes clevei Grun	0.5	0.5	1.0	0.7
Achnanthes oestrupii (A Cleve) Hust	—	—	—	1.0
Achnanthes exigua Grun	—	1.0	1.0	1.0
Achnanthes exigua var *heterovalvata* Krasske	0.5	—	—	—
Achnanthes peragalli Brun et Héribaud	0.5	—	—	—
Achnanthes minutissima Kütz	4.5	2.5	—	1.7
Amphora ovalis Kütz	0.5	0.5	1.0	0.3
Amphora ovalis var *pediculus* Kütz	1.5	0.0	2.0	1.3
Asterionella formosa Hass	0.5	0.5	0.3	0.3
Cymbella ventricosa Kütz	—	—	0.3	0.3
Cymbella sinuata Gregory	—	—	—	0.3
Cymbella microcephala Grun	0.5	0.5	0.3	0.7
Cocconeis placentula (Ehr) Cleve	4.5	4.0	2.7	3.7
Cocconeis disculus Schum	—	0.5	1.0	—
Cyclotella comta Kütz	2.0	2.0	1.3	1.3
Cyclotella kützingiana Thwaites	—	0.5	1.0	0.3
Cyclotella ocellata Pant	6.0	3.5	2.0	1.3
Cyclotella comensis Grun	1.0	1.0	0.7	0.7
Cyclotella antiqua W Smith	0.5	—	—	0.3
Diploneis ovalis (Hilse) Cleve	—	0.5	1.3	0.7
Diploneis oculata (Brébisson) Cleve	—	—	—	0.3
Epithemia sorex Kütz	2.5	1.0	0.3	1.7
Epithemia zebra (Ehr) Kütz	2.5	—	—	0.3

TAXON	Depth below surface (cm)			
	494	502	510	518
Epithemia turgida (Ehr) Kütz	—	0.5	0.7	—
Epithemia hyndmanni W Smith	0.5	—	—	—
Eunotia pectinalis var *minor* (Kütz) Rabenh	—	—	—	0.3
Fragilaria pinnata Ehr	2.5	1.5	2.3	6.0
Fragilaria construens (Ehr) Grun	3.0	4.5	8.7	4.7
Fragilaria construens var *binodis* (Ehr) Grun	0.5	0.5	0.3	1.0
Fragilaria construens var *venter* (Ehr) Grun	3.0	6.0	5.7	7.7
Fragilaria brevistriata Grun	4.5	6.0	7.3	3.7
Fragilaria vaucheriae Boye Pet	0.5	0.5	1.3	0.3
Fragilaria lapponica Grun	12.0	10.5	11.3	5.7
Frustulia vulgaris Thwaites	—	—	—	·0.3
Gomphonema olivaceum (Lyngbye) Kütz	—	—	—	0.7
Gomphonema angustatum (Kütz) Rabenh	3.0	1.0	0.7	1.0
Gomphonema acuminatum v *trigonocephala* (Ehr) Grun	—	—	0.3	—
Gomphonema acuminatum var *coronata* (Ehr) W Smith	1.0	—	—	—
Gomphonema abbreviatum (Agardh) Kütz	—	—	0.5	—
Gyrosigma attenuatum (Kütz) Rabenh	0.5	—	—	—
Navicula järnefeltii Hust	—	1.0	1.0	1.0
Navicula radiosa Kütz	—	—	—	0.3
Navicula hungarica Grun	0.5	—	0.3	0.3
Navicula cryptocephala Kütz	—	—	—	0.3
Navicula rhyncocephala Kütz	—	0.5	0.3	—
Neidium iridis (Ehr) Cleve	—	—	—	0.3
Nitzschia fonticola Grun	—	—	—	0.3
Nitzschia denticula Grun	—	—	—	1.3
Opephora martyi Héribaud	—	3.0	0.7	1.3
Rhoicosphenia curvata (Kütz) Grun	1.5	0.5	0.7	0.7
Rhopalodia gibba (Ehr) O Mull	1.5	—	—	0.3
Stauroneis anceps Ehr	—	—	0.3	—
Stephanodiscus hantzschii Grun	—	—	—	0.3
Stephanodiscus astraea (Ehr) Grun	4.0	4.0	2.7	3.0
Stephanodiscus astraea var *minutula* (Kütz) Grun	—	1.0	0.3	0.7
Synedra ulna (Nitz) Ehr	—	—	0.3	0.3
Synedra parasitica (W Smith) Hust	—	0.5	—	—
Synedra ulna var *spathulifera* Grun	—	—	0.7	—
(e) Halophobous				
Cocconeis diminuta Pant	—	1.0	0.3	0.3
Fragilaria virescens Ralfs	1.0	—	—	0.3
Melosira italica subsp *subarctica* O Mull	6.5	8.5	5.3	9.3
Tabellaria flocculosa (Roth) Kütz	1.0	—	0.3	0.7
Tabellaria fenestrata (Lyngb) Kütz	0.5	3.0	0.3	0.3
(f) Unknown				
Caloneis latiuscula (Kütz) Cleve	—	—	0.7	—
Diploneis decipiens A U	—	—	—	0.3
Navicula cf *wuestii*	—	—	—	0.3
Navicula cf *anglica*	—	—	—	0.3
Synedra affinis Kütz	—	0.5	0.3	0.7

Table 43 Diatoms recorded at Sandelford V

principally *Thalassiosira decipiens*. The oligohalobous taxa include planktonic and periphytic forms from the River Bann and Lough Neagh. The species composition of this group resembles the pre-eutrophication diatom flora of Lough Neagh (Battarbee 1978) and it is especially similar to the flora of the diatomite beds at Toome and Newferry (cf Battarbee in Woodman 1977) which were accumulating as seasonal flood deposits on the margins of Lough Neagh at about the same time as the Sandelford

Depth below ground surface*	Lab no	¹⁴C age	
(cm)		(bp)	(bc)
111–116	Lu-2130	6120 ± 70	4170 ± 70
151–156	Lu-2129	6430 ± 70	4480 ± 70
467–477	Lu-2128	6980 ± 70	5030 ± 70
507–517	Lu-2127	7440 ± 70	5490 ± 70

* Ground surface = 1.09 m OD

Table 44 Radiocarbon dates for Sandelford V

muds. The presence of *Fragilaria lapponica* in the diatomites and at Sandelford but not in the deepwater sediments of Lough Neagh is especially notable. A survey of samples at higher levels in the sediment sequence shows that marine diatoms are present throughout.

DATING

Radiocarbon dating of four samples was carried out at the University of Lund Radiocarbon Laboratory and the results are shown in Table 44. The dates show that the 4 m of estuarine muds (from −4 m OD) accumulated in about 1300 years as sea level rose during the Boreal and early Atlantic periods.

The primary interest in the Sandelford site, however, is its proximity to Mount Sandel and the possibility that the lowermost sediments are similar in age to the dates from Mount Sandel. From the pollen diagram (Fig 58) it can be seen that the base of the sequence falls somewhere between the rational boundary for *Quercus* and *Ulmus* and the rational boundary for *Alnus*. The rational boundary for *Quercus* and *Ulmus* at Garry Bog, about 7 km away, is 8010 ± 95 bp (UB-2194, Pearson 1979) and this date is similar to dates at other sites in the north of Ireland (cf Smith and Pilcher 1973). The rational border for *Alnus* has been dated variably from 7500 bp (Ringneill Quay, Morrison 1961) to 5145 bp (Ballynagilly, Pilcher 1970) although most dates fall at about 6500 bp. For Garry Bog the date is 6645 ± 100 bp (UB-2193, Pearson 1979). Interpolation between Lu-2129 and Lu-2128 (Table 44) for Sandelford gives a date of 6800 bp for this feature. The base of the Sandelford diagram is dated to 7440 ± 70 bp (Table 44). This date is in substantial agreement with all the pollen evidence and it can therefore be concluded that the beginning of the sequence at Sandelford post-dates the early occupation of Mount Sandel by approximately 1000 years.

Discussion

The sites in the Bann estuary show that a rapid rise in sea level took place on the north coast of Ireland during the Boreal and early Atlantic periods. The Sandelford data indicate that the Bann was estuarine before about 7500 bp when sea level was 4 m lower than the present, and the Bann Estuary site has evidence for estuarine conditions somewhat earlier, during the *Corylus* maximum in the mid-Boreal and at about −5 m OD. Both these conclusions are in substantial agreement with Carter's sea-level curve (Fig 55). Neither of the sites, however, has deposits of Mount Sandel age, 8500–9000 bp. A search for older sediments is clearly required, and other forms of evidence need to be considered. An evaluation of hydrological and morphological conditions in the river in the Early Mesolithic is especially necessary, and of crucial importance is the depth of the buried channel. Other influential factors are likely to be river discharge levels, tidal ranges, and whether the system, as today, functioned as a wedge estuary, allowing marine water to penetrate upstream below descending freshwater. However, until older sediments are found or until these factors have been fully evaluated we can only conclude that it is uncertain whether estuarine conditions prevailed as early as the Mount Sandel occupation, although the river at Mount Sandel was clearly estuarine 1000 years later.

Acknowledgments
We should like to thank Peter Woodman for bringing our attention to the Sandelford site and for helpful discussion during the production of this paper. We also had useful discussions with Bill Carter and thank him for allowing us to present a version of his sea-level curve here. We are grateful to Claudette John for typing the manuscript, to Sarah Skinner for drawing the diagrams and Chris Cromarty for photographic reproductions of the diagrams. Fieldwork was carried out with the financial assistance of University College, London, and the Department of the Environment for Northern Ireland.

References

Battarbee, R W (1978): 'Observations on the recent history of Lough Neagh and its drainage basin', in *Phil Trans Roy Soc B 281* (1978), *303–345*.

Carter, R W G (1982): 'Sea-level changes in Northern Ireland', in *Proc Geol Assoc 93*(1) (1982), *7–23*.

Hustedt, F (1957): 'Die Diatomeenflora des Fluss-systems der Weser im Gebiet der Hausestadt Bremen', in *Abhr naturw Ver Bremen 34* (1957), *181–440*.

Jessen, K (1949): 'Studies in late Quaternary deposits and flora history of Ireland', in *Proc Roy Irish Acad 52B* (1949), *85–290*.

Morrison, M E S (1961): 'The palynology of Ringneill

Quay, a new Mesolithic site in Co Down, Northern Ireland', in *Proc Roy Irish Acad* 61C (1961), *171–182*.

Pearson, G W (1979): 'Belfast radiocarbon dates IX', in *Radiocarbon* 21 (1979), *274–90*.

Pilcher, J R (1970): *Palaeoecology and radiocarbon dating of sites in Co Tyrone, Northern Ireland* (unpublished thesis, Queen's University, Belfast, 1970).

Smith, A G and Pilcher, J R (1973): 'Radiocarbon dates and vegetational history of the British Isles', in *New Phytol* 72 (1973), *903–14*.

Woodman, P C (1977): 'Recent excavations at Newferry, Co Antrim', in *Proc Prehist Soc* 43 (1977), *155–199*.

CHAPTER 11

Site organization

With a site of this complexity it is essential that each phase of occupation be considered separately. Therefore, as the later phases of occupation have left relatively slight traces which do little more than indicate the presence of man at Mount Sandel, they will be considered first in an attempt to remove some of the random interference from Mesolithic settlement. These later phases are obviously of interest but, apart from the post-medieval occupation, they probably would not in themselves have warranted excavation.

Post-Mesolithic Phases of Occupation

Many features were found which were later than the Mesolithic phase of occupation, but unfortunately relatively few contained anything diagnostic. Those which can be associated with specific phases of occupation will be discussed first and then, where possible, a relative sequence of the remainder will be suggested (Fig 60).

NEOLITHIC
The main concentration of evidence for Neolithic activity was on the northern edge of the site where a number of pits were found. Along this edge an old ground surface was preserved below a layer of dumped soil. The soil had been used to fill up a slight depression (at most 8 by 5 m) in the extreme south-west corner of the field. Although occasional sherds of souterrain ware were recovered from layer (2) (in the extreme SW corner) none were found in the pits, while one pit, F114, contained Neolithic pottery. Therefore it is possible that the scatter of pits with rather lighter fills could belong to the Neolithic. The distribution of the potsherds suggests that a Neolithic settlement may originally have lain to the north and east of the excavation. Occasional sherds were also found in the western area, sometimes embedded in the top of the Mesolithic occupation soil, while several stray sherds were found on the south-eastern edge of the site.

The main scatter of potsherds in layer (2) coincided roughly with the distribution of flintwork. As noted earlier (Chapter 3), in layer (2) there was a slight shift towards multi-platformed cores typical of later prehistoric industries. Although not documented by square metres there was also a small concentration of later retouched tools in this area. The material was concentrated in two small patches, probably resulting from differential erosion.

Neolithic sherds were found in F114, and a similar fill occurred in other features on either side of F82: 110/0, 113, 115, 118, 122, 123, 132, 136, 139, 140, 141 and 142. Some of these features, such as 110/0, were demonstrated by excavation to be later than the main Mesolithic phase of occupation, and 110/0, 113, 123 and 136 were found in the same area and were of roughly the same shape and character. Two other Neolithic sherds were found in features: one was in a small pit, F158, with dark brown fill, and the other was found in the upper fill of F11, but no other traces of Neolithic activity were found in this area. (The significance of these sherds will be discussed below.) The other groups of potsherds appear to be in tree-falls, in FS304, 29 and 77. The implication of the material in the tree-falls is that there was a slight scatter of Neolithic material over the whole area, but this scatter was only preserved in places such as the western area where occasional sherds were found in the occupation soil.

BEAKER PERIOD
No specific traces of structures can be assigned to this period although part of a barbed and tanged arrowhead was found in a disturbed context. No Beaker pottery was recovered from this site but several sherds were found at Mount Sandel (Lower) (Collins 1983). On the basis of comparison with the structures at Newgrange (O'Kelly 1973) it would be tempting to ascribe the northern structure to the Beaker period, but in the absence of any pottery this is stretching typological comparison too far; also, as noted earlier, some of the later prehistoric pits cut across the northern structure (Fig 1).

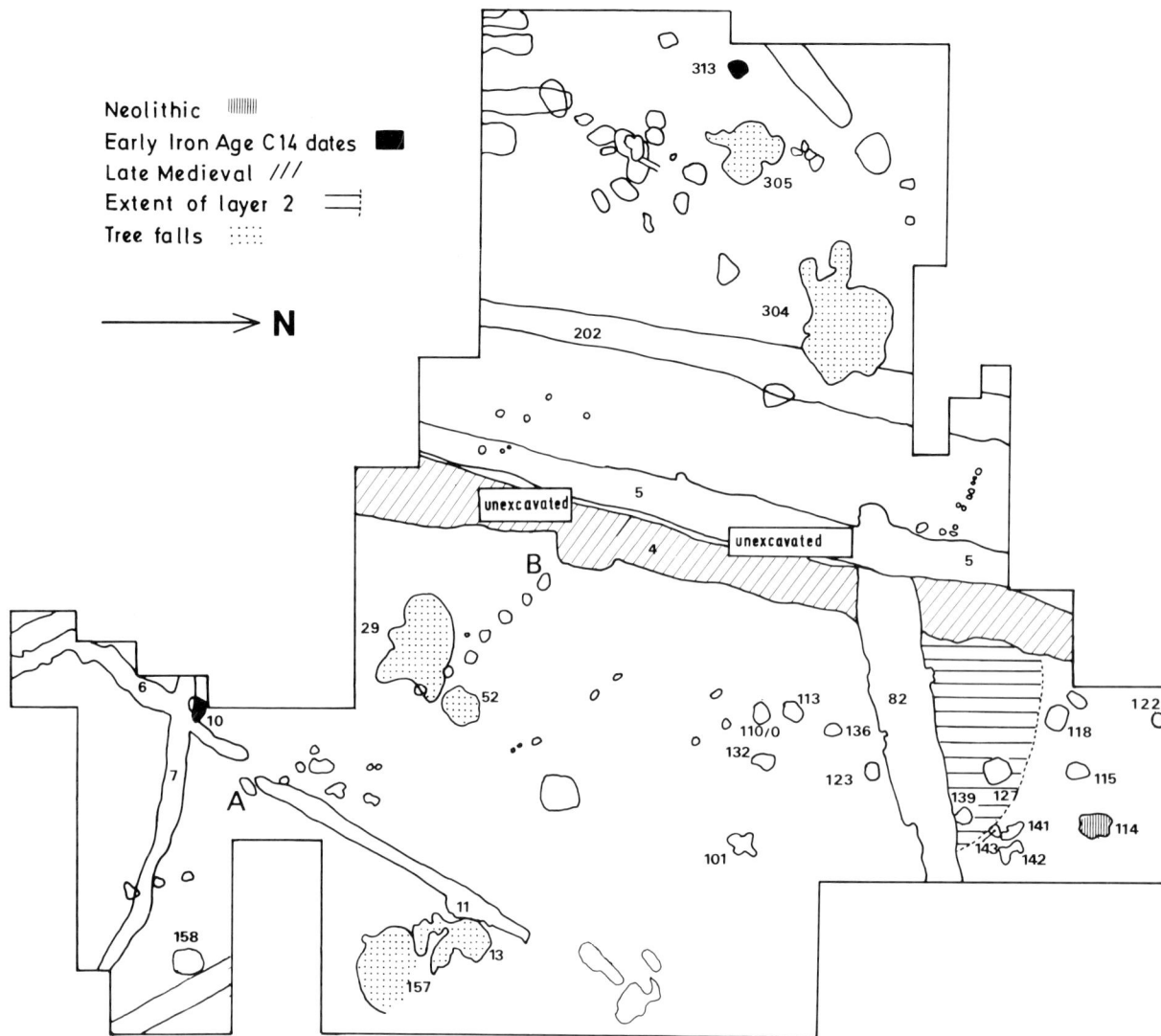

Fig 60   Distribution of later features

LATER PREHISTORIC PERIOD

The Later Bronze Age and Early Iron Age are represented by ^{14}C dates from F10 and F313 (Table 49), and the glass beads from the latter feature. Extensive traces of occupation of this date could be difficult to find in a site where much of the material was disturbed. If these dates belong to an aceramic period it is entirely possible that the relatively rapid stripping of the disturbed upper levels would have resulted in any other Early Iron Age material having been missed (Appendix 4).

EARLY CHRISTIAN PERIOD

Several sherds of souterrain ware were found, though unfortunately these never occurred in a significant context.

MEDIEVAL AND LATER PERIODS

A small scatter of wheel-thrown pottery was recovered, though never associated with any features. The possibility that it was connected with a late 12th-century refortification of Mountsandel Fort is discussed in Appendix 4. Sherds of post-medieval pottery were rather more common, though again they were usually found in disturbed contexts. One group, which included late medieval sherds and a hand-made everted-rim pot, was found at the base of the V-shaped east-west ditch, F4. These sherds occurred in lines 22–24 and were associated with the mortar slick. Stratified above them in the ditch fill were sherds of tygs and tripod-based pitchers. The only other associated find was a portion of a tyg found in stones at the base of the demesne bank. All other post-medieval material was unassociated. This includes the stoneware and Staffordshire pottery, much of which was found in the upper levels of the western area. The flat-bottomed ditches (FS5, 82 and 202) post-dated the main phase of post-medieval occupation and it is presumed that at this point the demesne bank was built roughly on the line of the earlier V-shaped ditch.

DISCUSSION

Relatively few features could be ascribed with any confidence to specific later phases of occupation. Unfortunately as so little excavation has taken place in the areas around ring-forts and on post-medieval military encampments there is little hope of dating groups of features by comparison with known dated examples.

The tree-falls appeared to post-date the Neolithic as several contained Neolithic potsherds, but none contained post-medieval pottery. The run of post-holes noted in Fig 60 as line A–B cut across tree-fall F29, which could make this line almost a modern field boundary. The other fixed point in a relative chronology is the ^{14}C date for F10 (Table 49). The foundation gully (F6) pre-dated it while F7 post-dated it.

Finally a dating sequence can be suggested for the later features, but it must be seen as a series of suggestions based on very little evidence.

Two types of features dominated the western area: long, relatively shallow gullies which could have belonged to any period, and several small rectangular pits whose fill was sterile. The pits could date from the post-medieval period, when large wooden structures could have been erected. It was one of the major disappointments of the excavation that traces of post-medieval activity in the western area were so scanty. In the central area a line of post-holes with rather lighter fill cut across the Mesolithic deposits. These lay at right angles to the ditch systems and may have marked a gap in the bank. It is almost certainly significant that it was in the adjacent part of F4 that the post-medieval pottery occurred. The bank itself consisted of such amorphous brown soil and was so heavily disturbed by tree roots and rabbit burrows that there was no evidence of any layers or phases of construction. However, it is probable that the bank consisted of two phases: an initial post-medieval defence which ran out from the fort, and a refurbishing of the bank in more recent times.

In the eastern part of the site was a scatter of pits which appeared to post-date the Mesolithic phase of occupation. Some, such as F114 and F158, contained sherds of Neolithic pottery, and it is therefore tempting to see all the other pits as Neolithic in date. The long foundation trench (F6, F11) also contained one sherd of Neolithic pottery, which might

encourage the suggestion that this was one wall of a Neolithic house. There are, however, two reasons why this may not be part of a house: no second wall was located, and no concentration of pottery or Neolithic artefacts was found in this area. It is highly improbable that so little Neolithic material would have been found either in surface collection or excavation if this was indeed a house site. Therefore perhaps the single potsherd in an area of disturbance is best seen, like the few microliths, as an accidental intrusion. Ultimately it is a question of assessing the ^{14}C date of 435 ± 70 bc and its context (Table 49). It did apparently overlie the foundation trench which would suggest that this structure must have been Bronze Age or Early Iron Age in date. The other gully (F7) is best seen as Early Christian (Later Iron Age) in date as it was like several found on the open settlement of Gortgrib, Co Down (Warner, personal communication). The only outstanding group of features were the lines of post-holes running NW/SE across the eastern part of the site. These were only dated in relation to the tree-falls and were distinguished by their lighter fill. Unfortunately Wimpey's test pit cut across the point where this line of post-holes should have met the V-shaped post-medieval ditch.

SUMMARY

The Neolithic remains can be best described as a thin scatter of material across the site. No significant structures could be associated with this period but it appeared to be best preserved on the western and northern edges of the site. Later traces of activity were even rarer, and it was only in the post-medieval period that specific activity could again be identified. This was the V-shaped ditch which appeared to join with a ditch round Mountsandel Fort (Appendix 4).

Mesolithic Occupation

The Mesolithic material will be examined in its separate component parts and only finally will there be any attempt to provide an integrated picture of the site. The material will be discussed under the following headings: layer and pit types; the hut area and other structures; distribution of material; and interpretation of ^{14}C dates.

LAYER AND PIT TYPES

Unfortunately the exact categorization of the layer types has been hampered by what we have described as the minimal expectations for the site (above, page 4). The richness of the faunal remains in certain layers was seen as of primary importance and therefore no overall sampling programme was created, with the result that there was a bias towards retaining material from what were considered to be rich layers while other layers which were deemed to be of less interest were often not sampled. There is therefore no objective record of chemical composition or of the density of faunal remains, charcoal, hazel nut shells, artefacts, etc, in the full range of layers within a range of pit types. The soil chemistry results analysed in Chapter 7 were obtained from a restricted series of samples, but these do allow some assessment of their nature.

Four distinctive layer types can be recognized. (1) *Occupation soil*, a rather general term, has been used to describe soil which was usually black because of the addition of particles of comminuted charcoal. This type of layer filled many of the pits or was found on top of other more organically rich layers. (2) *Black organically rich layers* contained large quantities of charcoal or burnt hazel nut shells, and sometimes also some quantities of bone and artefacts. (3) *Light organically rich layers*, of light-coloured soil, were often associated with large quantities of burnt bone and in some instances numerous burnt artefacts. This layer type was not only found in the pits but could occasionally be found in small patches in the occupation soil. (4) *Greasy black layers* were only recognized as a distinctive type at a late stage in the excavation programme. Besides some charcoal they sometimes contained numerous fragments of burnt stone.

As certain rather similar layer types were found within apparently different feature types a detailed analysis of the soil was carried out. This analysis was limited to a number of samples which had been kept back from sieving (Chapter 1). Even the simple, normal, pedological investigations done in the Department of Geography, Queen's University, Belfast, have shown that certain layers which were distinguished in the field as organically rich were very high in phosphates (Appendix 2a), but these methods did not allow for any distinction within these richer layers. The work of Hamond on trace elements and Doggart on magnetic susceptibility (Chapters 7 and 8) has shown that the processes which led to the formation of these layers may have been very complex. Ironically groups of related dark and light organically rich layers often appeared to be similar in character when analysed for trace elements and magnetic susceptibility, yet groups of similar layers in different pits appeared to have different origins. Thus F31/0, a central hearth, had trace elements which Hamond has suggested were associated with food preparation and according to Doggart contained traces of burning, while certain layers in F100/2 and F31/5, which were not hearths, had much more evidence of burning. Doggart in particular has shown that there may be a significant difference between a burnt layer and a layer which contains elements such as charcoal. The presence of charcoal does not imply

that a fire was necessarily lit at the point where charcoal was found. It is unfortunate that there were few control samples from the centre of the site from layers which were not apparently rich, as some of the pits which appeared to contain only occupation soil could have contained unburnt organic material. Hamond has already noted the presence of extra organic matter in the trace-element analysis. The work at Mount Sandel on the different origins of certain layers, and thus the primary and secondary functions of pit and hearth types, can hardly be described as satisfactory, but the discovery of such complex methods of formation may stimulate others to approach this problem with a greater awareness of its complexities.

Apart from problems of chemical composition there appeared to be significant differences in certain types of artefacts in distinctive layer types. Unfortunately many individual layers in certain complex features were not recognized sufficiently early during excavation and therefore the numbers of instances where totals of artefacts associated with specific layer types can be relied upon is seriously reduced.

A simplified table (Table 45) shows clearly that there were significant differences between the various types of organically rich layers on the one hand and a range of material found in occupation soil on the other. F56/1 and F29 were taken as representative of the range of material found in occupation soil in features.

The most noticeable difference was the significant increase in the numbers of microliths found in the organically rich layers, 21% to 43%. Obviously it would be unrealistic to compare the western area alone (2%) with these layers, but even the hut area (7%) and the F56/1/F29 group (11%) had lower proportions of microliths. One other significant variation was in the proportion of the material which was burnt. In the occupation soil usually 5 to 15% of the material was burnt, but in the organic layers the proportion of burnt material usually exceeded 30%. The numbers of microliths which were burnt can often exceed 75%. This apparently includes both individual types of microliths and the class as a whole.

Two conclusions can be drawn from this information. First, though the organically rich layers contained the remains of fires they had a significant addition of material which was unburnt. The implications of the chemical analysis were also that these layers contained material which, as it had not been burnt, had deteriorated and was discovered only through soil chemistry. The second conclusion is that microliths were deliberately being burnt, as exceptionally large numbers of burnt fragments have been found in these layers. It is almost certain that they were burnt because they were parts of broken

	Bone rich	Char rich	Char & bone	Hut occup	Indust	F56/1 & F29
Blades	125	139	183	1270	1579	403
Burnt	57	50	61	124	78	53
Flakes	36	22	29	255	1379	177
Burnt	18	3	13	63	120	39
Total weight	1.416 kg	1.173 kg	1.851 kg	12.073 kg	40.563 kg	6.034 kg
Burnt	0.731 kg	0.610 kg	0.952 kg	2.803 kg	2.953 kg	1.427 kg
Scalene triangles	54	38	39	92	38	44
Burnt	45	27	28	28	13	14
Narrow rods	24	25	18	45	10	14
Burnt	19	16	13	12	1	5
Broad rods	1	3	11	22	13	6
Burnt	1	0	5	7	5	2
Needles	5	8	5	17	6	9
Burnt	4	3	4	2	0	2
Other microliths	6	16	12	28	16	13
Burnt	5	12	4	4	0	3
Blades	125	139	183	1270	1579	403
Triangles	54	38	39	92	38	44
Ratio of blades to triangles	43%	27%	21%	7%	2%	11%
% Burnt triangles	83%	71%	72%	30%	34%	32%
% Burnt blades	45%	36%	33%	10%	5%	13%
Total weight burnt	52%	52%	51%	23%	7%	24%

Table 45   Selected categories and selected ratios of artefacts found in certain layer types

composite implements, and less effort is required in making fresh implements than in repairing or, using Schiffer's term, 'laterally recycling' portions of a broken artefact (1976). In fact the manufacture of

Feature	Mean diameter mm	Actual depth mm	Nos of microliths
F31/0	1000	180	65
F31/4	460	270	18
F31/5	500	240	27
F31/3	500	200	8
F56/5	980	210	12
F56/4	1150	280	47
F56/2	970	240	32
F27	830*	180	11
F46	500	200	1
F23	550	150	20
F22	420	190	14
F9	740	150	1
F16	1040	200	12
F36	850	110	3
F40	550	180	—
F105	900*	130	1
F107	1000	120	—

Table 46   Feature volume against frequency of microliths (*indicates only 50% preserved)

microliths would require virtually no effort, while making the wooden parts of these implements and hafting the microliths—presumably held in place with resin—would need much more time. The significance of the large numbers of burnt microliths and their association with certain types of faunal remains has already been discussed in Chapter 3.

There was no quantitative correlation between the numbers of microliths and the volume of the layers within which they were found; there was also only a marginal difference between dark and light organic layers and numbers of microliths. The apparent lack of distinction between the two layer types can be seen above in Table 45, while the absence of any even correlation between microliths and volume can be seen in Table 46.

There is, of course, a potential increase between volume of layers and number of microliths, which is a law of nature rather than anything derived from the excavation, but in fact this potential is not always realized in an increased number of microliths. The only noticeable correlation was that when a pit had larger quantities of burnt hazel nut shells and a bone layer that pit would usually contain larger numbers of microliths. The implication is that burnt hazel nut shells were more likely to occur round a household hearth rather than an outside fire, and thus the replacement of microlithic forms would appear to have been a social activity carried out near a communal hearth.

Tree-falls

At least six examples were found during the excavation (Fig 60). In the area of Mesolithic occupation they were characterized by the appearance of a dark annular ring cut into the subsoil, but on excavation it became clear that the inner area of subsoil was in a secondary position. This can be seen in Fig 11B (F29). These features ranged in size from 3.20 m maximum width, F29, to examples such as F52 which was only 1.30 m across.

The most common type is characterized by F29 where there was a large depression, often close to 1 m deep. The base was filled with a mixture of occupation soil and sand lenses, and this was sealed by a thick layer of sandy loam, the redeposited subsoil. These features occurred on the rather loamier portion of the site where the trees may have been more deeply rooted. Tree-falls have been noted on many sites of many periods and their implications have been discussed by Newell (1981). However, his Dutch examples appear to have filled to the top with lenses of occupation soil and subsoil (Fig 61A) while the Mount Sandel examples filled first with occupation soil and then with redeposited subsoil. The difference may lie in the nature of the subsoil: at Mount Sandel it was perhaps more compact, and if the roots were left leaning over the hole then eventually much of the soil from amongst the roots

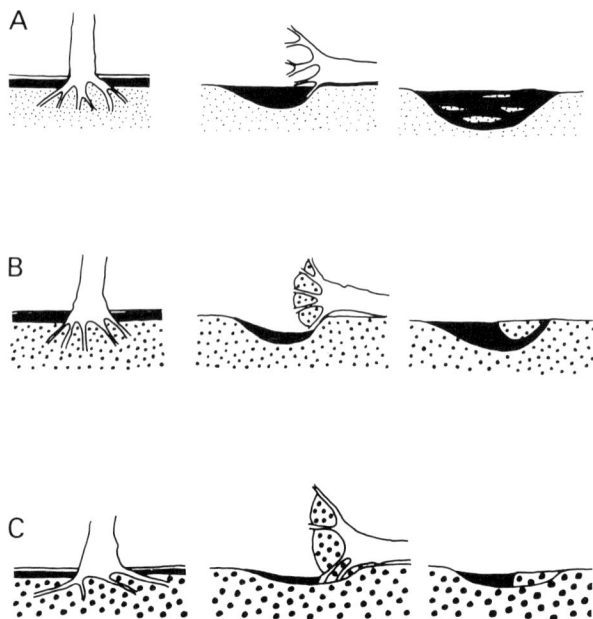

Fig 61   Tree-falls: (A) soft sandy subsoil, (B) loam-clay subsoil, (C) compact gravels

would fall back in large lumps, but probably only after much of the occupation material adjacent to the hole had been washed into it (Fig 61B).

A second, less distinctive type of tree-fall was found. These were two rather shallow examples, F157 and F13, found in an area where the subsoil was a compact gravel. F157 was partly excavated during the last season and revealed a section in which the occupation soil was limited. Even allowing for erosion this tree-fall was rather shallow and the occupation soil ended abruptly. The difference between the two forms could be accounted for by the trees causing the second type having rather shallow root systems, and the roots on sliding forward into the hole thus impeding the accumulation of occupation soil (Fig 61C).

Essentially these forms were annular in shape though with extensions which could be lines where roots were dragged out of the ground. They usually had relatively shallow-angled slopes compared with their depths. The one obvious exception was F52, which had the annular ring of black soil and was filled with redeposited natural. It had, however, relatively steep sides and so must be regarded as a problematic member of the group.

Obviously, as noted in Newell 1981, recognition of these forms has several interesting implications, not the least important of which is reconsideration of whether there are any genuine Mesolithic pit-dwellings.

Pits

Numerous pits and hearths of many different sizes were excavated, and separating them into meaningful groups proved to be one of the major problems of the excavation. They were not only scattered over a large area but varied in size and contents. It was originally hoped that a correlation might emerge between layer types and pit sizes.

The layers have been divided into major groups dependent on their co-occurrence and contents. They can be considered relatively homogeneous in character, and so few classificatory divisions are necessary. These are (0) occupation soil, (1) dark organic layer, (2) dark and light organic layers, (3) light organic layers, and (4) greasy black layer with burnt stones. Layer types 1–4 were often found below a layer of occupation soil (0). Where this upper occupation soil was missing it was almost certainly either because it had been ploughed off or because the pit was cut through occupation soil and the uppermost layer had inadvertently been excavated during removal of spreads of occupation soil.

The pits selected for examination were those considered to be Mesolithic in date and sufficiently intact to provide a reliable estimate of original size. Those on the eastern edge of the site, where

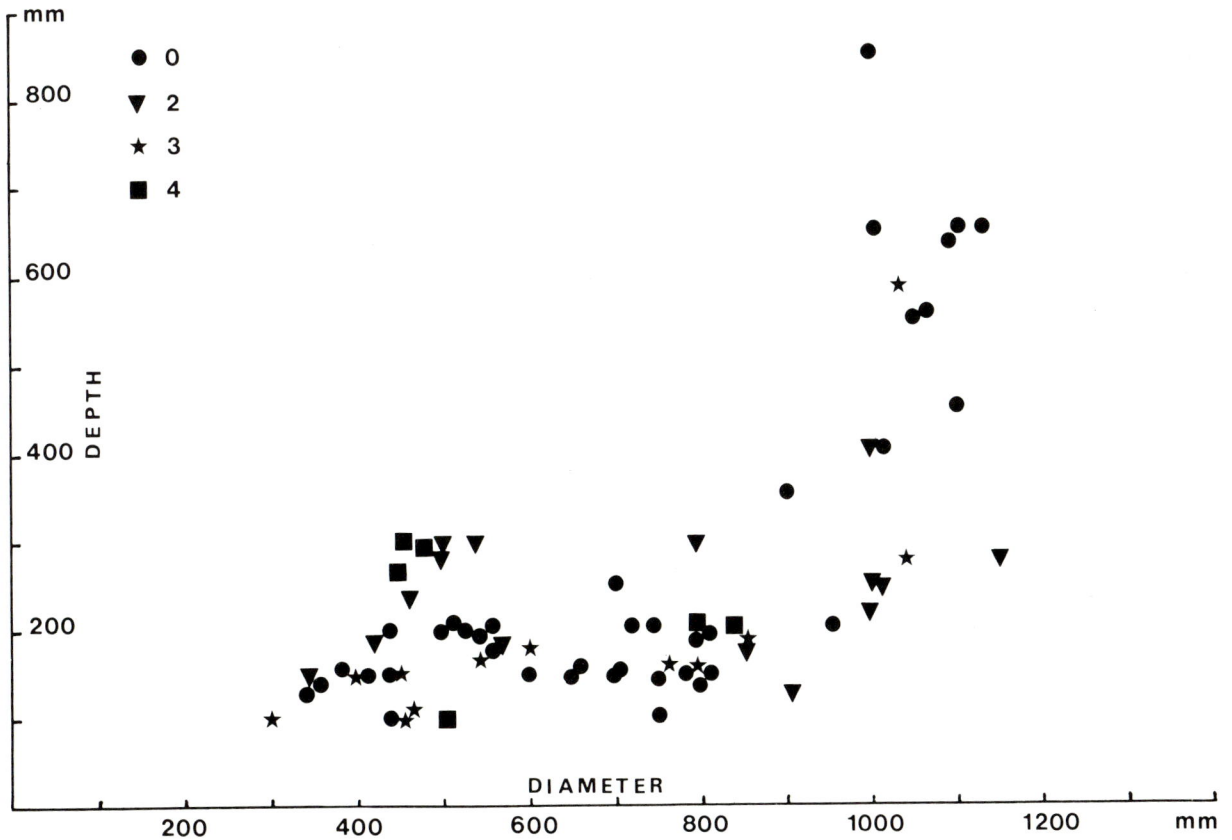

Fig 62   Scatter diagram of depth/diameter and types of fill associated with Mesolithic pits

ploughing had done most damage, have had an arbitrary 50 mm added to their depth to compensate for partial destruction.

Figure 62 shows that there was a relatively poor correlation between layer types and pit sizes. The only possible grouping was that of the larger, deeper pits which were lacking in the organically rich fills, but this does not necessarily mean that there was a direct correlation between depth and fill. Fig 62 does suggest three distinct sizes of pits. Amongst those less than 400 mm deep (in fact usually 300 mm or less) there is a bimodal tendency: (1) small pits less than 600 mm across and (2) those more than 700 mm across. Between these two groups there is little proportionate increase in depth as the diameter increases. There is also group (3), those over 400 mm in depth which are usually more than 1 m across.

The one variable which appears to explain most adequately the correlation between pit size and fill is that of location. Most of the organically rich layers were found in the area adjacent to the huts, while the largest pits tended to be found away from the huts. An *a priori* assumption was made that the huts were centred on the hearth group, 56/2–56/7, and all pits were plotted according to whether they were (A) within 5 m of a point at the centre of the

hearth group, (B) within 10 m of the central point, or (C) more than 10 m from the central point. (These lie with two exceptions between 10 and 15 m.) Fig 63 illustrates the change between the inner and outer areas.

The outer area was characterized by numerous large deep pits and a scatter of small pits. The fill was

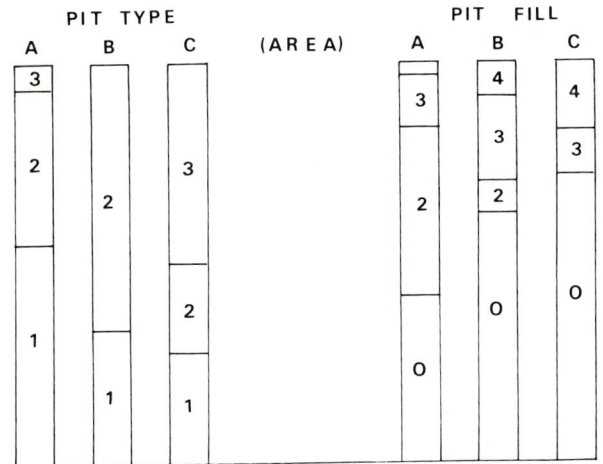

Fig 63   Location (A, B, C) against pit type and layer type (each column represents 100% in each area)

usually occupation soil with occasional examples containing some bone. The innermost area had a very high proportion of organically rich layers and fewer large deep pits. Therefore one can argue that the fill of the pits was related to the area in which they lay rather than to the type of pits. The only possible exception is that the pits with rather greasy black fill and burnt stones were rather deeper than would be expected and, as can be seen from Fig 63, they often lay out on the edge of the site.

DEEP PITS   In one sense these were represented by complementary attributes to those which characterized the tree-falls. They seem to have been steep, straight-sided pits which, on the basis of the size scatter diagram, were over 400 mm deep. In fact many were over 500 mm deep. Where an individual pit could be distinguished, such as F56/1 or F74, it was roughly 1 m in diameter. There was one particularly large group, F209/211, where several pits cut one another, and F56/1 also appeared to have been recut (Fig 11A). The major problem is whether the large secondary recutting of F209/211 and its refilling with subsoil was Mesolithic in date. The shape of the pit suggests that this was an artificial phenomenon and not a tree-fall. Although the thin layer of occupation soil in the secondary portion cannot be accepted as firm evidence, the absence of later artefacts and Neolithic or later pottery is a strong argument (albeit circumstantial) that the secondary recutting of this group of pits was Mesolithic in date. In fact F74 was also refilled with the local subsoil and was only found as a result of differential drying.

There was thus a minimum of five deep pits in one small area and two others which might have been obliterated by the secondary phase of recutting. The eastern edge of F304 (a tree-fall) was also reminiscent of one of these deep pits, and this edge lay within a metre of the western edge of F209. Not only was there a tendency for the large pits to occur in the outer part of the site, but many of them appeared to have been placed in the same specific area.

While it is possible to identify some of the processes associated with the location of these pits, little is known about their precise function. As noted earlier the contents of the various types of pits do not relate to their function. Three reasons for digging these pits can be suggested: that they were 'borrowing pits' (sources for earth), flint quarries, or for storage. The objections to the first two suggestions are almost identical: the pits appear to be too regular in shape for holes that were either supplying raw material for walls or flint nodules, and the tendency to dig a pit in roughly the same locality where much of the upcast would be occupation rubbish is not consistent with either of these explanations. A further

weakness in the flint quarry explanation is that much of the flint used on the site appears to have come from a beach deposit.

The third suggestion is that they were storage pits. As will be shown below (Chapter 12) there is every reason to believe that there could have been a food-procurement crisis in the second half of the winter and therefore food storage would have been essential. Storage would not necessarily have been in pits, but examples of possible meat-storage pits are known from the Palaeolithic, and there is archaeological evidence for storage of salmon in pits on north-west Canadian sites which date from the last two thousand years (Ames, personal communication). One possible way in which meat and fish could have been stored would have been in dried or smoked form. Plant foods could also have been stored. Obviously in the wet conditions which might have existed in the winter anything in pits would have needed protection, and the presence of slight depressions on the floor of F56/1 and possible stake-holes for pegs on one wall might suggest that the pits were lined.

One major problem outstanding is that there is no way of telling whether the slightly shallower pits such as F100/2 and F74 were used in the same fashion as F56/1.

SHALLOW PITS   The pits of this type have been divided according to their mean diameter into broad and narrow shallow examples. There is no correlation between depth and diameter, and this suggests that many may have been used to contain fires and that the need for a good oxygen supply limited their depth.

Broad shallow pits   Amongst those over 700 mm in diameter some had a definite bowl-shaped section and a few had a hard, cinder-like concretion round the edge. These pits do not appear to have had any particularly characteristic type of fill.

Only five pits had cinder concretions round the edge. These were FS56/2, 56/4 and 56/5 in the central hollow, while F91 in the centre of another hut also had the same type of concretion. The only pit with the concretion which appeared to have been outside a hut was F109, which may have been outside a small tent-like structure on the northern edge of the site (see below). F31/0 could have had a similar edge but because of ploughing its top had been destroyed. Several stones were, however, placed round the edge of this pit where it had cut through an older refilled feature. The only other pit which contained stones was F56/5.

The distribution of these pits appears at first sight unremarkable. They were slightly more common in the 5 to 10 metre band than in the 0 to 5 metre area. Those in the inner area included almost all the examples which were over 900 mm across, the exceptions being F91 and F16, which was possibly at the centre of another hut. These features could therefore be considered as fireplaces which, like some at Pincevent (Leroi-Gourhan and Brezillon 1966), have been used so extensively that they have been extended. The larger hearths appear to have been associated with the arcs of post-holes while a scatter of rather smaller, perhaps transitory, hearths in this group were found outside the hut areas.

Narrow shallow pits These pits tended to be rather straight-sided in comparison with the bowl-shaped profile of the broader group. Although scattered across the site they were most common in the inner area of activity. While there was only one very obvious group of broad pits, those interpreted as the central hearths, the narrow forms occurred more frequently in little groups and had often been recut (Fig 13). At least three of these groups can be identified in or around the hut area (Fig 64).

There are many possible explanations for these small pits, including cache pits or even (Binford, personal communication) bedside hearths. However, many appeared to be close to the edges of the huts and in some instances were stratigraphically very late (see below for analysis of blade declinations), while one (associated with F31/0) cut across a hearth which in turn cut across the edge of one of the huts with which the pit might have been associated as an internal feature. In particular F23 pre-dates the post-holes of huts V or Z (see below) and therefore also pre-dates hut W, so it is unlikely to have been an internal pit. Similarly FS46, 20 and 22 may post-date the build-up of occupation soil associated with these huts.

The small pits could have been used for numerous different purposes but they are simple in form and little evidence survived to indicate their range of function. One can only note the tendency for some to occur in small groups as if to support some structure although, as can be seen in Fig 64, within each group there were some pits which had been recut and this suggests that each group represented more than one phase of activity. This clustering, clear in Fig 64, suggests that they could have been used to hold large posts for substantial structures such as storage racks, and the evidence of frequent recutting suggests that the structures were frequently re-erected on the same spot.

While small pits do occur on many Mesolithic sites their function remains unknown. One of the most obvious groups for comparison are those from Moita de Sebastiao (Roche 1960) but these tend to be rather narrower and deeper than the smaller pits at Mount Sandel and must belong to a very substantial structure or structures.

Discussion of pits
There was one noticeable difference between the central hearths and the other pits. Four of the five hearths which contained faunal remains had a large quantity of fish bones, and these features also had a rather more homogeneous fill. Unfortunately no other pits could be designated with certainty as central hearths, but an obvious possibility is F31/0, which contained pig bones and little else. The other possible example of an internal hearth is F27, though this suggestion is based purely on size. Again it contained large quantities of pig bones. The smaller pits and F100/2, which appeared to contain rubbish (often more heavily burnt), exhibited a less selective trend towards either fish or pig bones than any individual hearth. This could be a reflection of the difference between individual events and a general gathering-up of rubbish.

There is of course a temptation to explain away the huts of the central hollow as smoke-houses for curing salmon, though there are certain problems with such a simple interpretation. One problem relates to the seasonality, in that more evidence of eel-smoking would be expected as eels tend to run later than salmon and so would be used as a stored resource. The locational evidence of tools and evidence for other forms of food processing also suggests a much more general use of the hut area (see below, page 138).

THE HUT AREA AND OTHER STRUCTURES
As a preliminary to any discussion of the organization of the hut area we must determine to what extent the various features and post-holes associated with it derive from a single or numerous phases. The latter possibility was suggested by the observation that many features were filled with the same black soil as constituted the occupation soil, and so it is possible that they were cut through the occupation soil and belonged to a somewhat later phase. One test for this was to measure the declination away from the horizontal for every blade found *in situ* in a 5 by 5 m strip of the overlying occupation soil. These measurements may indicate areas of disturbance, since there is a greater tendency for blades to lie at an angle when the soil has been disturbed, for example if pits have been cut through. The result of the measurements can be seen in Fig 65. Numerous angled blades were found close to the edge of certain pits, but the numbers involved were unfortunately not sufficiently large for statistical analysis. If the total numbers of blades in each group listed at the bottom of Table 47 are examined, it is clear that fewer than 1 in 10 are disturbed by 40°+, but it is also obvious that several features had much higher frequencies of blades lying at 40°+ than would be expected in an undisturbed context. These include FS56/1, 100/6, and 46, which were almost certainly

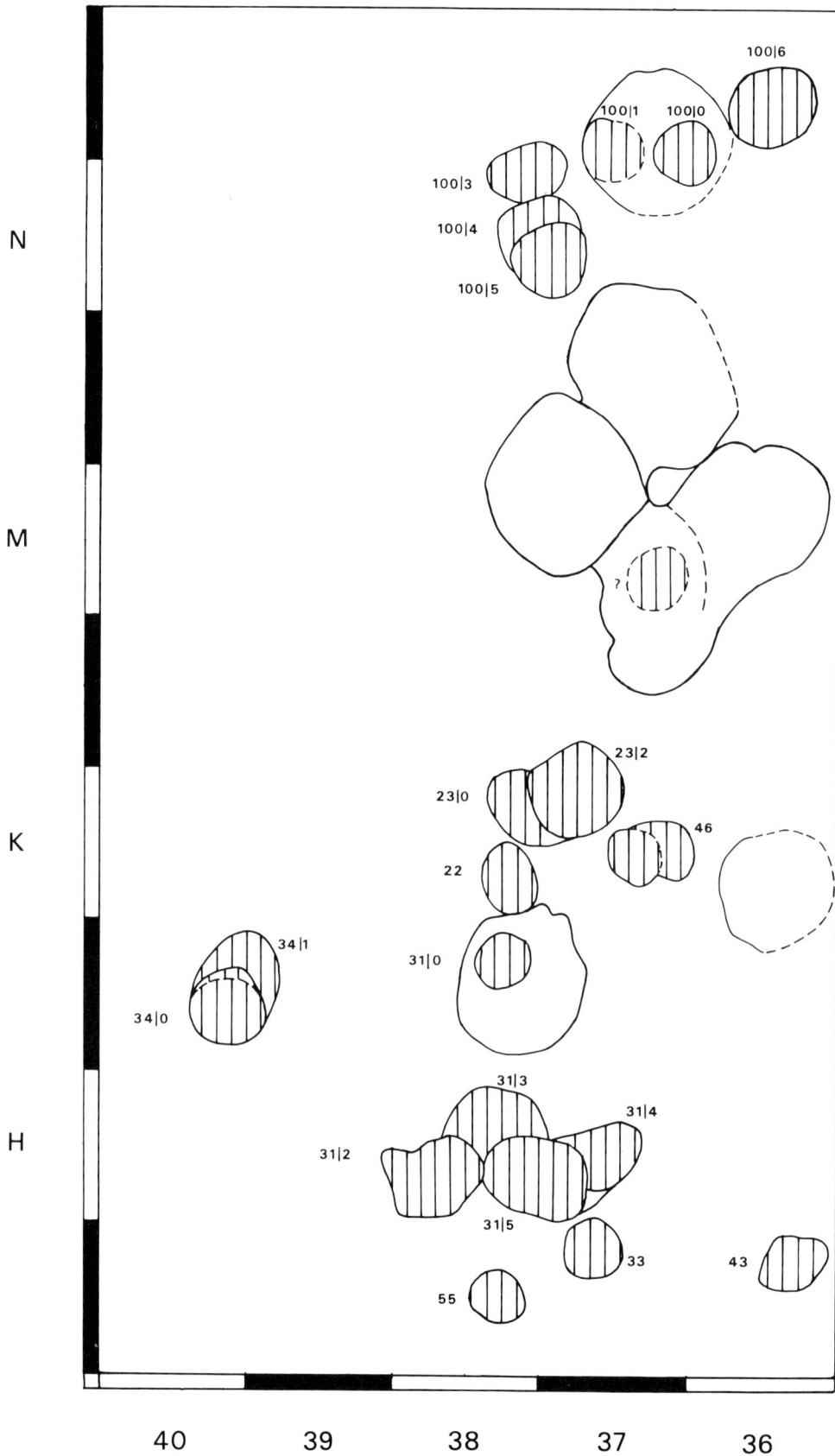

Fig 64   Location of narrow pits (shaded) in hut area

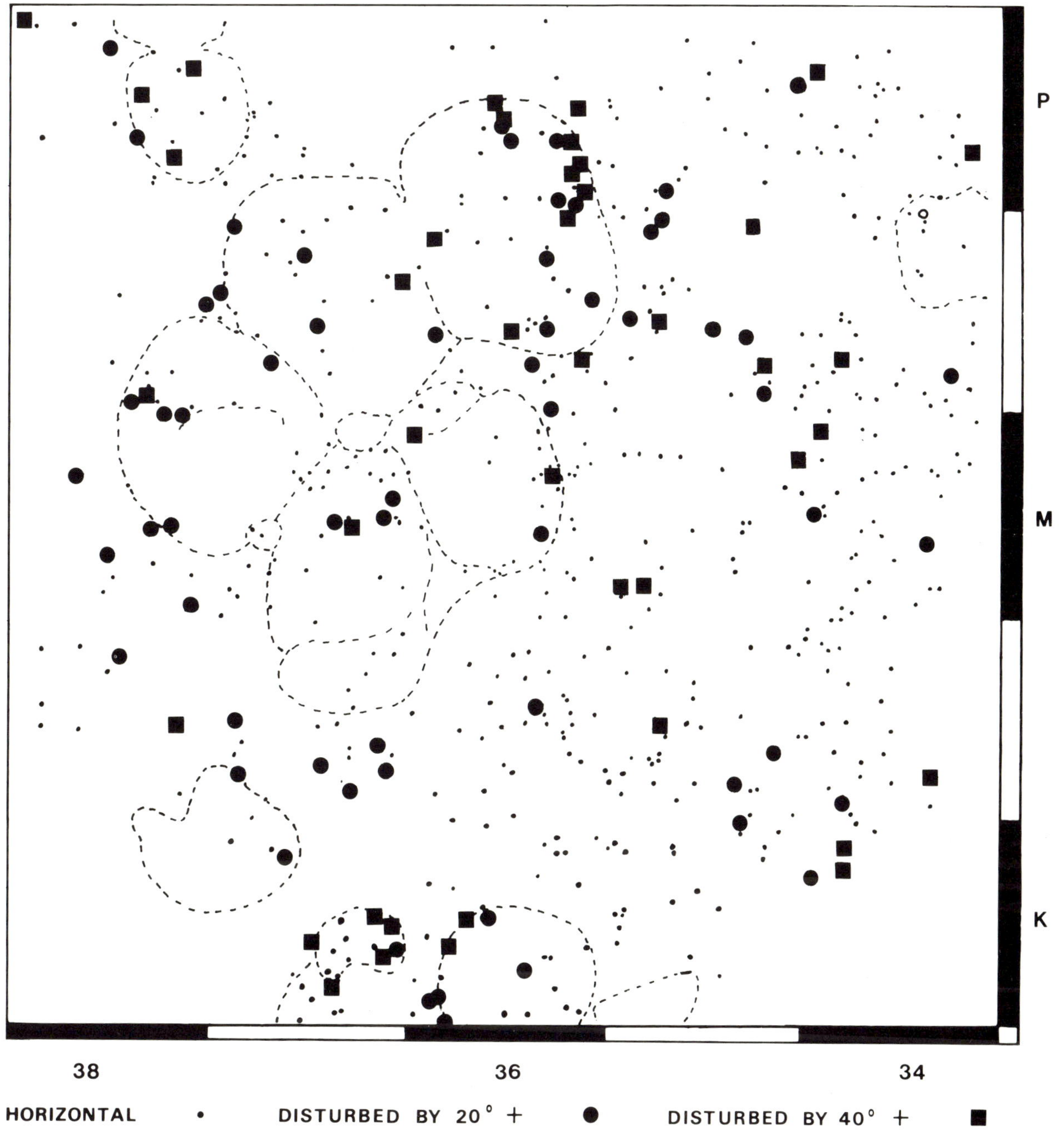

Fig 65 Blade declinations in hut area

HORIZONTAL • DISTURBED BY 20° + ● DISTURBED BY 40° + ■

intrusive pits. The four central hearths are not included in the obviously intrusive group.

Other more circumstantial forms of evidence exist which also suggest that some of the features post-dated the main phase of occupation. There was a markedly higher concentration of burnt hazel nut shells in the grid squares within which FS100/0–2 and 22 occurred. The underlying features also contained large quantities of burnt material, and so the upper portions of these features may have been excavated as part of the occupation soil.

The central hearths and the post-holes represent the main body of evidence for the huts, but the obvious implication of the blade declinations is that there were also other huts erected elsewhere, resulting in pits cutting through the area of the hut hollow where the occupation soil had survived.

While it has been possible to define hearths, large

Feature	0–20°	20–40°	>40°	Total	Comment
F100/6	7	1	3	11	>40 possibly higher
F56/3	8	4	1	13	20–40 possibly higher
F56/2	5	1	0	6	No significance
F56/4	17	4	1	22	No significance
F56/1	19	8	8	35	>40 possibly higher
F56/5	23	3	1	27	No significance
F23	4	2	0	6	20–40 possibly higher
F46	7	1	3	11	>40 possibly higher
F20	10	4	2	16	>20 possibly higher
F50	7	0	0	7	No significance

Totals measured within area tested

468	61	39	568

Table 47   Distribution of declination of blades from vertical in occupation soil above selected features

pits and small pits, there are numerous examples of hearths which could have been placed outside, unassociated with any hut. Some, such as F16, which was the same size as the central hearths, were also almost certainly hearths, but with the erosion of the old ground surface many post-holes had been obliterated. There is therefore little chance of establishing how many huts were erected on the site and how many fires were associated with each specific building phase. Instead the analysis of the hut structures must concentrate on identifying a few of the huts in one specific area, admitting that there will always be a certain random 'background noise' associated with building phases for which most of the evidence has been destroyed. This is obviously a less than ideal solution as it means that no explanation can be offered for many of the post-holes on the site, leaving the excavator open to the charge that the shapes of the huts are fabrications with no basis in reality. However, the arc of post-holes round the lip of the hollow does create the basis for a working hypothesis that the huts were circular and that there were several huts in the dwelling hollow, with at least one other to its north. Therefore the purpose of this section is to attempt to identify the shape and components of an individual hut, as well as to estimate how many were built in the hut area and in the area to the north (see Fig 1 for feature numbers and Figs 9 and 15 in Chapter 2).

Unlike foundation trenches, post-holes rarely cut each other and in an apparent palimpsest such as the hut area the few overlapping post-holes and other features do little to provide a detailed horizontal stratigraphy. The presence of Feature 31/0 cutting the arcs of post-holes in J/37–38 shows that as well as the individual pits referred to earlier, there could have been huts with central hearths which post-dated

the main building phase in the hut area. Unfortunately it was not possible to identify an overlap between huts centred on FS91 and 83 and those around 56/2–56/7. The latter group of hearths can be shown to have some stratigraphic sequence in that F56/5 cut F56/7, and F56/2 cut F56/4. The later pair were both two-phase hearths as F56/5 also cut 56/6 and F56/2 also cut F56/3.

The suggestion has been made that these huts were essentially curvilinear and that they had a central hearth. There is no evidence that the huts were built with internal support. Inclination of many of the post-holes suggests that saplings may have been bent over and tied to another member on the opposite side of the hut. Setting the posts into the ground at an angle reduces the strain on the walls and obviates the need to clutter the centre of the hut with supporting posts.

The arc of post-holes round the lip of the hollow suggests that the huts may have had a radius of between 2.5 and 3 m. However, if circles are drawn from the presumed centre of the original hearths (on the assumption that there were four huts) it can be seen that the assumption of approximately circular huts does not quite fit the evidence of the post-hole pattern. In particular the concentration of post-holes in line 34 lies slightly too far north to delimit circular huts. The evidence suggests that the huts may have been almost egg-shaped, with the flattened end of the ellipse lying south of the hearths.

If ethnographic archaeology can be appealed to, it is clear that there is no reason why these huts could not have been asymmetrical in plan. In the case of the Alacaleuf hut (on which Fig 66 is partly based: Bird 1946) the post-holes are not equally distributed round the edge of the hut. It is possible that the walls of the Mount Sandel huts would have been made up of short runs of substantial posts, which created the framework, with lighter stakes driven in between. This pattern of short runs of small stake-holes can be seen in J/35–37 and in L–M/33.

Unfortunately there was usually no clear difference in the colour of the fill within the post-holes, and it was impossible to identify a sequence of huts on the basis of fill. Generally the post-holes were filled with slightly charcoal-stained soil (Munsell colour 7.5 YR 3/2). The only instances where differences could be observed were where post-holes had cut one another. Here rather subtler colour differences could be seen, and it was noted that the earlier post-holes would not be so impregnated with charcoal (Binford *et al* 1966). But these differences are so slight that they cannot be used to distinguish between specific huts.

A record of the charcoal recovered from each post-hole was examined in the hope that one hut might have burnt down, but the post-holes with the greatest quantity of charcoal proved to be those

Site of
entrance

Site of hearth

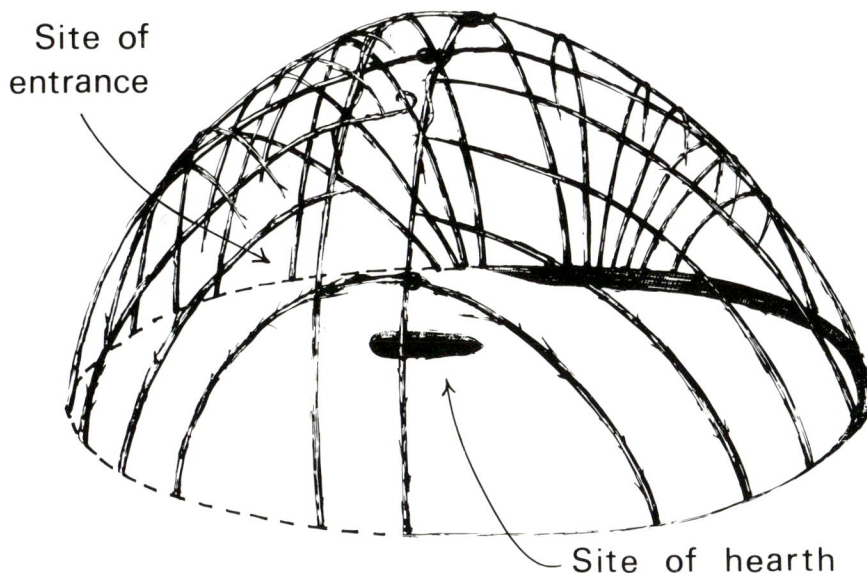

Fig 66   Hypothetical reconstruction of hut framework during construction

adjacent to the area where charcoal was commonest in the occupation soil. Only one post-hole, ph 184, contained sufficient amounts of charcoal to suggest that it had held a post which burnt down *in situ*.

Because of the difficulty of determining the sequence of the post-holes we are left with two different hypotheses for the hut area: first, that there was only one large hut built in the hollow, and the hearths and post-holes represent a continuous process of minor adjustments, and second, that there were several different structures built in the hollow, each with its own central hearth. To pursue this question a simplified site plan has been produced for part of the eastern area, with different weightings for various types of post-holes (Fig 67). Those which were angled are marked in a heavier outline and have an arrow, while other oval post-holes which may originally have been angled are marked with simply a heavier outline. Deep post-holes (100 mm+) which are narrow in comparison with their depth are also noted. This simplified plan shows that the structural post-holes, the large angled examples, were found over such a wide area that they cannot be part of a continuous rebuilding of one hut. Portions of arcs of other huts can also be identified to the north. It is also noticeable that the angled post-holes pointed inwards toward the centre of the huts. Therefore there is every reason to believe that a series of huts was built, each curvilinear in outline and each with a central hearth.

The solution outlined in Fig 67 for the number of huts can only be considered the most feasible, and it would therefore be pointless to attempt to attribute each post-hole to a specific hut, as in several places an individual post-hole could be attributed to three huts.

The destruction by later pits and tree-falls has also seriously impaired any chances of defining a complete arc, but there are enough post-holes to suggest that these were enclosed huts rather than simple open shelters.

It has already been noted that F56/4 (hut X) and F56/7 (hut V) were earlier than F56/2 (hut Z) and F56/6 (hut W) respectively and two groups of post-holes did cut across each other: ph 321 cut 319 and ph 301 cut 300 (Fig 9). This evidence suggests that hut W, associated with F56/5, was the latest in the sequence. It was also the hut with which the small arcs of stake-holes marked on Fig 67 were associated.

In summary, therefore, it is suggested that most of the huts were roughly 6 m in diameter, though they were not absolutely circular. They appear to have had a hearth set slightly off-centre. The northern edges of the huts were built in a rather more robust fashion than the southern edges. There were no traces of any entrances but these were probably on the south and south-western perimeter, an area which has been disturbed by later activity. The problem of the hut entrance, and internal divisions, will be further discussed below (page 138).

To the north two other arcs of post-holes survived (Figs 15 and 67). One, which ran round F91, appeared to be associated with a slightly larger hut than those further south. Unfortunately, the post-holes in the south-east quadrant were too badly damaged to be attributed to this hut with any certainty. The western edge has been obliterated by the post-medieval ditches, which had also destroyed most of another hut. On the opposite (W) side of these ditches there was no clear continuation of this arc: although there were numerous post-holes in the

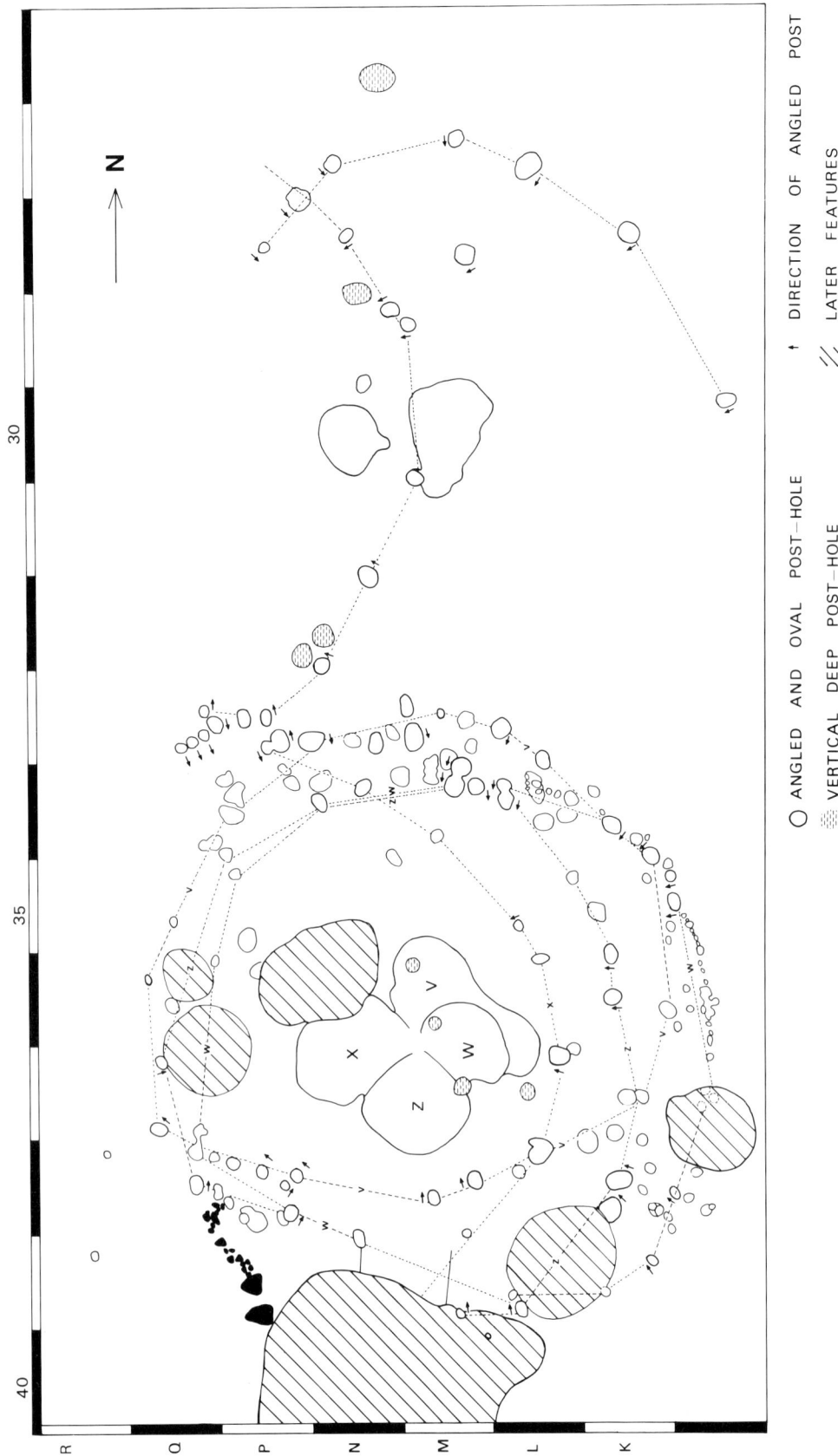

Fig 67   Schematic representation of hut outlines in eastern area (letters refer to suggested phases of construction)

○ ANGLED AND OVAL POST–HOLE

▨ VERTICAL DEEP POST–HOLE

↑ DIRECTION OF ANGLED POST

∥ LATER FEATURES

appropriate area, none were large enough to be clearly identifiable as structural posts for the edge of the hut.

One of the most difficult problems is that of the method of roofing the huts. If, as suggested below (Chapter 12), the site was an autumn-winter base camp then a substantial form of covering might be expected to provide insulation. One reason for the rather heavier, robust nature of the northern edge of the hut structures could be that the sods removed from the hut floor were used to build up a wall round the outside of the hut. (The absence of palaeosol in the hut area has already been noted in Chapter 2.) The clearing of the whole of the floor of a hut would have created an area of over 25 square metres of sod which could have been used to build quite a high wall round the hut. The height and extent of the wall remain uncertain, but there is no reason why a wall over 1 metre high could not have been built round the hut.*

This, of course, raises the possibility that each hut could have been left up between seasonal visits to the site, and each structure used for several seasons. This method of construction using sods would mean that only a limited area would be roofed with hides—probably deer-skin. The total area of a hemisphere of 6 metres diameter is 56 m², and using sods perhaps only 50% would be covered by skins. This would have the advantage of reducing the quantity of hide required and the need for transport, as one square metre of good deer-skin could weigh between 1 and 1.5 kg. When a new hut was built, probably in part by cannibalizing material from the standing hut, this would entail removing the extant wall and replacing it with a new one. This may have been a limiting factor in hut construction. This problem, combined with soil accumulation round the hut and problems of hearth relocation, could have forced the eventual moving of the hut to an entirely new location.

The surviving hut area must therefore be seen as part of a larger sequence of hut construction at Mount Sandel. The sequence within the hut area suggests a desire to keep the hut in this little hollow. The sequence of huts based on central hearths could be X (F56/4), Z (56/2), V (56/7), W (56/5) (Fig 67), and perhaps the artificial enlarging of the hollow was associated with the second two hearths.

Other structures

There were traces of a smaller, slighter structure on the northern edge of the site (Fig 68), defined by four shallow gullies which outlined an area 3 m across, not apparently associated with post-holes. It may have

been a tent whose edge was held down by a small bank; it may have been similar in character to Poggenwisch (Von Rust 1972). Owing to erosion little of the old ground surface was preserved inside the structure, but the gullies contained only a small scatter of Mesolithic artefacts. Two other feature complexes lay east of this structure. There was a group of post-holes whose plan might suggest a porch, and a hearth. These features were so contiguous that they were unlikely to have been contemporary. As there were other post-holes nearby it would seem more reasonable to assume that they were part of some other unidentifiable structure, and as the post-holes were quite substantial it is unlikely that they would have supported a porch outside a tent (Fig 68).

The hearth had, like those in the main hut hollow, a cinder-like concretion round its edges. There was also a scatter of stones running out to the north-east of the hearth, some of them burnt. A thin layer of occupation soil had survived in the area adjacent to the hearth, but the extent of surviving occupation soil seems to have been conditioned more by the limits of the hollow than by the soil's original distribution. The extent of scatter of archaeological material was therefore almost certainly conditioned by post-occupation erosion. Another problem arising in this area was that several pits were impossible to attribute to any period. It has already been suggested (above, page 24) that most of these were rather later in date than the Mesolithic phase of occupation.

There were slight traces of other structures which were not necessarily huts or pits. The most noticeable were groups of up to four angled post-holes. At least four sets can be identified. Two of these sets lay on the edge of the hut area (Fig 9). One group in Q/33, based on post-holes 143–144, was relatively clear, while the other group in P/35, based on ph 324, was rather less certain. The other two groups lay on the north-western edge of the site (Fig 82, A'–C'/27–28). So far it has not been possible to identify any support in front of these post-hole groups. The post-holes were as large as those associated with the huts, which suggests that large posts had been placed together in a group.

A second, equally enigmatic feature was the gully running NNW/SSE from the northern edge of the hut hollow (F42, Figs 9 and 15). It may have been a drainage gully but it did not appear to run down a slope. It did not protect the hollow, nor serve as a drip-trench.

There are obviously still a large number of post-holes which have not been explained. Some could have belonged to huts which were not sufficiently well preserved to be detectable, but a number of post-holes need not be explained in this fashion. The most notable example was the post-hole

---

* Taylor (personal communication) has found a Mesolithic structure at Priddy (Somerset), slightly more irregular in outline than at Mount Sandel, and roofed with earth.

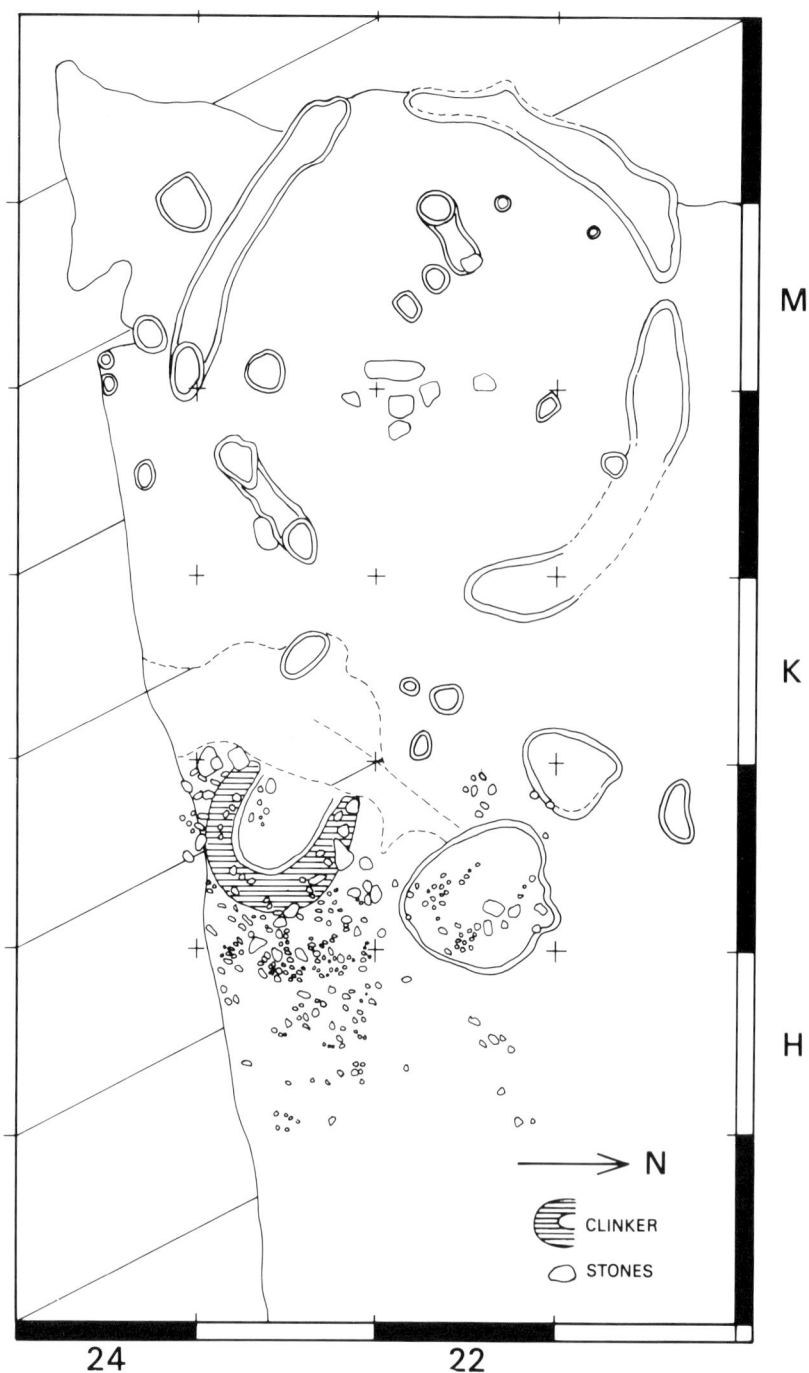

Fig 68   Composite schematic plan of northern hut area (diagonal hatching indicates FS4 and 82)

stratified below the cinder concretion which divided F56/2 and F56/5. This, and several other relatively deep post-holes (Fig 10, no 544) in the same area, some of which clearly post-dated the hearths, did not fit into any pattern of huts and were vertical rather than angled. As many of them were over 300 mm deep they could have been parts of substantial structures. Further north other similar, large, deep post-holes were found, which could have been parts of the extra-hut site facilities. Many meat-drying racks were relatively flimsy structures which would not have required substantial posts (Binford 1978, figs 3, 5–11), but fish-drying and storage racks, such as those illustrated by Schalk (1977), are much more extensive and it is possible that some of the post-holes at Mount Sandel survived from this type of structure.

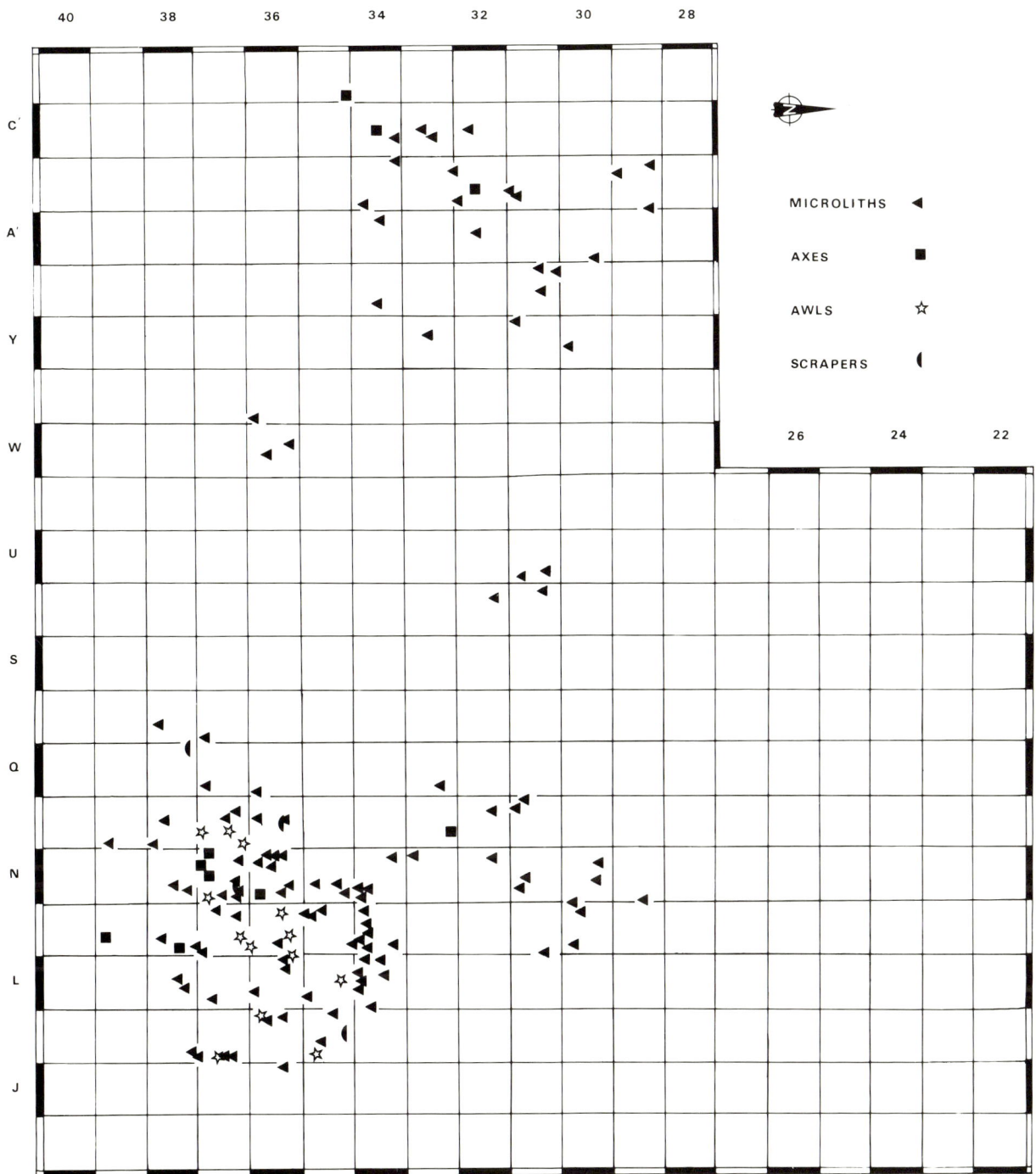

Fig 69 Distribution plan of point-plotted retouched tools

DISTRIBUTION OF MATERIAL

Most Mesolithic sites are rather lacking in structural remains and a heavy reliance has usually been placed on the distribution of the stone artefacts (Price *et al* 1974), but as Mount Sandel has produced a certain level of structural information, an attempt will be made to compare the distribution of artefacts with various site facilities.

Unfortunately owing to the croded nature of the site only certain specific areas of occupation survived, with the result that methods of analysis such as nearest-neighbour-analysis could not be employed because of boundary problems. Some problems in presentation also arise from a change in recording systems mid-way through the excavation.

Both the point-plotted distribution of retouched tools (Fig 69) and the gridded distributions of various categories of material (Figs 70–76: microfiche) show how discontinuous the areas of survival were. Therefore instead of analysing the material from the site as a unit, certain recognized areas will be examined for intra- and inter-unit variation.

The hut area

The major problem in assessing the significance of intra-site variations for the hut area was that the occupation soil had been partly ploughed away and so there was no easy method of pinpointing significant clusterings of material. Figs 70–76 clearly indicate that the archaeological material was most concentrated in the northern half of the hut area and, as the section shows (Fig 6), this was where the occupation soil was at its thickest. Therefore any simple analysis

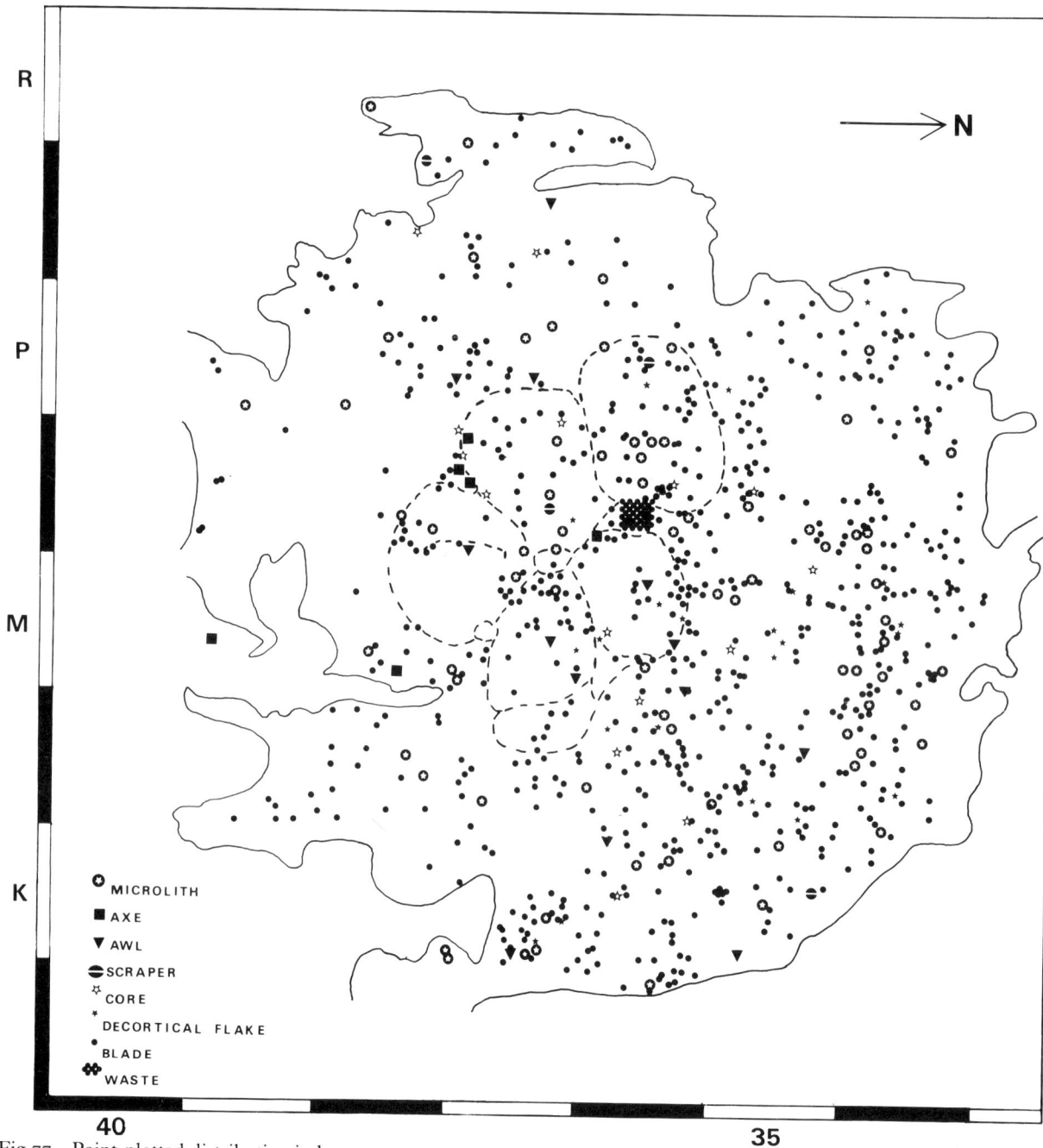

Fig 77   Point-plotted distribution in hut area

would tend to reveal that most types of artefacts and waste were found to the north-east of the hearths.

Fig 77, which marks the location of some of the retouched tools, shows that there are some tendencies to clustering which cannot be explained by the relative thickness of the surviving occupation soil. It shows the overall distribution of microliths, with large numbers being found in the north-eastern part of the site. With the thicker layer of occupation soil in

that area, this is the type of distribution which would be expected, but it is notable that the micro-awls and axes did not cluster in the same areas as the microliths and it is, perhaps, also possible to argue that the scrapers were found in areas where microliths were relatively few.

Similar tendencies to clustering can be seen by examining the gridded material (Fig 78). Here the advantages are larger quantities of material and a

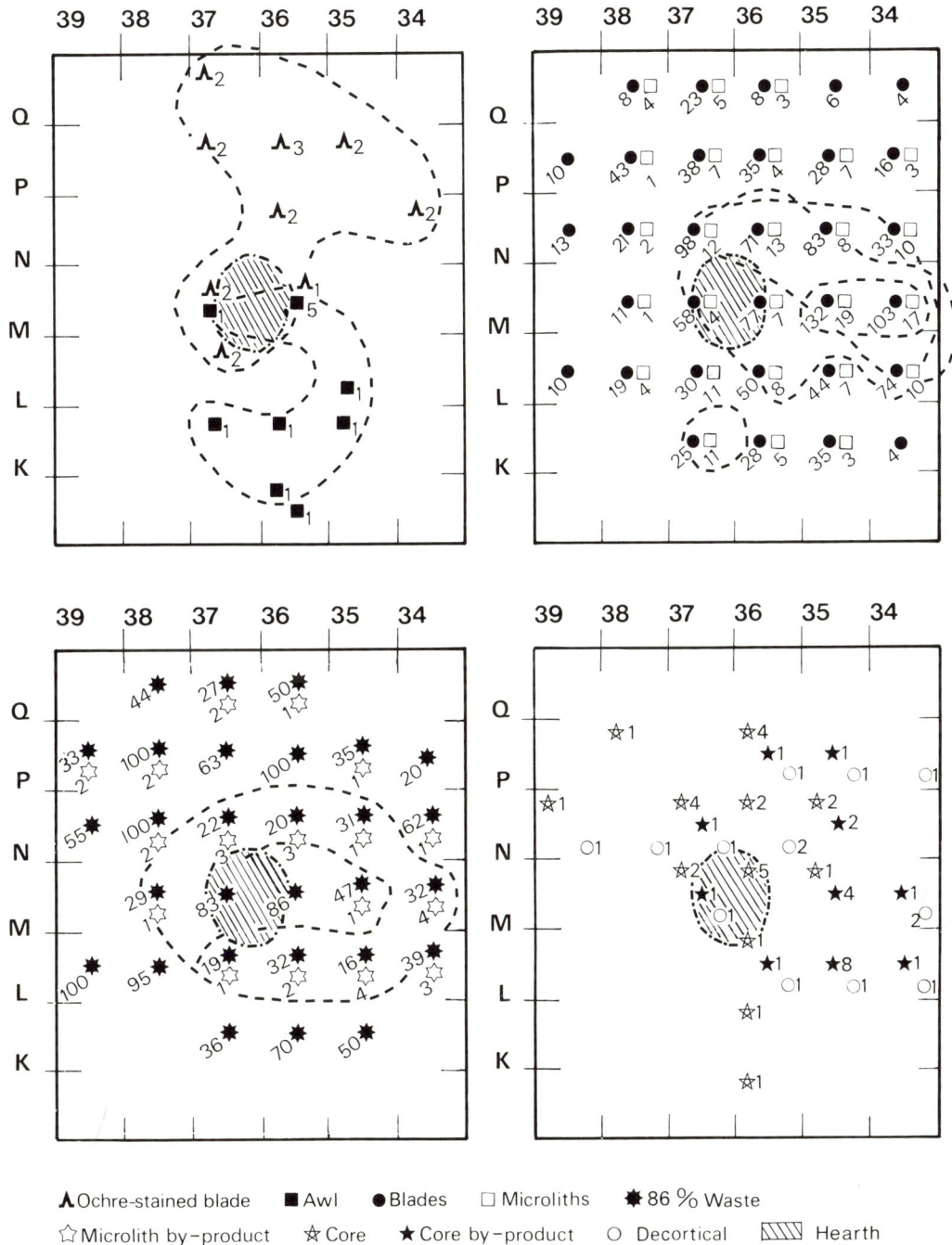

Fig 78 Distribution of material by metre square in hut area

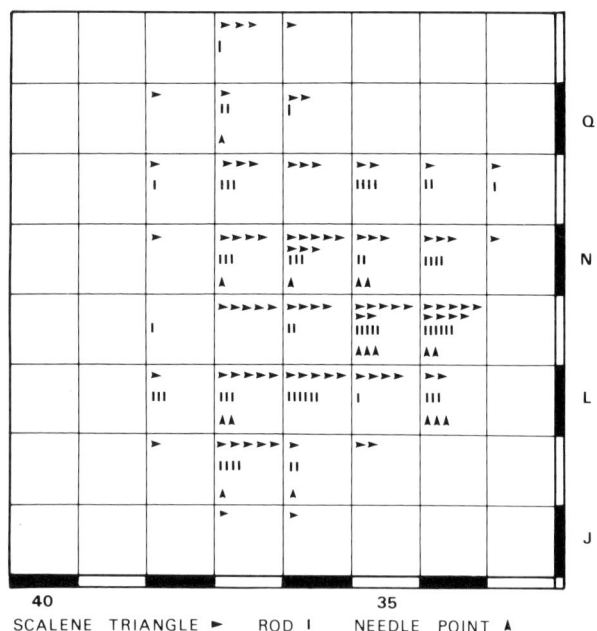

SCALENE TRIANGLE ▶   ROD ▮   NEEDLE POINT ▲

Fig 79   Distribution of different types of microliths by metre square

greater range of types, but these advantages have to be weighed against the change from point analysis with all its potential to a system where there is a restricted number of units. In order to overcome the problems of partial survival of data, ratios between types of material as well as absolute numbers need to be examined.

Within the gridded material discrete clusters can be identified and these include the micro-awls (noted already) and ochre-stained blades. The former concentration lay north-east of the hearth area, while the latter lay to the north-west. Discrete clustering of different types of microliths is not detectable (Fig 79), except for the needle points found in the north-eastern corner. The only other noteworthy concentration of material was the large quantity of charcoal in the northern part of the hut.

One major problem arises from the large quantity of material inside the hut. In particular, there appears to be extensive evidence of blade production which one might not expect inside a hut. It could therefore be argued that these blades did not belong to the phase of occupation of the site when the huts were being used, or belonged to a phase when the hut still stood but had been abandoned, being used perhaps as a windbreak. However, the ^{14}C dates suggest rough contemporaneity within the main phase of occupation, and as certain pits, dated slightly later, such as 46, 100/0–2 and 22, cut through this occupation soil, this material does not apparently represent reoccupation of the site at a significantly later date. The fact that in the north-eastern corner,

where a substantial layer of occupation soil was preserved, there was no evidence that the blades were stratified above the microliths (Fig 7) also suggests rough contemporaneity with the rest of the material in the hut hollow.

If the total weight of material is taken as an index of production then it can be seen that there is a greater accumulation of material in an area running NE/SE on the north-west edge of the hearths 56/2 and 56/4 (Fig 70: microfiche). As has been noted earlier this is not entirely commensurate with the distribution of the greatest density of artefacts. In order to overcome problems of variation in numbers across the hollow, the ratio of blades to debitage was plotted as a rough index of where flint-working activities may have taken place (Fig 80). This suggests an annular concentration of waste material which, unfortunately, point-plotted distribution did not reveal, as it did not extend to all material but (as noted on page 4) only to retouched tools, blades and certain types of industrial waste.

It is particularly instructive to examine the distribution of the micro-burins and microliths (Fig 77) in relation to this probable annular flint-working area. Not only are micro-burins absent from the

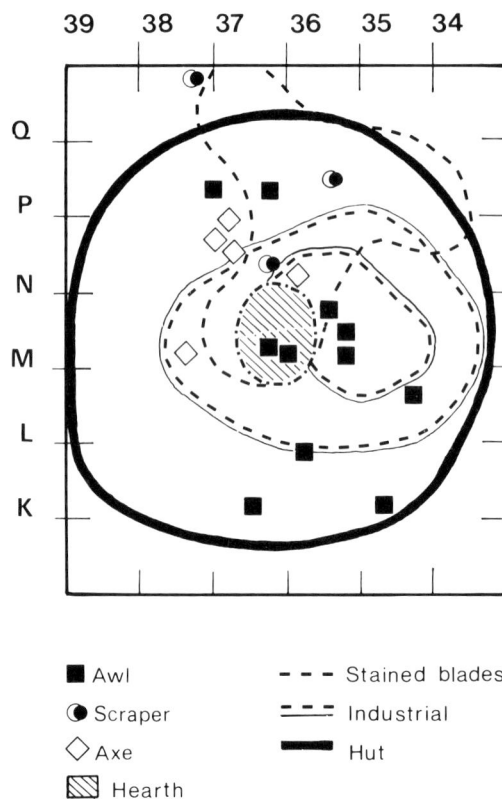

■ Awl   - - - Stained blades
◑ Scraper   ▬ ▬ Industrial
◇ Axe   ▬▬▬ Hut
▨ Hearth

Fig 80   Synthesis diagram of main activity zones in hut area

central area but microliths are also rather rare: possibly we have the results of rubbish cleared off a skin, creating a blank area, or a gradual accumulation of debris round a worker. The latter is a less likely explanation according to both Binford (1978a) and Newcomer and Sieveking (1980) as small debitage (primary rubbish by its size) would almost certainly fall in front of a worker who was facing the light, while an annular pattern would seem to indicate rubbish disposal. In fact the small concentration of flakes noted in N/36 (Fig 77) could be in part the by-product of the manufacturing of an axe, and a number of axe-manufacturing flakes were found in this area, while they were relatively rare elsewhere in the hut. This distribution would equate with the type of pattern Newcomer achieved manufacturing an axe while sitting on the floor. The micro-burins appear to be products of microlith manufacture while—as appears to be confirmed by Dumont (Chapter 4)—the microliths found in this area are the used discards from broken composite tools. This would explain the relative lack of discrete clustering of specific microlith types in the north-eastern corner. This is again emphasized by the lack of correlation between the left-hand/right-hand ratio of micro-burins and microliths in the occupation soil: left-handed, 19 microliths and 2 micro-burins; right-handed, 11 microliths and 31 micro-burins.

Binford has suggested that certain patterns of discarded material can be recognized. The first is a 'conversational' pattern of small items dropped on the spot. This is annular in shape, usually round a hearth as noted by him at the Mask site (Binford 1978a). This can often be associated, when outside, with a tendency to discard larger items over the shoulder. The second is a pattern for work areas which, when inside, are usually placed at an angle to the hearth and in the front part of the hut, thus taking the best advantage of the light from two sources (Binford forthcoming). The distribution noted in the Mount Sandel hut does not appear to conform to either pattern. A possible solution could be that outlined in Fig 80, where a small initial flint-working area can be postulated alongside the hearth. The cores from this area were discarded along its southern edge, towards the inside of the hut (Fig 78), and possibly towards the entrance. If the hut existed when the flint-knapping was taking place this would be a natural process as suggested by Binford—to face the light and perhaps discard the cores in front. This pattern was interrupted by two events. F56/1 had cut through the western edge of this area, and thus most of the cores appeared to lie on the southern edge. Secondly, on the eastern edge the inner part of the chipping floor appeared to have been swept away, mostly into squares M/34 and L/35, thus leaving a relatively clear space in M/35 adjacent to the hearth, and particularly in M/36 where the largest concentration of awls and blades was also found. Other industrial by-products were equally rare in this area, such as micro-burins and core-rejuvenation flakes.

It can thus be argued that there was a small flint-working area within the hut, where large flakes were often used as the core pre-forms. The rather broad flake facets and the large numbers of core-rejuvenation flakes also suggest that this may have been a rather *ad hoc* session of flint-working.

It could be argued that this work took place in a prime area, beside the fire and in front of the sleeping area, which was cleared for reuse—marked by the large numbers of blades which may have been used in their own right and by the little group of awls. The other small concentration of artefacts on the extreme edge of the hut, the awls and microliths around K/36–37, may have been a cache.

The lack of material in the southern part of the hut can be explained by the thinness of the occupation soil, but it is of interest to note that the tree-fall, F29, appeared to contain the equivalent of at least six square metres of occupation soil (based on ground area and an assumption of a minimum thickness of 100 mm of occupation soil), and this feature contained relatively little in comparison with F56/1, which contained volumetrically the same amount of occupation soil or less. Therefore, as it can be postulated that artefacts and waste would accumulate in the area round the entrance, the paucity of material in F29 suggests that the entrance did not lie towards the south. Again it can be noted in Fig 80 that the ratio of debitage to the south and east of the hearth area is very low.

In summary, several specific activity areas can be identified in the hut and from their distribution it can be suggested that the entrance to the hut generally lay south-west of the hearth. So the scrapers and stained blades would have lain near the entrance, and we can recall that Dumont has detected traces of hide polish on the latter. Behind these, north of the hearth, lay the small chipping floor, and immediately adjacent to the hearth was a larger concentration of blades and micro-awls.

Ultimately we must return to the question of how many occupations are represented by the material found in the hut area. Hopefully we can safely suggest that the material recovered does not belong to a phase of occupation which post-dated the hut, and that due to rubbish disposal and clearing of the hut only a random sample of material from phases of occupation towards the end of the use of the hut hollow has been recovered. It is possible that if the huts were floored several phases of occupation of the hut area could have been present, but the material found in the hut area cannot be separated out into individual occupations. One can only note that on the northern edge the microliths usually occur in the middle of the occupation soil. It could even be that the thin scatter of material found above the level of the microliths represents either post-occupation accumulation or an inwards collapse of a sod wall round the edge of the hut. As there was almost certainly occupation on the site before the huts in the hollow were erected, it is likely that material had already accumulated in the sod. Of course these occupation layers are not absolute horizons and even a minor disturbance within huts would have inverted the stratigraphy. Therefore one can only note that whether the material relates to one or more hearths its distribution appears to take cognizance of the central hearth area and is consistent with a series of activities taking place within an enclosed area.

Other areas
Unlike the hut, the material in the western area appeared to lack any evidence of differential clustering. This can be seen in Fig 81. Here, as noted earlier, there was some clear evidence that extensive

flint-knapping took place and material had been dumped where it was worked. A small hearth (F335) was excavated in $B^1/31$–32 (Fig 82). There is always the possibility that the hearth was associated with the industrial area, but none of the outside patterns of accumulation noted at the Mask site (Binford 1978) could be identified round the edge of this small hearth. An incomplete ring of small items, as though small flakes had accumulated round the fire, was noted while a more diffuse pattern of large items was found outside this area. Instead, rather more specific concentrations of material in small heaps were found, in particular in B^1–$C^1/33$ and in $B^1/34$–35. While the limit of the concentration in W/36 was obviously a product of rabbit burrowing, this may have exaggerated another accumulation of waste. In Fig 82 areas where more than 15 and 25 pieces per 20 cm^2 were recorded have been delineated. These do not take cognizance of the existence of the hearths, and in fact one concentration partly overlay F335. The shape of this concentration may have been in part created by cutting by a later feature whose upcast could have

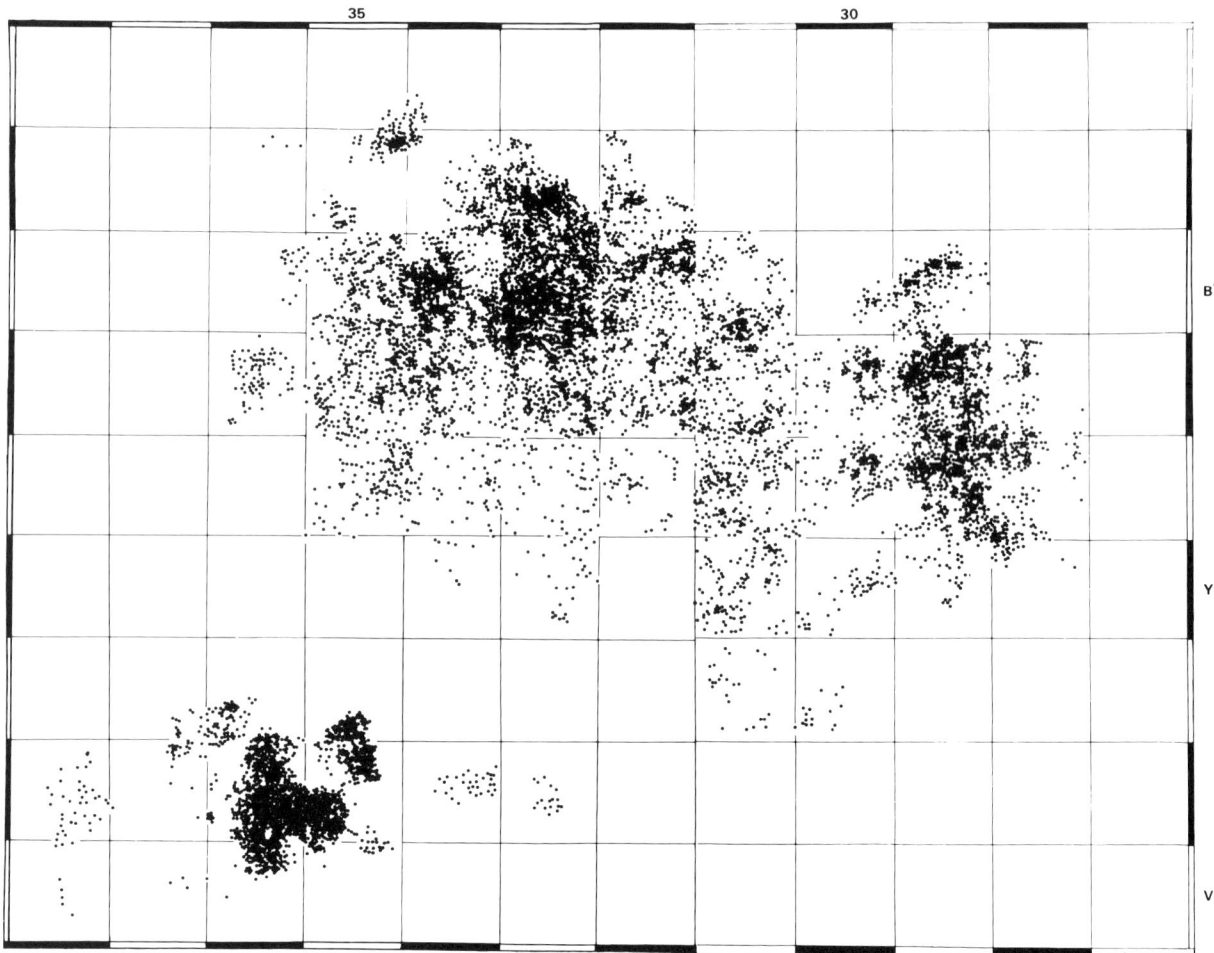

Fig 81   Distribution diagram of *in situ* material in central and western areas

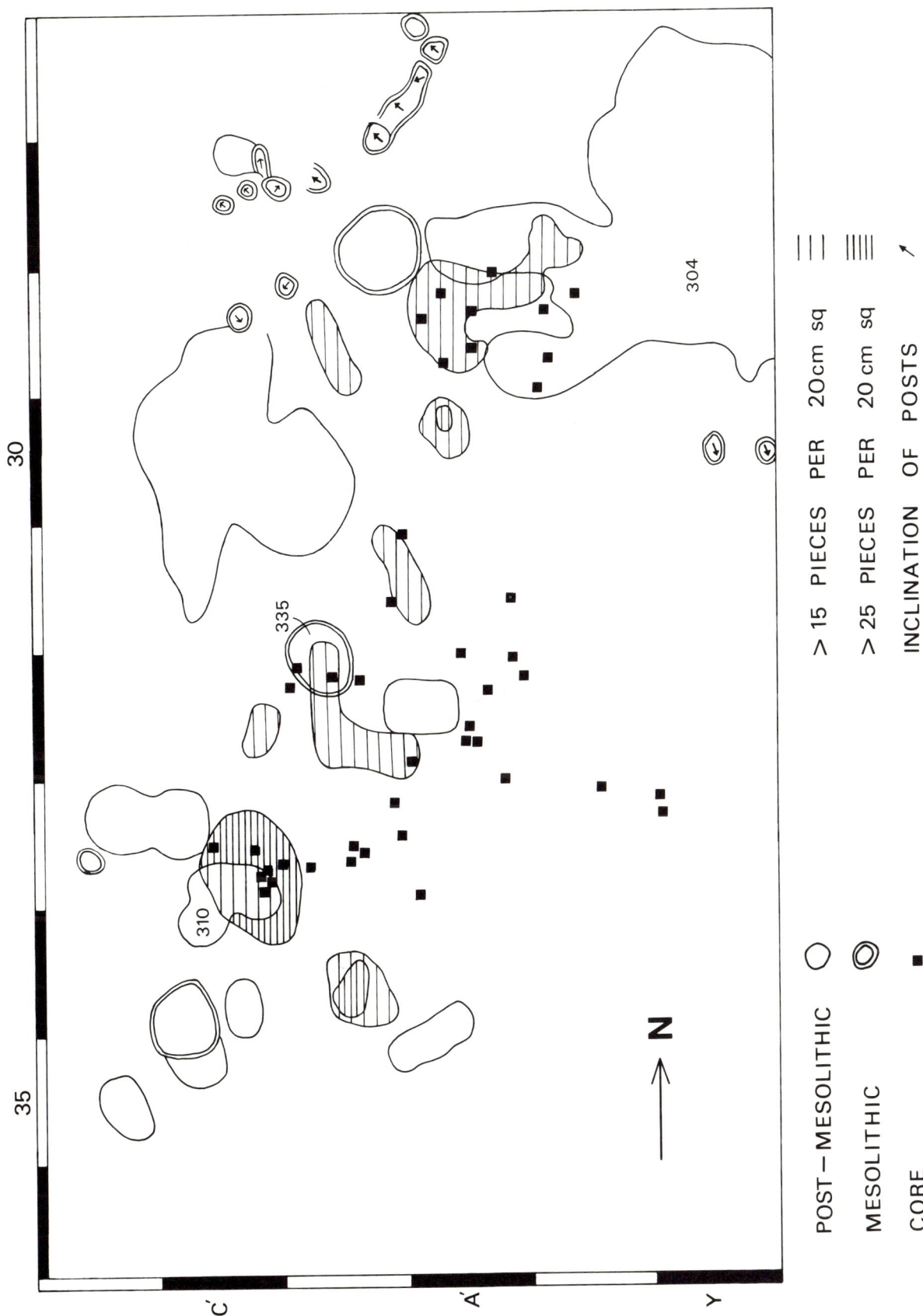

Fig 82 Synthesis of distribution map and related features

increased the density. Similarly the most northerly concentration, which had an irregular outline, could have resulted from the upcast from a tree-fall, F304. A third example was found near F310, where a more recent feature may have cut through. Therefore there were few specific concentrations which could with any certainty be assumed to have survived without post-depositional disturbance. In the few undisturbed areas the cores appeared to have been scattered outside the concentrations, possibly up to several metres away, perhaps indicating work going on outside rather than in an enclosed space. Unfortunately as these areas were often very close together it was impossible to separate specific events. One can only note that there was an area of flint-working activity along the western edge, and that in the area Y–Z/32–34 where the occupation soil was equally thick there was relatively little material.

It can be suggested that the hearths and perhaps the small scatter of microliths, many of which show signs of use (Dumont, Chapter 4), may belong to another phase of activity. Unfortunately most of the material was found within a band 80 mm thick which had suffered a certain amount of disturbance, and it is hardly surprising that no stratigraphic distinction could be found. It is tempting, however, to see two more groups of microliths, one associated with F335, and a more northerly group which may be associated with the hearths and post-holes in the north-western corner of the site.

There were other small areas of occupation soil, such as that on the northern edge of the site. This area, around F109, contained relatively little. Similarly the area immediately north of the hut, L–N/28–33, was neither sufficiently extensive nor contained sufficient quantities of material for detailed interpretation. It is probable that the latter represented the remnants of another dwelling area, while the number of cores in and around F109 suggested that this was, at least in part, an industrial area.

Comparison between hut and industrial area
It is not easy to justify a comparison between the hut and industrial area since there was no clear evidence that they were even part of the same phase of occupation. In fact, in spite of the degree of disturbance, there were obviously several specific work areas which could individually have belonged to different occupations of the site, such as A^1–B^1/29–30 and A^1–B^1/32–34. Conjoining of flint flakes at sites such as Pincevent (Leroi-Gourhan and Brezillon 1966) and Meer II (Van Noten *et al* 1978) has proved an effective method of demonstrating contemporaneity between disjointed activity areas. Unfortunately the lack of characteristics peculiar to individual nodules, combined with the homogeneous nature of the raw material (almost entirely cretaceous flint) and

significant changes within the individual nodule, make it virtually impossible to identify blade and flake joins. It can only be suggested that, as these flint nodules were probably not available in the immediate locality (see below, Chapter 12), these industrial areas represent components of larger, more complex sites rather than specific sites in their own right.

The observed differences in archaeological material which derives from these two areas is not so great as to permit one to make clear-cut distinctions between specific activity areas. First, differences in absolute numbers are a reflection of local factors such as flint availability: thus cores will be discarded more frequently on sites where flint is easily accessible, such as Glynn (Woodman 1977), while on sites where there is virtually no flint the cores will be used until they are exhausted. Thus absolute numbers of cores and decortical flakes could be a reflection of both duration of activity and availability of raw materials. A second problem is that as trends rather than absolute distinctions are being measured, it is hardly surprising that occasional small hearths should be found in the industrial area while some traces of industrial activity are found in the hut area.

If areas which are thought to represent different spheres of activity are identified, the distinction between these areas might be best seen in the relative differences in make-up of the assemblages found in them. It can be suggested that most finished products would be found in the hut area while most of the elements characteristic of manufacturing would be found in the postulated industrial area.

An assumption has been made that if there was no significant difference between the two areas then other elements should be found in the same proportion as the cores or total weight of flint. The actual differences are recorded in Table 48 and Fig 83.

Western area		Hut area	
107	Cores	25	
1579	Blades	1270	Significantly higher at 0.001
1379	Flakes	255	
8879 gm	Debitage	5965 gm	Significantly higher at 0.001
112	Decortical flakes	25	
19	Core by-products	15	Significantly higher at 0.001
8	Micro-burins	39	Significantly higher at 0.001
	Retouched tools		
17	Axes	8	Possibly just significant
83	Microliths	210	Significantly higher at 0.001
13	Other tools	36	Significantly higher at 0.001

Table 48 X^2 test of differences between hut and industrial areas using ratio of cores as a norm

Table 48 shows the application of a *chi*-squared test in which each group of material is tested against the number of cores. Many retouched tools are signi-

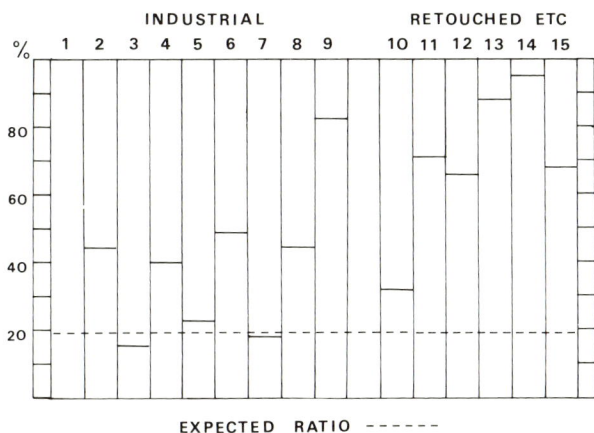

Fig 83 Relative differences between hut and industrial
area (dotted line marks presumed percentage
differences based on cores)
   1 Cores   2 Blades   3 Flakes   4 Debitage
   5 Weight of unretouched material
   6 Weight of burnt material
   7 Decortical flakes   8 Core by-products
   9 Micro-burins   10 Axes
   11 Microliths   12 Scrapers   13 Awls
   14 Stained blades   15 Retouched blades

ficantly more common in the hut area, as would be
expected, but many categories of what might have
been described as waste are also significantly more
common there than would have been expected. These
differences are also illustrated in the percentage
divisions of material in Fig 83.

The retouched tools in Fig 83 are divided into two
groups: those such as micro-awls, retouched blades,
and scrapers which were commoner in the hut, and
the axes which were relatively common in the western
area, though significantly fewer than might have been
expected. Schiffer (1976) has noted that the disposal
of different types of implements could be affected by
differential discard patterns, while Gould (1977) and
others (including Hayden 1977) have noted that
objects on which substantial time has been spent, for
example in hafting, will be looked after or curated
and not necessarily discarded at the location of use.
Schiffer (1976) has suggested that rubbish can be
defined as primary (disposed of on the spot) and
secondary (disposed of away from areas of use). One
criterion besides curation is size. Smaller simple
tools, such as awls or scrapers, would be good
examples of the type of object which might be
discarded in the area of use while axes, particularly if
hafted, are unlikely to be disposed of in a casual
fashion at a point of use, and as they are also complex
objects they would be cared for and cached. Thus the
scatter of flake and core axes in industrial areas
cannot be explained away as objects which have been
casually discarded during use. They could represent

cached objects or even unfinished examples. Again,
as in the hut area, a small concentration of
micro-burins was found near the hearth (F335), and it
is possible that the microliths found were those being
replaced either as new components or through the
manufacture of completely new artefacts. All tools
have a life history from manufacture through use to
discard. Obviously the more complex the artefacts,
the longer and more complex the use-life, and these
complicated tools are therefore very dubious indicators of the use of a site or activity area.

When Schiffer's warnings about the differences in
methods of disposal for different types of archaeological material are taken into consideration, and added
to the implications of work on curation of complex
artefacts, then obviously care must be taken in using
retouched tools to estimate the nature of an activity
area. Other more casually discarded waste products
may provide better indicators of the nature of activity
areas.

Not only is there a difference in the percentages of
retouched tools present in both areas, but there is a
much higher incidence of burnt flint, stained flakes
and blades in the hut area, while in the industrial area
there is a much higher ratio of flakes and unburnt
debitage. This is of course the natural and expected
division, with the character of the hut area and its
more intense occupation indicated by larger numbers
of fires and therefore more burnt flint.

There are in the hut several notable exceptions to
the expected trends. One is the proportion of
debitage. This was increased above its expected level
by the extensive burning of flint in the hut area which
increased the number of small pieces of flint as well
as the proportion of burnt debitage. A second
exception is the number of core by-products. This
can be explained by the number of poorly worked
cores which may have required more core-
rejuvenation. The numbers of blades and micro-
burins found in the industrial area are also much
lower than expected. The number of micro-burins in
relation to the numbers of microliths might have been
expected to be higher in an industrial area. The
implication of their lack is again that there is not
necessarily a total correlation between early and later
stages of manufacture of an implement. The obvious
explanation is that the blades were produced in an
industrial area and that the microliths were made
elsewhere, therefore numerous blades could have
been removed from the industrial site. This of course
in part explains the relatively high proportion of
blades found in the hut area. There were several
indications that the blades were not entirely produced
in the hut area. First, the cores found in that area
were relatively poor, often made on small flakes, and
the ratio of cores to blades was low (allowing for the
fact that a minimum number blade-count has been

used). The presence of micro-burins and *lamelles-à-cran* indicated that a certain amount of microlith manufacture had taken place. While many microliths could have been made without the micro-burin technique, the number of blades found during excavation may represent only a proportion of those originally present in the hut area, and as the numbers were still so high it would not be surprising to discover that unretouched flint blades were being used in composite implements. It is therefore of interest that Newell has noted similar concentrations of blades around the huts at Bergumemeer (Newell 1981). Also, as noted in the previous section, the concentration of blades beside the hearth could be a secondary concentration after the cores used were cleared away.

Ultimately one must conclude that industrial areas within larger, more complex, settlements need not be marked by large quantities of all industrial by-products. Also, in the case of Mount Sandel it is difficult to identify what could be characterized as occupational or dwelling area debris. It is even possible to argue that the high concentration of microliths is in part a product of a secondary type of industrial activity, and that the actual traces of activities associated with maintenance tasks are very slight and almost masked by the blades, cores and microliths. It is therefore the presence of higher quantities of burnt flint and enlarged hearths which may indicate more intensive occupation, while the thin scatter of awls, scrapers and stained blades may represent discarded material from maintenance activities. It is the apparent association of this material with the structural evidence which suggests that these maintenance activities were carried out inside a shelter.

Distribution of topsoil material
In spite of the somewhat cavalier treatment of the topsoil (Chapter 1) certain trends in the topsoil material were still evident. Certain areas were excavated by metre squares, and one strip across the site was also sieved. Therefore the problem of bias in recovery has been partly obviated by only examining these areas. In the case of microlith distribution, only the strip which was sieved has been considered (Fig 84A).

The distribution recorded in Fig 84 shows that in spite of the extensive agricultural disturbance there was still a remarkably high coincidence between the concentration of material in the topsoil and the hut area, thus confirming Newell and Vrooman's suggestion (1972) that ploughing does not necessarily obscure the more general trends in distribution of material. This high reading for the hut area would still be clear even if a decrease of 30% is allowed for the use of sieves in line L.

The excavation of line K/41–50 showed that there was a significant concentration of material to the south of the hut area, in an area where no occupation soil and few features had survived; in fact the recovery of a significant quantity of material in A/50 suggested that there was an extensive area where the original traces of settlement had not survived *in situ*. One minor problem is that this does not necessarily imply Mesolithic settlement, as occasional sherds of Neolithic pottery were found on the southern edge of the site. The distribution of microliths across the sieved area did, however, clearly indicate that there was a Mesolithic activity area south of the hut complex (Fig 84).

The distribution of material along the eastern edge of the site is rather more problematic. There was undoubtedly less material along this edge of the hut, but as the topsoil was thinner here this could have been a simple function of the volume of soil. Analysis by Hamond (Chapter 7) showed that features in this area had a low concentration of phosphates, and this could confirm the relative lack of archaeological material on the eastern edge of the site.

While it is impossible to suggest exact limits to the distribution of material there was a definite fall-off to the east and south of the hut area, and it can be argued that the limits of the excavation lay just within the 95% limit of scatter used by Whallon *et al* (1974) or Yellen's Limit of Most Scatter Total (LMST, 1977).

INTERPRETATION OF RADIOCARBON DATES
The ^{14}C dates from Mount Sandel (Upper), Mount Sandel (Lower) (Collins 1983) and Castleroe (Appendix 5) are listed in Table 49. As the final convention for feature numbers has been altered from the initial field notation a key has been included as an appendix to allow correlation with earlier publications (Appendix 1g).

It is immediately clear that the two Groningen dates are later than samples from the same pits dated in Belfast. Warner has shown that the two samples from F100/2 are significantly different in date, but because of the larger standard deviation on the UB samples from F56/1 there is no very significant difference between UB and GRN samples in that case. While the implications of this possible inter-laboratory variation could be of great importance for the origins of the Irish Mesolithic (see below, Chapter 13), it must be remembered that any such variation will have little bearing on the internal consistency of the Irish Mesolithic. In order to examine the problem of intra-site variation in date the Groningen samples can be excluded so that only one potential variant is being considered.

As can be seen from Table 49 many dates have relatively large standard deviations. This arises from

A   3   2   9   9   3   1   2   4   6   3   0   0   1   0   6   4   1   2   4   0

B

Row A: 2 13

12

Row D: 5

8   14

4   10   5   9   17   2   9   7

Row G: 9   4   10   7   7   8   9   5

13   5   8   7   7   4   4

8

Row K: +23   19   +13   +16   21   7   14   21   15   11   9   13   11   13   17   10   7   9

20   13   25   22   25   17   16   14

Row N: 24   17   12   28   21   16   17   15   14

19   23   18+   9

9   14+   10+   10

35   40   45   50

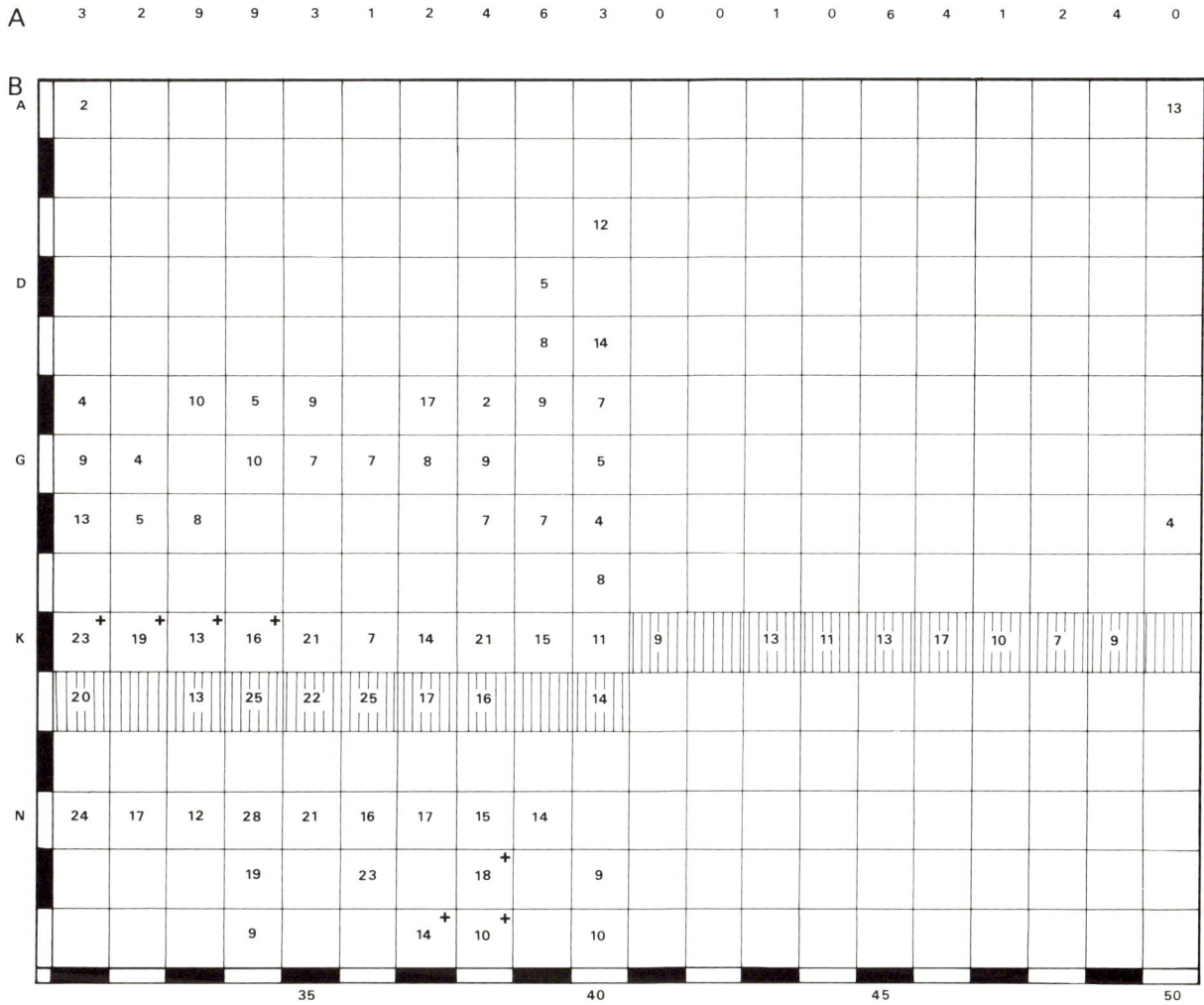

Fig 84   Distribution of topsoil material: (A) number of microliths found by metre square in sieved area, (B) number of blades by metre square (sieved area hatched; cross indicates material kept only from lower 2/3 of square)

the nature of the samples. Many come from specific layers in pits and so the sample size could not be increased as amalgamating samples even from two adjacent layers would have made the increase in accuracy rather pointless. Similarly the samples from the occupation soil could only be taken from areas where there was little chance of contamination from pits underlying or cutting through the occupation soil. The dates from the site cannot be considered as belonging to one specific short phase of occupation. The dates from the main hut hollow and those from the hut round F91 are very similar, but there is a high probability that the features which cut the main hut hollow belong to a phase of occupation which is significantly later, perhaps as much as 200 years later if only the UB dates are taken into consideration, but 400 years if the GRN dates are considered (Fig 85).

There is a slight trend in that the oldest samples associated with the hut area are all dominated by charcoal. This would negate suggestions that charcoal derived from hazel nut shells, probably being collected in a single year, might have picked up an annual fluctuation in ^{14}C, thus causing some samples to be older. While F74 also contained charcoal it could belong to a later phase of activity. Warner (1976) has suggested that a potential age lapse for charcoal samples should be allowed, though perhaps his 200 years is excessive in the Early Mesolithic, where only substantial pieces of Scots pine could be expected to live long enough significantly to bias the samples. Therefore an age lapse of 100 years has been allowed. Having made allowance for this possible source of bias the relative stratigraphic position of samples which existed in the hut hollow and cut across it can be plotted (Fig 85).

Summary

The combination of extensive surface erosion and the numerous reoccupations of the site has left a

MOUNT SANDEL (UPPER)

Mesolithic contexts

	No	Feature	Context	Date
Hazel nuts & charcoal	UB 912	F100/2	(4)	6775 ± 115 bc
Hazel nuts & charcoal	UB 913	F31/0	(1)	6605 ± 70 bc
Charcoal	UB 951	F56/1	(3)	6840 ± 185 bc
Charcoal & hazel nuts	UB 952	F56/5	(2)	7010 ± 70 bc
Hazel nuts & charcoal	UB 2008	F27	(1)	6490 ± 65 bc
Hazel nuts & charcoal	UB 2007	F31	(2)	6845 ± 135 bc
Charcoal	UB 2356	L-M-N/35	occup	6815 ± 135 bc
Charcoal	UB 2357	N/31, P/31–32	occup	7005 ± 185 bc
Charcoal & hazel nuts	UB 2358	F56/4	(1)	6845 ± 135 bc
Charcoal	UB 2359	F10/9	(1)	5935 ± 120 bc
Charcoal & hazel nuts	UB 2360	F56/1	(1)	6720 ± 100 bc
Charcoal	UB 2361	F74	(2)	6595 ± 165 bc
Charcoal	UB 2362	F99	(1)	7040 ± 80 bc
	GRN 10470	F100/2	(2)	6430 ± 50 bc
	GRN 100471	F56/1	(3)	6480 ± 60 bc

Later occupation

Charcoal	UB 2205	F10 (overlying a palisade trench)	(1)	435 ± 70 bc
Charcoal	UB 2446	F313 (containing two glass beads)	(1)	220 ± 40 bc

MOUNT SANDEL (LOWER)

Charcoal	UB 591	Cut A		5770 ± 525 bc
Charcoal	UB 592	Cut C		5410 ± 695 bc
Charcoal	UB 532	Cut C		6540 ± 210 bc

CASTLEROE

Charcoal	UB 2171	Occupation		6805 ± 135 bc
Charcoal	UB 2172	Feature 1		6610 ± 75 bc

Table 49   Radiocarbon dates

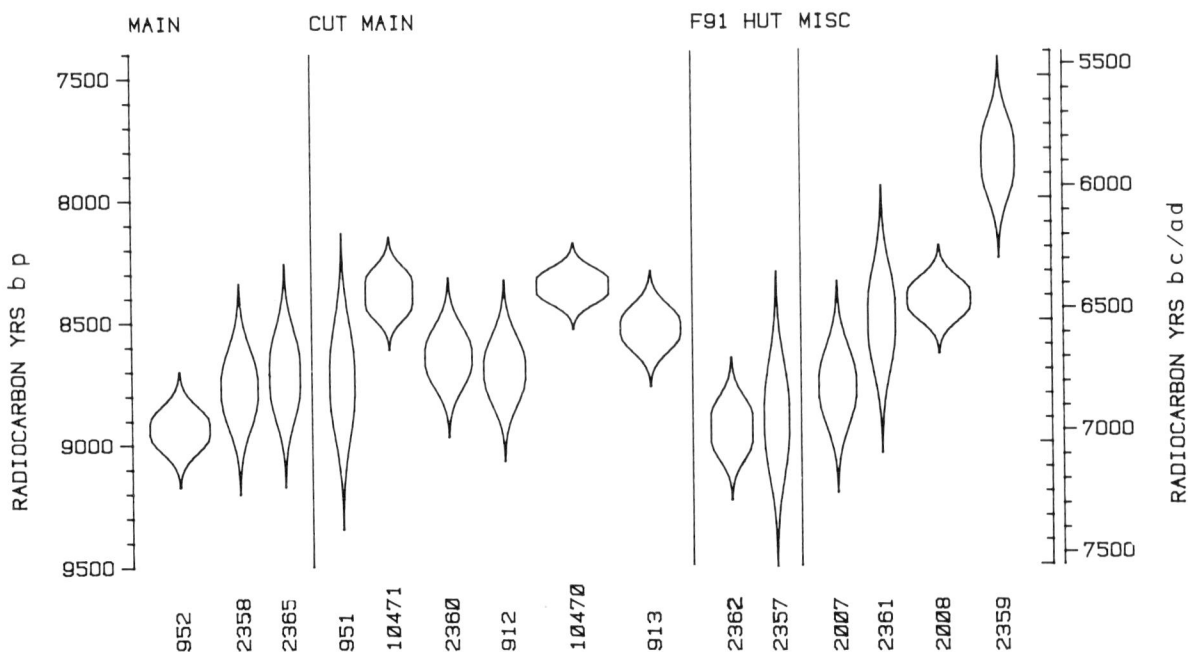

Fig 85   Radiocarbon dates sorted by area, with age-lapse

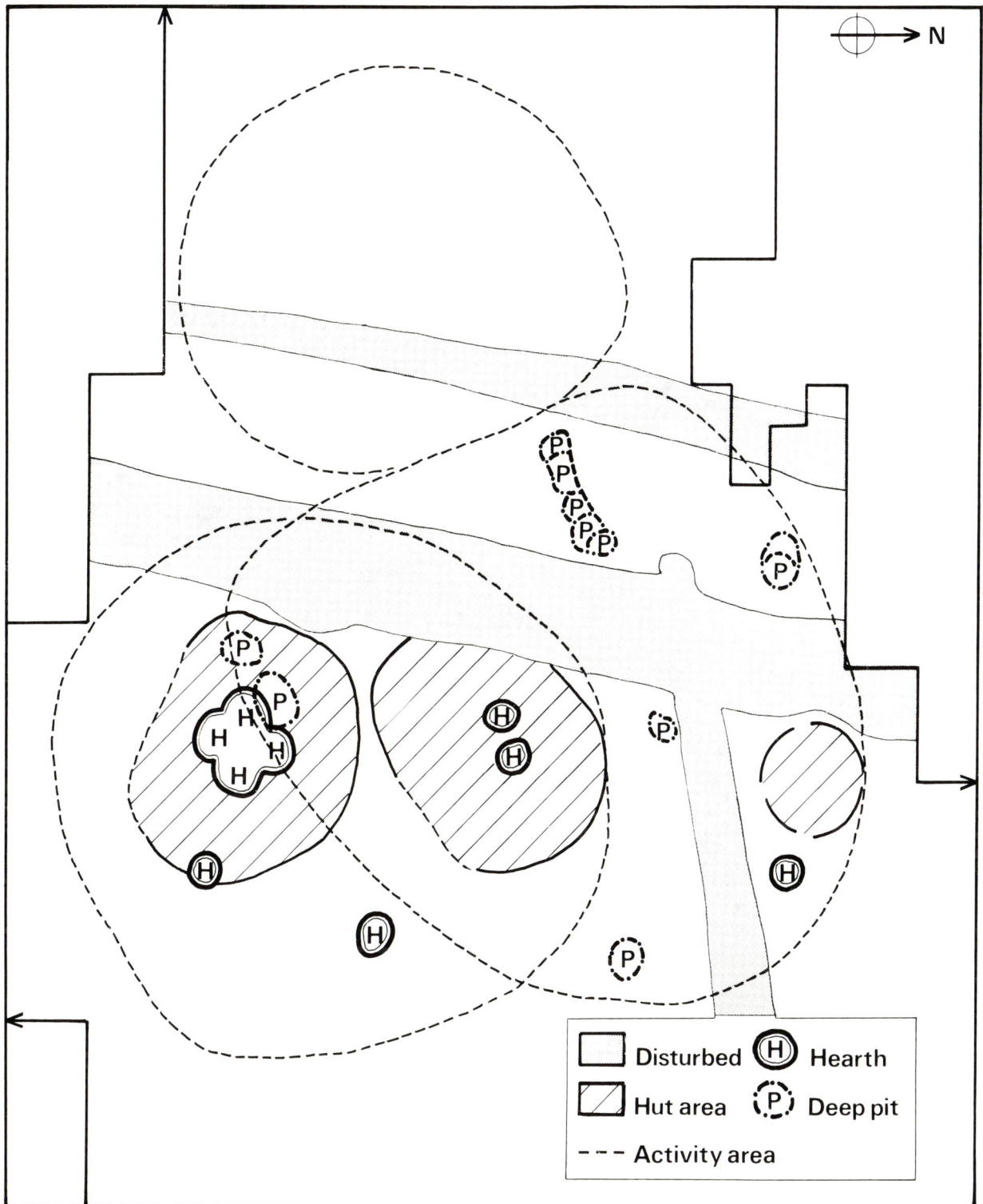

Fig 86   Generalized site plan showing hut and industrial areas and deep pits

bewildering array of archaeological material and features. The problem has been to identify all the components which make up the individual camp sites and distinguish those which are anomalous.

The suggestion has been made that most of the Mesolithic material and features were associated with a series of Mesolithic huts, each of which may have been about 6 metres in diameter. These huts seem to represent numerous reoccupations of the site rather than a series of contemporary huts. The one exception was the rather lighter northern structure which may have been a tent, and this could have been part of a rather transitory summer settlement in which a smaller shelter was erected and an outside hearth used. The essentially different nature of this end of the site may be explained by the fact that the hearth, F109, was dated to 5935 ± 120 bc. The whole nature of the Mount Sandel area may have changed in the period after the main phase of settlement, from 7000 to 6600 bc. This was probably a result of the rising sea level changing the nature of the river estuary at Mount Sandel (Chapter 10).

The main phase of occupation appears to have been centred on the huts, each of which had at its centre a relatively large hearth (Fig 86). Placed some distance away from each hut was a large pit—perhaps used for storage—and scattered around the settlement were smaller hearths. The main reason for a difference in size between the internal and external hearths could have been the restriction of location for the central hut hearths. Other structures must have been built on the site, as was clear from the few deep but vertical post-holes found. Some of these were definitely not associated with the construction of the huts and could

have been for storage or drying racks. A similar though more enigmatic facility is suggested by the small group of posts which were placed in the ground at an angle. These were more or less contiguous and rather different in their placing from those associated with hut construction.

Pits which were clearly associated with extensive food preparation—stone boiling, etc—were rare. One (F109) may belong to a later phase of settlement. At least four other examples were found. These were possibly lying on the outer edge of the settlement zone.

The range of artefacts and waste products associated with an individual settlement remains rather more problematic than the site facilities. It can be suggested that the industrial areas belonged with at least one of the huts, but with the destruction of so much of the occupation layers there was little point in attempting blade- and flake-joining. The inclusion of the industrial material as part of the settlement is based on the fact that the flint appears to have beach-rolled cortex and so would have to have been brought from some distance to the site. Finally, from the poor sample of topsoil material it has been possible to detect at least one small concentration of material south of the hut area. This could well remind us of the social component as distinct from the functional one.

Therefore from the disjointed fragments of evidence, perhaps the remnants of many individual occupations, it is possible to show through the location and association of groups of huts, hearths and industrial areas how an individual settlement was articulated nearly nine thousand years ago.

CHAPTER 12

The social and economic interpretation of the site

In attempting an overall assessment of the site at Mount Sandel the most important consideration must be the partial nature of the surviving evidence. Obviously any archaeological site suffers from post-depositional disturbance, the absence of artefacts lost off-site so that the activities of the group are not fully reflected in the surviving archaeological remains, and differential butchering practices which will have a similar effect on the faunal remains. In the case of Mount Sandel it has been emphasized that there was considerable disturbance through ploughing and later activity which resulted in a very partial record surviving. The acidity of the soils also meant that only the burnt bone fragments survived, and these can represent only a small proportion of the faunal remains which would originally have been left around the site. The two main questions which will be examined in this chapter are first, the nature of the site and secondly, the seasonal duration and economic strategies.

Type of Settlement

In recent years considerable attention has been given to dividing hunter-gatherer settlements into various categories (Mellars 1976; Newell 1973; Price *et al* 1974). Authors have usually been concerned with the identification of site type from the variability within scatters of artefacts. They stress the difference between small, specialized extraction sites with a narrow range of artefacts and large sites where a broader range of material has been found. A second line of enquiry has been pursued through the use of ethno-archaeology: Yellen (1977), for example, argued that longer-term settlement is marked by an accumulation of activities on a site, while Murray (1980) focused on organized rubbish disposal as the best indication of longer-term occupation.

The problem of the archaeological approach is that with a restricted range of evidence such simple approaches to the data are almost self-justifying and cannot be tested. Therefore, this discussion will attempt to assess the nature of the settlement at

Mount Sandel against Yellen's suggestion that a longer period of occupation is not marked by an increase in site size but by a greater number of activities being carried out, and Murray's theory that base camps will be characterized by more organized rubbish disposal.

Ideally the archaeological data rather than the seasonal evidence should be sufficient to provide an estimate of the nature of the site, but without other sites against which the Mount Sandel data can be tested this line of reasoning is of limited value. However, the faunal information will be used to support the argument that Mount Sandel was a base camp occupied for a large part of the year.

THE ARTEFACTUAL EVIDENCE
The quantity of material from Mount Sandel is impressive, but given that there could have been recurrent occupation of the site it is the least important factor. In fact it could be argued that any site which is largely typified by one form of material might represent, as in the case of Star Carr, a specialized component of a larger settlement system (Clark 1954 and 1972; Pitts 1979).

Initially the narrow range of artefacts found at Mount Sandel might appear to suggest that the site falls within the specialized site category. But several factors have conspired to create a high concentration of microliths in relation to other artefacts. This can be partly explained by a practice of disposing of composite tools into fires, causing the high concentration of triangles on the site (Chapter 11). Besides this behavioural biasing of the data, a comparison with the Later Mesolithic assemblages of the English Mesolithic (Mellars 1976) is rather misleading as scrapers and burins do not appear to play such a prominent role in the Irish Mesolithic (Woodman 1978). (The significance of the relative scarcity of scrapers will be discussed below.)

If the material from the occupation soil in the hut and other areas is taken as representative of the activities carried out on site, and the material from the pits is excluded as over-emphasizing certain aspects of the inhabitants' activities, allowing for the scarcity of scrapers, a broad range of activities would appear to have been carried out.

		%
Microliths	357	77
Awls	18	4
Stained blades	24	5
Retouched blades	29	6
Scrapers	6	1
Burins	4	1
Axes	28	6

Table 50   Major categories of retouched tools found in occupation soil

We can note that this list could be compared with roughly similar lists from some of the larger Mesolithic sites in England which appear to have the same general type of assemblage (Mellars 1976, type B1).

Examination of material in the hut area (Chapter 11) has shown quite clearly that there was a small flint-working area and that most finished items were not found in this area. The one implement type found in large numbers with the industrial waste was the microliths. It is possible to argue that these were the discards whose replacements were being manufactured beside the hearth. Dumont's work (Chapter 4), although at a preliminary stage, demonstrated that much of the material on the site had been used. This included not only the more characteristic retouched tools, including the microliths, but also small worked blades.

A major weakness—due to the partial survival of the site—is the lack of evidence for the inter-relationship between the hut and industrial area. As noted earlier, no attempt was made at flint-joining as so much of the site had been destroyed and the flint was unsuitable. It could therefore be argued that the detailed identification of the range of activities implied by the stone artefacts must be fraught with pitfalls and must also wait for a more complete microwear study. Certain trends, however, do emerge.

The microlithic material appears to represent at least two different implement types: those containing triangles, which may have been associated with hunting, and those with rods which, on the basis of association with different types of layers, were used perhaps for plant-food processing or fishing. It is even possible that the needle points may have been all that remained of a different type of artefact such as a lighter form of arrow.

The microwear examinations also point to a variation in the use of microliths. Although few triangles showed traces of polish this has been identified by Dumont (Chapter 4) as mostly meat or hide polish. On the other hand, Dumont has suggested that different types of rods may have been put to different uses.

The axes again are not a single group but contain at least three distinctive functional types: the core axe, a narrow chopping tool, the flake axe, a broad-edged adze or chisel, and picks and borers. Dumont has already shown that some of these had been extensively used.

The other artefacts, such as awls, stained and retouched blades, may well represent general maintenance equipment. Again all show signs of extensive use. The most enigmatic group are the ochre-stained blades. These could be simply associated with preparation of ochre for paint, but it is more likely that the ochre was to be used for other purposes such as helping in animal hide preparation (Chapter 4).

It is tempting to correlate the relative absence of scrapers and burins with the absence of red deer from the faunal remains. This is not to suggest that red deer was not hunted, but rather that the hunting and processing of red deer may not have played an important role while the Mount Sandel site was occupied. Skins and artefacts procured from red deer could have been brought to the site. However, it would be simplistic to assume that the end scraper was the only implement which could have been used for hide preparation. A significant proportion of the Danish Later Maglemosian lacks scrapers, while red deer were most certainly hunted (Brinch-Petersen 1972; Henricksen 1976). It is, therefore, possible that the ochre-stained blades could have been a by-product of hide preparation, which would explain the large quantities on sites such as Pincevent (Leroi-Gourhan and Brezillon 1966).

Another problem is whether the industrial area represents a totally separate phase of activity which did not relate to the hut area. Although it is a subjective assessment, much of the flint appears to have come from a beach and a small quantity has fresh cortex. Similarly at Mount Sandel (Lower) a significant quantity of flint appears to be beach flint (Collins 1983). There is no evidence of extensive use of the local glacial erratic flint from the Armoy Ice Sheet. This flint could therefore have been derived from the coast, either in the Portrush area to the east of the Bann or the Downhill area to the west. The industrial area produced some evidence of axe manufacture but it is important to note that there was little evidence of early stages of core production. The decortical flakes which occur are all relatively small, and it could therefore be argued that the cores which were used were brought to the site as pre-forms.

Binford (1979a) has argued that collection of raw material is part of an embedded procurement strategy which is tied into the gathering of other resources. Therefore, as there is some slight evidence for the exploitation of the marine environment, it could be that flint was brought back to Mount Sandel from the coast at a time when small groups were exploiting the open coast. Gould (1980) has noted that lithic raw materials are used in two fashions: first, opportunist use, when a simple implement is made from the most convenient usable rock type (see also Binford 1979a), utilized, and then usually discarded on the spot, and secondly, planned use, when a specific raw material is collected and brought back to a camp site. It could be argued that the Mount Sandel flintwork falls into the latter category and that flint-working is best explained as one of a series of activities carried out at a camp site.

In attempting an assessment of equipment it must be realized that much will never be recovered because it is used off-site and, as Oswalt has noted (1976), fishing communities tend to use more complex equipment which will leave little trace in the lithic artefacts found on a settlement. Structures such as fish-traps (Brinch-Petersen *et al* 1979) or the Antrea net find (Clark 1975) are good examples of this type of equipment. The wide range of wooden artefacts at Tybrind Vig (Andersen 1980), canoe, paddles, bows, traps and fish-hooks, illustrates how much the stone artefacts found on settlement sites represent the production of the means of procurement rather than the hunting or fishing equipment itself.

In the light of potential off-site use of many artefacts it is important to assess the range of artefacts in terms of use and curation. As noted earlier (Chapter 11) different types of artefacts will have different use-lives, and those which have required extensive preparation in manufacture and hafting will be used and repaired rather than discarded. The axes therefore probably represent the single most important artefactual group, as these would have been the most highly curated pieces on the site. The core axes and picks were probably resharpened on numerous occasions. Gould (1977) has listed the number of adzes or flakes used each year by aborigines of the Australian Western Desert as on average 23. While northern European communities may have had more opportunity and need for woodworking than aborigines, the ability to resharpen the core axes and the remarkably robust edge of the flake axe, combined with the problem of hafting the axe, would suggest that relatively few were used each year. On the other hand, the numerous microliths in the hut area could well represent a single specific phase of retooling somewhere between ten and twenty artefacts. The other artefacts may represent a much more casual discarding of pieces which had a very limited lifespan. This would include awls (for drilling) and the stained blades for ochre preparation or skin-working.

It is instructive to compare Mount Sandel with the site of Meer II in Belgium (Van Noten 1978). The excavators have claimed that the site produced evidence of an 'expedient' technology (Cahen *et al* 1979) in the form of cores, implements and waste still lying together in concentrations. This apparent *ad hoc* production, use and rapid discarding of artefacts would typify an expedient technology. In spite of the authors' assertions, however, it is by no means certain that Meer II represents one particular phase of occupation. It may be little more than an area where several disparate and unrelated activities took place (Dunnell 1979).

In contrast it is impossible to illustrate the same types of associations within the Mount Sandel assemblages. Even aside from the partial preservation of activity areas we can note the relative absence of microliths and blades from the industrial areas, while much of the material in the hut area appears to belong to a discard phase which is in no way associated with the limited evidence of production. Similarly Dumont (personal communication) has failed to join any axe-sharpening flakes to axes. Thus the Mount Sandel assemblage appears to be rather more organized, and probably most of the material used was discarded off-site.

In summary, the artefactual material reflects traces of a number of different activities which relate to both the manufacture and use of artefacts on and off the site at Mount Sandel. Perhaps the range of axes and the implications of their role in a range of woodworking activities illustrate best the number of activities which were carried out at the site.

SITE ORGANIZATION

Many individual aspects of site organization have already been discussed in Chapter 11. The two main questions which arise concern the number of activities identifiable on the site and the evidence of organization of discrete activity areas and rubbish disposal.

The artefactual evidence has already been used to show that a broad range of activities took place but, as Binford (1978) and Gould (1980) have noted, maintenance tasks are not always carried out at base camps. Hunting stands in particular can be associated with routine maintenance tasks, as the considerable periods of free time spent waiting for one's prey are ideal for this work, hence Binford's alternative interpretation of Pincevent I (Leroi-Gourhan and Brezillon 1966) as a hunting stand rather than a camp site.

At Mount Sandel it is the evidence for various types of facilities which indicates that this site was more than a watching point for fish runs. Besides the large substantial structures with which some of the archaeological material was associated (Chapter 11) there were a series of large pits, possibly for storage, smaller outside hearths and pits, and groups of angled post-holes which had little to do with the main huts and may have been associated with storage, skin stretching, etc. Finally, the few large post-holes found scattered around the site could have been associated with other site facilities such as storage racks. Therefore, although much of the distribution of different types of evidence overlaps, an impression is gained of a complex organized site which would be best explained as a base camp which had been occupied for a significant part of the year.

The possibility of relating the type of evidence left on most archaeological sites to activity areas has generated considerable discussion. Yellen (1977) has suggested on the basis of the Kung Bushmen camps that it may be impossible to identify specific activity areas on a settlement. Whallon (1978) has also suggested that simple distribution of stone tools may provide an inadequate record of human activity. Binford (1978; 1979) has argued that even allowing for curation and rubbish disposal, there should be a recognizable pattern of activity, while Murray (1980) has indicated that the changing nature of the settlement between transitory and sedentary will induce a change towards more organized rubbish disposal. Mount Sandel provides an ideal test case for these problems. The partial destruction of the site has reduced the number of units of evidence surviving but even with this restricted range a pattern is identifiable.

The centre of the site must have been the hut area where there was a higher concentration of retouched tools than elsewhere. As explained in Chapter 11, the division of material between the surviving hut and industrial areas was not as simple as might have been expected, and there were small hearths and some possible occupation debris in the industrial area. However, the trend towards certain roughing-out activities in the industrial area was clear while the hut area was associated with various routine maintenance tasks.

Similarly it is possible to show that the pits—in particular the larger pits—were usually placed some distance from the area where the huts were usually built, so again the hut area provides a notional central area which was avoided. The pit fills illustrated quite clearly a pattern of rubbish disposal. The central hearths appeared to contain remarkably homogeneous layers, not all of which showed signs of intense burning, while several other pits, though clearly not hearths, did contain mixtures of material which may have come from hearths. These not only have larger concentrations of burnt bones and charcoal, but magnetic susceptibility studies show that these had been intensely burnt (Chapter 8). This deliberate transfer or disposal of hearth material into pits adjacent to the huts could be regarded as evidence of

more organized rubbish disposal. Presumably areas of rubbish scattered over the old ground surface have long since disappeared and only those in the pits have survived.

The evidence outlined above has obviously survived from only a tiny fraction of the activities carried out on the site. In particular there would probably have been a butchering area where bones and unwanted portions of animals would have been left, but in the acid soils of Mount Sandel none of the bone would have survived. Broadbent has noted (1979, fig 62) that this might have been an area where few stone tools would be found, and at Lundfors he recorded a high concentration of phosphates in an area where few stone tools were found. The area south of the huts produced numerous microliths and may have been a centre for various activities in an area where occupation soil had not survived and where no pits had been dug.

The most enigmatic group consists of the small pits filled with burnt stones. Some may represent stone-boiling activities carried out round the edge of the site but in one instance, FI09, the hearth could be associated with the smaller northern structure. Certainly this hearth was later in date than the main part of the settlement. Even without FI09 there is no doubt that this type of pit and fill is peripheral, and it could represent a different activity towards the edge of the site.

In summary there is evidence that the Mount Sandel settlement did have a high degree of organization and that specific activity areas did exist.

SIZE OF SETTLEMENT

Besides being used as indicators of the nature of the site, site size and hut size have been used to estimate population size. Mount Sandel has provided some evidence that the area of occupation of a Mesolithic site cannot always be considered as a single unit, as multiple reoccupations are possible. In the case of Mount Sandel, however, there appears to have been a high degree of overlap between different reoccupations. This could in part result from reuse of standing structures, but it does make it difficult to estimate the total area of occupation.

Fortunately the limits of the site could be roughly determined. Little of consequence was found in the field north of the main excavation. The only small concentration was close to the northern structure. The eastern edge of the site contained little, for example FS13 and 157; a test for levels of phosphates in several of the peripheral features here, such as FI57, showed that there was little trace of occupation preserved in the form of high phosphate readings along the eastern edge of the site (Chapter 7). A significant concentration of material was found in the topsoil south of the huts, stretching to at least line 50.

The western edge was more difficult to assess as large quantities of material of unknown origin were found along the western edge of the industrial area, at least as far as line G[1].

As has been noted in discussion of the topsoil material (above, page 146), it is impossible to provide a systematic quantification of this material but it would seem reasonable to assume that 90% of it would lie within a 15 m radius of the notional central point defined in Chapter 11 (Price *et al* 1974). This would be the rough equivalent of Yellen's LMS (limit of most scatter) although he would consider that this included 95% of the material. The distribution of material would not be circular but might be biased more towards the south and west of the hut area. The total area of settlement would therefore be in the region of 700 m² (Fig 86). This, of course, represents the surviving portions of a number of occupations.

It can be suggested, on the basis of ethnographic analogy, that most activities during an individual settlement at Mount Sandel would have taken place within at least a radius of 10 m from the centre of the settlement and that an individual settlement would have its limits of most activity, such as those described above, at roughly 300 m². This figure naturally invites an assessment of the number of people present on a site of this size. The most commonly used estimator of population size is the logarithmic formula of Weissner (1974) which is again based on 90% of the area of scatter. A settlement of the area of 300 m² would suggest a figure in excess of 25 people. Yellen's formula for LMS, $\neq 0.5$ m² + 9.03 = number of occupants, produces a figure of 24. Of course the tendency for these two computations to support each other is the result of using the same data source, the Kung Bushmen, and it is questionable whether their type of village organization could be transferred to temperate zones. In fact at the other extreme Binford noted in his work amongst the Nunamiut that a protohistoric winter camp site, the Kakinya site, occupied for 130 days during two winters, appeared to have covered several hundred square metres with only one house, as did the occupation round each of the houses at the Phalanga site (Binford 1978; more detailed report in preparation). This would suggest that the population level at a site such as Mount Sandel would have been much lower—in fact the Kakinya house was occupied by only five people.

If an assumption of one hut per occupation is used, then a second estimate of population can be made. House or hut size is often used for estimating population size, though obviously, as Binford and others have noted, Naroll's theorem of 10 m² per person does not work for hunter-gatherer populations. In the case of Mount Sandel the hut area of just under 30 m² would suggest a group of three. In the light of the previous discussion, however, this seems unlikely. Cook and Heizer (1968) have suggested a figure of 14 m² for a hut containing up to six people and 9.3 m² for each further person.

Inevitably much of our data is derived from sources which cannot be regarded as comparable to the Irish Early Boreal environment, but Binford (personal communication) has suggested that on the basis of the Nunamiut data it is difficult to believe that the numbers in each hut would be higher than ten. If instead of huts the personal family area, or Yellen's (1977) 'Nuclear Area' or hut and family space in front, is taken as the equivalent of the floor space of a temperate zone hunter-gatherer base camp hut, then an area of 4 to 5 m² per person might be expected. By this reckoning again fewer than ten people would have lived in one of the Mount Sandel huts. Ultimately there appears to be a limit to the size of structure which can be built by hunter-gatherers. Huts of 6 to 7 m in diameter would appear to be the usual size and so it must be assumed that there was an upper limit to the numbers living in each hut, and that once a certain threshold was passed new huts were built for separate social units.

In comparison with Bergumemeer (Newell 1981), where it has been suggested that there were several contemporary structures with a population as high as 71 to 82 (Odell 1980), the population levels at Mount Sandel appear remarkably low. It will be argued below that there are good environmental reasons for this low population level, but some consideration must be given to the possibility that Mount Sandel (Upper) is one component only within a dispersed base camp. Only two other traces of settlement have been identified. Even allowing for erosion, the traces noted by Hamond were slight (Chapter 7). The site excavated by A E P Collins (1983) produced what could have been the last remnants of another base camp and hut hollow of a slightly later date on a terrace south-west of Mountsandel Fort. No other traces were, however, found in the fields on either side of Mountsandel Fort, and lower terraces similar to the one which Collins explored are virtually non-existent. Where possible the edge of the escarpment was searched for other traces of occupation, without success. (Including the work of the May family much of the area now covered by houses has been explored.) It therefore appears unlikely that there were a number of contemporary huts spread along the escarpment edge in the immediate area. Within the area excavated the huts were so close together that they are presumed to belong to different phases of occupation.

Unfortunately it is often beyond the competence of archaeology to work out whether two Mesolithic structures are exactly contemporary or roughly contemporary. Similarly lithic typology does not provide a good means of establishing a relationship. In fact, allowing for the possibility of minor individual stylistic variations in microliths as well as chronological variations, it may never be possible to separate any two occupations. At Mount Sandel the ^{14}C date of 6540 ± 210 bc for the Lower site is so much later than the dates for the Upper site (in spite of its large standard deviation) that there is a reasonable probability that Mount Sandel (Lower) is later than the main hut area at Mount Sandel (Upper) (Table 49).

It should be remembered that Wobst (1974) has argued for a level of organization equating with the band. This usually implies a large enough group to provide for all day-to-day contingencies, and he has suggested that group mean size of 25 would be ideal. The Mount Sandel site would appear to fall below this level, and a dispersed population would suit the type of economy and environment discussed below. The number 25 has no magic qualities, but as the suggested Mount Sandel population figures fall below even fifteen, and as there is no evidence of several huts having been erected at once, it is possible that several communities may have lived within relatively easy access of each other in the area immediately south of the Bann estuary. Thus sites such as Castleroe (Appendix 5) could be contemporary with Mount Sandel. Castleroe is within 2 km of Mount Sandel but is on the other side of the river. A loose grouping of this type would still allow co-operation and sufficient organization to dispatch smaller, specialized task groups.

Seasonality and Economy

The problem of seasonal occupation at Mount Sandel is a fundamental one which impinges on the mobility of Mesolithic communities and the extent of their annual territory. Present day and recent hunter-gatherer societies have a range of economic strategies which generally require seasonal mobility. Some hunter-gatherers can maintain a sedentary existence, such as the Nootka of the Canadian Pacific coast, but no assumption of sedentary occupation should be made for Mesolithic communities (Caulfield 1978). Indeed, few assumptions can be made about Mesolithic economies: Larsson (1980) has even noted different strategies on either side of the sound dividing Zealand from Skåne. Therefore the seasonality of a site such as Mount Sandel can only be examined in the context of the contemporary environment and landscape.

In Chapters 9 and 10 Hamilton and Battarbee have attempted to reconstruct the landscape and environment contemporary with the Mount Sandel Mesolithic occupation. The vegetation would have been a birch-pine-hazel forest, with hazel increasing in importance and gradually replacing birch. The exact importance of hazel is rather difficult to ascertain. There is considerable evidence from various pollen diagrams that water levels in many lakes were considerably lower than today (O'Sullivan et al 1973). There are many areas where bog now exists but where in the Early Boreal open water would have been present (Chapter 6), though these lakes were often smaller than in later post-glacial times (Pilcher and Smith 1979), and in some cases water-logged areas and small lakes may have temporarily dried out (Chapter 6).

Battarbee has shown that the sea level was considerably lower than today, in eustatic terms 15–20 m lower, but that because of the isostatic depression of the north the relative sea level may have been only 5 to 10 m lower than today's. He has also noted that with saline wedges and the possibility of a deeper mid-stream channel the sea could have penetrated quite close to Mount Sandel. Therefore this area may be seen as an area of rapids just upstream from the river estuary. The Lower Bann drains over 50% of Northern Ireland and would always have been a major river, though if, as has been suggested by many climatologists, the Boreal period was drier than today (Lamb et al 1966), the river may have been slightly smaller in the Mesolithic period.

The climate is also thought to have differed slightly from that of today. Lamb has suggested (1966) that, due to the presence of ice sheets in Canada, cyclonic winds were directed slightly further north and that the Gulf Stream may have also run further south than today. This would have resulted in a more continental climate with longer colder winters and lower sea temperatures.

ARCHAEOLOGICAL EVIDENCE

As the faunal and macrobotanical remains were not found in a normal midden deposit, and as the only organic material which survived had been burnt, the problem arises of interpreting the economy, and in this case seasonality of occupation, from a very unrepresentative body of data.

The main indicators of seasonality have already been discussed in Chapter 5. Summer occupation is clearly indicated by the large quantities of salmonid bones found in several features, while winter occupation is indicated by the fusion rates of pig bones and by the presence of foetal pig bones. Late summer occupation could be indicated by the occasional presence of water-lily and apple/pear(?) seeds, while hazel nuts could attest to occupation from late autumn onwards. But collecting seasons need not directly correlate with the period of consumption and occupation. Hazel nuts, for example could have been collected in the late autumn but stored and consumed much later. Schiffer (1976) has helped explode the myth that there is necessarily a correlation between artefactual use and discard, but there is an equivalent 'assumption of immediacy' that collection of food and its consumption are closely related in time.

Two particular aspects of the Mount Sandel evidence need careful consideration. The rather substantial huts cannot be described as transitory, and this may have some bearing on the question of seasonal movements associated with the site. In particular the very existence of substantial structures may have attracted occupation at several seasons of the year without this occupation necessarily being continuous. The contexts in which the evidence was found also need to be considered. Most of the material was found in pits where there was a possibility that unique or short phases of occupation might be represented. There may also be (as was shown in Chapter 7) a certain variation in the way that various deposits accumulated—hence the relative homogeneity of many of the hearths which was often not evident in other pits.

The different seasonal interpretations which can be placed on the contents of hearths 56/2 and 56/4 on the one hand, and the occupation soil in the hut area on the other, epitomize the problem. The hearths contained large quantities of salmonid bones with some water-lily seeds: this could suggest summer occupation. The occupation soil on the other hand contained a scatter of pig bones. Van Wijngaarden-Bakker (Chapter 5) has noted that the pig remains in the occupation soil had the same general characteristics as all the pig bones: there was a significant quantity of young pigs just under one year old, and this suggests occupation at the end of the winter. Similarly if Table 51 is examined numerous seasonal indicators can be found together in the one pit. In some instances these indications occur in different layers—often the bones are in one layer while the macrobotanical remains are in another—but both Hamond and Doggart have shown that layers in the same pit which visually appear different may be part of the same formation process. The problem therefore is whether the layer contents represent an amalgam of debris from numerous activities carried on across the site, or whether storage of certain resources has created an apparent amalgam of different seasonal activities.

To avoid problems with multiple season deposition F100/2 and F56/1 have been excluded, the former because a number of events have clearly taken place, and the latter because it could have been filled with older occupation soil.

The central hearths, FS56/2, 56/4, 56/6 and 91, all contained large quantities of fish bones and varying quantities of hazel nut shells. These could represent summer-autumn occupation. The hearths contained large quantities of salmonid bones, and these fish are presumed to have been present in large numbers from late spring to midsummer. The water-lily seeds could have been collected towards the end of this period. Other features, in particular F27 and F31/0, contained large quantities of pig bones from animals caught during the winter as well as quantities of hazel nut shells. These are best explained as resulting from a winter occupation in which hazel nuts had been kept in storage and used throughout the winter. The tendency towards winter occupation is emphasized by the presence of foetal pig bones in FS31/0, 31/1, 31/5 and 31/4. In spite of the fact that these were closely associated, the smaller pits were part of a group which cut across F31/0 and so were probably not contemporary; similarly FS100/0–2 obviously represented several events.

The central hearths, with the exception of F31/0, which was by no means certainly a hearth, contained fish bones and would appear to belong to a phase of occupation from summer to autumn. On the basis of the proportion of salmon to eels, with the trout also possibly becoming more important after the salmon runs, it could be argued that F56/2 was earlier than F56/4 or F91. However, all these pits also contained numerous hazel nut shells, and in F91 these were stratified below the fish bones. Therefore it can be argued that these really represent the expected range in what were virtually unique events some time in the autumn. This implies salmon as a good source some time after its run is today supposed to end, possibly through a lowering of the river water temperature delaying the salmon run.

On the other hand there were the pits in which pig was of greater importance. Of these F31/3 was rather transitional in character. The others had relatively few fish bones, and though salmon bones still occurred, the actual numbers were smaller and they were often not as common amongst the fish bones. Van Wijngaarden-Bakker has noted that several of these pits, FS31/0, 31/1, 31/4 and 31/5, had foetal pig bones, and this helps reinforce the idea that the pigs were caught at the end of the winter. The fact that hazel nuts occurred in the same pits suggests that some reliance was also placed on the use of stored resources.

The absence of pig which could have been killed in the autumn suggests a possible discontinuity of occupation, though this could arise from the nature of the data: deposits resulting from unique events rather than deposits in which faunal remains gradually accumulated. Thus it is possible to interpret the faunal remains from the pits as representing either a continuum or two phases of occupation.

Feature	Salmon	Trout	Eels	Bass	Pig	Birds	Plants
27	7	5	—	—	69	—	+80% Hazel nuts
31/0	6	7	—	—	69	*Ana., T. phil.*	+80% Hazel nuts
31/3	30	18	12	—	7	*Col., Lagop.*	+80% Hazel nuts
31/4	10	6	—	—	16	*Col.*	+80% Hazel nuts
31/5	30	21	1	4	12	*G. stell., Lagop.*	+80% Hazel nuts
35	15	4	—	—	—	*Col., Scolop.*	?
56/2	126	11	1	11	—	*Col., Ana.*	−60% Hazel nuts Water-lily seeds
56/4	375	147	22	2	—	*Ana., G. stell. Accip., Lagop.*	+80% Hazel nuts
56/5–6	23	3	1	8	—	*Pass., Accip.*	+80% Hazel nuts
100/0–2 upper	15	3	7	9	17	—	+80% Hazel nuts
100/2 lower	39	25	3	23	21	*Ana., Scolop. T. phil., Lagop.*	+80% Hazel nuts
91	35	58	17	15	3	*Accip.*	
Hut area exc L/37+ N/37	18	5	15	3	12	*Ana., Lagop. Scolop., Col. G. stell., F. atra*	<20% Hazel nuts

Table 51   Distribution of specific types of faunal remains against hazel nut shells (see Table 15 for bird species)

The apparent rarity of eels represents a very serious problem. The possibility of storage helping to eke out meagre food supplies has already been considered. Storage of fish has been a very important strategy for many hunter-gatherers, but it is usually one adopted in the autumn, just before resources begin to get scarce: the Ainu, for example (Watanabe 1972), catch salmon throughout the summer, but the most important round of fishing is in October and November when the dog salmon are caught and dried, smoked and stored as the staple food for winter. Thus at the time when eels run, which occurs at monthly intervals for a few days, it would make sense to set up camp in the area of the winter base camp before the onset of winter. As hazel nuts would be at their best towards the end of the period when eels were running (Fig 88), and as large quantities could be gathered, one would expect sites such as Mount Sandel to be occupied by late September or early October. Again it would make sense to harvest the hazel nuts in the area of the camp. The crucial factor is that the eel runs are relatively short, so that if extensive use was made of them the problem would be, as Schalk (1977) has noted for salmon, to catch, process and preserve them in large numbers in a short period. This would probably be best carried out close to the fishing site, and if these fish were filleted then few bones would turn up on the settlements.

A short gap in occupation can therefore be envisaged, accepting that a significant proportion of the refuse on a site could belong to a *de facto* rubbish category or immediate post-abandonment phase, as described by Schiffer (1976). This could explain the apparent contradiction between the seasonality of the hearths and the occupation soil in the hut area. Perhaps a pre-existing hut was occupied during the summer and, on reoccupation later in the year, this hut may have been replaced before the onset of winter. Again, if these huts were kept clean then the refuse left in them would belong to the end of the winter occupation, of which the bones found in the hut hollow occupation soil would also be part.

There are also several indications that the site was not occupied during spring. There is no evidence of a spring run of salmon in the form of small eel (elver) bones. While today the Bann is not noted as a spring salmon river, this could be a result of the practice of netting which is known to reduce the numbers of salmon available in the spring. Sampson (1802) noted that during the 17th-century civil wars, when commercial fishing stopped, salmon of 6 feet in length were found in the tributaries of the Bann. Although they lie on the edge of the territory, the sea cliffs on either side of the Bann estuary would have provided an abundance of sea birds during the nesting season, yet none have been found on the site.

While these absences may have other explanations, it is not unusual for hunter-gatherers to abandon long-term winter camps as they have often exhausted the resources of the immediate vicinity.

Therefore, depending on whether or not the surviving evidence is accepted as representative of the totality of the fauna, totally different interpretations of the duration of seasonal occupation can be arrived at.

ECONOMY

As can be seen from the previous section, in spite of the fact that the duration of seasonal occupation is somewhat uncertain, a summer occupation and a late autumn to winter occupation at least can be justified (Chapter 5). The discussion of the economy will therefore proceed on the assumption that the site was occupied at these periods, and some consideration will also be given to the strategies adopted at other seasons of the year.

The small sample of bones drawn from different seasons of the year makes it difficult to produce a definitive study of the economic strategy of the Mesolithic inhabitants of this area, but at least several major trends can be seen. There appears to have been a concentration on fishing during the summer and perhaps into the autumn, with a greater emphasis on mammal hunting and use of stored resources during the winter. The reasons for this have already been discussed by the author (Woodman 1978): there are few freshwater fish native to Ireland, and the anadromous and catadromous fish would not be available in winter. In the case of Mount Sandel the location of the site would also have an impact on the economic strategy. It has been assumed by many, for example Paluden-Muller (1978), that river estuaries are a constant source of food throughout the year, but much depends on the nature of the river estuary. Thus Larsson (1980) has noted that there may have been a shorter seasonal occupation of estuarine sites on major rivers in Skåne.

In summary this site can be described as being on the upper limits of the Bann estuary, within easy reach of the open sea cliffs; it was also ideally placed in a wide, relatively well drained plain which would have contained several small lakes and which would not as yet have become clogged up with more recent (holocene) deposits. The only significant area of high ground would have been the northward extension of the Sperrin Mountains, which is several km west of the site, while the high Antrim Plateau lies 25 km to the east.

Fish

Battarbee has shown that the Mount Sandel site may have been placed close to its contemporary river estuary and more than likely just above it (Chapter 10). As the River Bann drains a substantial proportion of Northern Ireland, it is a river which would be subject to very significant discharge downstream. In the summer, even in the 19th century, the Bann could be reduced to a trickle so that one could walk across the Bar at Toome on Lough Neagh, while in the winter Lough Neagh could be 10 to 15 feet higher. The result of this massive increase in water would be the shifting of the river estuary much further downstream. After the September spring tides, the Mount Sandel site would often be placed relatively further upstream from the coast.

If other local information is added to that used by van Wijngaarden-Bakker (Chapter 5, Figs 40 and 42), the result is Fig 87 which shows some of the other species which are liable to be present in the Bann estuary and in the open sea. On the evidence of Dubourdieu (1812) a spring salmon run has been added. The marine species have been placed in two groups. Mullet and flounder are considered typical of the fish which penetrate the upper reaches of the estuary, usually during the summer. Bass is more intermediate in character but is less likely to be found in the inner estuary. Pollock and cod are thought to be more typical of the outer estuary and open sea.

If a comparison is made between the relative numbers of fish found at Mount Sandel and Fig 87, a slight paradox emerges (Chapter 5 and Appendix 1d). The migratory fish, in particular the salmonid, are the most important in the Mount Sandel fauna, while those which most commonly penetrate the inner estuary are not particularly common. This suggests fishing in two different environments: the freshwater area immediately adjacent to the estuary (Chapters 9 and 10), and the outer estuary. The noticeable absences are species typical of the inner estuary.

The strategy of catching most of the fish just above the river estuary during the summer months can be seen from the faunal remains and by examining the recent traditions of fishing in the estuary. The fact that flounder and other fish like mullet which can penetrate the upper reaches of the estuary are virtually absent indicates that extensive fishing did not take place in the estuary. This suggests that fish were not netted but rather caught in traps or similar devices in the rapids area. An apparent contradiction is the presence of bass. These are a species which today belong in the outer estuary. They are not usually found round the northern coast of Ireland, but according to Linnane (1980) they are found in Lough Foyle and off the Bann estuary. This species could be evidence of coastal exploitation—perhaps in connection with flint collection from the coast and, if the one bevel-ended pebble is an indication, shellfish exploitation. The Bann estuary with its extreme variations in salinity would render the inner estuary

POLLOCK

COD

BASS

MULLET

FLOUNDER

ELVERS

SILVER EELS

SPRING RUN ?

SALMON

A MY JN JY AG S O N D JA F MR

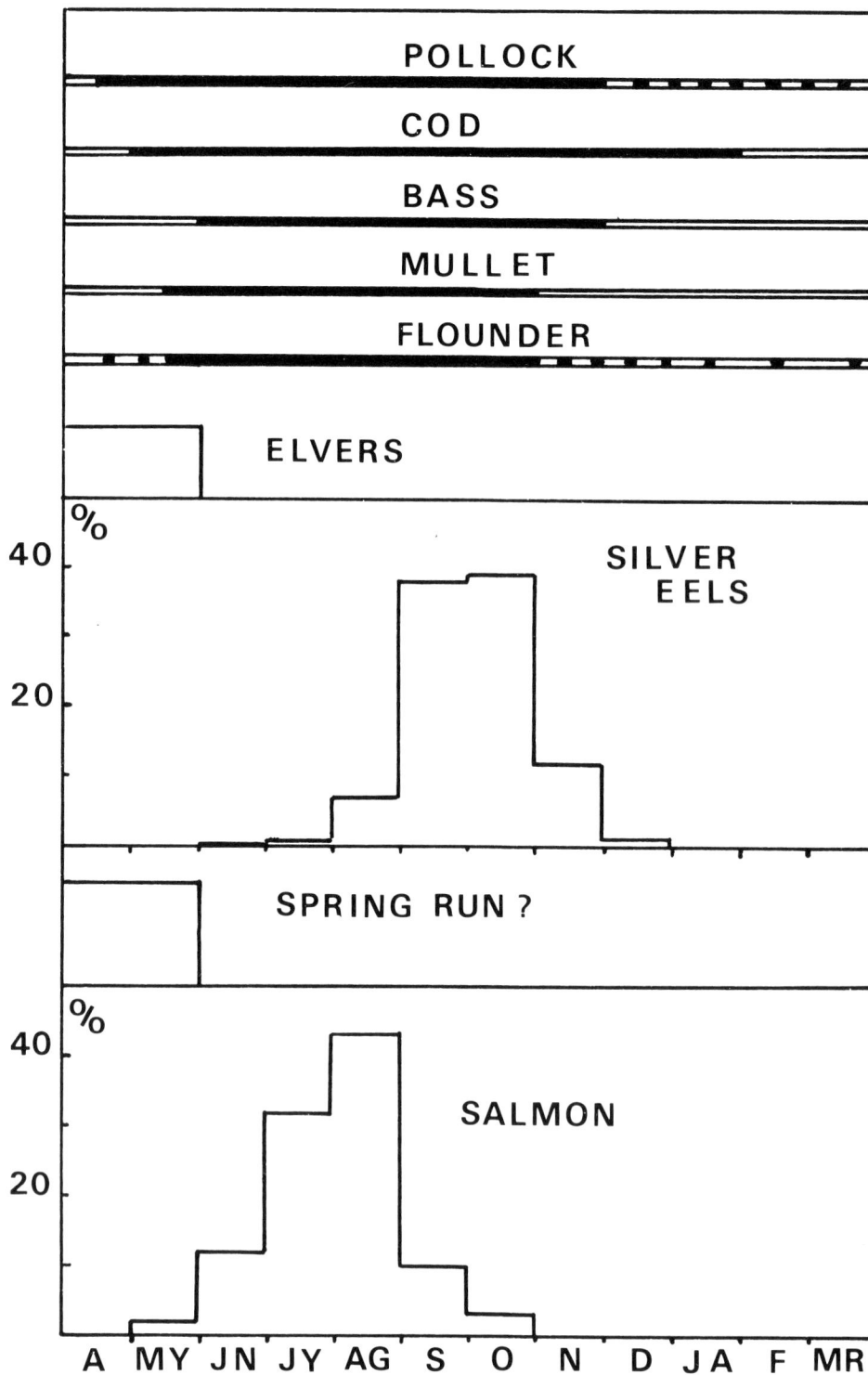

Fig 87   Monthly distribution of fish resources

unsuitable for shellfish exploitation, therefore shellfish and in particular limpets would be best collected on the rocky shores which lie beyond the edges of the river estuary.

Even today the estuary changes character during the winter. The tenfold increase in freshwater discharge down the River Bann reduces the salinity of the water in the estuary, so that even with a saline wedge forcing its way into the estuary there is a massive decrease in marine species during the winter: a few flounder survive in the estuary by eating nereid worms, for example, while in the summer they would have a wider range of food. The result is that species such as cod and pollock cannot easily be caught in areas adjacent to Mount Sandel, and their absence cannot be used to suggest a lack of winter occupation.

There is, of course, the possibility that fish migration patterns were different in the Mesolithic period. In particular Taylor (1980) and Lamb *et al* (1966) have suggested that the climate of Early Boreal times may have been more continental and the winters longer and colder. Because of the presence of more extensive ice caps, the Gulf Stream may not have run so far north and sea temperatures would have been lower. Taylor (1980) has even suggested that the temperature differences between northern and southern parts of the British Isles would have been much greater than today. Therefore certain species may not have established migratory patterns round the north coast of Ireland. However, the presence of bass does suggest that other species should have been present as bass, though found today off the mouth of the Foyle, is more common further south. Therefore the absence of mullet, flounder and similar species could result from fishing strategies rather than represent a genuine absence.

The main emphasis on fishing just above the estuary appears to be backed up by Dubourdieu in his observations on the early 19th-century commercial salmon fisheries of the Bann (1812). These suggest that fishing with dip nets and traps was regarded as more efficient than fishing with nets in the estuary. Though Bonsall has noted the importance of netting the Esk estuary in Cumbria (1981), and in spite of the Antrea find (Clark 1975) and the Barre Mosse birch-bark float (Welinder 1971), the role of fishing with traps and dip nets was probably more important than netting in the Mesolithic period. Indeed many of the methods of netting used in Ireland are a relatively recent introduction (Went 1964). The probable use of traps and dip nets again emphasizes the positional importance of the Mount Sandel site. Fig 1 shows that from the point of view of hunting there is a little advantage in this location, as the flat land formed by the Armoy Ice Sheet runs for several miles along the Bann, as does the steep-sided valley in which the river runs. Therefore areas such as the Cutts and Loughan Island, where the river was narrower and access was easier, were probably the most important as in the 19th century. In these areas if simple traps were used they could be reversed to catch eels coming downstream, a tactic the Ainu used to catch returning salmon (Watanabe 1972).

It is impossible to estimate the summer carrying capacity of this area. Even allowing for the fact that the prodigious quantities of salmon and eels caught in recent times result from commercial fishing, the numbers of fish in the Bann would have been very large. The limiting factor would probably have been points of access, and if 'fixed engines' were used then it is possible that each point of access would have been controlled by a small group or even an extended family. This could have been through ownership, as with many of the north-west coastal tribes in North America, or through access to the details of certain rituals associated with fishing, as with the Ainu (Coon 1976). Problems of access could have reduced population levels well below the theoretical carrying capacity of the terrain.

Mammals
In discussing the strategy of mammal hunting which might have become more important in the autumn and winter, one returns to the remarkable absence of red deer from the faunal remains. While certain biasing of the record can be expected through the nature of the faunal remains, this total absence of red deer must reflect its relative lack of importance as a major food resource in the area around Mount Sandel. But this is not to say that red deer was unimportant within the Mesolithic of north-east Ireland. This animal would have been a necessary source of skins for clothing, tents, etc, though there is so far no evidence in Ireland that its antlers were used as raw material for the manufacture of implements— at least during the Mesolithic. As this was probably an area where deer could have foraged throughout most of the year, particularly at this time when the forest was still rather open, one can assume that some deer would have been available. However, from the viewpoint of their skins these animals are best killed in autumn when their coats are improving in quality. Perhaps the numbers of deer were so small that expeditions away from the camp were necessary to kill them. The association of Star Carr with skin-working has been noted by Pitts (1979). Binford (1978) has noted that it is more advantageous to move to the kill and processing sites to consume the meat available and this, perhaps, rather than following fish runs upstream, could have caused either a temporary abandonment or reduction in population levels at sites such as Mount Sandel. If, as with the Bushmen (Yellen 1977), these animals were killed within about two hours' walk or even paddle of the site, then even through differential butchering practices some bones would find their way back to the site. Ultimately one must conclude that most deer were killed far enough away from the base camp, or in such small numbers, for their remains not to be reflected in the faunal record. As with so many problems where an

assessment of the Irish post-glacial fauna is essential it is impossible to balance the equation.

A similar failure has to be admitted when the economic strategies for pig hunting are discussed. Van Wijngaarden-Bakker (Chapter 5) has emphasized the solitary nature of the pig, which would lead to hunting in small groups. The one period when pigs gather in larger numbers is in autumn, in areas where large quantities of nuts are available. Thus as hazel could well have flourished on the slopes below Mount Sandel, as it did a thousand years later (Chapter 9), numerous pigs may have been present in this area during the autumn. There is no clear evidence for this, however, and the presence of foetal bones of pig shows that they were present on the site slightly later in the year. Again, is this a genuine absence or biasing of the data? Not every group of animal bones should belong to the latest part of the year's occupation.

Despite this problem, there is no doubt that pigs were extensively hunted and that their small numbers would have encouraged fission of larger groupings of people to hunt in smaller units. This would be consistent with the suggestion that the Mount Sandel site was occupied by a small group of people, perhaps only just into double figures. Jochim (1976) nd Bay-Petersen (1978) both offer sets of figures which are roughly comparable and suggest a range of 60 to 500 pigs within a 10 km radius. There is a usual assumption that coniferous forests have a relatively low carrying capacity. While it is difficult to assess the nature of Boreal environments, Grigson (1982) has noted that pigs are diversivores and that beech nuts and acorns are usually an important part of their diet. Therefore, while they will eat anything from ground-nesting birds to rotting fruit and vegetables, they would be rather restricted in the birch-pine-hazel forest. So even on the assumption of 120 pigs within this territory and with the young forming up to 50% of the population, rather than 20% as suggested by Bay-Petersen, pigs would have formed a limited source of food, even if 50% of the total population could be culled (Chapter 5).

The potential effect of having to rely extensively on pigs rather than on a broader range of ungulates can be seen below. If an assumption of 10 people living at Mount Sandel is made, and if a mean of 2500 calories per person per day is also taken* and the winter period is assumed to last 125 days, then 3.12 million calories would be required for each winter occupation.

At twice the minimum number of pigs in a 10 km^2

area, this would give approximately 11,000 kg in terms of body weight of pig (Bay-Petersen 1978). 70% could be regarded as consumable (White 1953), giving a total of 7700 kg of meat including heart, liver, brain, etc. It is impossible to provide an accurate estimate of the calorific value of this range of food, but van Wijngaarden-Bakker (1980) has suggested that for wild pigs 300 calories per 100 gm could be considered reasonable: thus in total 7700 kg equals 23.1 million calories. There are, of course, several limiting factors such as the 50% cull rate (at a maximum), and if this was happening continually a large proportion of the animals caught would be young. Thus the 50% cull might consist of small animals, perhaps again only 50% of the expected weight. The potential food value would thus be just below 6 million calories. Again Jochim (1976) has noted that winter territories are usually smaller, so that if efficient hunting was reduced by half then only one group could live extensively on pigs in a territory about 7.5 km in radius. This implies that even a group of ten people, living entirely on pig, is an over-estimate for the population of Mount Sandel, and that perhaps little more than one extended family would have lived there.

Obviously these figures are subject to numerous alterations. Pigs could have been more successful at this time but against that, as an island population, there could have been a reduction in animal size. Obviously red deer, though not represented, could have made a contribution. Small game could have played a role but of those native to Ireland (Woodman 1974a; van Wijngarden-Bakker 1974) only Irish hare would usually be hunted. This animal could, of course, be caught by trapping but would only be a marginal addition.

Birds

Unfortunately the avifauna contain no real indicators of seasonal occupation. In general the presence of red-throated diver (*G. stellata*) and grouse (*Lagopus*) would point to autumn and winter occupation, but as these are not entirely seasonal migrants, it is consistent presence on the site which could suggest this. Individual bones in certain hearths cannot be used to support attribution of a certain season to specific features.

Little can be said of the bird remains. They constitute such a small number that they are best seen as an additional source of food rather than a staple one. In spite of the range of bird bones, which may reflect both the opportunist nature of their contribution to the diet and the way in which they have been preserved, it is the absences which are remarkable. There is no significant contribution from sea birds, and this could be both a locational and seasonal indicator: sea birds are at their most vulnerable

---

* Wing and Brown (1979) have shown that many children need large numbers of calories while growing, and nursing mothers need even more, so an assumption of at least 2500 calories is justifiable.

during the nesting season (late spring/early summer). These bones have been found in significant numbers in the Later Mesolithic coastal middens of Ireland. Also notable for their absence are the larger water fowl, such as geese and swans. These could have made a substantial contribution to the diet, and might be expected to congregate on the nearby small lake which would have existed under Garry Bog and further upstream on the Bann. While (as noted earlier) the absence of sea birds may be seasonal, the hunting strategies for both these groups of birds would have been much more organized and their absence suggests a rather more casual trapping strategy for birds close to the camp (Chapter 5).

Plant foods
These must represent the most biased fragmentary resource of all. Both water-lily seeds and apples could have been used as a staple food during the summer and autumn, as is clear from their presence with salmon bones. These plants and others could have been collected in the area round the settlement by women, children and the elderly. Binford (personal communication) has pointed out that water-lily seeds can be stored and are often used as a last reserve during late winter. Therefore, though these seeds occur in F56/2, they could also represent part of the gathering of winter reserves.

While water-lily seeds could have been used as winter staple foods, they are remarkably bulky in relation to their calorific value. In comparison hazel nuts would have been an ideal resource. There is evidence that these would have been used throughout the winter in that they have been found with foetal pig bones (Chapter 5). These nuts could have been collected in large quantities in the area adjacent to Mount Sandel. Bonsall (1981) has correctly criticized Clarke (1976) for using figures derived from controlled hazel stands, thus creating the impression of hazel nuts existing in exceptional abundance. On the other hand, Jacobi (1978a), on the basis of figures from pollen diagrams at Hockham Mere, has suggested that for a winter of four months 25% of the diet of a community of four families would require the collection of nuts in an area between 0.7 and 1.6 square miles of hazel scrub. Godwin has pointed out (1956) that we know very little about the nature of the hazel forest which existed in early post-glacial times and therefore estimates of this nature must be treated with caution. Even if Clarke's estimate of a half tonne of hazel nuts per hectare is exceptionally high, the careful exploitation of the hazel crop before the nuts fell from the trees and the placing of the camp site adjacent to areas where hazel was common could lead to large numbers of nuts being collected from a small area. Thus, even though Mount Sandel is dated to before the hazel maximum, large areas (4 sq km

suggested by Jacobi) would not have had to be scoured for nuts as some areas, such as the slopes below Mount Sandel, could have been very rich in hazel scrub. Hazel would almost certainly have existed in such locations in large quantities before some other areas were extensively colonized. In pollen diagrams a certain spurious average increase can be created when regional diagrams are used, rather than diagrams derived from close to a site: Garry Bog for example, discussed in Chapter 9, does not provide local information for Mount Sandel, and there could have been a local abundance of hazel at Mount Sandel without this appearing at Garry Bog.

If an average 20% of the diet of our notional community were hazel nuts, 5000 calories a day for 125 days would be required, that is 625,000 calories altogether. Unshelled hazel nuts provide approximately 100 calories per 100 gm, and 5 kilos in volume represent less than 2000 cc. If this resource was to last 125 days, roughly 625 kilos, or over half a metric tonne, would be required. It is intriguing that the deep pits had an average volume slightly greater than would be required to keep this supply of hazel nuts. Even if Clarke's figures for the potential of hazel are optimistic and the usual level of production of hazel nuts was only one-fifth of what he suggested, it would have been possible to collect sufficient nuts along the slope below the site without having to go more than 0.5 km from the camp.

As Bonsall (1981) has noted, most other plant foods do little more than provide occasional supplements. This can be seen by comparing nuts with apples (Table 52). Apples are rich in carbohydrates, but the volume of apples required is considerably larger than the volume of hazel nuts, thus presenting storage problems. While acorns are a very rich food source, even at 6500 bc they would not have been very plentiful. Ease of collection, arising from ready availability, and storage were probably the two major determinants in deciding what plant foods would be collected, as it is probable that more than would be required would have been available, even before 6500 bc. Another limiting factor may have been, as Bonsall pointed out, the body capacity to absorb coarse fibrous plant foods. While they would have been useful, there may have been a limit to the extent to which they could have been relied upon. This may not, however, have been as restrictive as he suggests. Californian Indians relied extensively on acorns. This is a plant food which is virtually inedible in its natural state but with lengthy processing it was made edible and nutritious enough to become the main part of their diet.

Therefore, the preceding estimates could have significantly under-estimated the importance of plant foods. The main restricting factors would have been availability in an Early Mesolithic context and, for

	Water %	Protein %	Fat %	Available carbo-hydrate %	K cals per 100 gm	Waste %
Acorns						
Quercus robur	13.9	7.9	4.6	67.8	353	20
Hazel nuts (shelled)						
Corylus sp.	41.1	9.0	36.0	6.8	398	64
Mushrooms						
Agaricus camp-estris	91.5	1.8	Tr	0	7	25
Blackberries						
Rubus sp.	82.0	1.3	Tr	6.4	30	0
Gooseberries						
Ribes uva-crispa	89.9	1.1	Tr	3.4	17	1
Crab apples						
Malus sylvestris	81.1	0.4	0.3	17.2	68	—
Watercress						
Nasturtium officinale	91.1	2.9	Tr	0.7	15	23
Dock						
Rumex sp.	90.9	2.1	0.3	4.5	28	—
Sea kale						
Crambe maritima	95.6	1.4	Tr	0.6	8	26

Table 52   Composition of certain selected plant foods (based on Bonsall 1981) (Tr = trace)

winter consumption, an ability to be stored. The relative lack of obvious archaeological evidence of plant processing equipment is one of the striking characteristics of the European Mesolithic.

ARCHAEOLOGICAL CONTEXT

It has been suggested that the Mount Sandel site contained evidence for only a portion of the expected activities for a year-round cycle of occupation and that there are good reasons to believe that its inhabitants may have moved elsewhere at certain seasons of the year. Unfortunately the quality of material from the other north-eastern sites makes it impossible to assess the nature of the sites from the stone artefacts. Because of the problems of multiple use and curation it is almost impossible to assess the significance of a site even when a selection of stone tools from an excavation is available, but when there is a poor selection of surface-collected artefacts, dominated by axes, the problem is insurmountable. In spite of these difficulties, an attempt will be made in this section to see how the archaeological evidence now available for the Irish Mesolithic can be interpreted in social and economic terms.

Unlike many parts of mainland Europe, it has been possible to show the presence of man on the coast of Ireland before 6000 bc. The best known material is from the lower gravels at Cushendun (Movius 1940; Woodman 1978) and Glynn (Woodman 1977), both in Co Antrim. Early Mesolithic material has been

found along the north coast at Portrush and Portballintrae (Woodman 1978) and in the Mount Sandel area are several other excavated sites (Fig 88). At Mount Sandel (Lower), part of a hut was uncovered as well as material which could derive from manufacturing activities (Collins 1983); at Castleroe a small rescue excavation uncovered a sample of material, faunal and structural remains similar to those from Mount Sandel (Upper) (Appendix 5); and a scatter of flint blades comes from the ford at Sandelford just below Mount Sandel (Fig 1). Scatters of material have been found further up the River Bann in rather similar locations to Mount Sandel, on ridges of slightly higher ground where the river is relatively narrow. These sites are Movanagher, Portna, Glenone and Culbane (see Woodman 1978, area 1, for detailed descriptions). On the shores of Lough Neagh material has been found at Maddens, River Maine estuary, Coney Island and at Maghery, while a small scatter of microliths was found away from the shore at Tullywiggan, Co Tyrone (Woodman 1978, area 1b).

Further south, scatters of material have been found on the shores of Strangford Lough, Co Down, and in coastal areas in Leinster. Recent excavations have produced an extensive scatter of Early Mesolithic material on the shores of the now peat-filled Lough Boora, Co Offaly (Ryan 1980). The bias towards north-eastern sites is obviously an historical bias arising from the large numbers of collectors. There is

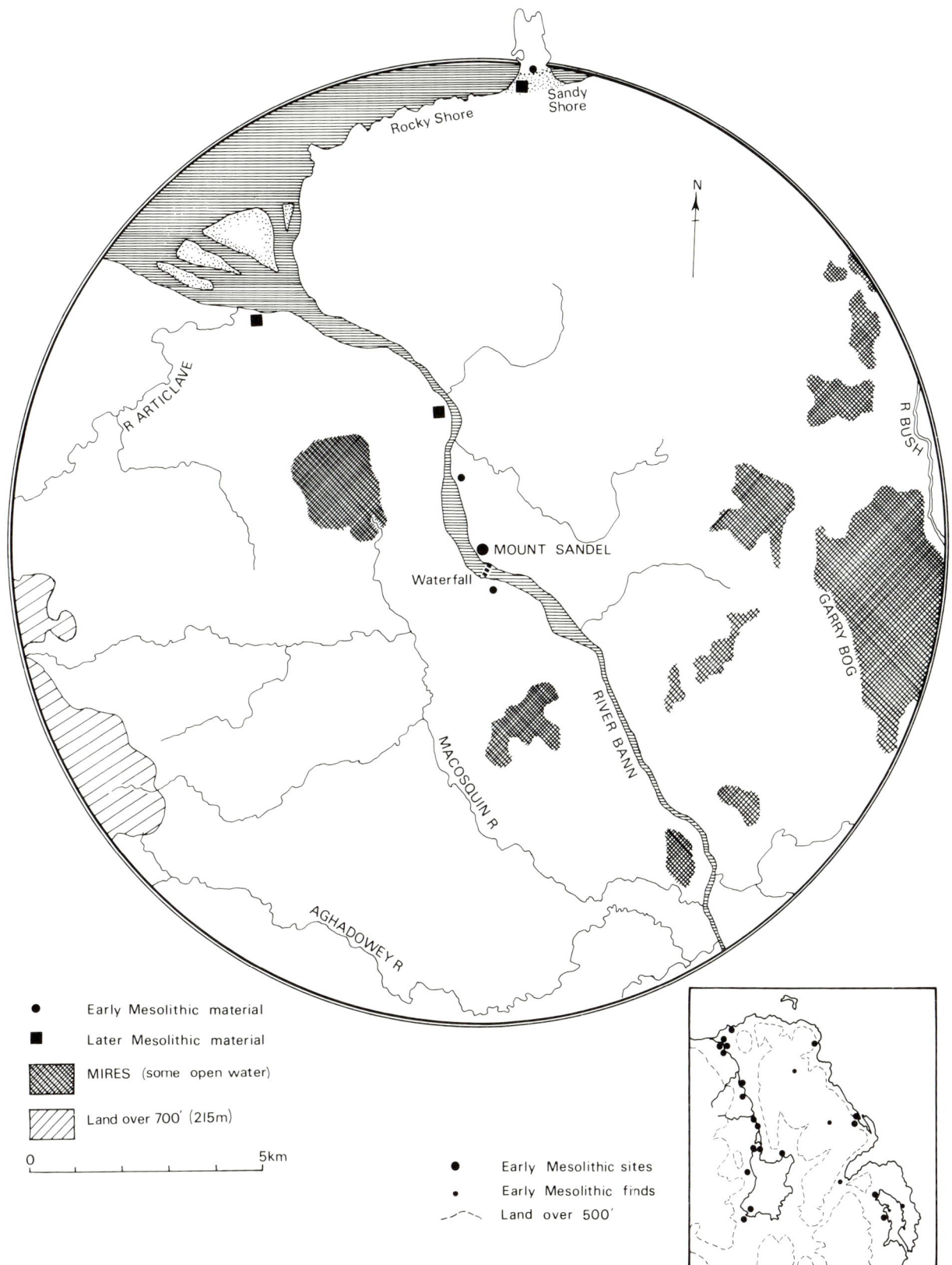

Fig 88   Distribution map of Early Mesolithic sites in the area adjacent to Mount Sandel and (lower right) north-east
Ireland

a noticeable lack of upland sites in Co Antrim. Significant quantities of Neolithic material have been found on the Antrim Plateau, but there is no equivalent to the substantial scatter of Mesolithic material found in Great Britain in the Pennines. This has led to the suggestion that red deer may never have played a significant role in the Irish Mesolithic (Woodman 1974a).

Obviously the Mount Sandel (Lower) site could be another occupation site in the Mount Sandel area, and in spite of the large standard deviation for the one reliable ^{14}C date (Table 49) it could be suggested that it represents a significantly later occupation than that centred on the main hut at Mount Sandel (Upper). On the other hand the Castleroe site appears to be roughly contemporary with Mount Sandel (Upper) and so could be part of a pattern of dispersed occupation. The Sandelford material is the least satisfactory as it is rather difficult to find amongst the boulders on the ford, but with virtually no finished artefacts and little waste material the selection of blades could be derived from a fishing and processing site.

It is tempting to arrange the few other known sites within the framework of the general model which is often used to explain seasonal movement in coastal areas, for example to the coast in spring and inland during summer (Larsson 1980). Thus sites such as the Portrush Springhill, situated on top of a rocky promontory, could be positioned to take advantage of the beginnings of the coastal salmon runs. This fishing tradition continues even today along the rocky shores of north Antrim. Similarly shellfish and sea birds would be available in large quantities along the rocky shore in this area. Unfortunately the Mesolithic shoreline where shell middens would have existed has been buried below later post-glacial deposits.

Certain sites on the shores of Lough Neagh, such as Maddens and River Maine, have produced a small but significant number of scrapers and, in the case of Maddens, a few burins. These sites, from their material and location, are reminiscent of Star Carr as shoreline processing sites.

The other inland sites present a greater problem. They could represent occupation of a rather more transitory nature during a seasonal movement inland, or they could represent base camps of other groups. The problem with the former explanation is that there is no real need for these communities to follow fish runs upstream. The runs are liable to have lasted for a few months, and the advantage of remaining at Mount Sandel is that the sea and estuary present alternative ecological niches which could have been exploited much more conveniently. In fact, with a fall-off in fish densities as one moves inland, there is little point in moving away from the estuary after fish. A problem in Ireland is that there is little

evidence of residential fish populations (Woodman 1978). *Coregonus Autumnalis* (pollan) must have established itself in Lough Neagh during late glacial times but it can be caught most easily during the winter, while during the summer months it feeds on the bottom of Lough Neagh (Wilson 1979). Pike, which was fished extensively in Scandinavia (Larsson 1978; Henricksen 1976), and the carp family, fished in central European lakes (Jochim 1976), are not native to Ireland. A further problem is the undoubted bias in the distribution of sites. Any extensive summer riverside settlements like those which existed in the Later Mesolithic, such as Newferry (Woodman 1977a), would now be buried under more recent deposits or be eroded away.

While the significance of coastal settlement in the Early Mesolithic of southern Scandinavia is a subject of active debate, in Ireland the main problem appears to be the extent of inland settlement. The report on the faunal remains from Lough Boora is awaited with interest as this might establish whether there were any residential freshwater fish populations in early post-glacial Ireland and whether red deer played a significant part in the economy of the Irish Mesolithic. From its location and relatively large concentration of scrapers the Lough Boora site would seem to be another shoreline processing site, like Maddens. In fact it could well be a summer-autumn site where fishing, hide-working and, because of the availability of chert nodules on the lough shore, chert-working took place. The major problem must be whether it was related to base camps in its immediate area or sites closer to the coast. The presence of a significant number of flint microliths and blades is suggestive of some form of contact with the coastal parts of Leinster (Woodman 1981).

A problem which arises with sites such as Lough Boora or the inland scatters of material in the north-east is that they could represent camps of small specialized task groups, rather than the result of a full family group moving. Therefore it is possible that we may eventually find totally different environments being exploited at the same time by different members of the same family group. With this possibility in mind we must be able to identify the nature of a site before we can begin to reconstruct any overall economic interpretations.

The site at Mount Sandel must also be seen within the broader context of a social grouping, though here one returns to the vexed question of the extent of occupation in Ireland before the settlement at Mount Sandel. This will be discussed further in Chapter 13, but there is sufficient evidence to show that a significant, though unknown, period may have elapsed between the initial colonization and the use of the Mount Sandel site. Therefore those living in the Mount Sandel area must be seen as having contacts with other groups, perhaps living in the Larne Lough or Strangford Lough areas. There are also indications, through Ryan's excavations at Lough Boora, that the centre of Ireland was extensively exploited at this time, but that more recent peat development has covered these traces of activity. It is also intriguing to note the presence of occasional chert microliths at Mount Sandel. There are no known occurrences of chert in the north-east of Ireland, and no natural mechanism is known by which it could have travelled there, so some population movement must be postulated to explain their presence. The possibility of contact between Mount Sandel and sites as far south as Lough Boora seems remote, but the chert microliths could imply exploitation in a rather transitory fashion of areas at the northern end of the Irish midlands, where chert is found in abundance. The slight scatters of material around Lough Neagh, such as the two or three composite implements from Tullywiggan and the possible evidence for processing sites at Maddens and River Maine, could suggest small hunting parties moving inland away from the coast. It is not necessary to envisage a large-scale movement inland from the coast.

While much of the previous discussion indicates that the Early Mesolithic of Ireland was essentially coastal, it is important to remember that the inland areas have not been extensively searched and there is evidence of extensive exploitation of the Lower Bann during the Later Mesolithic. While the economic strategy of this phase is not fully understood, the presence of thousands of large blades and hundreds of axes in areas such as Culbane and Newferry shows that at a certain time of the year the Lower Bann played a very important role in the Mesolithic of the north-east of Ireland. This could, of course, be due to the change in environment, but the possibility that similar Early Mesolithic sites exist buried beneath Atlantic period deposits must be real.

Summary

It is of course impossible to provide a detailed assessment of the relative importance of the different sources of food used throughout the period when Mount Sandel was occupied. We can, however, suggest that as the site was occupied for a substantial portion of the year a number of different strategies would have been employed to produce food.

With the availability of plant foods as well as large quantities of fish the summer months would have been a period of plenty when there would have been no limit to the population which could have been supported in the area. In fact it is possible that at this period small groups were dispatched from the main areas of settlement. This would explain both the scatters of material in inland areas and the occasional

presence of exotic raw materials at Mount Sandel. If, as suggested above, the carrying capacity of the interior was not particularly high it makes sense to dispatch groups during a time of plenty, resulting in less intensive use of the Mount Sandel area resources during the late summer and early autumn, something which seems to be reflected in the surviving evidence.

The limiting factor for this area was clearly the winter when, as noted by the author (Woodman 1978), there is a rather restricted availability of fish. The potential for extensive exploitation of pig in the Boreal forest would not have been particularly great, and with red deer providing a restricted part of the diet there seems to have been a relatively poor potential for any large groups to survive the winter. Therefore, with food in short supply, a 'least risk' policy was probably adopted. Instead of relying on an extensive culling of pigs which, as shown earlier, has its limitations and would also effectively drive away game as the area was hunted more and more intensely, storage would provide a 'least risk' solution. Autumn storage of fish and, as is clear from many pits, hazel nuts would provide an effective buffer against winter shortages. Thus, while small game and bird hunting could have provided additional sources of food, there is no reason why winter mammal hunting should have provided more than 50% of the food needed throughout the winter. The potential seasonal variations have been summarized in Fig 89.

In general, as has been noted by van Wijngaarden-Bakker (Chapter 5), this type of economy, even with its extensive use of storage, would have led to a rather dispersed winter settlement. The apparent presence of only one hut at a time at Mount Sandel appears to fit in with this type of economic strategy, while other sites such as Castleroe could be contemporary with Mount Sandel. The proximity of settlement sites would then be decided by the size of the group living at each site and by the extent of reliance on mammal hunting.

Binford (1980) has suggested that the Bushmen and Nunamiut represent two contrasting strategies, the Bushmen having a foraging strategy and the Nunamiut a 'mapping-on' strategy. The former involves a high degree of mobility of camp site while the latter is associated with more strategic placing of base camps and few moves. The major problem with the model offered by Binford is that the contrast between the near-sedentary mapping-on strategy and his alternative seasonal foraging strategy epitomizes the alternatives of the European Mesolithic—seasonal mobility or near-sedentary occupation. Perhaps the interpretation of a single site in a unique environment for Europe may not seem important for testing Binford's suggestions, but few other sites in western Europe appear to have produced such a range of

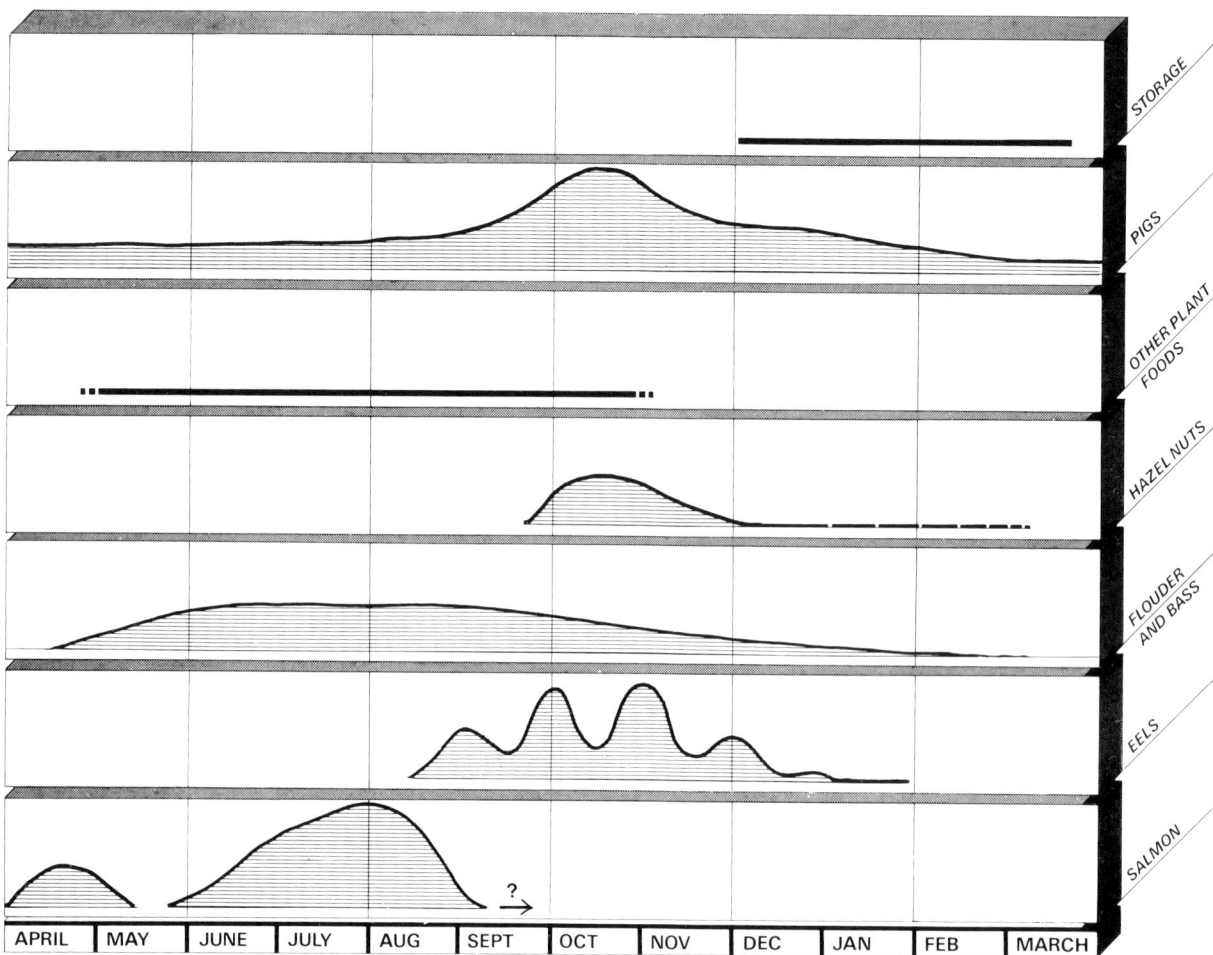

Fig 89   Distribution of seasonal resources

seasonal information combined with extensive structural evidence, and even here at Mount Sandel, as van Wijngaarden-Bakker has noted, there is a real possibility that the site was abandoned in the autumn. Thus the interpretation of Mount Sandel as a long-term base camp hinges on either accepting the faunal remains at face value or pleading that off-site butchering or processing and bias through behaviour have created a false impression of abandonment. While it is tempting simply to note that the wealth of structural remains at Mount Sandel implies that the site was occupied for much of the year, comparison with the range of data found at the archaic levels at the Koster site (Wolynec 1977; Streuver and Holton 1979) underlines how much is lacking from most European Mesolithic settlement sites.

In spite of these problems of seasonality, positive statements can be made about certain main aspects of the settlement at Mount Sandel. It was a substantial base camp, where not only a dwelling but other contemporary activity areas can be defined. In spite of the impoverished nature of the faunal evidence, it has been possible to show that this community exploited a wide range of fauna and plant foods. These indicate that occupation may have taken place during the summer and winter and that only a relatively small group could have lived on the site. The discovery of chert microliths suggests that the community was able to draw on raw materials throughout a significant portion of Ireland, through either mobility or exchange systems. The remaining questions of autumn occupation and the role of the red deer must be seen as vexing enigmas which limit, rather than totally impair, our understanding of the nature of the Mesolithic settlement at Mount Sandel.

CHAPTER 13

Mount Sandel in its broader Mesolithic context

Introduction

The preceding chapters have concentrated on the problems of interpreting the data collected during the excavations at Mount Sandel, but the site has also to be seen in a broader context. In terms of artefacts, faunal remains and ^{14}C dating it is now one of the linchpins of the Irish Early Mesolithic. On the other hand, an excavation report is not the place for a detailed discussion of all aspects of the Irish Mesolithic and therefore discussion will be confined to three specific topics: the chronological position of Mount Sandel, the origins of the Irish Mesolithic, and the implications of the structures found at Mount Sandel.

The Chronological Position of Mount Sandel

When the first samples from Mount Sandel were ^{14}C-dated in 1974 it became clear that this site was earlier than the traditional beginnings of the Irish Mesolithic, in about 6000 bc. Evidence for a phase of the Irish Mesolithic which used microliths, small flake and core axes, flake scrapers and a controlled knapping technique is now amply confirmed by dates from Castleroe (Table 49 and Appendix 5) and Lough Boora, Co Offaly (Ryan 1980). The tantalizing prospect of an even earlier Mesolithic has since been uncovered by Burenhult (1980) at Woodpark, Co Sligo. Here the site produced an early ^{14}C date of 7490 ± 100 bc, but unfortunately insufficient diagnostic artefacts were found during a test excavation. There is a strong possibility that the ^{14}C date came from a piece of very old wood washed up on the Littorina shoreline, yet there is always the possibility that this date could indicate an even earlier Mesolithic than at Mount Sandel.

One of the most vexing problems arising with the Early Mesolithic industry concerns its relationship to the broad-bladed Later Mesolithic. If the ^{14}C date from F109, that is 5935 ± 120 bc, relates to the adjacent scatter of material found on the northern edge of the Mount Sandel site, then the narrow-blade industry could have survived to around or even

significantly later than 6000 bc. The material found in the area of F109 is identical to that found in the rest of the site. There is no evidence of a change to the forms which occur in the Later Mesolithic.

The peculiar distinctiveness of the Later Mesolithic shows that the dichotomy cannot be explained by population change, as many of the type fossils of the Later Mesolithic are best explained as local developments from earlier types (Fig 90). The industry changed from a controlled percussion to a direct percussion technique resulting in larger, broader blades. Microliths disappeared, and a range of implements made on large heavy blades came into existence. At the moment no convincing explanations can be offered for the virtually total replacement of the lithic equipment of the Irish Mesolithic. It could have been a product of the distribution of raw materials or a change in economy, though most lithic artefacts do not relate so directly to procurement strategies. At a more general level the change may have resulted from a build-up to a population level that was sufficiently viable to allow the development of its own stylistic traditions (Woodman 1981). At this stage we cannot explain the mechanism for change but can only suggest that the factors which allowed the creation of the potential for change were probably as much social as environmental.

These problems are perhaps highlighted by the large concentration of dates that come from only two sites, Mount Sandel (Upper) and Newferry site 3, but there are also some other slight traces of human

Toome	Y 95	5630 ± 110 bc
Cushendun (lower silts)	I 5134	5720 ± 140 bc
Cushendun (lower silts)	UB 689	5445 ± 65 bc
Newferry site 3 (zone 9)	UB 888	6225 ± 145 bc
Newferry site 3 (zone 9)	UB 487	6240 ± 140 bc
Newferry site 3 (zone 8)	UB 641	5680 ± 195 bc
Mount Sandel F109	UB 2359	5935 ± 120 bc

Table 53   Radiocarbon dates from the poorly documented part of the Irish Mesolithic

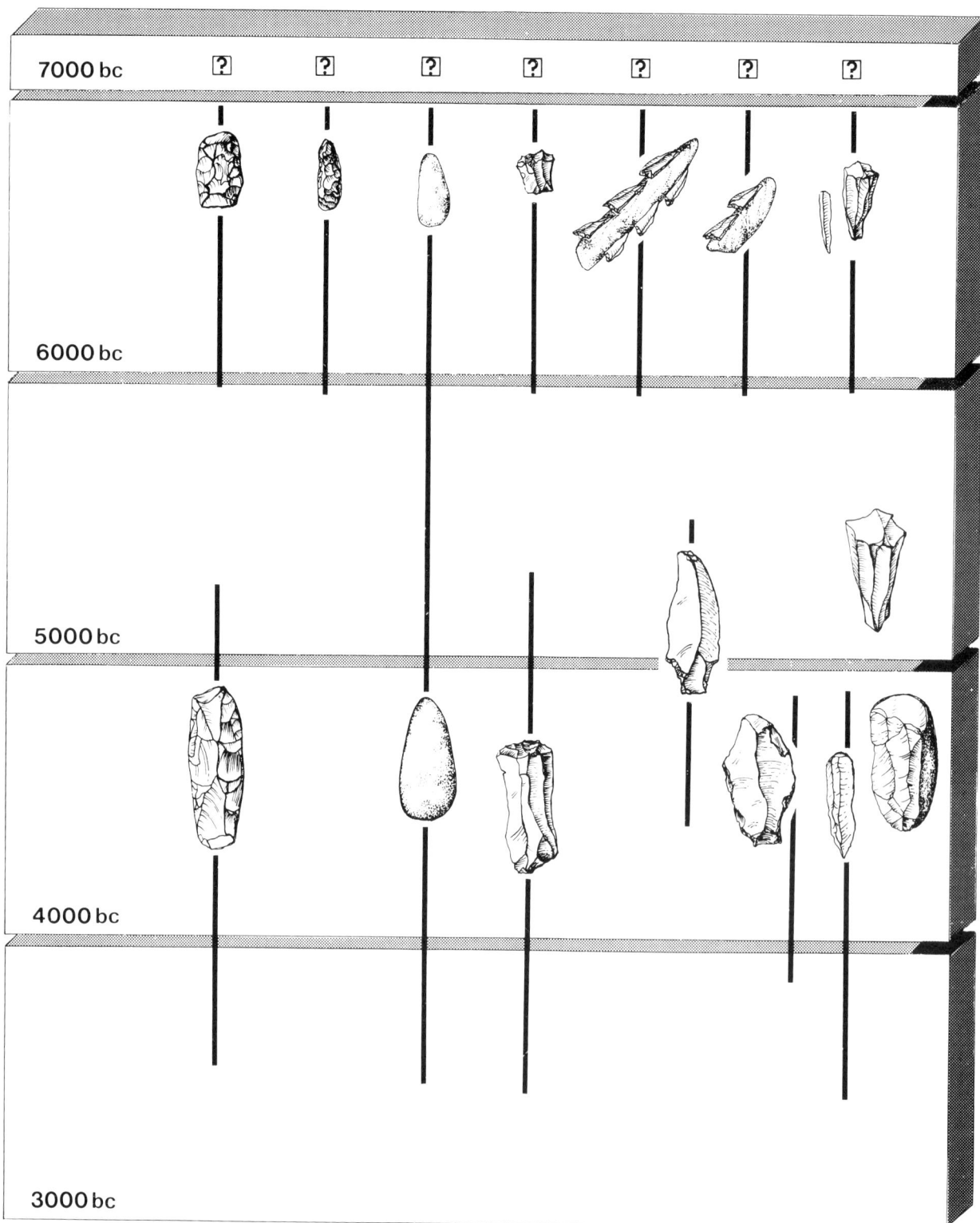

Fig 90   Chronological chart of the Irish Mesolithic

activity which show that man was present in Ireland between 6500 bc and 5000 bc. These are dates from a basal layer at Newferry (zone 9) which contained a stone setting, charcoal associated with a stone setting at Toome, and the lower lagoon silt at Cushendun, as well as FI09 at Mount Sandel (Table 53).

The Origins of the Irish Mesolithic

The relatively early dates for the Mount Sandel site mean that the whole mechanism of the colonization of Ireland must receive some consideration.

The insular character of certain aspects of the Mount Sandel assemblage, notably the needle points and perhaps the presence of true flake axes,* suggests that Mount Sandel is not a site of the initial colonizing phase. It can be argued (Woodman 1981) that there is no reason why Ireland could not have been colonized at a much earlier date and that the surviving evidence is biased, as many of the shoreline and lakeside settlements would have existed at a period when the sea and lake levels were so much lower than today and are therefore rarely recoverable.

The alternative is to accept that Ireland was not colonized before the development of the British narrow-blade industries and that the spread of man to Ireland was somehow tied in with the apparently sudden appearance of the elongated scalene triangles in northern England. Jacobi (1973) has suggested that this could be associated with the inundation of the North Sea and possible dislocation of populations. This apparently abrupt change could, however, be exaggerated by the rather specialized nature of many of the sites dated, as these are usually upland sites which have a relatively restricted range of artefacts.

Whichever solution is accepted, problems do still exist. In particular the range of dates from Mount Sandel is remarkably early for this type of industry. Only Filpoke Beacon and Aardhorst Vessem are nearly as early as several of the dates from Mount Sandel (Jacobi 1976). With this problem in mind two samples were submitted to Groningen (through the good offices of Dr J Lanting and Miss A Brindley). They were taken from pits from which samples had also been taken for dating in Belfast (Table 49). We have seen that in the case of GRN 10470 the date is significantly later than the sample dated in Belfast, UB 912, but the second sample, due to the bigger standard deviations on UB 951 and UB 2360, cannot be stated with any certainty to be later in date. While the variation in dates between laboratories could simply be a product of the inherent uncertainty within the ^{14}C dating method, the fact that the Belfast Mount Sandel dates are consistently early could also

suggest inter-laboratory variation. A fuller discussion of this problem is beyond the scope of this report and the competence of the author. At one point it was believed that early dates could be a product of ^{14}C fluctuations in samples of exceptionally limited lifespan, such as hazel nuts, but an examination of Table 49 shows that hazel shell samples are, if anything, slightly younger than wood samples. A third solution could lie in the relatively poor dating of the transition between the Early and Later Mesolithic in England. The dates from Yorkshire all have large standard deviations so that it is impossible to state with any certainty that the English Earlier Mesolithic can be dated as late as 7000 bc. Thus, as yet, there is no satisfactory explanation for the earliness of these Mount Sandel dates.

The excavations at Mount Sandel and Lough Boora have resulted in one major change of attitude. There is now no reason to believe that man came to Ireland by the shortest sea route, that is from Argyll (Fig 91). Mercer (1974) suggested that the sites in south-west Scotland where scalene triangles dominate can only be found after 6000 bc, and that the broad microlithic tradition preceded it on Jura. Recent publication of his early site at Lussa Wood does not confirm his earlier suggestions, as this site can now be seen to have a strong scalene triangle element (Mercer 1980). However, given the general trend in Scotland (Morrison 1980), earlier sites contemporary with Mount Sandel could well belong to the broad microlithic tradition. Therefore, while man could have crossed from Argyll, industries of the same general type, and nearly the same date, can be found in northern England from 6800 bc, for example Filpoke Beacon (Jacobi 1976). The author has shown that during the 7th millennium bc there was a significant alteration in relative sea level in the Isle of Man basin (Woodman 1981), and it seems likely that the inundation of the coastal plain may have induced movement of colonists to Ireland. This is, of course, a solution for which there can be little hope of finding evidence, particularly if the settlement was coastal. Bonsall (1981) has found traces of settlement in the Esk estuary in Cumbria which were associated with a phase when the sea level began to stabilize, while the ^{14}C date from a hearth at Redkirk Point (Galloway), 6060 ± 65 bc, is the earliest evidence for man in southern Scotland (Masters and Longhorne 1976). These finds and the material on the Isle of Man (Woodman 1978a) must belong to phases when the sea level had risen, inundating a significant area around the Isle of Man basin.

There are various other points from which Ireland could have been colonized, but there is often a distinct lack of information about them, though the Broomhill site, Hants (O'Malley and Jacobi 1978), shows that the same type of industry was present in

---

* Though these do exist at early Pre-Boreal sites in southern Scandinavia (Fischer 1978).

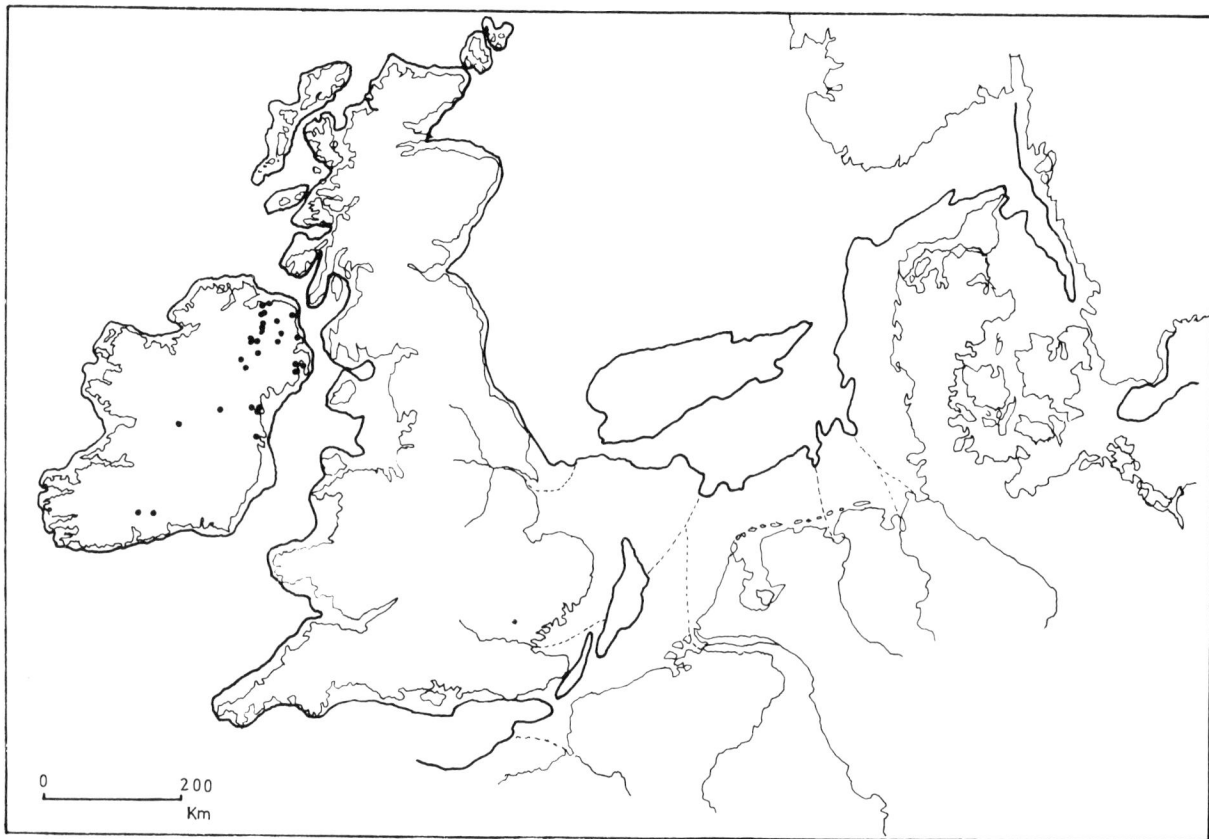

Fig 91   Map of the North Sea area in the 8th millennium bc, showing Early Mesolithic material in Ireland (20 fathom
contour marked)

southern England at roughly the same date as Filpoke
Beacon and Broomhead Moor V. Entry into Ireland
would be theoretically possible further south, particularly if a significantly earlier colonization had taken
place. However, it has been suggested that perceptual
distances caused by the presence of mountains are
probably more important than real ones (Woodman
1981); thus a narrowing of the Irish sea in an area
where there is no high ground was probably less
important than the presence of high mountains,
combined with an area of high marine productivity
where a well established marine-orientated economy
might have existed. Just as there is no evidence for a
post-glacial landbridge to explain the origin of the
Irish mammalian fauna, there appears to be no
significant probability that Ireland was colonized
across a landbridge. Even if one existed, probably in
the southern part of the Irish Sea, it would have been
so narrow that it would have been a route across
which only very small groups could have crossed.

The excavation of Mount Sandel on the northern
coast of Ireland has thus helped to show that the
notion of an extreme north-eastern point of entry into
Ireland has been based on the convenient presence of
a narrow sea-crossing rather than on archaeological

evidence. This has been amply confirmed by M
Ryan's excavation at Lough Boora, Co Offaly, and by
the recent discovery of microliths at Kilcomer Lower,
Co Cork, in the Blackwater valley (Fig 91).

It must be admitted that the addition of an extra
thousand years to the Irish Mesolithic has not solved
the problems of its origin. No matter how early the
date to which the colonizing phase is pushed back,
there will probably always be problems in understanding how Ireland was colonized, and in particular
how the initial colonizing group managed to survive
and establish itself on a permanent basis on this
island (Woodman 1981).

The Implications of the Structures

There is little point in using this study as a vehicle for
listing all the dubious, probable and certain Mesolithic huts. Newell (1981) has already provided a
critical reassessment of the evidence available in
western Europe. He shows how remarkably few sites
in Europe have produced clear evidence for hut
construction, and it is noteworthy that traces of at
least seven structures can be recognized at Mount
Sandel, which equals the number of sites in Newell's

table 2 'post-hole alignment for enclosed space in open air' category.

While post-holes have occasionally turned up on other sites—even in Ireland at Sutton, Co Dublin (Mitchell 1956), and Bay Farm, Carnlough, Co Antrim—few large, substantial structures have been found in Europe. This could be partly on account of the type of area excavated. In many areas low-lying wet sites will produce a range of faunal remains and artefacts made from organic materials, but these may often be locales which were used in a rather transitory fashion, where there would have been little reason to invest in a substantial structure. Thus it is noticeable that the extensive excavations of low-lying sites in south Scandinavia have produced only a small number of substantial huts. Similarly, at the end of the Mesolithic, waterlogged deposits and middens have attracted archaeologists but, as noted in practice by Albrethsen and Brinch-Petersen (1976), the richness of the remains in these deposits has drawn attention away from potential dwelling and cemetery areas to areas of rubbish disposal. Therefore it seems likely that more excavations in areas of slightly higher ground, more suitable for long-term settlement, would produce many more Mesolithic huts. Of course the ideal environment for the excavator would be waterlogged deposits adjacent to raised dwelling areas, such as have been identified both in the Vedbaek project (Brinch-Petersen *et al* 1979) and Ringkloster (Andersen 1974).

The nature of the economic strategy and environment may have enhanced certain characteristics of the Mount Sandel site. It has been argued that the site was occupied throughout the winter and possibly for a longer portion of the year. It is therefore hardly surprising that substantial, well built dwellings were erected. If these were in part 'earth houses' then the structural members would need to be even more robust than for surface structures.

It is worth considering Mount Sandel in relation to other known structures of hunter-gatherers. There appear to be two different hut types at Mount Sandel: first, the small hut, 3 m in diameter, on the northern edge of the site, with a possibly contemporary hearth outside, and second, the larger huts, 6 m in diameter. This could reflect a basic division into large winter huts with an internal hearth and smaller summer huts which usually had a hearth outside.

If the enclosed dwellings listed by Newell are examined, excluding Moita de Sebastiao (Roche 1960) which is not necessarily a dwelling, the same division is evident. There are huts around 10 m² or smaller and others around 20 m² or larger. Several interesting hypotheses can be suggested. The larger huts would be those built at base camps, and these are relatively rare structures. Those at Ulkestrup are amongst the best (Andersen, forthcoming): hut I (the best preserved) was slightly more rectilinear than the Mount Sandel examples, but as at Mount Sandel its hearth was placed towards the front. Unfortunately because of later disturbance it was impossible to analyse the distribution of material inside the hut as the back end of the hut had been extensively damaged. Both huts were over 25 m² and had posts about 10 cm in diameter. From the size of the posts used, this appears to have been a relatively light structure which would have been abandoned with little loss, but it was noticeably as large as those at Mount Sandel.

The Ulkestrup huts were not winter camp sites, as their location on a small island in the centre of a lake suggests that they could have been inundated by the winter floods. They were probably dwellings for family groups rather than huts for specialized task groups. In temperate zones the flimsy nature of a structure may be a better indication of a short-stay summer camp site than its size. It appears to have been difficult to roof a structure over 6 m across without internal support, and it is noticeable that many of the clear-cut Upper Palaeolithic dwellings seem to fall into this size range, for example, Plateau Parrain (Bordes 1968). Even some of the Russian sites, such as Moldova (Sklenar 1976), could be in this category but many of the large structures, such as those at Kostienki, could well be figments of the imagination. Post-pits several metres in width and depth, and dwellings which are larger than most of the largest *Bandkeramik* houses, are difficult to accept. It is intriguing that the apparently more outlandish mammoth-jaw structures of Mezin, etc, are of a more reasonable size. Suggestions that the large pits at Kostienki were winter dwellings should be treated with the same caution as Newell treated Mesolithic pit dwellings. They are unlikely to be tree-falls, but as many of the Steppe dwellings could have been earth lodges it is possible that these large pits were 'borrowing pits' similar to those found round the *Bandkeramik* long houses. Their location at some distance from the hearths is rather reminiscent of those on *Bandkeramik* sites. It is more likely that these hearths and pits belong to several rebuildings than to one larger dwelling.

The smaller dwelling at Mount Sandel equates with many other rather transitory structures, such as those excavated by Coles at Morton (1971), and probably most of the rather small discrete patches of flintworking in the Pennines. The problem with the Pennine sites is that a concentration of material does not represent a hut, and even a hearth close to a working area is no indication of an enclosed dwelling. The Pennine sites would probably have had small tents not requiring the placing of posts to any depth in the ground. The limiting factors here would probably have been time and, if a tent was being used, the size and weight of the skin covering to be transported. Many of these sites probably belonged to small specialized task, rather than family, groups.

Binford, in a forthcoming study of hunter-gatherer behaviour in relation to their dwellings, has noted a similar division into large winter huts and small, rather transitory, summer tents, again with the hearth placed outside (Binford, forthcoming).* This he believes to be a common division amongst many hunter-gatherers throughout the world. One interesting division could be seen at the Phalanga site (Binford 1978), where a small hut was built to house the men for the few days it took them to build a larger dwelling. Again, the diameters of the huts were 3 m and 6 m respectively. The larger hut was occupied for two successive winters with only the addition of a second birch-bark floor. Therefore in general, and in relation to Mount Sandel in particular, one should not assume that one hut equals

---

I would like to thank Professor L R Binford for sharing with me, in advance of publication, his interpretations of ground plans based on his work with the Nunamiut.

one season of occupation. Binford has also shown that many activities around summer huts take place outside so that the hut itself can be kept relatively clean, but that rubbish from different activities will often accumulate against or some metres away from the huts.

One possible explanation of the variation in hut types at Mount Sandel has already been given: the small structure could be one thousand years later, when the environment of the area may have changed rather radically and this may no longer have been such an important location. Its presence illustrates the point that there is probably no distinctive type of Mesolithic dwelling structure, but rather that the nature of the dwelling depends on environmental factors, season and economy. The main Mount Sandel huts were strategically placed at an important location which could have been used for a substantial part of the year. They were therefore large dwellings, in keeping with the economy and environment of the site at that period, while the small structure may reflect a change in the environment which made the Mount Sandel area less attractive.

CHAPTER 14

Summary

Summary of Finds and Conclusions

1 Mount Sandel townland lies south of Coleraine, near the upper limits of the estuary of the River Bann. The excavation took place between 1973 and 1977 in the fields immediately adjacent to Mountsandel Fort.

2 An area of approximately 700 square metres was opened, revealing partly preserved traces of a major Mesolithic settlement along with traces of later occupation. Small scatters of Neolithic material were found, particularly to the north and west of the site, while two radiocarbon dates indicate activity during the Late Bronze or Early Iron Age. Traces of Early Christian, medieval and post-medieval occupation were also found, perhaps associated with nearby Mountsandel Fort.

3 The site has produced a series of radiocarbon dates. While one lies around 6000 bc, most dates lie between 6500 bc and 7000 bc with six between 6800 bc and 7000 bc.

4 The most significant area found during the excavation was the hut area where a natural hollow had been enlarged artificially. Several huts—possibly four—had made use of this hollow. Delimited by arcs of post-holes, and about 6 m across, the huts were built by placing posts in the ground at a 60° angle so that they could be flexed and tied to posts from the opposite side of the hut, avoiding the need for internal roof supports. Each hut seems to have had a central hearth which was dug into the compact subsoil rather than ringed with stones. These hearths were, in some instances, recut.

5 The excavated evidence indicates a limited number of occupations: allowing for the very extensive destruction of much of the site, perhaps no more than ten different huts had been built. These were represented by arcs and incomplete arcs of post-holes and large shallow pits which were reminiscent of the central hearth of the hut area.

6 The huts were concentrated in the central part of the site, while to the west was an area where large quantities of industrial waste from flint-working were found. Although less clearly separated, there also appeared to be a tendency for the larger, deeper pits to occur north of the hut area. Other site facilities were indicated by small groups of posts placed contiguously in the ground at an angle, and other post-holes possibly suggesting storage racks.

7 The fill of the pits correlated better with the area of the site rather than the type of pit. Organically richer layers were found closer to the huts than elsewhere. Trace-element analysis suggests that the refuse layers in the central hearths may have been associated with food production, while magnetic susceptibility shows that layers of intensely burnt material can be found in contexts which were not those of hearths. This implies some sort of organized disposal of rubbish on the site.

8 The archaeological material associated with this Mesolithic occupation is dominated by microliths. These include scalene triangles, rods and needle points. The exact ratios of these forms on the site is probably not so much a cultural or chronological characteristic of the assemblage as a product of the function of the different types and the survival of different types of contexts: the correlation between pig bones and scalene triangles is notable. Other artefacts found include core and flake axes, awls and ochre-stained blades.

9 Microwear examination has shown that many of the artefacts had been discarded after use. Differing wear traces were found on microliths and hide polish was found on ochre-stained blades. Research on the microwear traces continues.

10 The faunal remains consisted solely of fragments of burnt bones which were most abundant in specific layers in certain pits. The faunal material was

dominated by pig and fish. One dog bone was also recovered. Amongst the fish salmon, trout and eels were the most common. While bird bones were found, these gave the impression of resulting from opportunist rather than organized capture. The recovery of capercaillie was of special interest.

11 Traces of plant foods were rare. The main exception was the large quantities of burnt hazel nut shells found in several pits. Some water-lily seeds and an apple/pear(?) seed were also recovered.

12 A study of the sediments accumulated downstream from Mount Sandel suggests that the Mesolithic site was located just above the contemporary river estuary.

13 The evidence indicates that the site was occupied for a substantial part of the year. The catching of salmon during the summer(?) may have marked the beginning of the occupation, while the presence of young pig and foetal pig bones may mark the end of the occupation in late winter or early spring. The large quantities of burnt hazel nut shells, which would have been collected in the autumn, recovered from the same layers as foetal pig bones suggest the use of stored resources.

14 The site was probably occupied by one small group throughout the winter. The environment would probably still have been dominated by Boreal forests whose carrying capacity was not particularly high, but with the use of fish, which could have been stored, as could certain plant foods, small groups could have survived the winter by hunting pigs.

Main Problems Outstanding

1 One obvious problem arises from the difference between ^{14}C dates produced in Belfast and Groningen. The variation is within an accepted range, but the fact that the Groningen dates are both later than the Belfast dates from samples from the same pits must require further investigation.

2 Because of the extensive destruction of so much of the site it remains difficult to be certain whether all the various components, such as industrial areas and huts, belong together as part of the same settlements.

3 A series of small pits was found, scattered across the site though mostly in the area of the hut, but no explanation for their function can be suggested.

4 Apart from the presence of hazel nuts, which would have to have been *collected* in the autumn, there are few indicators of autumn occupation. The problem remains of whether this means a genuine lack of autumn occupation or whether the very fragmentary nature of the surviving seasonal indicators (small groups of bones in pits) has created a false impression of broken occupation of the site.

MOUNT SANDEL EXCAVATION DATA

a   Description of Mesolithic features (microfiche, with Fig 92)

b   Distribution of lithic material by features (microfiche)

c   Attributes in the analysis of stylistic variations of selected microliths (microfiche)

d   Distribution of faunal remains (microfiche) *by* Louise H van Wijngaarden-Bakker

e   Catalogue of medieval and later pottery, including clay pipes *by* M L Simpson

f   The coins *by* R Heslip

g   Cross tabulation with field notation used in previous publications

---

CATALOGUE OF MEDIEVAL AND LATER POTTERY, INCLUDING CLAY PIPES

M L Simpson

Pottery

The following abbreviations have been used in the catalogue: int = internal; ext = external; dec = decorated; undec = undecorated; adj = adjoining; u/p = unprovenanced Mu indicates the finds catalogue number.

The pottery has been sorted according to fabric types and, where possible, its origins. The vessel counts should be taken only as rough approximations and are intended as a general guide.

MEDIEVAL POTTERY

Although most of the following are small body sherds, they are probably all from jugs.

8 body sherds, reduced fabric, white margin under ext green glaze, hard fired; 3146 is strap handle attached to 3144/3145; probably same vessel as 3187, 3271 and 3485
P/23, F4 (mortar surface)   Mu 3139–46

body sherd, fabric as above
Q/27–28 (topsoil)   Mu 3187

body sherd, fabric as above
E'/25–28   Mu 3271

body sherd, fabric as above
Q–W/25–40   Mu 3485

body sherd, soft fabric, oxidized except for ext surface, red inclusions, green glaze ext
u/p   Mu 3630

body sherd, reduced, hard fired, dark green/brown glaze ext
A–E/34–40   Mu 3833

body sherd, possibly medieval, green glaze ext, pronounced int rilling
E'/25–28   Mu 3272

Sherd total: 14
Minimum vessel count: 4

POST-MEDIEVAL POTTERY

Tin-glazed, polychrome
Mid 18th-century
Although from different vessels, the two sherds listed below evidently originated from the same set of pieces. Their identification as French (or possibly Belgian) has been confirmed by D M Archer of the Victoria and Albert Museum (see Noel-Hume 1972, *141*).

rim sherd, pink/buff fabric (Fig 38.2)
u/p   Mu 4521

rim sherd, buff fabric
u/p   Mu 4186

Sherd total: 2
Minimum vessel count: 2

Tin-glazed, blue/white
17th/18th-century

base sherd, buff fabric, mottled blue dec int
Q/25   Mu 3422

body sherd, very fine buff fabric, blue dec int, and part of inscription ext
Q–W/25–40 (bank)   Mu 3513

body sherd, fine buff fabric, blue dec ext
B'–E'/25–28 (topsoil)   Mu 3525

body sherd, fine buff fabric, blue dec ext
F–H/42–47 (topsoil)   Mu 3858

base sherd, buff fabric, red inclusions, blue dec int
u/p   Mu 4129

3 body sherds, buff fabric, traces of blue dec but all
degraded
P/20–21 F4/5   Mu 3900–2

Sherd total: 8
Minimum vessel count: 6

Tin-glazed, white
17th/18th-century

body sherd, pink/buff fabric
B′–C′/25–28 (topsoil)   Mu 3526

body sherd, pale buff fabric
G (gully)   Mu 3705

rim sherd and body sherd, buff fabric, same vessel
u/p   Mu 4183, 4131

1 rim sherd and 4 body sherds, pale buff-pink fabric,
probably all from different vessels
u/p   Mu 4135, 4142, 4260, 4463, 4522

Sherd total: 9
Minimum vessel count: 6

Stoneware, Bellarmine
17th-century, probably Cologne/Frechen

mask fragment–beard (Fig 38.3)
F200 (sandy bank)   Mu 3243

medallion fragment (Fig 38.4)
A′/25–28 (top fill)   Mu 3479

Sherd total: 2
Minimum vessel count: 1

Stoneware, brown salt-glazed, no decoration
17th-century

body sherd, same fabric as 3270 and 3480
D–E/44–49 (lower topsoil)   Mu 3088

body sherd, same fabric as 3088 and 3480
E′/25–28   Mu 3270

body sherd, same fabric as 3088 and 3270
A′/25–28   Mu 3480

body sherd
u/p   Mu 4523

Sherd total: 4
Minimum vessel count: 2

Stoneware, brown, yellow etc
19th-century and later

rim sherd, glossy brown glaze
u/p   Mu 3636

body sherd, brown, same fabric as 3654
u/p   Mu 3639

body sherd, brown, dec, with rouletting, same fabric as
3639
u/p   Mu 3654

body sherd, light brown/dark brown, same fabric as 4524
u/p   Mu 3665

base sherd, brown
H–K/41–43   Mu 3797

base sherd, light brown, same fabric as 3665
u/p   Mu 4524

part of brown stoneware object
u/p   Mu 4520

Sherd total: 7
Minimum vessel count: 5

Staffordshire scratch blue
This type of pottery is generally dated to *c* 1740–80
(Mountford 1971, *48*); this particular vessel is perhaps
1750–60 (Fig 38.1)

rim of fine, small tea bowl, same vessel as 3923
F82 (western end)   Mu 3777

base of tea bowl, same vessel as 3777
M–Q/27–30   Mu 3923

Sherd total: 2
Minimum vessel count: 1

Other stoneware with cobalt decoration
18th-century

body sherd, probably Westerwald
N/45–46 (topsoil)   Mu 3876

body sherd
u/p   Mu 4525

body sherd, probably modern
D–E/44–49 (lower topsoil)   Mu 3094

Sherd total: 3
Minimum vessel count: 3

Staffordshire white salt-glazed stoneware: decorated plate rims
Mid 18th-century: the 'Barley' pattern is usually dated to *c*
1740s/50s and the 'Bead and reel' pattern to *c* 1750s/70s
(Noel-Hume 1972, *115–117*).

2 rim sherds, 'Barley' pattern, possibly same vessel
u/p   Mu 4218, 4261

2 rim sherds, 'Bead and reel' pattern, probably not same
vessel
u/p   Mu 4127, 4196

Sherd total: 4
Minimum vessel count: 3

Undecorated white salt-glazed stoneware
18th/19th-century

base sherd
extension to R18/19   Mu 3275

5 rim sherds (4159 and 4177 probably same vessel)
all u/p   Mu 4159, 4177, 4325, 4371, 4450

6 base sherds, two with footrings (all different vessels
except for 4172/4198)
all u/p   Mu 4172/4198, 4208, 4215, 4434, 4383

4 ridged body sherds
all u/p   Mu 4125, 4285, 4321, 4384

18 undec body sherds
all u/p   Mu 4122, 4146, 4184, 4191, 4200, 4209, 4219,
4238, 4243, 4253, 4280, 4284, 4316, 4327, 4328, 4388,
4392, 4428

handle ?
F–K/24–26   Mu 3992

Sherd total: 35
Minimum vessel count: 9

Staffordshire-type combed slipware
Early 18th-century

> rim sherd
> N/22 Mu 3021
>
> 3 base sherds, 2 adj
> F200 (sandy bank) Mu 3240–2
>
> body sherd
> Q/27–28 Mu 3399
>
> body sherd
> D'/26–28 Mu 3516
>
> body sherd
> D'/26–28 Mu 3556
>
> body sherd
> F82 (western end, lower fill) Mu 3592
>
> base sherd
> u/p Mu 3613
>
> handle, probably from combed slipware tankard
> Q–W/25–40 (topsoil from bank) Mu 3493

Sherd total: 10
Minimum vessel count: 2

Press-moulded slipware
Early 18th-century

> plate rim, piecrust edge
> Q/25 F4/5 Mu 3420
>
> body sherd
> u/p Mu 3619
>
> plate rim, combed dec, mixed clay fabric
> u/p Mu 4416

Sherd total: 3
Minimum vessel count: 3

Other Staffordshire-type decorated slipwares

> body sherd, yellow spots on dark brown ground
> W/26 F202 Mu 3311
>
> body sherd, as 3311
> u/p Mu 4529
>
> rim sherd, dark brown spot on yellow ground
> u/p Mu 3693

Sherd total: 3
Minimum vessel count: 2

Staffordshire/Nottingham type 'manganese' decorated brown slipware
18th-century

> base sherd, buff fabric
> L/39 (upper topsoil) Mu 3601
>
> body sherd, mixed clay fabric
> L/39 (upper topsoil) Mu 3059
>
> body sherd, buff fabric
> N–S/25–26 (ditch) Mu 3395
>
> body sherd, pink/buff fabric
> K/21 Mu 3570
>
> body sherd, buff fabric
> u/p Mu 3685
>
> body sherd, buff fabric
> P–T/25–26 Mu 3753

> body sherd, with handle, buff fabric
> E/37–40 (topsoil) Mu 3880
>
> body sherd, buff fabric
> u/p Mu 4564

Sherd total: 8
Minimum vessel count: 3

Sgraffito
Probably 18th-century, all with coarse, soft, oxidized fabric; slip and glaze very worn. South Somerset type, but could be local.

> rim sherd
> B'/25–28 Mu 3544
>
> rim sherd
> M–Q/27–30 Mu 3933
>
> 6 rim sherds
> u/p Mu 3786, 3787, 3827, 3890, 4526, 4527
>
> 2 body sherds
> u/p Mu 3682, 4528
>
> body sherd, fabric as rest but with splash of green glaze
> u/p Mu 3624

Sherd total: 11
Minimum vessel count: 8

Plain yellow slipwares
Probably 18th-century, all with fairly fine buff fabric

> base sherd
> F–J/24–26 Mu 3965
>
> complete base
> u/p Mu 4530
>
> 3 base sherds
> u/p Mu 4517, 4531, 4532
>
> 2 body sherds, each with handle
> L–N/22–26 (topsoil) Mu 3603, 3608
>
> handle frag
> u/p Mu 3867
>
> body sherd
> N/45–46 (topsoil) Mu 3879
>
> 2 body sherds
> B/31–35 Mu 3974, 3981

Sherd total: 11
Minimum vessel count: 5

Coarse slipware
18th/19th-century, all with soft, coarse oxidized fabric, white slip, yellow lead glaze, very worn

> 2 body sherds
> D–E/44–49 (lower topsoil) Mu 3089, 3090
>
> body sherd
> Q/20–21 (topsoil) Mu 3232
>
> body sherd
> F–L/27–28 Mu 3410
>
> body sherd
> U–V/35–40 (top of natural) Mu 3532
>
> 2 body sherds
> u/p Mu 3612, 4565
>
> base sherd
> u/p Mu 3796

body sherd
A–E/34–40   Mu 3834

body sherd
L/23   Mu 3913

body sherd
J–K/17–18   Mu 3916

body sherd, fabric as rest but with splash of green glaze
L/40 (topsoil 2nd spit)   Mu 3016

Sherd total: 12
Minimum vessel count: 4

Miscellaneous green, lead-glazed earthenware
body sherd, buff fabric, green-glazed int and traces of glaze ext, probably Saintonge, 17th-century.
u/p   Mu 3934

The following sherds are all from the same handled, tripod-footed vessel, decorated with grooves and ridges around the upper part (Fig 38.7). Probably 16th/17th-century.

2 rim sherds and 1 body sherd, all adj
F4   Mu 3175, 3176, 3177

1 other rim sherd
u/p   Mu 3377

5 base sherds, 3 with feet
M/20   Mu 3138, 3155, 3156
F4   Mu 3142
Q–W (2nd level of bank)   Mu 3534

1 body sherd with handle and 2 body sherds, all adj
F4   Mu 3172, 3173, 3174

22 other body sherds
Four from F4, rest from various contexts, some unprovenanced

Sherd total: 33

The fabric of the following sherds is similar to, although coarser than, the North Devon gravel-free wares and could well be a local type. All of these sherds are very worn. 17th/18th-century.

base sherd
Q–W/25–40   Mu 3487

body sherd
E'–?/34–36   Mu 3495

body sherd
Q–W/25–40   Mu 3517

body sherd
U–V/31–32   Mu 3731

3 body sherds
u/p   Mu 3509, 4533, 4534

Sherd total: 7
Minimum vessel count: 3

Blue-shell-edged pearlware
Late 18th/ early 19th-century (c 1780s–1830)
rim sherd
L/39 (upper topsoil)   Mu 3062

4 rim sherds
all u/p   Mu 4358, 4425, 4459, 4460

Sherd total: 5
Minimum vessel count: 5

Full details have not been listed for the remaining categories of pottery, either because the sherds are too small to say anything very useful or because they have little relevance to the archaeological interpretation of the site.

Tygs
17th-century
Virtually all the following are very small sherds, probably coming from only four vessels, so it was not thought worthwhile to record the exact provenances here, except for the two bases which have been illustrated. These details are, however, included in the site archive.

complete base and lower part of body with handles (Fig 38.6)
V–W/28–29   Mu 3478

base sherd and 2 body sherds with handle, all adj (Fig 38.5)
N/20   Mu 3154, 4567, 4568

Sherd total: 9 bases, 12 rims, 9 body sherds with handles attached, 6 handles, 56 body sherds
Minimum vessel count: 4

Coarse red fabric, black/brown lead-glazed wares
17th–19th-century
A wide range of fabrics and forms are included in this category; one would suspect that many came from locally-made vessels but until more research has been done on this type of pottery little can be said about it. Full details are in the site archive.
Sherd total: 35 rims (5 from 1 vessel), 17 bases, 6 handles, 2 lids, 217 body sherds

Other earthenware
Probably 19th-century
buff fabric, light brown glaze
Sherd total: 1 rim, 4 body sherds
buff fabric, brown glaze
Sherd total: 1 base
red fabric, some reduced, green/brown glaze
Sherd total: 4 rims, 2 bases, 16 body sherds

Porcelain
Although both Chinese export and English vessels appear to be represented, the sherds are so small they are not listed in detail here.
Sherd total: 23

Transfer-printed and other decorated wares, creamware etc
Mainly 19th-century
Sherd total: 226 undec, 168 transfer-printed and other types, dec, 7 pieces of Spode tile

Unglazed oxidized pottery
A total of 41 sherds of this category was recovered; with the exception of one rim sherd and one base sherd they were remarkably featureless and probably fairly modern in date. They have therefore not been listed here but full details are included in the site archive.

Fired clay
39 fragments of fired clay were found; some are evidently from bricks but because they are so small they have not been listed or described here. More information can be found in the archive.

Clay pipes

All are from topsoil unless otherwise stated. Types as defined by Oswald 1975.

17th-century pipes

1 bowl, heel/spur missing, no milling. Mark: 'mulberry' on sides of bowl. Type 7/18, *c* 1660–80 (Mu 3317).

1 bowl, with heel, no milling. Mark: AD on heel. Type 5, *c* 1640–60. Q–W second level of topsoil from bank (Mu 3319).

1 bowl, with heel, and milling round mouth. Mark: uncertain, on heel. Type 5, *c* 1640–60. Q–W second level of topsoil from bank (Mu 3321).

1 bowl, with spur, and milling round mouth. No marks. Type 18?, *c* 1660–80. Q–W second level of topsoil from bank (Mu 3320).

1 bowl, with spur, mouth missing. No marks. Type 17? *c* 1640–70 (Mu 3332).

1 bowl, with heel, no milling. No marks. Type 5, *c* 1640–60 (Mu 4542).

1 bowl, with spur, milling round mouth. No marks. Type 17, *c* 1640–70 (Mu 4543).

1 bowl, with spur, milling round mouth. No marks. Type 17, *c* 1640–70 (Mu 4544).

1 bowl, with spur, no milling. No marks. Type 17, *c* 1640–70 (Mu 4545).

1 bowl fragment, with heel, mouth missing. No marks. Probably Type 5, *c* 1640–60 (Mu 4550).

1 bowl fragment, with very small heel, mouth missing. No marks. Dutch? Early to mid 17th-century (Mu 4549).

1 bowl fragment, heel/spur missing, milling round mouth. No marks. Probably Type 5, *c* 1640–60 (Mu 4552).

1 bowl fragment, heel/spur missing, milling round mouth. No marks. Probably Type 5, *c* 1640–60 (Mu 4553).

1 bowl fragment, heel/spur missing, possibly traces of milling round mouth. No marks. Probably Type 5, *c* 1640–60 (Mu 4554).

Early 18th-century pipes

1 bowl fragment, with heel, mouth missing. Decorated heel. Probably Type 10, *c* 1700–40 (Mu 3323).

1 bowl fragment, with spur, mouth missing. No marks. Does not fit standard bowl shapes, but could be Type 19–21, ie between 1690 and 1740 (Mu 3322).

1 bowl fragment, with spur, mouth missing. No marks. Does not fit standard bowl shapes, perhaps first half of 18th-century (Mu 4547).

19th-century pipes

1 bowl, with spur, no milling. Mark: 'COCK OF THE NORTH' in cartouche on front of bowl. Late 19th-century (Mu 4541).

1 bowl, with spur, no milling. Mark: cross-hatched heart on left side of bowl, cross-hatched diamond on right. Late 19th-century (Mu 3315).

1 bowl fragment, spur missing, no milling. mark: stylised feathers under bowl, ? harp on right side. Mid 19th-century (Mu 4548).

1 bowl, with spur, no milling. No marks. Late 19th-century (Mu 3316).

1 bowl, with spur, no milling. No marks. Late 19th-century (Mu 3318).

1 bowl, spur missing, no milling. Finely made. No marks. 19th-century (Mu 4546).

1 bowl fragment, with spur, mouth missing. No marks. 19th-century (Mu 4551).

1 stem fragment. Mark: (DER)RY. Late 19th-century (Mu 4560).

1 stem fragment. Mark: DER(RY). Late 19th-century (Mu 4561).

Others

5 bowl fragments, too small to date (Mu 4555–4559).

106 stem fragments, no marks, mixed in date, but not measured (Mu 4562).

10 stem fragments, no marks, mixed in date but not measured (Mu 3100, 3102, 3106, 3107, 3216, 3267, 3282, 3283, 3300).

2 stem fragments, no marks, from F203 (Mu 3236, 3237).

2 stem fragments, no marks, from F200 (Mu 3250, 3251).

2 stem fragments, no marks, from F202 (Mu 3309, 3310).

Total:		
29 bowls	17th-century: 14	
7 marked bowls	Early 18th-century: 3	
124 stems	19th-century: 9	
2 marked stems	Date uncertain: 127	
	(122 of these stems)*	

References

Mountford, A R (1971): *The illustrated guide to Staffordshire salt-glazed stoneware* (London, 1971).

Noel-Hume, I N (1972): *A guide to artifacts of colonial America* (New York, 1972).

Oswald, A (1975): *Clay pipes for the archaeologist* (Brit Archaeol Reports 14, Oxford, 1975).

---

* It has not yet been possible to measure bore diameters, but it might be worth measuring the diameters of the stems from features 200, 202 and 203.

THE COINS

R Heslip

1 IRELAND, Elizabeth I, copper penny of the type issued in 1601 and 1602 (Dowle and Finn 1969, *255–6*; Seaby 1970, *4510*). This coin is very corroded and almost totally featureless, only a few fragmentary letters being visible. Any identification must be tentative.

2 IRELAND, 18th-century copper halfpenny, probably issued by George II, dated between 1736 and 1760. If issued under George III the latest date of this type of coin is 1782. The piece appears more corroded than worn and again the identification depends solely on a few letters.

3 ENGLAND, Victoria, bronze halfpenny, young head type, issued between 1860 and 1884. Corroded but apparently with little wear.

4 FRANCE, Louis XIII, copper double tournois, dated 1643, *type de Warin*, mint mark H for La Rochelle (Gadoury and Droulers 1978, *12*).

All the coins were found in surface collecting and none were in good condition, apparently because of the action of the soil, with the exception of no 4. This made identification in the case of nos 2 and 3 almost impossible, and the assessment of wear extremely difficult.

Number 1 is an almost smooth disc and the identification is put forward merely as a suggestion. If the coin is indeed an Elizabeth I penny, it will be argued in a forthcoming paper that such pieces probably disappeared from circulation, to all intents and purposes, by 1623.

Double tournois (no 4) are almost ubiquitous finds from sites in the north of Ireland occupied during the latter half of the seventeenth century. In spite of this almost nothing appears to have been written about them, and suggestions regarding the period during which they circulated must remain tentative. Some of the locally-issued traders' tokens are found over-struck on these French pieces so it would be reasonable to assign a similar period of circulation, that is 1653 to 1679. These coins are mentioned in Scottish legislation, but I have seen no documentary evidence for Ireland.

The other two coins (2 and 3) may probably be assumed to have been lost only a few years from their dates of issue.

References

Dowle, A and Finn, P (1969): *The guide book to the coinage of Ireland* (London, 1969).

Gadoury, V and Droulers, F (1978): *Monnaies royales françaises, 1610–1792* (Monte Carlo, 1978).

Seaby, P (1970): *Coins and tokens of Ireland* (London, 1970).

CROSS TABULATION WITH FIELD NOTATION USED IN PREVIOUS PUBLICATIONS

These publications are Woodman 1978 and 1978b.

F31 + F31A = F31/0	Pit 100Y = F56/1	Pit 100A = F100/0
F31B = F31/1	Pit 100Z = F56/2	Pit 100C = F100/1
F31D = F31/2	Pit 100T = F56/3	Pit 100B = F100/2
F31E = F31/3	Pit 100X = F56/4	Pit 100F(B) = F100/4
F31F(A) = F31/4	Pit 100W(A) = F56/5	Pit 100F(C) = F100/5
F31F(B) = F31/5	Pit 100W(B) = F56/6	Pit 100G = F100/6
	Pit 100V = F56/7	

COMMENTS ON THE INITIAL ANALYSIS OF SOIL SAMPLES

J G Cruickshank

The values for certain properties measured show little difference from what might be expected on any subsoil sample on basalt till in Co Antrim, but others show a spectacular difference due to the modification caused by human activity (Table 54). The properties will be discussed by these two groups, and subdivided to consider particular samples.

One important limitation in this evaluation of results is the lack of data from a control site outside the excavation area. The relative difference of values in this set of results is compared with my own personal experience of what can be expected in agricultural soils derived from basalt till in Co Antrim.

Properties similar in value to those expected in surrounding area
pH—range is quite small, pH 4.7 to 5.1, for most samples, and is considered to be slightly acid.
% Base Saturation—is always related to pH, so likewise is mostly in a narrow range in the slightly acid part of the scale. These results are to be expected in sub-surface, well-drained and leached horizons.

Exchangeable cations
Calcium values are in the moderate part of the scale (5–10 me %)
Magnesium values are in the moderate part of the scale (1–3 me %)
Sodium values are in the moderate part of the scale (0.3–0.7 me %)
Potassium values are in the very low part of the scale (less than 0.3 me %)
The above applies to all samples as all values are again in the same narrow band of each scale of values, and are what

would be expected in sub-surface, middle horizon basalt soils. Basalt soils are always deficient in potassium K.

Organic Carbon
Again, values are all moderate (mostly 3–5%) and in a narrow range. In all cases, less than 10% Wt organic matter would be present.

Nitrogen
There is a slightly greater range of values, but most are again in the moderate range (0.1 to 0.25%). There are one or two high values over 0.4% to be found in the lowest layers of the pits.
C/N values are related, and are also in the moderate range and only low where the nitrogen is high.

Properties high and very high in value compared with those expected outside

Total exchange capacity
These are almost all over the very high value of 40 me %, and some over 60 me % would be exceptionally high. Such very high values are expected in samples with high humus content (not apparent here) or high clay content (not given in these results). Because of the type of clay minerals found in basalt soils, values of 35–40 me% would be normal in the surrounding area, so possibly these results are not *relatively* unusual.

Total Phosphorus
This is the single soil property where exceptionally high actual and relative values are found. Agricultural soils have 0.05 to 0.3 %P, so all results here being above 0.4 %P will be in the very high part of the scale, and samples in the pits (bone layers in particular) fall between 3.0 and 5.79 %P which places them *10 times higher than normally high values.*

	Sample	Particle size % Sand	% Silt	% Clay	pH	% Org C	Total P %	Exchangeable ions me/100 g Ca²⁺	Mg²⁺	Na⁺	K⁺	me/100 g TEC	me/100 g CEC	% N	% Base sat
F100/2	Layer 1	76.40	17.60	6.00	5.60	3.60	4.3	10.00	4.60	0.43	0.77	15.80	46.56	0.30	33.93
	Layer 2	74.00	18.00	8.00	5.50	3.30	3.7	15.00	4.60	0.54	0.64	20.78	44.16	0.29	47.10
	Layer 3	78.40	15.60	6.00	5.50	3.60	4.7	17.50	5.40	0.54	0.64	24.08	44.16	0.35	54.53
	Layer 4	74.80	17.20	8.00	5.50	3.90	3.9	17.50	5.60	0.54	0.64	24.28	48.24	0.35	50.33
	Layer 5	79.20	14.80	6.00	5.60	2.40	3.8	17.50	5.60	0.54	0.70	24.34	44.16	0.31	55.12
F56/2	Layer 2 & 4	69.20	18.80	12.00	5.40	6.00	4.3	20.00	5.60	0.54	0.64	26.78	57.92	0.39	46.24
	Layer 3	71.20	16.80	12.00	5.40	2.40	7.4	11.25	3.40	0.54	0.64	15.83	47.36	0.38	33.42
	Layer 4	66.00	26.80	7.20	5.30	5.10	3.8	22.50	6.80	0.54	0.70	30.54	54.72	0.45	55.81
F31/5	Layer 1	73.20	16.80	10.00	5.00	4.20	1.9	13.75	3.00	0.43	0.77	17.95	50.72	0.25	35.39
	Layer 2	73.20	19.80	9.00	5.00	4.50	2.8	7.50	2.20	0.32	0.64	10.66	53.04	0.27	20.10
	Layer 3	71.20	19.80	9.00	5.10	3.90	4.2	8.75	2.40	0.65	0.64	12.44	54.64	0.21	22.77
	Layer 4	75.60	10.40	14.00	5.10	3.60	2.0	13.75	4.00	0.43	0.77	18.95	57.04	0.26	37.13
L/37		71.20	14.80	14.00	5.40	4.20	1.7	22.50	6.00	0.43	0.64	29.57	49.12	0.25	60.20
Q/38		82.80	13.20	4.00	5.60	2.70	1.8	23.75	7.80	0.54	0.70	32.79	42.72	0.14	76.76

Table 54 Analysis of soil samples—analyses on <2 mm fraction

EXAMINATION OF RED OCHRE SAMPLES

P Francis

The examination was by binocular microscope. The samples were taken from the square or feature stated.

1 A^1/30 Extremely altered fine-grained basalt, containing many crystals of iddingsite (an alteration product of olivine), and dark coloured sub-spheroidal clay inclusions which can be interpreted either as infilled vesicles or as altered remnants of immiscible globules of glassy lava. The alteration of the rock probably occurred by lateritization, suggesting that this sample originated in one of the two main inter-basaltic (lateritic soil) horizons in north Antrim. It could also have arisen from an oxidized flow top, but the lack of amygdale minerals other than clay does not support this suggestion.

2 U/28 Altered fine-grained basalt, comprising hard, light buff to yellow rock which clearly shows the original crystalline structure (ie lithomarge), enclosed by softer deep red lateritic clay. This rock seems to be a product of lateritic weathering and is therefore probably from a similar source to sample no 1. It would seem to be too hard and too variable in texture and colour to be of use as a good red ochreous pigment.

3 A^1/29 Totally dissimilar to the four other samples examined, as it did not originate in the Tertiary basalts.

This is a purple to black coloured (producing a dark red streak) dense (SG 2.6) schistose rock, containing aligned mica-like flakes of unaltered specular haematite with interpenetrating cryptocrystalline quartz. It almost certainly originated in metamorphic schistose rock such as those which are developed in the Dalradian sequence of north-east Antrim, Co Londonderry and Co Tyrone.

4 F31/1 Uniformly very fine-grained, bright red clastic rock which is capable of taking an exceptionally smooth polish. This is the most suitable of the five samples examined for use as red ochreous pigment. There is no visible indication of an original crystalline state, which therefore suggests an origin as an oxidized fine-grained volcanic ash (tuff), such as those interpreted (J Preston, QUB, Geology Department) as commonly being preserved between individual lava flows throughout the Antrim basalt pile. It could conceivably have arisen by other means, however, for instance by palagonitization or lateritization of a basaltic glass.

5 U/32 Slightly coarser in grain size than no 4, but still extremely fine-grained with no evidence of a visibly crystalline state originally, although small rounded grains can occasionally be distinguished. This sample probably originated in a similar manner to sample no 4.

PETROLOGICAL ANALYSIS OF TWO POLISHED STONE AXES

Iain Johnston

Thin sections from two implements were examined (catalogue nos Mu 2018 and Mu 2024.)

Mu 2018 is a coarse unbedded siltstone (grains up to 0.02 mm diameter) which has been slightly metamorphosed. It consists of about 50% angular quartz grains in a matrix of muscovite and chlorite. No bedding is evident in either the thin section or the hand specimen. A small vein of quartz is present and this has also suffered metamorphism.

Mu 2024 consists of fine bedded (0.01–2 mm) fine silt or coarse clay-sized particles (grains of up to 0.005 mm).

These are quartz (about 50%) and muscovite and chlorite micas, the proportions varying in the different bands. Pyrite is present and this has been altered. The micas show two preferred orientations at acute angles to bedding. This specimen has also been slightly metamorphosed.

No specific place of origin can be suggested for these rock types although it would seem likely that they came from the Carboniferous system which crops out mainly in Tyrone, Fermanagh and much of central Ireland. Rocks of this system are not generally metamorphosed and therefore the alteration seen in these two specimens suggests a local source of heat such as a dyke or sill.

A PALYNOLOGICAL INVESTIGATION OF KETTLE-HOLE SEDIMENTS AT MOUNT SANDEL

A Hamilton, L R Dalzell, B P Lenehan and B J McDonagh

Introduction*

Knowledge of regional variation within Irish late-glacial vegetation is still limited. This paper describes a preliminary palynological investigation of the late-glacial vegetation of Mount Sandel, situated 7 km from the north coast and within the area of the late Midlandian advance of

Scottish ice, the limits of which are marked by the Ballycastle-Armoy-Ballymoney moraine (Stephens *et al* 1975). The sediment site is a kettle-hole lying at an altitude of about 30 m close to the River Bann (Fig 93). This kettle-hole (grid ref D856305) lacks surface drainage and is surrounded by glacial deposits. No detailed map of the superficial geology is available, but field observations show

---

* The references for Appendix 3 will be found on page 192.

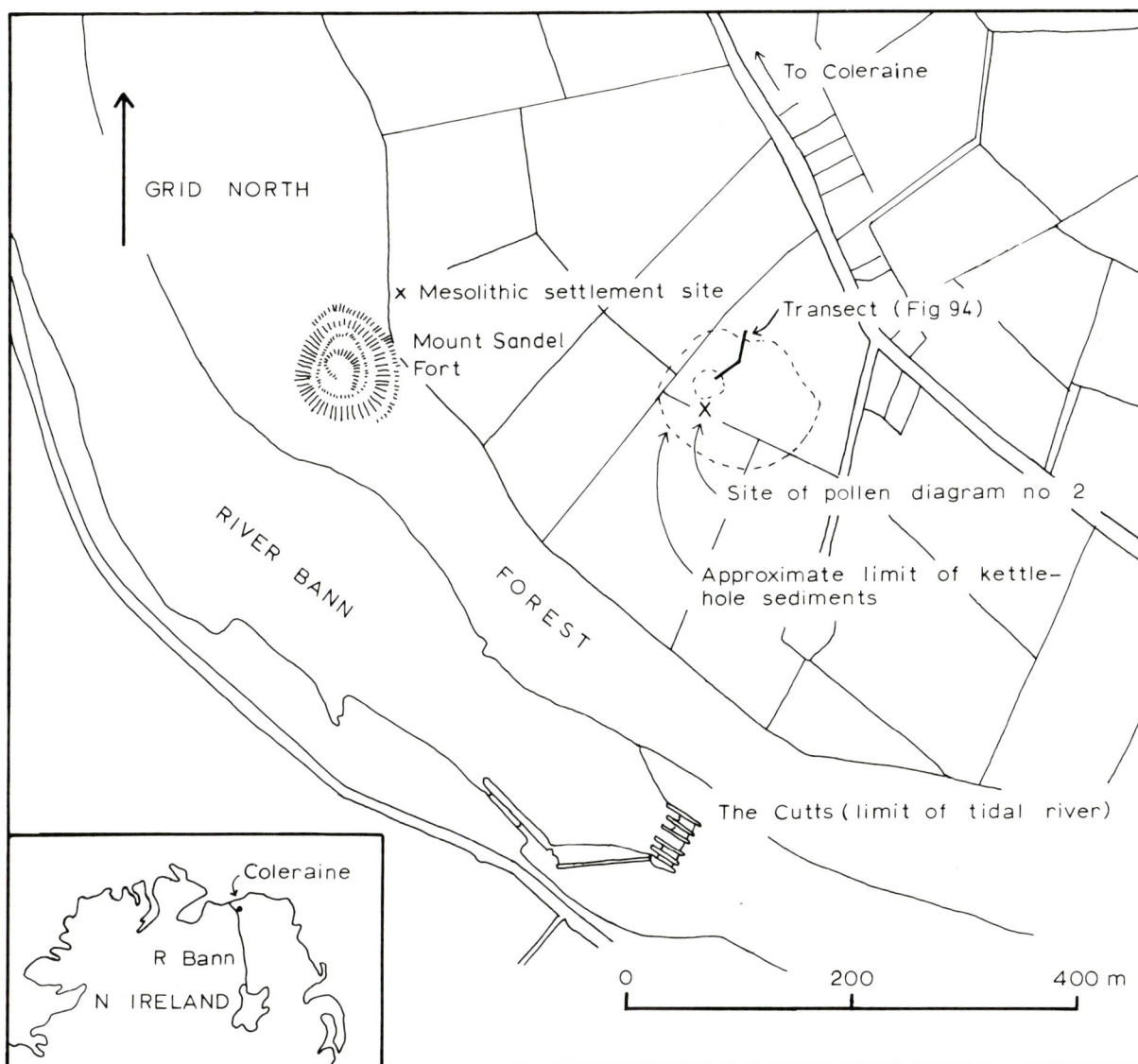

Fig 93   Map showing location of kettle-hole

that slopes to the east are composed predominantly of sand and gravel and those to the west of glacial till. In the centre of the kettle-hole there is a small till inlier, presumably deposited during melting of the kettle-hole ice.

Although most of the sediment in the kettle-hole is of late-glacial age, the uppermost peats are post-glacial and palynological examination of these provides some evidence of early post-glacial environments. It is unfortunate, however, that there appear to be no sediments dating to the time of the Mesolithic occupation at Mount Sandel.

The Kettle-Hole Sediments

The stratigraphy of the sediments (Fig 94) was investigated along a transect line by means of pits and corings made with a Hiller Sampler. Samples were collected for pollen analysis from one of the pits, the position of which is shown on Fig 93. The resulting pollen diagram (no 1) is given on Fig 95. In the following description depths refer to this pit.

A   0–16 cm   Topsoil.
B   16–25 cm   Dark brown, well-decomposed peat, containing some silt. Modern roots present.
C   25–31 cm   Light brown peat, with much inorganic matter. Modern roots present.
D   31–107 cm   Blue-grey silty clay, with frequent macrofossils (including mosses, seeds and, near the northern end of the transect, leaves).
E   107–122 cm   As above, but with very abundant macrofossils.
F   122–142 cm   Light brown, little-decomposed monocotyledon peat, becoming dark brown and well-decomposed towards the centre of the basin.
G   142–162 cm   Blue-grey silty clay, with occasional macrofossils. A band of *Drepanocladus* (160–162 cm) was seen in the pit at the base of this stratum, but not in the borings.
H   162–186 cm   Blue-grey, without obvious macrofossils. Sand and gravel become more abundant towards the base and margins of this stratum. Laminations, probably varves, were seen in the basal parts of this layer at the points indicated on Fig 94.
I   186 + cm   Sand.

The uppermost peat horizons (B and C) along the transect were considered too disturbed by ploughing and cattle-trampling to be useful for detailed palynological investigations. A pit was dug off the transect line to sample the upper sediments at a site at which a relatively thick layer of apparently undisturbed peat was preserved (locality shown on Fig 93). The resulting pollen diagram (no 2) is shown on Fig 96. The stratigraphy was as follows.

0–12 cm   Topsoil.
12–25 cm   Dark brown, well-decomposed, very crumbly peat, containing little visible inorganic matter. Apparently undisturbed by ploughing and trampling. Some modern roots present.
25–41 cm   Light brown, well-decomposed crumbly peat; inorganic matter increasing towards base.

41–70 cm   Blue-grey clay, with light brown mottles. Occasional pebbles up to 1 cm across. Macrofossils present, especially mosses. Becoming more organic below 70 cm.

Pollen Identification

The following notes refer to Diagram 1 (Fig 95).
Artemisia   Some at least is *A* cf *norvegica* (thick-walled and noticeably echinate).
Cyperaceae   Those at the base of the diagram (levels 160 and 170 cm) differ morphologically from those at higher levels.
Ericaceae/Empetrum   Separation of these pollen types proved very difficult and their counts have been amalgamated.
Juniperus   A difficult pollen type to identify, varying considerably in size between levels. The counts are thought to be quite accurate.
Lycopodium   Many of the grains are *L selago*, but *L* probably *alpinum* is the only taxon at level 30 cm.
Myriophyllum   Mostly *M alternifolium*.
Populus   Perhaps a few of the unsplit grains which have been referred to *Juniperus* could be *Populus*. Most possible grains occurred in Zone C.
Salix   *Salix* pollen in Zone A is of a different and larger type to that elsewhere.

Rarer pollen types have been excluded from both diagrams. In the case of Diagram 1 it is valuable to record these excluded pollen types (zones of occurrence in brackets): *Butumus* (M1), *Callitriche* (M2), *Chenopodium* (M2, M4), Gentianaceae (M1), *Hippuris* (M3), Liguliflorae (M2, M4), Liliaceae-type (M3), *Menyanthes* (M3), *Potentilla* (M1, M3, M4), *Polygonum viviparum/bistorta* (M1, M2, M3), Pteridophytes (Monolete) (M1–4), *Ophioglossum/Botrychium* (M2), Rubiaceae (M1, M3), *Rumex* (normal type) (M3), Saxifragaceae undifferentiated (M1, M3), *Selaginella* (M3), *Sphagnum* (M1, M2, M4), Tubiflorae (M1, M4), *Urtica* (M3).

Pollen Assemblage Zones

Two pollen sums used for the two diagrams differ, that of Diagram 1 including all pollen types belonging to terrestrial taxa (*sensu* Birks 1973) and that of Diagram 2 including only tree and shrub pollen. Four pollen assemblage zones (M1–M4) (referred to below as zones) are recognized on Diagram 1, and two (M5, M6) on Diagram 2. Their characteristics are as follows.

DIAGRAM 1 (Fig 95)
Zones M1–M3   These three zones have several common features: low or very low percentages of tree pollen, high values of Cyperaceae, Gramineae and *Juniperus* and the presence, sometimes in considerable quantity, of the pollen of various herbs of open habitats, such as *Artemisia* and *Rumex acetosa/acetosella*. *Myriophyllum* is generally the most abundant aquatic.
Zone M1   This differs from Zones M2 and M3, especially towards its base, in its higher values of tree pollen (mostly *Alnus*, *Corylus* and *Pinus*) and in its lower values of

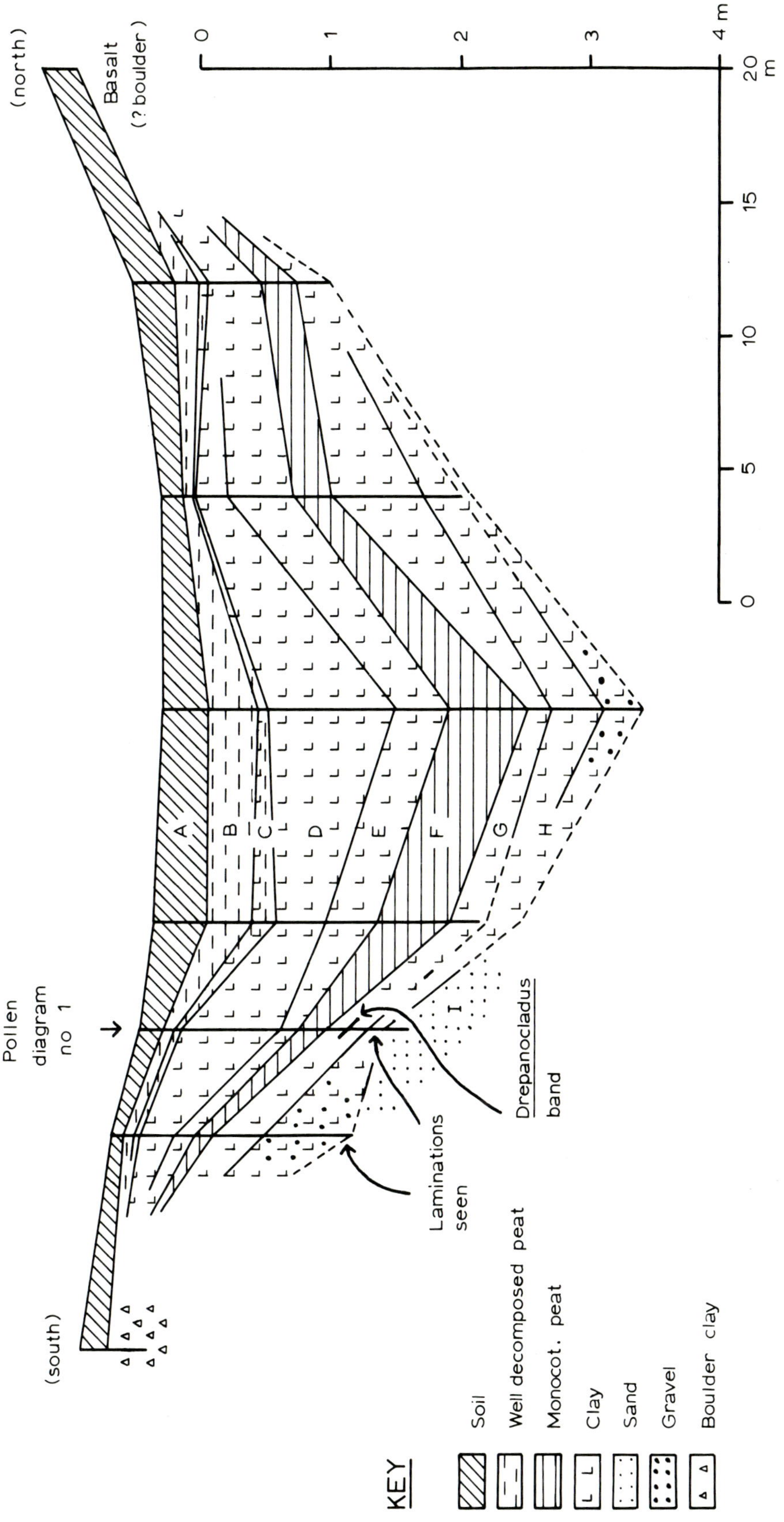

Fig 94 Kettle-hole sediments (line of transect shown in Fig 93)

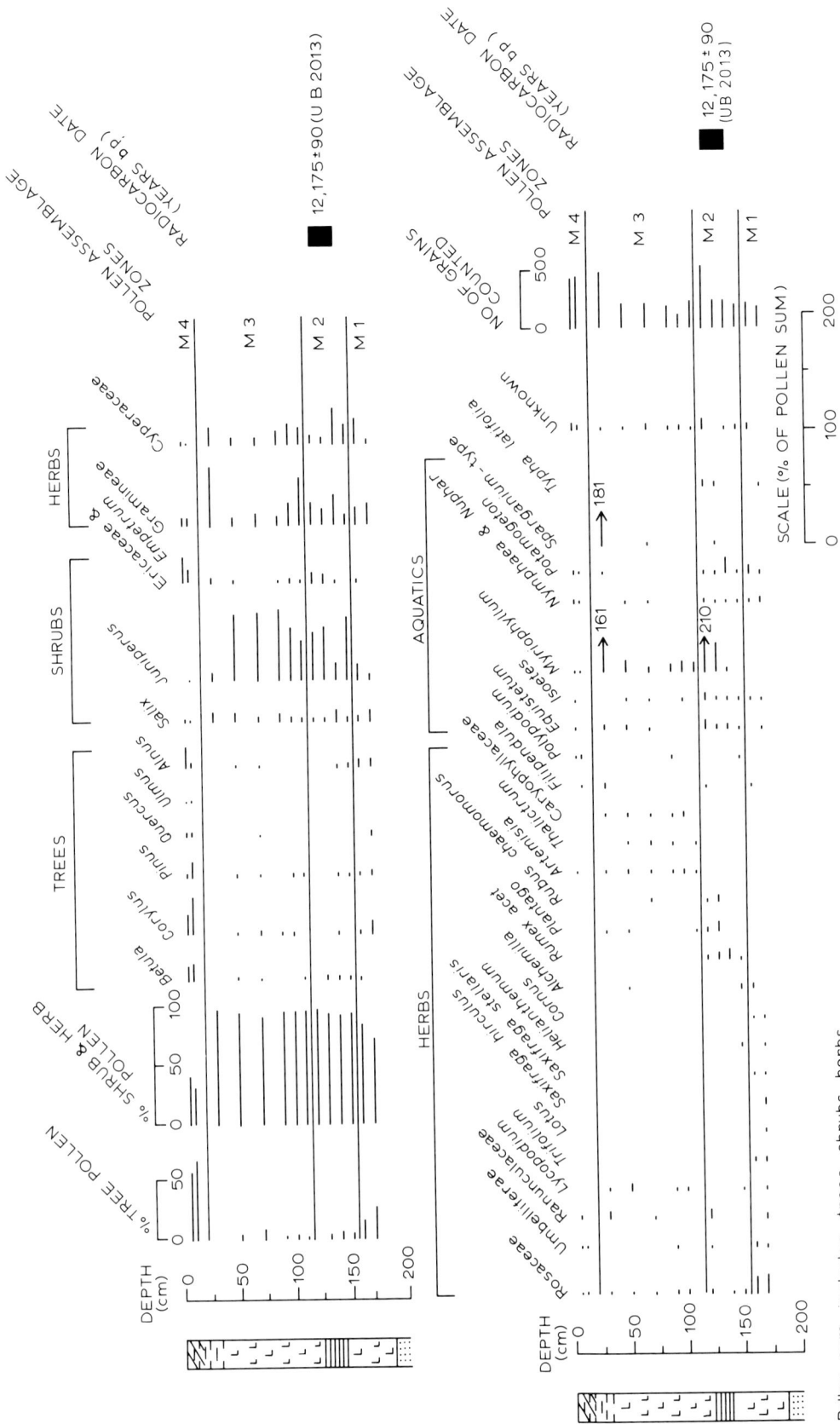

Pollen sum includes trees, shrubs, herbs
Sediment symbols as in stratigraphic column

Fig 95   Kettle-hole pollen diagram no 1: late-glacial

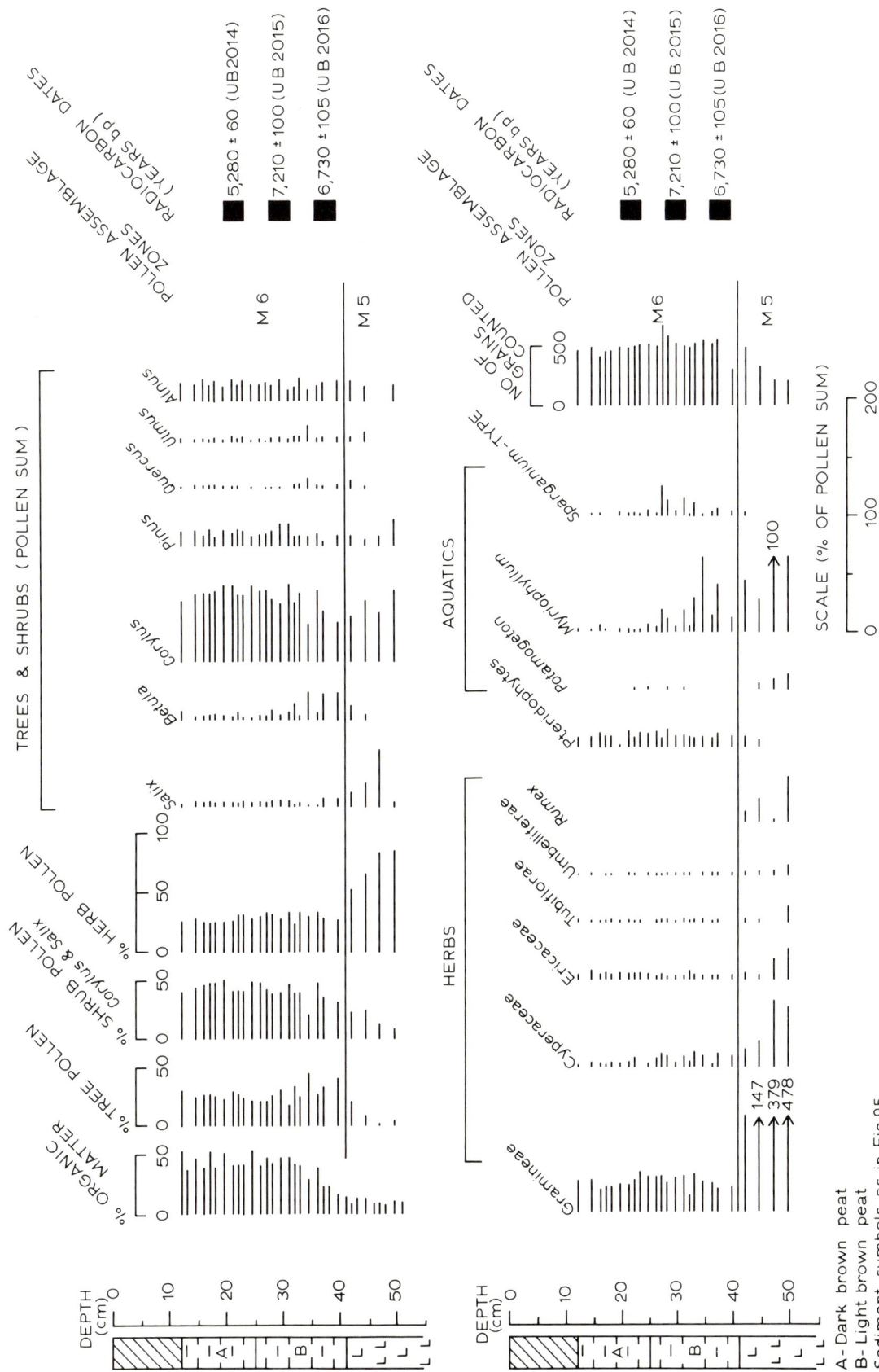

Fig 96   Kettle-hole pollen diagram no 2: post-glacial

Juniperus. Most of the tree pollen is corroded and obviously derived. Its abundance indicates that influx of polliniferous inorganic material was occurring. Rosaceae pollen is abundant. The following pollen types are confined to this zone: *Cornus*, *Helianthemum* (also in the lowermost sample of Zone M2), *Lotus*, *Saxifraga hirculus*, *S stellaris* and *Trifolium*. Among aquatics, the outstanding feature is the absence of *Myriophyllum*. *Nymphaea/Nuphar* and *Potamogeton* are relatively abundant.

Zone M2 Relatively common pollen types include Ericaceae/*Empetrum*, *Plantago*, *Rubus chaemomorus* and *Rumex acet*. Aquatic pollen differs from Zone M1 mainly in the presence of *Typha latifolia* and *Myriophyllum*, the latter being very abundant at some levels.

Zone M3 *Artemisia*, Caryophyllaceae and *Thalictrum* are particularly characteristic of this zone. *Myriophyllum* remains abundant. The uppermost level of this zone is unusual for its total absence of tree pollen, low percentage of *Juniperus* and high values of Ericaceae/*Empetrum*, *Myriophyllum* and *Sparganium*-type.

Zone M4 This zone differs from Zones M1–M3 in possessing much higher values of tree pollen, especially of *Alnus*, *Betula*, *Corylus* and *Pinus*.

DIAGRAM 2 (Fig 96)

Zone M5 This zone is characterized by values of tree pollen as low as those of Zones M1–M3 of Diagram 1. There is a tendency for tree pollen values to rise towards the upper part of the zone. Among shrubs, *Salix* is abundant but *Juniperus* is unrecorded (in this case perhaps due to observer inexperience). Values of Gramineae are very high and other relatively well represented herbs include Cyperaceae and *Rumex*. *Myriophyllum* is the dominant aquatic.

Zone M6 This zone contains relatively high values of tree and shrub pollen. With the exception of a rise in *Betula* towards its base, percentages of tree and shrub pollen remain fairly constant throughout the zone, at approximately the following values: *Alnus* 15%, *Betula* 4% (rising to 24% at base), *Corylus* 60%, *Pinus* 12%, *Quercus* 1%, *Ulmus* 3%. Percentages of Gramineae are much lower than in Zone M5. Other herbs present include Cyperaceae, Ericaceae, Tubiflorae and Umbelliferae, all with fairly constant percentages. In the lower half of the zone there is a gradual replacement of *Myriophyllum* by *Sparganium/Typha*, but both of these, as well as other aquatic pollen types, are rare in the upper half of the zone.

CORRELATION BETWEEN THE DIAGRAMS

Pollen spectra indicate that Zones M5 and M6 of Diagram 2 are correlated, respectively, with the uppermost part of Zone M3 and with Zone M4 of Diagram 1. This conclusion is supported by similarities in sediment stratigraphy.

Radiocarbon Determinations

The following radiocarbon determinations are available.

Diagram no	Depth	^{14}C date		Reference
2	19.5–23.0 cm	5280 ± 60 bp	3330 ± 60 bc	UB 2014
2	27.5–31.0 cm	7210 ± 100 bp	5260 ± 100 bc	UB 2015
2	35.5–39.0 cm	6730 ± 105 bp	4780 ± 105 bc	UB 2016
1	122–142 cm	12,175 ± 90 bp	10,225 ± 90 bc	UB 2013

Age of the Sediments

Subdivision of late-glacial sediments in Ireland was originally based on sediment stratigraphy and macrofossil content (Jessen 1949), but there has been a tendency in recent years to rely more on pollen zones (Mitchell 1976; Singh 1970; Smith 1961 and 1970; Watts 1963; but see the note of caution in Morrison and Stephens 1965). In the case of Mount Sandel both sediment and pollen stratigraphy support correlation of Zone M3 with Pollen Zone III of Watts (1963), which is identical with the *Artemisia* Pollen Assemblage Zone or Nahanagan Stadial of Mitchell (1976). The high values of *Juniperus* at Mount Sandel are unusual, but the relatively low values of Gramineae and the presence of *Artemisia* and Caryophyllaceae are characteristic (Watts 1963). According to Mitchell (1976) the opening and closing dates of the Nahanagan Stadial are about 10,500 and 10,000 bp respectively, though it is noted that an older date of between 11,000 and 10,800 bp has been suggested as more typical of the date of commencement of this cold period in Britain (Birks 1973; Morrison and Stephens 1965).*

The radiocarbon date of 12,175 ± 90 bp indicates that Zone M2 lies within the Woodgrange Interstadial, the onset of which occurred at about 14,000 bp (Mitchell 1976). (Note that Birks (1973) states that a younger date of about 12,800 bp is more typical of the opening of the equivalent Allerød Interstadial in the British Isles.) Although there is lack of complete agreement between pollen and sediment stratigraphy, which is a not unusual feature of Irish late-glacial deposits (Singh 1970, Smith 1961), the peat band within Zone M2 is also indicative of a climate warmer than that of Zone M3. The pollen curves of Zones M1 and M2 have several unusual features in the Irish context. One is the maintenance of high values of *Juniperus* from the beginning of Zone M2 into Zone M3. Another is that the sequence appears to be truncated, with a transition from the open ground vegetation of Zone M1 to the *Juniperus* rise of Zone M2 without the intervening *Rumex* peak which is so characteristic of Irish late-glacial sites (Mitchell 1976; Singh 1970; Watts 1963). Stephens *et al* (1975) suggest a date of about 13,500 bp for retreat of ice from the Armoy State and it is postulated that the late date of deglaciation at Mount Sandel is responsible for the abnormal vegetational development. Judging by the relative thinness and inorganic nature of the sediment, Zone M1 could well fall within the Woodgrange Interstadial as recognized by Mitchell (1976).

In Diagram 2, as in Diagram 1, there is a good correlation between sediment and pollen stratigraphy, the clay being referred to pollen Zone M5 and the overlying peat to Zone M6. The three radiocarbon determinations from the peat all fall within the Atlantic Period (*sensu* Mitchell, see Smith 1970), which in Ireland is believed to extend from very roughly 7500 to 5000 bp (Smith 1970). Of the four pollen spectra of Zone M5, the lower two, with their very high herb pollen percentages, are of undoubted late-glacial age, but the upper two are possibly contaminated by infiltration of pollen downward from the peat. Even

---

* The normal form for radiocarbon dates in this volume is bc, but the authors' preference for bp has been respected in this appendix, as also their preference for cm over mm.

if this is so, the above evidence suggests that sediments dating from approximately the end of the late-glacial (about 10,000 bp) to approximately the beginning of the Atlantic Period are absent.

At least one of the radiocarbon dates is anomalous and it is necessary to consider whether pollen stratigraphy supports an Atlantic date for the peat. The Mount Sandel kettle-hole differs from the usual sites selected for post-glacial palynological research in Ireland in being a very small mire, rather than an extensive bog or a lake. During forested post-glacial times the site was probably closely surrounded by trees. Bearing in mind that pollen spectra from such sites tend to mirror local as opposed to regional vegetational composition (Goddard 1971), the pollen spectra of Zone M6 can be compared with those available from elsewhere in Ireland. In the present case the percentages of *Alnus* and *Pinus* are believed to be particularly informative. Values of *Alnus* in Zone M6 at Mount Sandel are sufficiently high to suggest an Atlantic or post-Atlantic date (Smith 1970). Compared with some other areas, *Alnus* expansion is said to have been very rapid in the lower Bann valley, where it is radiocarbon-dated at about 5000 bc (6950 bp) (Pilcher 1973). *Pinus* can remain abundant during the Atlantic (for example at nearby Cannons Lough, Kilrea (Smith 1961)), but it is rare thereafter and *Pinus* values as high as those of Zone M6 are unlikely to be encountered in post-Atlantic peats. These palynological considerations therefore support the conclusions from the radiocarbon determinations as to the age of the peat. The low values of *Quercus* and *Ulmus* are unusual and could be due to the suggested very local origin of the pollen at this site.

Reconstruction of Late-Glacial Vegetation

The work of Birks (1973) on the composition of surface pollen samples from modern plant communities which might be expected to provide analogues with late-glacial communities is invaluable for interpreting Diagram 1. At Mount Sandel four pollen types maintain rather constant and relatively abundant percentages throughout most of Zones M1–M3: *Juniperus*, Gramineae, Cyperaceae and *Salix*, with average values of about 50, 20, 15 and 4% of the pollen sum respectively. According to Birks (1973), high values of *Juniperus* pollen are today encountered only in tall, dense juniper scrub; high values of Gramineae are characteristic of subalpine communities on basic soils (dwarf *Salix* communities and derived tall and dwarf herb communities); and high values of Cyperaceae are found in the alpine zone. *Salix* pollen is greatly under-represented in surface samples from dwarf willow scrub, with values of 0.7–2.5% being recorded from plots with 45–68% *Salix* cover. These considerations suggest that *Salix* scrub, *Juniperus* scrub and open, sedge-rich communities occurred on the slopes around this kettle-hole during much of the late-glacial period.

With reference to late-glacial vegetation elsewhere in the British Isles, all three zones have similarities to the Gramineae-*Rumex* Assemblage Zone described by Birks (1973) and especially to its *Juniperus communis* Assemblage Subzone. This zone ranges from about 14,300 to 10,000 bp, with a generally northern and western distribution within Britain. Mount Sandel is somewhat atypical in its low values of *Rumex* (except in Zone M2) and also in several features more typical of the *Lycopodium*-Cyperaceae Assemblage Zone. The latter, which are particularly prominent in Zones M1 and M3, include, *inter alia*, high values of Cyperaceae (in all zones), and the presence of *Saxifraga stellaris* in Zone M1 and of *Artemisia* cf *norvegica* in Zone M3. Within Britain the late-glacial *Lycopodium*-Cyperaceae Assemblage Zone has a restricted distribution, being only known from montane areas of western Scotland, the Lake District and north Wales.

In the Irish context (Mitchell 1976; Morrison and Stephens 1965; Singh 1970; Smith 1961 and 1970; Watts 1963), noticeable features are the lack of a pronounced *Rumex* peak below the *Juniperus* rise, the abundance of *Juniperus* throughout and especially in Zone M3, and the absence of a marked *Betula* rise in Zone M2. The high *Juniperus* values may be related to the existence of oceanic climatic conditions close to the north coast (Singh 1970). The low *Betula* values support the suggestion of Singh (1970) that the genus was more abundant in southern than northern Ireland during the Allerød Period.

Sediment stratigraphy indicates soil instability in Zones M1 and M3 and more stable conditions in Zone M2. There is some palynological evidence for a greater extent of open vegetational communities in Zones M1 and M3 compared with Zone M2, but the floristic composition of these open communities in the two zones apparently differed. It is suggested that the parent species of at least some of the following pollen types occurred in these more open communities: in Zone M1—*Alchemila*, *Cornus*, *Helianthemum*, *Lotus*, Rosaceae, *Saxifraga hirculus*, *S stellaris* and *Trifolium*; in Zone M3—*Artemisia*, Caryophyllaceae and *Thalictrum*. Zone M2 is noteworthy for its higher values of Ericaceae/*Empetrum*, *Rumex acetosa/acetosella* and, to lesser degrees, of *Plantago* and *Rubus chaemomorus*. Birks (1973) mentions that *Empetrum* (at any rate) is under-represented in modern pollen spectra and it is thought likely that Ericaceae or *Empetrum* scrub may have become abundant on the slopes around the basin during Zone M2. Both *Plantago* and *Rumex acetosa* are high pollen producers, so that the abundance of their pollen may give a false impression of the abundance of their parent species in the vegetation. *Rumex acetosa* pollen has a good representation in modern spectra from subalpine dwarf willow scrub and derived herb and grass communities (Birks 1973).

Evidence for Post-Glacial Climates

The absence of Preboreal and Boreal sediments in this basin is attributed to two factors. Lack of inorganic sedimentation is believed to be a consequence of stabilization of the soil surface on the surrounding slopes under forested conditions, and the lack of organic sedimentation is held to be a consequence of a relatively dry climate. The dry climate could have persisted either throughout the Preboreal and Boreal Periods or be confined to part of the Boreal, in the latter case causing oxidation of previously accumulated organic sediments. This evidence for a change to a moister climate at the beginning of the Atlantic supports the views of Jessen (1949) and Smith

(1970). Many of the complicating environmental factors, such as successional changes and changes in water-table consequent to changes in sea level, which have created difficulties over interpretation of Boreal/Atlantic climatic changes, are thought to be unimportant at the Mount Sandel site.

Conclusions

1 A kettle-hole at Mount Sandel contains sediments of late-glacial and Atlantic ages. Absence of sediments of intermediate age is attributed partly to stable soil conditions on the slopes around the kettle-hole and partly to a drier climate in all or part of the Preboreal and Boreal Periods than in the Atlantic Period.

2 Three types of plant community were widespread on the slopes around the kettle-hole during much of the late-glacial: *Juniperus* scrub, dwarf *Salix* scrub and open, sedge-rich, communities. The vegetation had a more open character in the earlier and later parts of the late-glacial compared to a central interlude (part of the Woodgrange Interstadial), which was marked by spread of Ericaceae or *Empetrum* scrub.

3 Atypical vegetational development in the early late-glacial is regarded as a consequence of a later date of deglaciation at Mount Sandel than at many of the late-glacial sites which have been palynologically investigated in Ireland.

References

Birks, H J B (1973): *Past and present vegetation of the Isle of Skye: a palaeoecological study* (Cambridge, 1973).

Goddard, A (1971): *Studies of the vegetational changes associated with initiation of blanket peat accumulation in north-east Ireland* (unpublished thesis, Queen's University, Belfast, 1971).

Jessen, K (1949): 'Studies in late Quaternary deposits and flora history of Ireland', in *Proc Roy Irish Acad* 52B (1949), *85–290*.

Mitchell, F (1976): *The Irish landscape* (London, 1976).

Morrison, M E S and Stephens, N (1965): 'A submerged late-Quaternary deposit at Roddans Port on the north-east coast of Ireland', in *Phil Trans Roy Soc London* (B) 249 (1965), *221–255*.

Pilcher, J R (1973): 'Pollen analysis and radiocarbon dating of a peat on Slieve Gallion, Co Tyrone, N Ireland', in *New Phytol* 72 (1973), *681–689*.

Singh, G (1970): 'Late-glacial vegetational history of Lecale, Co Down', in *Proc Roy Irish Acad* 69B (1970), *189–216*.

Smith, A G (1961): 'Cannons Lough, Kilrea, Co Londonderry: stratigraphy and pollen analysis', in *Proc Roy Irish Acad* 61B (1961), *369–383*.

—— (1970): 'Late- and post-glacial vegetational and climatic history of Ireland: a review', in *Irish geographical studies in honour of E E Evans*, eds N Stephens and R E Glasscock (Belfast, 1970), *65–88*.

Stephens, N, Creighton, J R and Hannon, M A (1975): 'The late-Pleistocene period in north-eastern Ireland: an assessment, 1975', in *Irish Geography* 8 (1975), *1–23*.

Watts, W A (1963): 'Late-glacial pollen zones in Western Ireland', in *Irish Geography* 4 (1963), *367–378*.

THE MOUNT SANDEL AREA IN LATER PREHISTORIC AND HISTORIC TIMES

R Warner and N F Brannon

Part 1 Iron Age (R Warner)*

Earlier Iron Age

Two radiocarbon dates and some late objects necessitate a brief discussion of the late prehistoric and early historic nature of the site. Feature 313, a small pit whose fill contained several lumps of charcoal, produced also two glass beads (above, p 54 and Fig 36). The charcoal gave a conventional ^{14}C date of 2170 ± 40 bp (UB 2446), which can be calibrated on two alternative published 'smoothed' curves to give real dates of 270 ± 85 bc (the curve of Clark 1975) and 265 ± 105 bc (Damon *et al* 1974). The methodology of each calibration has resulted in rather different 'error' terms, but the means are in good agreement. If we take the date according to Clark, whose calibration seems to be favoured in Britain at present, we get a 95% probability range (2sd) of 440 to 100 BC (a 99.7% range, 3 sd, of 525 to 15 BC). This 'smoothed' calibration curve has the advantage of giving the calibrated date a Gaussian form, as was the original radiocarbon date, which can be treated statistically. It is now clear, however, that such a calibration curve does not properly represent the fluctuating property of the atmospheric radiocarbon reservoir, and the resulting 'wiggly' nature of the correct calibration curve. It is therefore generally regarded as best to calibrate on a 'wiggly' curve and replace the Gaussian convenience by a probability range. We may use, for the period before 300 BC, the recent precise curve of Pearson, Pilcher and Baillie (1983), and for the period after 300 BC the less precise curve of Michael and Ralph (1974). For this sample we obtain a 95% probability range of 380 BC to 135 BC (99.7% range of 390 BC to 10 BC). We must, however, consider the potential 'age-lapse' of the sample (Warner 1976a) to which, the sample being oak of unknown original biological age, we may give an estimated value of 200 years. The effect of this is to stretch the mean towards the present by 200 years, and to move all the upper limits by the same amount in the same direction. We thus conclude that the date of deposition of the sample, and of the creation of the pit, lies, with high probability, in the range 400 BC to AD 200. In other words it belongs either to the latest part of the obscure late Dowris phase of the Later Bronze Age or to the Earlier Iron Age.

The two glass objects from F313 were a small toggle of the 'dumb-bell' class, formed of two conjoined globes of greenish translucent glass, and a tiny annular bead of rich blue translucent glass, both in very good condition (Fig 36). Glass toggles, or dumb-bell 'beads', are not infrequent in Irish collections, but are rather difficult to date closely typologically. They have been found in a number of Irish Earlier Iron Age contexts, for instance in cremation burials at Kiltierney, Co Fermanagh (Raftery 1981, fig 39, no 3, *187*), and Grannagh, Co Galway (*ibid*, fig 32, no 4, *180*; Hawkes 1981, *60–3*). These sites produced objects securely dated to the 1st century BC or the 1st century AD. A translucent greenish toggle similar to that from Mount Sandel was found at Close ny chollagh on the Isle of Man with another like that from Kiltierney (Gelling 1958, *94*, nos 5, 6). They came from a midden which also produced a brooch of the earlier 1st century AD.

Although the ^{14}C date for the Mount Sandel pit is quite consistent with this evidence and precludes a post 2nd-century AD date for the beads, glass toggles did continue in Ireland well into the Later Iron Age,* translucent greenish toggles of the Mount Sandel type having come from post 7th-century AD contexts, for instance at Lagore (Hencken 1950, *139*, no 1471) and Clogher (Warner forthcoming). In the vicinity of Mount Sandel three dumb-bell beads are recorded: a translucent greenish one from the sandhills at Grangemore, at the mouth of the River Bann (Hasse 1891, *139*), and two from the Whitepark Bay sandhills (Knowles 1885, *122*, note 1). None of these is from a datable context. Greenish translucent glass is not particularly common in the Irish Earlier Iron Age, except as the base for some complex beads, nor is it common in Britain much before the 1st century AD, although widespread on the Continent from the 6th century BC onwards (Guido 1978, *11*). A number of plain beads of this colour were found in barrow no 8 at Carrowjames, Co Mayo (Raftery 1940, *28–37*), which also produced a bone toggle and a bronze toggle rather reminiscent of some objects from Romano-British levels at Traprain Law, Midlothian (Curle 1915, 34; Curle and Cree 1921, *176*, no 10), and from Newstead, Roxburghshire (Curle 1911, pl 77, 16). The bronze toggle may well be a British equivalent of the Irish glass toggle. Analysis of the trace-element content of the Mount Sandel bead (by XRF spectroscopy) showed it to belong to the same analytical group as a number of other dumb-bell beads, the absence of antimony being indicative of the Earlier Iron Age (Warner and Meighan 1981, *60*). The greenish colour is due to iron in the original sand (Guido 1978, *11*).

The tiny annular blue bead is of the rich, deep, translucent blue which I have found to be indicative of Earlier Iron Age Irish beads, contrasting with the usually limpid translucent blue beads of the Later Iron Age (that is, after the 5th century AD). This is due to the use of

---

* The references for Part 1 will be found on page 195.

* The author's preferred term for the Early Christian period.

manganese as a clarifier in the former and of antimony in the latter (Warner and Meighan 1981). Analysis confirmed the absence of antimony and the presence of manganese, though the size of the bead prevented quantitative estimation. Cobalt was also present in this blue bead, being, as in all Irish blue beads analysed (*ibid*), the cause of the coloration. Tiny annular blue beads have been widely found in Earlier Iron Age burials in Ireland. Many were found in inhumations at Knowth, Co Meath, belonging, as far as one can judge from the few bronzes found, to the first few centuries ad (Eogan 1974, *81–87*). Another inhumation here produced a greenish toggle bead of rather curious form (*ibid*, *87* and pl 29b). Sixty-five were found in a 1st-century AD burial (?) at 'Loughey' near Donaghadee, Co Down (Jope and Wilson 1957; Jope 1960). Several came from Grannagh (Raftery 1981) and single ones were found in ring-barrows at Clogher, Co Tyrone (Warner forthcoming) and Mullaghmore, Co Down (Mogey *et al* 1956, *19*). In Britain similar beads (Guido 1978, group 6 ivb) are found throughout the Early Iron Age and, particularly, in the early Roman period.

The beads are, therefore, quite consistent with the radiocarbon date range for pit F313 and indeed suggest we should narrow the date to the last century BC or the first couple of centuries AD. The purpose of the pit seems obscure, the absence of cremated bone and the unfused nature of the beads telling, perhaps, against interpretation as a cremational burial. Nor does it seem explicable as the remains of normal habitation. I am loath to suggest the convenient 'ritual' explanation, but there are examples of such 'caches' of personal ornaments, including beads, in clearly non-domestic situations. The geographically closest, which included an imported Romano-British bead, was inserted into the Bronze Age cairn on Lyles Hill, Co Antrim (Evans 1953, 57, fig 24.76). Pit F313 may be related to a number of other features on the site, such as three straight slots, of which the pair (F6 and F11) was overlain by a small deposit of charcoal (F10), which deposit was, in turn, overlain by another slot (F7: see above, p 7 and Fig 4). The charcoal deposit gave a ^{14}C date of 2385 ± 70 bp (UB 2205), to which the Clark calibration gives a real date of 480 ± 105 BC and a 95% probability range of 690 BC to 270 BC. The combined Pearson, Pilcher and Baillie and Michael and Ralph 'wiggly' curves calibrate the 95% range to 790 BC to 360 BC (99.7% range is 800 BC to 260 BC). This date is not significantly different from the radiocarbon date from pit F313, but is significantly different from the date of that pit as narrowed by the contained beads. If, however, we add the standard 200 year age-lapse estimate to convert the sample date to a deposit date we get for F10 an upper limit in the first century BC. There is thus no significant argument *against* pit F313 and either deposit F10 or one of the slots being contemporary, but neither is there associative or contextual evidence that they *should* be. Nor are the real time intervals between slot F7, deposit F10 and slots F6/11 known even approximately. It could be that a proportion of the coarse pottery from the site belongs to the general period of the pit and the deposit F10, but it is not, at present, datable either by context or typology.

It seems to have become accepted (after Reeves 1847, *342*, note k) that the adjacent Mountsandel Fort, to which slots F6/11 seem to be tangential, is the *Dún Da Bend* of early Irish literature (a claim repeated on the present Ordnance Survey maps, where the site is designated 'Dun da beann or Mountsandel Fort'). *Dún Da Bend* appears in the Old Irish 'Ulster Cycle' tales as a regional pre-Christian 'royal' (= ritual?) centre with a similar status to *Emhain Macha*, now Navan Fort, Co Armagh. It is true that the linear slots (F6/11) are reminiscent of 'roadway' fences of Latest Bronze Age or Earlier Iron Age date at the two great earthwork enclosures of Navan Fort (Waterman and Selkirk 1970) and Knockaulin, Co Kildare (phase 2, Wailes 1976, fig 3). But it is clear from the early Irish documentary sources that *Dún Da Bend* was *west* of the River Bann (Ó Ceallaigh 1951, *38–9*). The equation of Mountsandel Fort with *Dún Da Bend* must therefore be dismissed and, despite the slight similarity of the Mountsandel earthwork to a number of large ring-barrows of possibly Earlier Iron Age date (at Tara, Co Meath, for instance) and our demonstration of Earlier Iron Age activity in its vicinity, there is absolutely no reason to believe that Mountsandel Fort belongs to such an early period, or even pre-dates the medieval period (see further below and McNeill 1980, 6).

The extreme north-east of Ireland is particularly rich in finds of the Earlier Iron Age, mostly metalwork (for map, Warner 1982, fig 1). These finds, which include imported and native material, span both its phases (Warner 1976b, *268*). Within this north-eastern concentration a notable cluster is seen in the area within 15 km of Mount Sandel, east of the River Bann and from the river itself. A group of river finds 3 km south of Mount Sandel is related to the former existence of a major ford at Camus or Loughan Island (Warner 1974, *60*), and the large decorated stone from Derrykeighan (Waterman and Warner forthcoming), although in a secondary position, implies a contemporary site in its near vicinity. Unfortunately there is contextual ignorance of most of the material, including a horse-bit 'from Mountsandel' (Haworth 1971, *46*, no 39), and despite this material richness the only certain excavational evidence of Earlier Iron Age activity comes from the excavated Mount Sandel site.

Later Iron Age

A few words should be appended on the small scatter of Later Iron Age pottery, the so-called 'souterrain ware', from the site. There was no recognizable context for this pottery, or associated features, but it shows habitation in the very near vicinity at some time between about AD 700 and AD 1200 (Ryan 1973 for the souterrain ware class, although I would date its inception later than he does). The 12th-century name for Mount Sandel was *Cill Sanctain* (the equation can easily be traced in documents from the 12th to the 17th century: see Reeves 1847, *324–5*) and it may well be that the Later Iron Age material, albeit a very small quantity, relates to this ecclesiastical site. That whatever traces of the church that existed here were destroyed utterly by the building of John de Courcy's castle in 1197 is clear from its failure to be mentioned in any of the medieval visitations (eg Reeves 1847, 3ff).

Acknowledgments

I am grateful to Dr A Edgar of the Industrial Science Division of the Department of Commerce (NI) for putting his XRF facilities at my disposal.

References

Clark, R M (1975): 'A calibration curve for radiocarbon dates' in *Antiquity* 49 (1975), *251–266*.

Curle, A O (1915): 'Account of the excavations on Traprain Law . . . in 1914', in *Proc Soc Antiq Scotland* 49 (1915), *139–202*.

—— and Cree, J (1921): 'Account of the excavations on Traprain Law . . . in 1920', in *Proc Soc Antiq Scotland* 55 (1921), *153–206*.

Curle, J (1911): *A Roman frontier post and its people* (Glasgow, 1911).

Damon, P, Ferguson, C, Long, A and Wallick, E (1974): 'Dendrochronologic calibration of the radiocarbon time scale', in *American Antiquity* 39 (1974), *350–366*.

Eogan, G (1974): 'Report on the excavations of some passage graves, unprotected inhumation burials and a settlement site at Knowth, Co Meath', in *Proc Roy Irish Acad* 74C (1974), *11–112*.

Evans, E E (1953): *Lyles Hill: a late Neolithic site in Co Antrim* (Belfast, 1953).

Gelling, P (1958): 'Close ny chollagh: an Iron Age fort at Scarlett, Isle of Man', in *Proc Prehist Soc* 24 (1958), *85–100*.

Guido, M (1978): *The glass beads of the prehistoric and Roman periods in Britain and Ireland* (London, 1978).

Hasse, L (1891): 'Objects from the sandhills at Portstewart and Grangemore, and their antiquity', in *J Roy Soc Antiq Ireland* 21 (1891), *130–138*.

Hawkes, C F C (1981): 'The wearing of the brooch: Early Iron Age dress among the Irish', in *Studies on early Ireland*, ed B Scott (Belfast, 1981), *51–73*.

Haworth, R (1971): 'The horse harness of the Irish Early Iron Age', in *Ulster J Archaeol* 34 (1971), *26–49*.

Hencken. H (1950): 'Lagore crannog: an Irish royal residence of the 7th to 10th centuries AD', in *Proc Roy Irish Acad* 53C (1950), *1–247*.

Jope, E M (1960): 'The beads from the 1st-century AD burial at "Loughey", near Donaghadee: supplementary note', in *Ulster J Archaeol* 23 (1960), *40*.

—— and Wilson, B (1957): 'A burial group of the first century AD from "Loughey", near Donaghadee, Co Down', in *Ulster J Archaeol* 20 (1957), *73–94*.

Knowles, W J (1885): 'Whitepark Bay, Co Antrim', in *J Roy Soc Antiq Ireland* 17 (1885), *104–125*.

McNeill, T E (1980): *Anglo–Norman Ulster* (Edinburgh, 1980).

Michael, H and Ralph, E (1974): 'University of Pennsylvania radiocarbon dates 16', in *Radiocarbon* 16 (1974), *198–218*.

Mogey, J, Thompson, G and Proudfoot, B (1956): 'Excavation of two ring-barrows in Mullaghmore townland, Co Down', in *Ulster J Archaeol* 19 (1956), *11–28*.

Ó Ceallaigh, S (1951): *Gleanings from Ulster history* (Cork, 1951).

Pearson, G W, Pilcher, J R and Baillie, M G L (1983): 'High-precision ^{14}C measurements of Irish oaks to show the natural variations from 200 BC to 4000 BC', in *Radiocarbon* 25 (1983), *179–186*.

Raftery, B (1981): 'Iron Age burials in Ireland', in *Irish Antiquity*, ed D Ó Corráin (Cork, 1981), *173–204*.

Raftery, J (1940): 'The tumulus cemetery of Carrowjames, Co Mayo', in *J Galway Archaeol Hist Soc* 19 (1940), *16–71*.

Reeves, W (1847): *Ecclesiastical antiquities of Down, Connor and Dromore* (Dublin, 1847).

Ryan, M (1973): 'Native pottery in early historic Ireland', in *Proc Roy Irish Acad* 73C (1973), *619–645*.

Wailes, B (1976): 'Dun Ailinne: an interim report', in *Hillforts in Britain and Ireland*, ed D Harding (London, 1976), *319–338*.

Warner, R (1974): 'The reprovenancing of two important penannular brooches of the Viking period', in *Ulster J Archaeol* 36–37 (1974), *58–70*.

—— (1976a): 'Further notes for users of radiocarbon dates', in *Irish Archaeol Res Forum* 3(2) (1976), *25–44*.

—— (1976b): 'Some observations on the context and importation of exotic material in Ireland', in *Proc Roy Irish Acad* 76C (1976), *267–292*.

—— (1982): 'The Broighter hoard: a reappraisal and the iconography of the collar', in *Studies on early Ireland*, ed B Scott (Belfast, 1982), *29–38*.

—— and Meighan, I (1981): 'Dating Irish glass beads by chemical analysis', in *Irish Antiquity*, ed D Ó Corráin (Cork, 1981), *52–66*.

Waterman, D and Selkirk, A (1970): 'Navan Fort', in *Current Archaeol* 2 (1970), *304–308*.

Part 2   Medieval and Later (N F Brannon)*

Occupation within the Coleraine area in the years following the Anglo-Norman invasion is well attested in written sources, but these present considerable problems of interpretation. Reference is made in the early 13th century to two castles, at *Culrath* (Coleraine) and *Kil Santain*, variously spelt (Reeves 1847, *324*; McNeill 1980, *14–15*). McNeill, like Orpen earlier, identified *Kil Santain* castle, founded by John de Courcy, with Mountsandel Fort. Warner (above) favours this identification and also the likely existence of a church, the *cill*, probably destroyed by the construction of the castle.

The Antrim Inquisition of 1605 appears to support the identification of *Kil Santain* with Mountsandel, giving 'Killsantill alias Mount Sandall', but Reeves argued that this perpetuated an error made in antiquity (1847, *74* and *324*), and preferred to identify *Kil Santain* with the remains of a stone castle in Fish Loughan townland, slightly further upstream on the Bann. This site was close to a motte and an old burial ground in the next townland, Mill Loughan, and the church of *Loghkan* was valued at 2 marks in the 1306 taxation (*ibid*, *72–3*). Unfortunately the masonry remains

---

* The references for Part 2 will be found on page 198.

MOUNT SANDEL — GENERAL SITE PLAN

B

A

C

Section

B

C

A

LOWER
SITE

BRIDGE

PATH

W

L

A
60

50

40

UPPER SITE

0   20   60   100Feet

0   10   20   30Metres

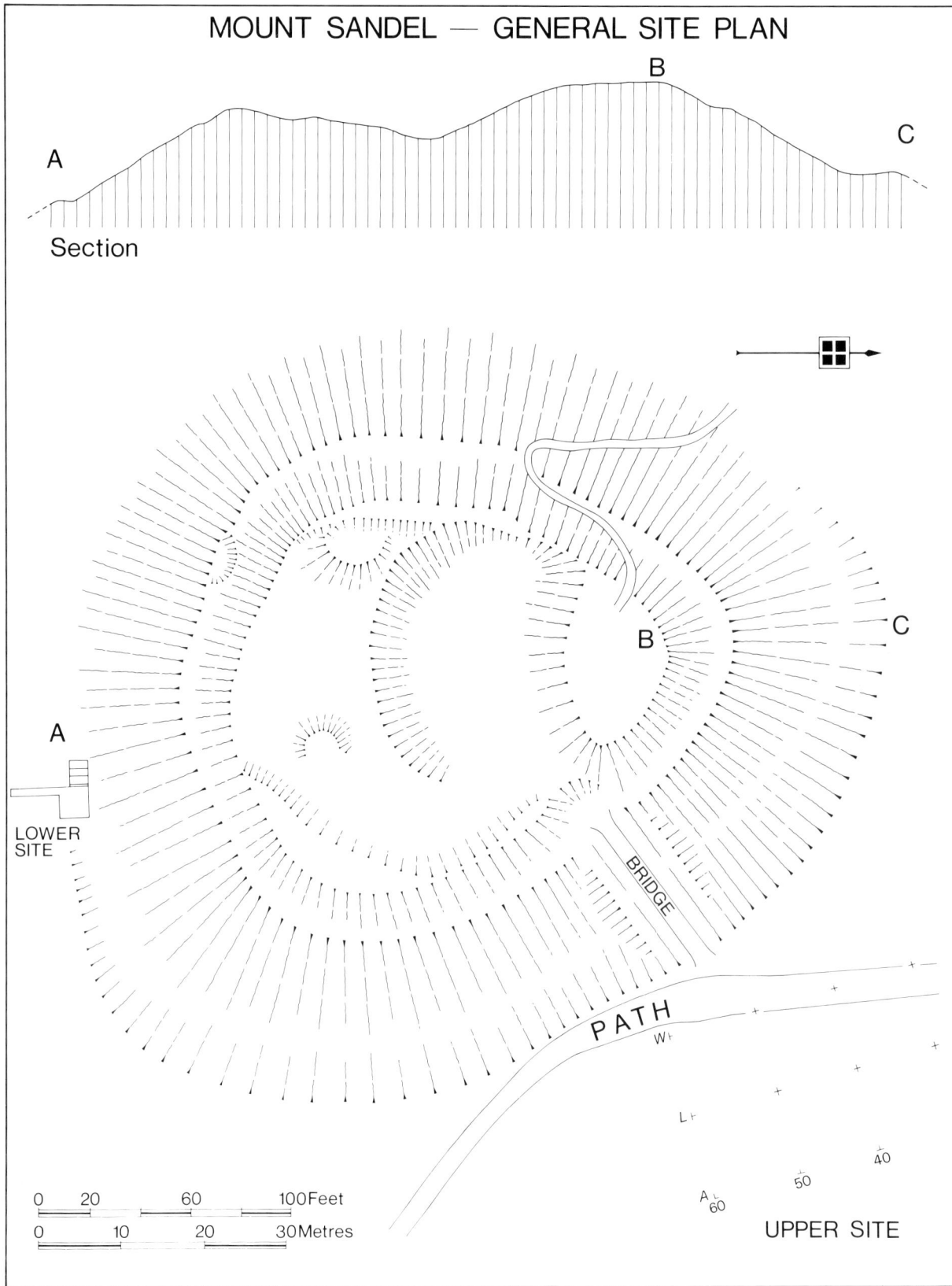

Fig 97   Mountsandel Fort: plan and section, showing upper and lower excavation sites

thought to be of the castle, described as seven feet thick in places, were destroyed in recent years without archaeological investigation and the site's chronology cannot now be tested. The motte and castle would have commanded the ford across the river to the church at Camus on the west bank.

Disagreement over the location of *Kil Santain* is not helped by the account of the Lord Deputy, the Earl of Sussex, in 1556: '. . . wee camped at ye river side, and by a hill called Knock Sandall . . . by ye hill of Knock Sendall there is a castle called Knock Caslen Loughan' (O'Laverty 1887, *166*). This seems to suggest two distinct sites, and if one follows Reeves's interpretation it is possible that 'Knock Sendall' (Mountsandel) was referred to because of its prominence as a landmark rather than as a functioning fortification. A survey of maps of the area from the late 16th and early 17th centuries in the Public Record Office of Northern Ireland has produced four from the 1600–1610 period which locate Mountsandel, using various spellings. Three of these (T1493/1, T2543/1, T1668/44) show Mountsandel as a mounded site.

Neither of the points of view given above is fully satisfactory. The association of *Kil Santain* with Mountsandel seems strong, but equally the evidence from the Loughans seems to have points in its favour. Perhaps the two can be reconciled by suggesting a chronological distinction? The profile of the earthwork at Mountsandel (Fig 97) has always been a subject of debate, especially its central hollow. Had this not existed and the mound been flat-topped, the identification of the site as a raised rath or motte would hardly have been disputed, and the identification of the site with the de Courcy castle of 1197 would not be in doubt. The uninterrupted ditch on the landward side is a motte feature, and there is no evidence that a causeway existed and has since been removed, but the top of the mound bears no relation to motte surfaces recognized elsewhere. It can be suggested that de Courcy did indeed start to build a motte, with the deep ditch on the landward side providing material for the existing mound. In his excavation at the edge of the mound A E P Collins also located a ditch at its S edge which contained a carbonized tree branch dated by ^{14}C to the mid 13th century, and regarded this as supporting the de Courcy connection (Collins 1983, *21*). Perhaps because of the physical difficulties of the site, or for unknown military or political reasons, the construction was never finished. Parallels for such an unfinished earthwork can be seen at the English Mount at Downpatrick and Piper's Fort, Farranfad townland, Co Down (*ASCD* 1966, *195–6* and *202–3*). Mountsandel would then take its place as an unfinished late 12th-century earthwork with a very short lifespan, possibly replaced by a stone fortification at Fish Loughan early in the 13th century and a castle in Coleraine. A small scatter of medieval glazed pottery was found in the excavations (above, page 58), but it was not plentiful, and this would be consistent with a short occupation.

As far as location is concerned the 13th-century references to Coleraine castle are almost as open to confusion as those for *Kil Santain*. In 1214 Thomas MacUchtred, who held land on both sides of the Bann, is reported to have built the castle of Coleraine from '. . . all the cemeteries, fences and buildings of that town, save the church alone' (*AU* 1214), suggesting probably a largely

stone castle. Since there was no bridge over the Bann, and the church was on the east bank (Reeves 1847, 247–8), it seems likely that Coleraine castle stood somewhere within the present Coleraine urban area on the east bank. No traces of it survive, however, and apart from a 1228 reference to repairs to the castle (*AU*) most later references to 'Coleraine castle' seem to belong to Drumtarsy, built on the west side of the Bann in 1248 (such as Bagenal's 1585 mention: Hore 1854, *149*).

The status of Coleraine as a medieval settlement has been discussed elsewhere (McNeill 1980, *92*). The assessment of it as an urban centre is based largely on written sources and has not yet been demonstrated by excavation.* One feature of note from the late medieval period, however, was a large ditch sectioned in several places in gardens behind Cross Lane. It produced a well stratified series of late medieval coarse ware cooking pots, unfortunately not very closely datable. It is likely, from their appearance, that the coarse ware sherds from the Mount Sandel site (above, page 55) are of this type. They share the characteristic glitter which seems to have been obtained by dusting the vessels with mica before firing. This feature was also noted on coarse ware sherds excavated from a ditch beside the medieval church at Macosquin, Co Londonderry (Brannon 1983), and it may prove to be a diagnostic feature of coarse ware vessels in the Coleraine area.

The post-medieval history of Coleraine has been dealt with extensively elsewhere (Moody 1939 and Mullin 1976). Though within the parish and liberties of Coleraine, Mount Sandel does not appear from documents to have been of particular interest to the Plantation settlers, and it is mentioned only occasionally in later Irish Society records, generally as a landmark by the name of Mount Sandy. There is, however, some archaeological evidence that the mound may have been reused for military purposes in the 17th century. Though no very clear picture of the post-medieval features emerged from the excavations, some could be interpreted as connected with a bank running out from the fort (Fig. 60 and above, page 123). A E P Collins found a scatter of lead musket balls on the top of the ditch fill round the mound and speculated that it could have been used as an artillery emplacement during the 1641 rebellion, when Coleraine held out against the rebels (Collins 1983, *21*). The post-medieval ceramics from Mount Sandel are insufficient in number and not clearly enough stratified for many conclusions to be drawn from them, but the absence of Lancashire and North Devon wares contrasts with the excavated assemblage from Coleraine. North Devon ceramics, particularly gravel-tempered tiles, were quite numerous in mid 17th-century deposits there, and it can be suggested that their absence at Mount Sandel relates to a scarcity of buildings with such roof embellishments in the immediate area.

Finally it is perhaps worth noting that the Ordnance Survey Memoir for Coleraine parish records the destruction of a nearby earthwork in the late 18th century 'for manure' (PRONI MIC 6, p 13). While there seems little likelihood that such damage occurred at Mountsandel Fort, since the

---

* There have been three main seasons of excavation in Coleraine town centre (1978–80) in advance of redevelopment, as well as smaller projects in 1981–2.

central hollow is the least accessible part of the site from the point of view of transport, its partial destruction in this way must remain a possibility if the unfinished earthwork theory proves unacceptable.

Acknowledgments

I would like to thank Richard Warner for discussion of the early sources for Mount Sandel, Chris Lynn for discussion of the physical aspects of the site, and Ann Hamlin for help with the text.

References

AU: Annals of Ulster, eds W M Hennessy and B MacCarthy, 4 vols (Dublin, 1887–1901).

ASCD (1966): *An archaeological survey of County Down* (HMSO, Belfast, 1966).

Brannon, N F (1983): 'Rescue excavations in Macosquin, County Londonderry', in *Ulster J Archaeol* 46 (1983), *93–99*.

Collins, A E P (1983): 'Excavations at Mount Sandel, lower site, Coleraine, County Londonderry', in *Ulster J Archaeol* 46 (1983), *1–22*.

Hore, H F (1854): 'Marshal Bagenal's description of Ulster', in *Ulster J Archaeol* 2 (1854), *137–160*.

McNeill, T E (1980): *Anglo-Norman Ulster* (Edinburgh, 1980).

Moody, T W (1939): *The Londonderry Plantation 1608–1641* (Belfast, 1939).

Mullin, T H (1976): *Coleraine in by-gone centuries* (Belfast, 1976).

O'Laverty, J (1887): *An historical account of the diocese of Down and Connor*, 1 (Dublin, 1887).

Reeves, W (1847): *Ecclesiastical antiquities of Down, Connor and Dromore* (Dublin, 1847).

RESCUE EXCAVATION AT CASTLEROE

The Excavation

This site on the west bank of the River Bann (Fig 1) was investigated over two days during August 1976. Service trenches had cut through the concrete floor of a small building beside the main part of the Spanboard factory at Castleroe (Fig 98) revealing what appeared to be the remnants of an extensive Mesolithic occupation site. Unfortunately the erection of the main factory some years earlier had led to the digging of a pit 'about 10 feet deep' to house a concrete raft. This, and the levelling of the surrounds, seemed to have obliterated most of the traces of this settlement. The service trenches had been almost completed when the Ulster Museum was contacted, so that most of the occupation soil had unfortunately been dug out before archaeological investigation.

One small area had survived total destruction (Fig 99, plan) and extensive sieving of the soil in this area, as well as a sample kept by a workman who noted the site's existence, produced sufficient material to make it clear that this was an Early Mesolithic settlement. The sections recorded (Fig 99, at A–B in Fig 98) show that this particular area had survived only by being in a small hollow, as the ground had been levelled through a cut and tip operation which entailed covering the hollow with a layer of red clay. Within the area of occupation was one small area where the soil was much blacker and larger quantities of charcoal were present. Fortunately it was part of this area which had survived intact (pecked outline in Fig 99). Excavation in

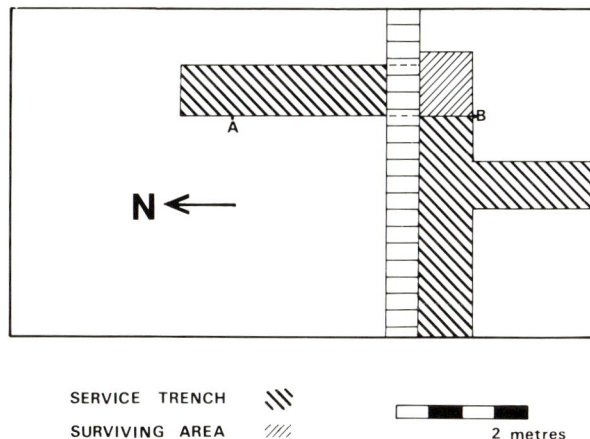

SERVICE TRENCH
SURVIVING AREA
WALL

2 metres

Fig 98 Castleroe: area plan

this deeper part of the hollow revealed traces of features similar to those found at Mount Sandel. Two pits, one 400 mm deep, and a substantial post-hole were located (Fig 99, plan).

Stone Industry

This material can hardly be described as coming from a controlled excavation.

Blades	38	Scraper	1
Flakes	4	Awl	1
Debitage	139	Microliths	13

Industry
In spite of the relatively small sample of material, the lack of cores and decortical flakes and the presence of burnt flint suggest that this was part of the dwelling area within the settlement. The blades show that this industry was identical to that found at Mount Sandel, with the blade size varying from 20 to 40 mm.

Retouched tools
Scrapers Only one very crude scraper was found and this was uncovered by one of the workmen. It is a flake scraper which has utilized a natural steep edge and so has only been retouched across half of its distal end.
Awl Again the only awl to be recovered was found by workmen. This is a rather small example which has only been retouched on its dorsal face.
Microliths (13) These were all recovered during the excavation. Scalene triangles: 7 These were rather fragmentary specimens, often burnt. Only one short edge was preserved and this was not concave. Like the dominant type from Mount Sandel these were rather narrow examples.
Narrow rods (2) Two rather small, undiagnostic examples.
Needle points (2) These both appear to be type 2, rather broad forms.

Faunal Remains

As with the Mount Sandel faunal remains, these consisted of burnt fragments of bone. Alwynne Wheeler (British Museum) has kindly identified the fish bones as salmon and eels, while there is a small selection of burnt mammal bones and one bird bone, unfortunately not identifiable as to species.

CONCRETE

RUBBLE

WALL

RED CLAY

GRAVEL

GREY OCCUPATION

BLACK OCCUPATION

--- EXTENT OF OCCUPATION

I METRE

N ↓

N-S SECTION

A

B

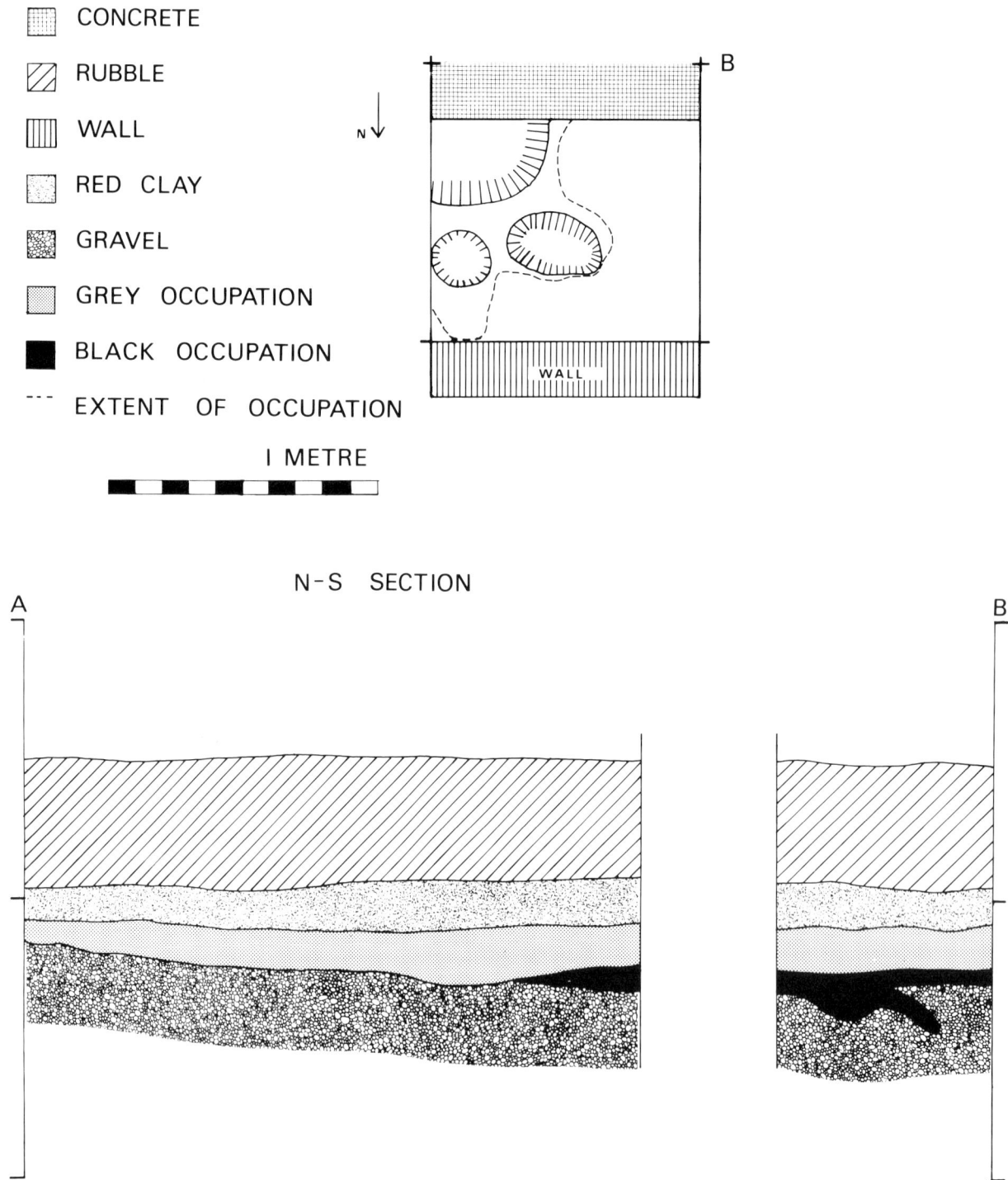

Fig 99   Castleroe: plan and section of area of *in situ* occupation

BIBLIOGRAPHY*

Albrethsen, S E and Brinch-Petersen, E (1976): 'Excavations of a Mesolithic cemetery at Vedbaek, Denmark', in *Acta Archaeologica* 47 (1976), *1–28*.

Andersen, S H (1974): 'Ringkloster: en jysk inlandsboplads med Ertebøllekultur', in *Kuml* (1973–74), *10–108*.

—— (1980): 'Tybrind Vig', in *Saertryk af Antikvariske Studier* 4 (1980), *7–22*.

Batty, J (1938): 'Some microliths from the Lower Bann Valley', in *Ulster J Archaeol* 1 (1938), *90–94*.

Bay-Petersen, J L (1978): 'Animal exploitation in Mesolithic Denmark', in *The early post-glacial settlement of northern Europe*, ed P Mellars (London, 1978), *115–145*.

Binford, L R (1978): *Nunamiut ethno-archaeology* (New York, 1978).

—— (1978a): 'Dimensional analysis of behaviour and site structure: learning from an Eskimo hunting stand'; in *American Antiquity* 43 (1978), *330–361*.

—— (1979): 'Comments on confusion', in *American Antiquity* 44 (1979), *591–594*.

—— (1979a): 'Organization and formation processes: looking at curated technologies', in *J Anthropol Research* 35 (1979), *255–273*.

—— (1980): 'Willow smoke and dogs' tails: hunter-gatherer settlement systems and archaeological site formation', in *American Antiquity* 45 (1980), *4–20*.

——, Binford, S R, Whallon, R C and Hardin, M (1966): 'Archaeology at Hatchery West' (*Southern Illinois University Museum Archaeological Report* No 25, 1966).

Bird, J (1946): 'The Alacaleuf', in *Handbook of South American Indians* 1, *Bureau of American Ethnology Bulletin* 143, ed J Steward (1946), *55–79*.

Bonsall, C (1981): 'The coastal factor in the Mesolithic settlement of north-west England', in *Mesolithikum in Europa, Veröffentlichungen des Museums für Ur und Frühgeschichte* 14/15 (Potsdam, 1981), *451–470*.

Bordes, F (1968): *The Old Stone Age* (London, 1968).

Brinch-Petersen, E (1966): 'Klosterlund–Sonder Hadsund–Bollund', in *Acta Archaeologica* 37 (1966), *77–185*.

—— (1972): 'A Maglemose hut from Svaerdborg Bog, Zealand, Denmark', in *Acta Archaeologica* 42 (1972), *43–77*.

——, Alexandersen, V, Vang-Petersen, P and Christiansen, C (1979): *Vedbaekprojektet* (Copenhagen, 1979).

Broadbent, N (1979): *Coastal resources and settlement stability: a critical study of a Mesolithic site complex in northern Sweden* (Uppsala, 1979).

Burenhult, G (1980): *The Carrowmore excavations (excavation season 1980)*, in *Stockholm Archaeological Reports* 7 (1980).

Cahen, D, Keeley, L H and Van Noten, F (1979): 'Stone tools, toolkits and human behaviour in prehistory', in *Current Anthropol* 20 (4) (1979), *661–683*.

Case, H (1961): 'Irish Neolithic pottery: distribution and sequence', in *Proc Prehist Soc* 27 (1961), *174–233*.

Caulfield, S (1978): 'Star Carr—an alternative view', in *Irish Archaeol Res Forum* 5 (1978), *15–22*.

Clark, J G D (1954): *Excavations at Star Carr: an Early Mesolithic settlement at Seamer, near Scarborough, Yorkshire* (Cambridge, 1954).

—— (1972): 'Star Carr: a case study in bio-archaeology', in *Addison Wesley Modules in Anthropology*, Module 10 (1972), *1–42*.

—— (1975): *The earlier Stone Age settlement of Scandinavia* (London, 1975).

Clarke, D (1976): 'Mesolithic Europe: the economic basis', in *Problems in economic and social anthropology*, eds G de G Sieveking, I H Longworth and K E Wilson (London, 1976), *449–486*.

Coles, J M (1971): 'The early settlement of Scotland: excavations at Morton, Fife', in *Proc Prehist Soc* 37 (1971), *284–366*.

Collins, A E P (1983): 'Excavations at Mount Sandel, lower site, Coleraine, County Londonderry', in *Ulster J Archaeol* 46 (1983), *1–22*.

Cook, S F and Heizer, R F (1968): 'Relationships among houses, settlement areas and population in Aboriginal California', in *Settlement Archaeology*, ed K C Chang (Palo Alto, 1968), *79–116*.

Coon, C S (1976): *The hunting peoples* (London, 1976).

Creighton, J R (1974): *A study of later Pleistocene geomorphology of north central Ulster* (unpublished thesis, Queen's University, Belfast, 1974).

Dubourdieu, J (1812): *Statistical survey of the County of Antrim* (Dublin, 1812).

Dunnell, W (1979): 'Comment on Cahen *et al*', in *Current Anthropol* 20 (4) (1979).

Fischer, A (1978): 'På sporet af overgangen mellen palaeoliticum og mesoliticum i Sydskandinavien', in *Hikuin* 4 (1978), *27–50*.

Flanagan, L N W (1970): 'A flint hoard from Ballyclare, Co Antrim', in *Ulster J Archaeol* 33 (1970), *15–22*.

Godwin, H (1956): *A history of the British flora* (Cambridge, 1956).

---

* This main bibliography refers to Chapters 1–3 and 11–14 and Appendix 5. At the request of Professor Woodman and his collaborators, contributions by other authors include individual lists of references.

Gould, R A (1977): 'Ethno-archaeology; or where do models come from ?', in *Stone tools as cultural markers*, ed R V S Wright (Canberra, 1977), *162–168*.

—— (1980): *Living archaeology* (Cambridge, 1980).

Gray, W (1888): 'Rough flint celts of the County Antrim', in *J Roy Hist Archaeol Assoc Ireland* ser IV, 8 (1888), *505–506*.

Grigson, C (1982): 'Pigs, porridge and pannage in Neolithic England' in *Archaeological aspects of woodland ecology*, eds M Bell and S Limbrey (Brit Archaeol Reports, international series 146, Oxford, 1982), *297–314*.

Hayden, B (1977): 'Stone tool functions in the Western Desert', in *Stone tools as cultural markers*, ed J V S Wright (Canberra, 1977), *178–188*.

—— (1979): *Palaeolithic reflections* (Canberra, 1979).

Henricksen, B B (1976): *Svaerdborg I* (Copenhagen, 1976).

Jacobi, R M (1973): 'Aspects of the Mesolithic age in Britain', in *The Mesolithic in Europe*, ed S Kozlowski (Warsaw, 1973), *237–265*.

—— (1976): 'Britain inside and outside Mesolithic Europe', in *Proc Prehist Soc* 42 (1976), *67–84*.

—— (1978): 'Northern England in the eighth millennium bc, an essay', in *The early post-glacial settlement of northern Europe*, ed P Mellars (London, 1978), *295–332*.

—— (1978a): 'Population and landscape in Mesolithic lowland Britain', in *The effect of man on the landscape: the lowland zone*, eds S Limbrey and J G Evans (London, 1978), *75–86*.

Jochim, M A (1976): *Hunter-gatherer subsistence and settlement: a predictive model* (New York, 1976).

Lamb, H H, Lewis, R P W and Woodruffe, A (1966): 'Atmospheric circulation and the main climatic variables between 8000 and 0 BC: meteorological evidence', in Sawyer, J S (ed), *World climate from 8000 to 0 BC* (Roy Meteorological Soc, 1966), *174–217*.

Larson, P A (1979): 'Comments on Lewis Binford's "Analysis of behaviour and site structure"', in *American Antiquity* 44 (1979), *590–591*.

Larsson, L (1978): *Agerod I:B—Agerod I:D. A study of early settlement in Scania* (Acta Archaeologica Lundensia 12, Lund, 1978).

—— (1980): 'Some aspects of the Kongemose culture of southern Sweden', in *Meddelanden från Lunds Universitets Historiska Museum* (1979–80), *5–22*.

Leroi-Gourhan, A (1976): 'Les structures d'habitat au Palaeolithique supérieur', in *La préhistoire française*, ed H de Lumley, I (1976), *657–663*.

—— and Brezillon, M (1966): 'L'habitation Magdalenienne no 1 de Pincevent près Montereau', in *Gallia Préhistoire* 9 (1966), *262–385*.

Linnane, K (1980): 'Sea angling', in *Fishing in Ireland*, eds D Warner, K Linnane and P Brown (Belfast, 1980), *85–144*.

McNeill, T E (1980): *Anglo–Norman Ulster* (Edinburgh, 1980).

Malmer, M (1969): 'Die Mikrolithen in dem Pfeil-fund von Loshult', in *Meddelanden från Lunds Universitets Histori-ska Museum* (1969), *149–152*.

Masters, L J and Longhorne, T (1976): 'A probable Mesolithic hearth at Redkirk Point, Gretna, Dumfries-shire', in *Discovery and excavation Scotland* (Edinburgh, 1976), *27–28*.

Mellars, P A (1974): 'The Palaeolithic and Mesolithic', in *British prehistory: a new outline*, ed C Renfrew (London, 1974), *41–99*.

—— (1976): 'Settlement patterns and industrial variability in the British Mesolithic', in *Problems in economic and social archaeology*, eds G de G Sieveking, I H Longworth and K E Wilson (London, 1976), *375–399*.

—— (1976a): 'The appearance of "narrow blade" microlithic industries in Britain: the radiocarbon evidence', in *Civilizations du 8 au 5 millénaire avant notre ère en Europe*, ed S Kozlowski (Nice, 1976), *166–174*.

Mercer, J (1974): 'New ^{14}C dates from the Isle of Jura, Argyll', in *Antiquity* 48 (1974), *65–66*.

—— (1980): 'Lussa Wood 1: the late glacial and early post-glacial occupation of Jura', in *Proc Soc Antiq Scotland* 110 (1980), *1–31*.

Mitchell, G F (1956): 'An early kitchen midden at Sutton, Co Dublin', in *J Roy Soc Antiq Ireland* 86 (1956), *1–26*.

Morrison, A (1980): *Early man in Britain and Ireland* (London, 1980).

Movius, H L (1940): 'An early post-glacial archaeological site at Cushendun, Co Antrim', in *Proc Roy Irish Acad* 46C (1940), *1–48*.

—— (1942): *The Irish Stone Age* (Cambridge, 1942).

Murray, P (1980): 'Discard location: the ethnographic data', in *American Antiquity* (1980), *490–502*.

Newcomer, M and Sieveking, G de G (1980): 'Experimental flake scatter-patterns: a new interpretative technique', in *J Field Archaeol* 7 (1980), *345–352*.

Newell, R R (1973): 'The post-glacial adaptions of the indigenous populations of the north-west European plain', in *The Mesolithic in Europe*, ed S Kozlowski (Warsaw, 1973), *399–440*.

—— (1981): 'Mesolithic dwelling structures: fact and fantasy', in *Mesolithikum in Europa*, Veröffentlichungen des Museums für Ur und Frühgeschichte 14/15 (Potsdam, 1981), *235–285*.

—— and Vroomans, A P J (1972): *Automatic artifact registration and systems for archaeological analysis with the Phillips P1100 computer: a Mesolithic test case* (Ooster-hout, 1972).

Odell, G H (1980): 'Towards a more behavioural approach to archaeological lithic concentrations', in *American Antiquity* 45 (1980), *404–431*.

O'Kelly, M J (1973): 'Current excavations at Newgrange, Ireland', in *Megalithic graves and rituals*, eds G Daniel and P Kjaerum (Aarhus, 1973), *137–146*.

O'Malley, M and Jacobi, R M (1978): 'The excavation of a Mesolithic occupation site at Broomhill, Braishfield, Hampshire', in *Rescue Archaeology in Hampshire* 4 (1978), *16–39*.

O'Sullivan, P E, Oldfield, F and Battarbee, R W (1973):

'Preliminary studies of Lough Neagh sediments I: stratigraphy, chronology and pollen analyses', in *Quaternary plant ecology*, eds H Birks and R G West (London, 1973), *167–178*.

Oswalt, W H (1976): *An anthropological analysis of food-getting technology* (London, 1976).

Paluden-Muller, C (1978): 'High Atlantic food gathering in north-western Zealand, ecological conditions and spatial representation', in *New directions in Scandinavian archaeology*, eds K Kristiansen and C Paluden-Muller (Copenhagen, 1978).

Pilcher, J R and Smith, A G (1979): 'Palaeoecological investigations at Ballynagilly, a Neolithic and Bronze Age settlement in County Tyrone, Northern Ireland', in *Phil Trans Roy Soc London* (B), 286 (1979), *345–369*.

Pitts, M W (1978): 'On the shape of waste flakes as an index of technological change in lithic industries', *J Archaeol Science* 5 (1978), *17–37*.

—— (1979): 'Hides and antlers: a new look at the gatherer–hunter site at Star Carr', in *World Archaeology* 11 (1) (1979), *32–43*.

—— and Jacobi, R M (1979): 'Some aspects of change in flaked stone industries of the Mesolithic and Neolithic in southern Britian', in *J Archaeol Science* 6 (1979), *163–177*.

Price, T D, Whallon, B and Chapell, S (1974): 'Mesolithic sites near Havelte, province of Drenthe (Netherlands)', in *Palaeohistoria* 16 (1974), *7–61*.

Radley, J and Mellars, P A (1964): 'A Mesolithic structure at Deepcar, Yorkshire, England, and the affinities of its associated flint industries', in *Proc Prehist Soc* 40 (1964), *1–19*.

Raftery, B (1969): 'Freestone Hill, Co Kilkenny: an Iron Age hillfort and Bronze Age cairn', in *Proc Roy Irish Acad* 68C (1969), *1–108*.

Roche, J (1960): *Le gisement Mesolithique de Moita de Sebastiao, Muge Portugal I: Archaeologie* (Lisbon, Instituto de Alta Cultura, 1960).

Ryan, M (1980): 'An Early Mesolithic site in the Irish midlands', in *Antiquity* 54 (1980), *46–47*.

Sampson, G V (1802): *Statistical survey of the County of Londonderry* (Dublin, 1802).

Schalk, R F (1977): 'The structure of an anadromous fish resource', in *For theory building in archaeology*, ed L R Binford (New York, 1977), *207–250*.

Schiffer, M B (1976): *Behavioural archaeology* (New York, 1976).

Sklenar, K (1976): 'Palaeolithic and Mesolithic dwellings: an essay in classification', in *Pamatky Archeologicke* 67 (1976), *249–340*.

Smith, A G and Collins, A E P (1971): 'The stratigraphy, palynology and archaeology of diatomite deposits at Newferry, Co Antrim, Northern Ireland', in *Ulster J Archaeol* 34 (1971), *3–25*.

Streuver, S and Holton, F A (1979): *Koster: Americans in search of their past* (New York, 1979).

Swisur, V R and Jacobi, R M (1975): 'Radiocarbon dates for the Pennine Mesolithi', in *Nature* 256 (1975), *32–34*.

Taylor, J A (1980): 'Environmental changes in Wales during the Holocene period', in *Culture and environment in prehistoric Wales*, ed J A Taylor (Brit Archaeol Reports 76, Oxford, 1980), *101–130*.

Van Noten, F (1978): 'Les chasseurs de Meer', in *Dissertationes Archaeologica Gandensis* (Bruges, 1978).

van Wijngaarden-Bakker, L H (1974): 'The animal remains from the Beaker settlement at Newgrange, Co Meath: first report' in *Proc Roy Irish Acad* 74C (1974), *313–383*.

—— (1980): *An archaeozoological study of the Beaker settlement at Newgrange, Ireland* (thesis, Amsterdam).

Von Rust, A (1972): *Vor 20,000 Jahren* (Neumunster, 1972).

Warner, R B (1976): 'Further notes for the use of radiocarbon dates, including a method for the analysis of a stratified sequence', in *Irish Archaeol Res Forum* 3 (2) (1976), *25–55*.

Watanabe, H (1972): *The Ainu ecosystem: environment and group structure* (Tokyo, 1972).

Went, A E J (1964): 'The pursuit of salmon in Ireland', in *Proc Roy Irish Acad* 63C (1964), *191–244*.

Weissner, P (1974): 'A functional estimator of population from floor area', in *American Antiquity* (4), *343–350*.

Welinder, S (1971): *Tidligpostglacialt Mesolithicum* (*Acta Archaeologica Lundensia*, Lund, 1971).

Whallon, R (1974): 'Spatial analysis of occupation floors I: the application of nearest neighbour analysis', in *American Antiquity* 39 (1974), *16–34*.

—— (1978): 'The spatial analysis of Mesolithic floors: a reappraisal', in *The early postglacial settlement of northern Europe*, ed P Mellars (London).

Whelan, C B (1938): 'Studies in the significance of the Irish Stone Age: the cultural sequence', in *Proc Roy Irish Acad* 44C (1938), *115–138*.

White, T E (1953): 'A method of calculating the dietary percentage of various food animals utilised by aboriginal peoples', in *American Antiquity* 14, *the*.

Wilson, J P F (1979): *Biology and the high pollan Coregonus Autumnalis pollan* (unpublished thesis, New University of Ulster, Coleraine, 1979).

Wing, E S and Brown, A B (1979): *Paleonutrition: method and theory in prehistoric foodways*.

Wirjoatmodjo, S (1980): *Growth of the flounder: Platichthys Flessus in* thesis, New University of Ulster.

Wobst, H M (1974): 'Boundary conditions for Palaeolithic social systems: a simulation approach', *American Antiquity* 39 (1974), *147–178*.

Wolynec, R B (1977): *The systematic analysis, the Koster site, a stratified archaeological site* North Western University, thesis.

Woodman, P C (1974): 'The chronological position of the latest phases of the Larnian', in *Proc Roy Irish Acad* 74C (1974), *237–258*.

—— (1974a): 'Settlement patterns of the Irish Mesolithic', in *Ulster J Archaeol* 37 (1974), *1–16*.

—— (1977): 'A narrow blade Mesolithic site at Glynn, County Antrim', in *Ulster J Archaeol* 40 (1977), *12–21*.

—— (1977a): 'Recent excavations at Newferry, Co Antrim', in *Prehist Soc* 43 (1977), *155–199*.

—— (1977b): 'Mount Sandel', in *Current Archaeol* 59 (1977), 375.

—— (1977c): 'Problems of a Mesolithic survival in Ireland', in *Irish Archaeol Res Forum* 4 (2) (1977), *17–28*.

—— (1978): *The Mesolithic in Ireland* (Brit Archaeol Reports 58, Oxford, 1978).

—— (1978a): 'A reappraisal of the Manx Mesolithic', in *Man and environment in the Isle of Man*, ed P Davey (Brit Archaeol Reports 54, Oxford, 1978), *333–370*.

—— (1978b): 'The chronology and economy of the Irish Mesolithic: some working hypotheses', in *The early post-glacial settlement of northern Europe*, ed P Mellars (London, 1978).

—— (1981): 'The post-glacial colonization of Ireland: the human factors', in *Irish Antiquity: essays and studies presented to Professor M J O'Kelly*, ed D Ó Corráin (Cork, 1981), *93–110*.

Yellen, J E (1977): *Archaeological approaches to the present* (New York, 1977).

Plate 1 Air view of River Bann looking north, with the Cutts in foreground, Mount Sandel in middle ground and Coleraine beyond (BKS Surveys Ltd)

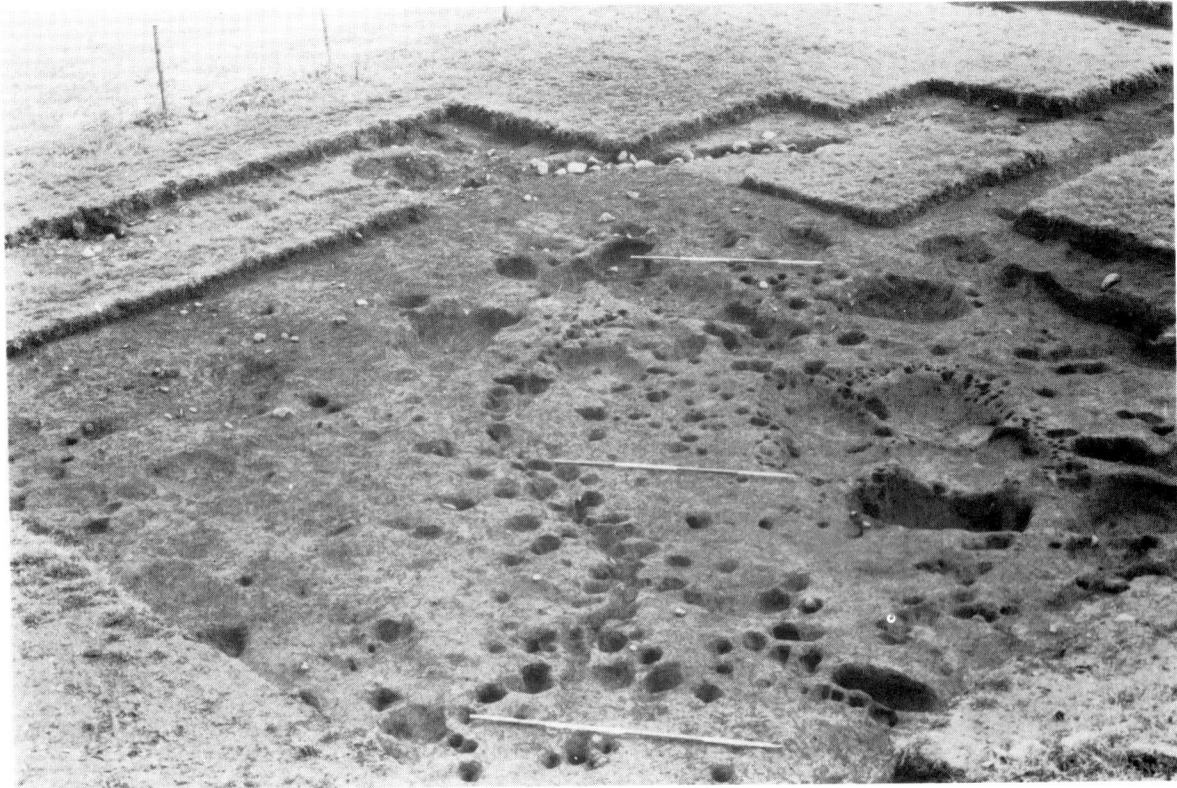

Plate 2 Main hut hollow after excavation, looking south-east, showing FII at south-east edge of area

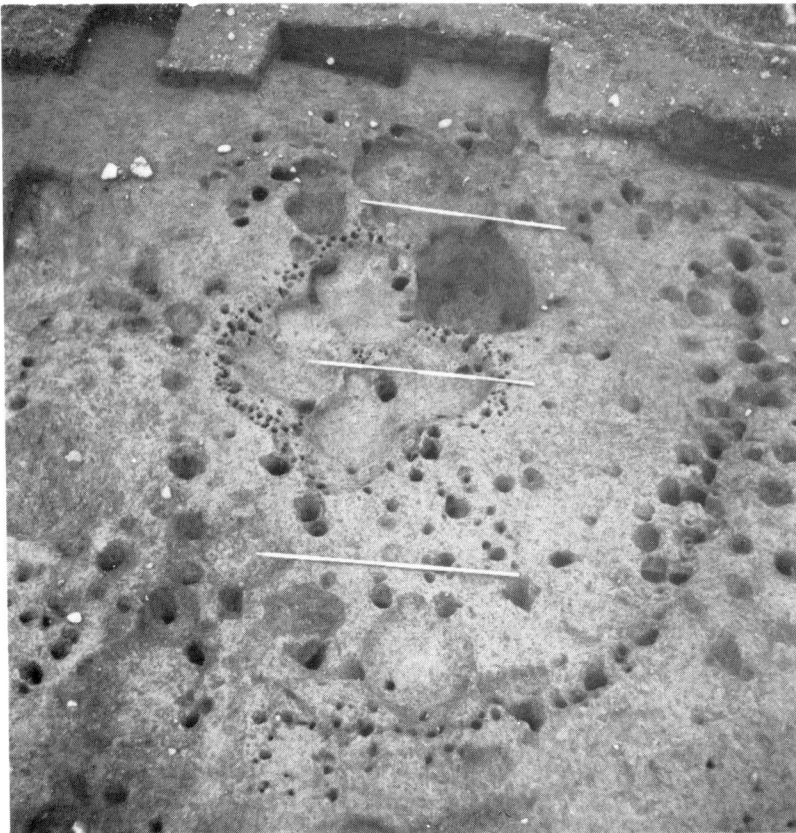

Plate 3 Main hut hollow, looking west, with central hearth complex at centre

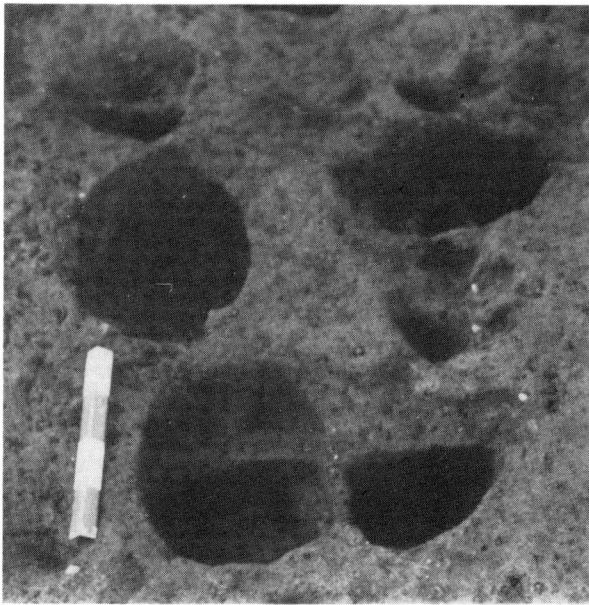

Plate 4   Post-holes on northern edge of main hut hollow

Plate 5   Section through F56/1

Plate 6   F56/2 showing both organic layers after removal of occupation soil

Plate 7   Small northern structure, looking east, showing obliteration of north-east part by F137

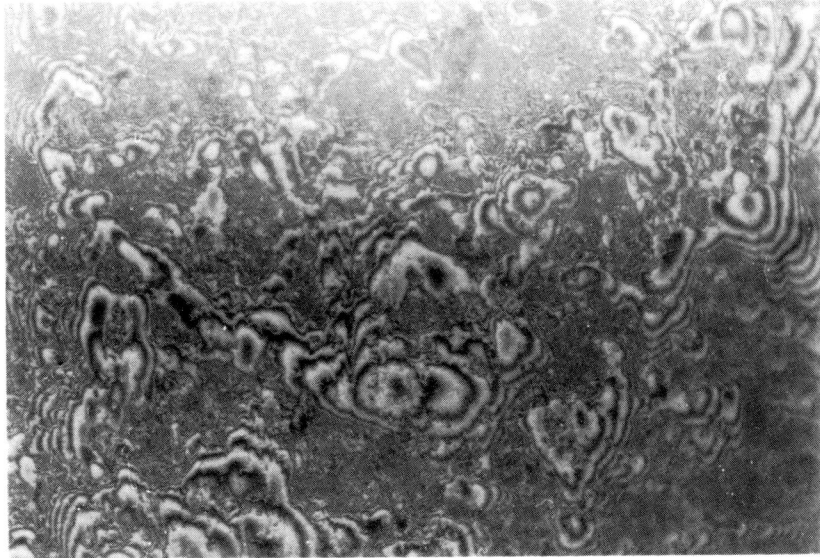

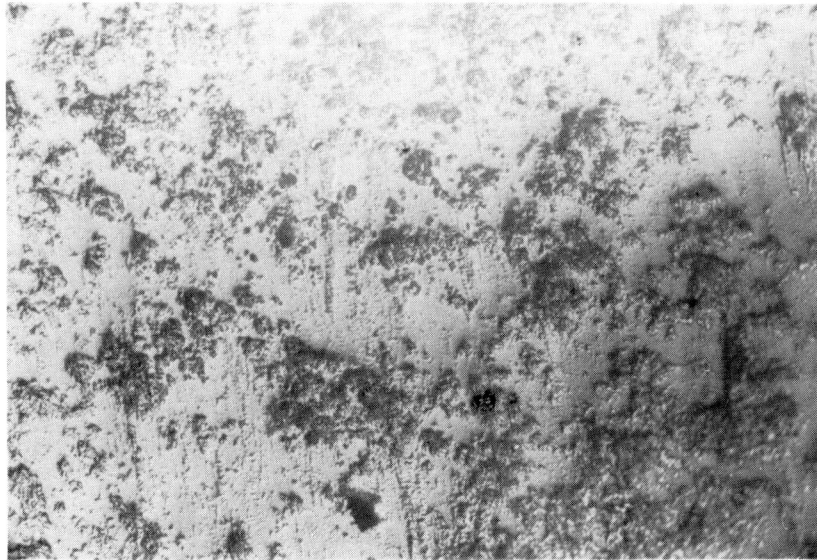

Plates 8,9. Interference pattern (8) produced by wood polish shown in 9
(magnification 200 diameters; length of photomicrographs 0.566 mm)
(see also Dumont 1982)

Plate 10   Bone polish (magnification 320 diameters; length of photomicrograph 0.354 mm)

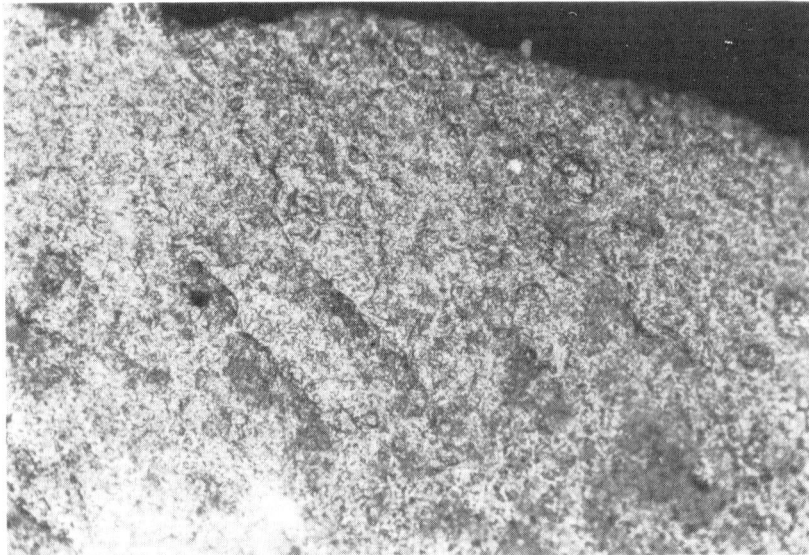

Plate 11   Meat polish (magnification 200 diameters; length of photomicrograph 0.566 mm)

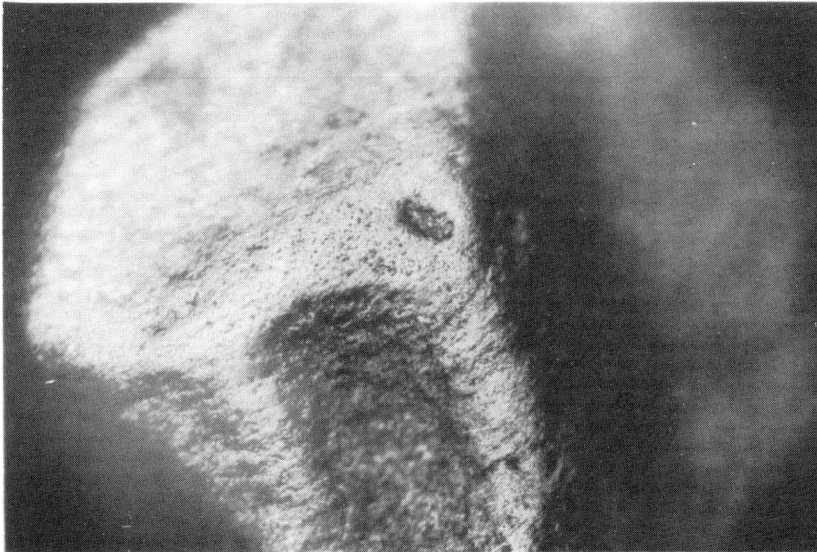

Plate 12   Hide polish (possibly dry hide). Note the extensive edge-rounding and micro-potlid fracture (magnification 200 diameters; length of photomicrograph 0.566 mm)

Plate 13   Antler polish (magnification 200 diameters; length of photomicrograph 0.566 mm)

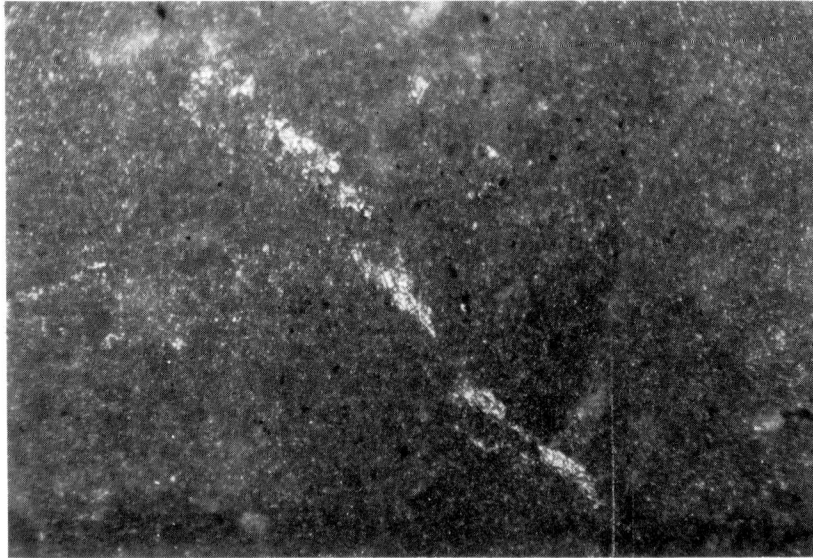

Plate 14   Linear arrangement of wood polish (magnification 100 diameters; length of photomicrograph 1.15 mm)

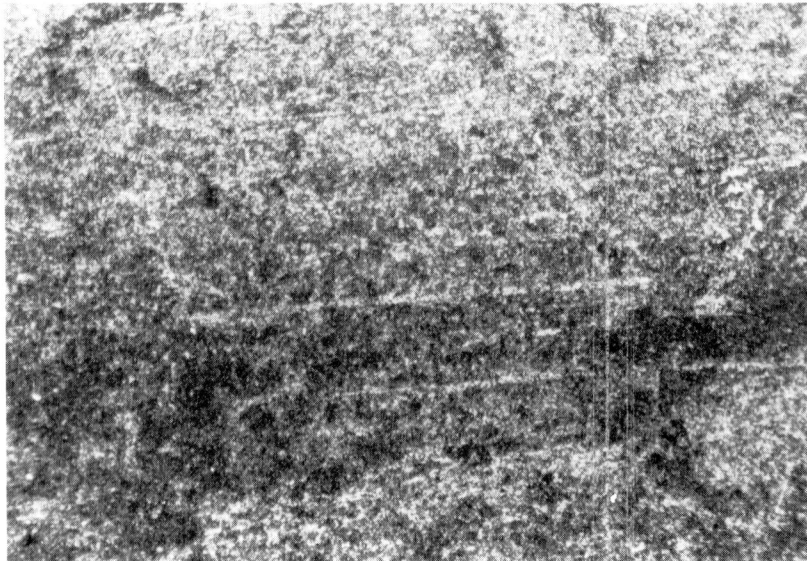

Plate 15   Linear arrangements of haematite deposits near and parallel to the working edge of an edge-damaged/retouched blade (magnification 100 diameters; length of photomicrograph 1.15 mm)

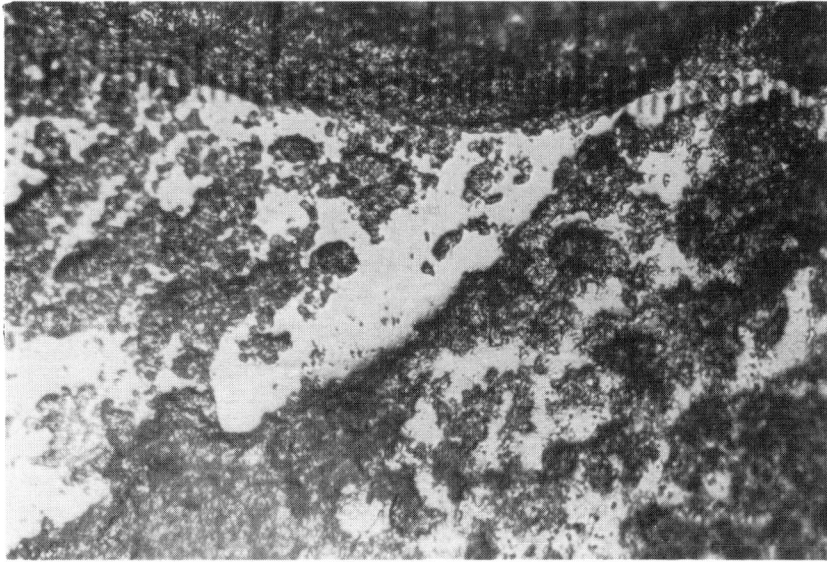

Plate 16   Stone-on-stone polish (magnification 200 diameters; length of
photomicrograph 0.307 mm)